BAD HABITS

BAD HABITS

A Duplex Collection
by Glenn McCoy

Andrews McMeel
Publishing, LLC

Kansas City

The Duplex is distributed internationally by Universal Press Syndicate.

Bad Habits copyright © 2006 by Glenn McCoy. All rights reserved. Printed in the United States of America. No part of this book may be used or reproduced in any manner whatsoever without written permission except in the case of reprints in the context of reviews. For information, write Andrews McMeel Publishing, LLC, an Andrews McMeel Universal company, 4520 Main Street, Kansas City, Missouri 64111.

06 07 08 09 10 BBG 10 9 8 7 6 5 4 3 2 1

ISBN-13: 978-0-7407-6195-9
ISBN-10: 0-7407-6195-1

Library of Congress Control Number: 2006926007

www.andrewsmcmeel.com

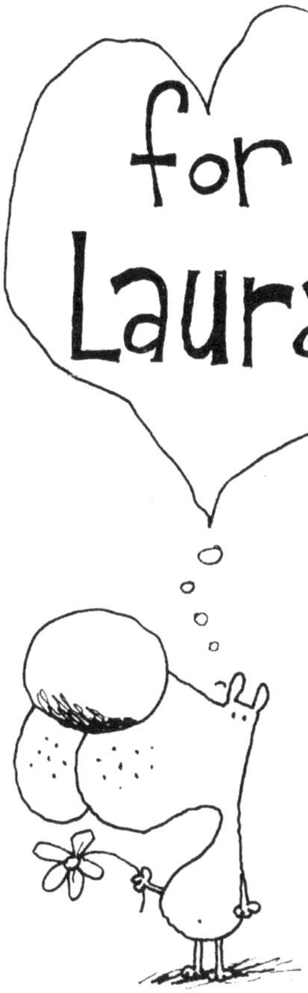
for
Laura

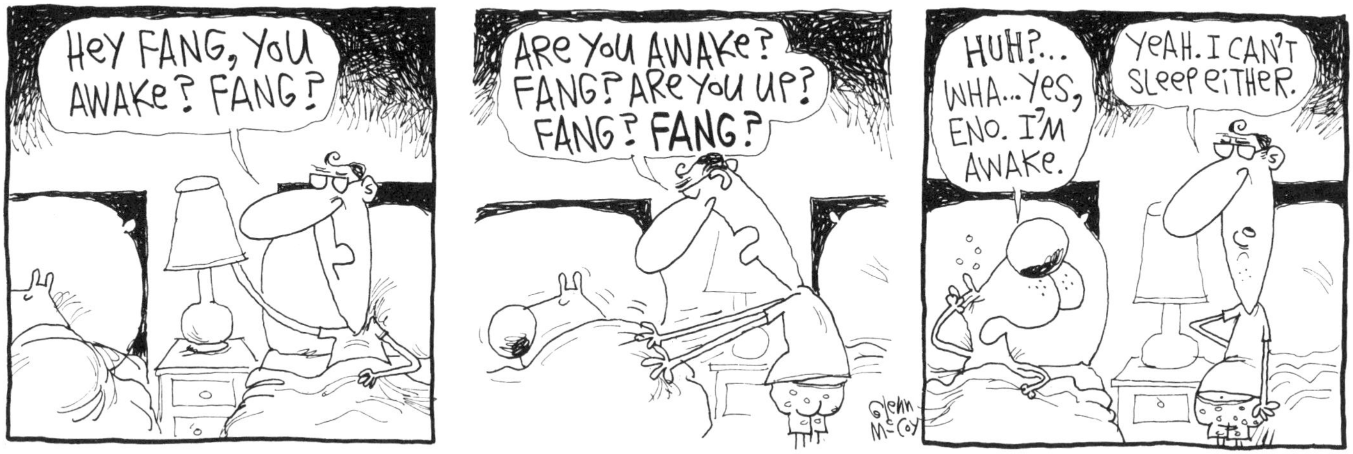
HEY FANG, YOU AWAKE? FANG?
ARE YOU AWAKE? FANG? ARE YOU UP? FANG? FANG?
Glenn McCoy
HUH?... WHA... YES, ENO. I'M AWAKE.
YEAH. I CAN'T SLEEP EITHER.

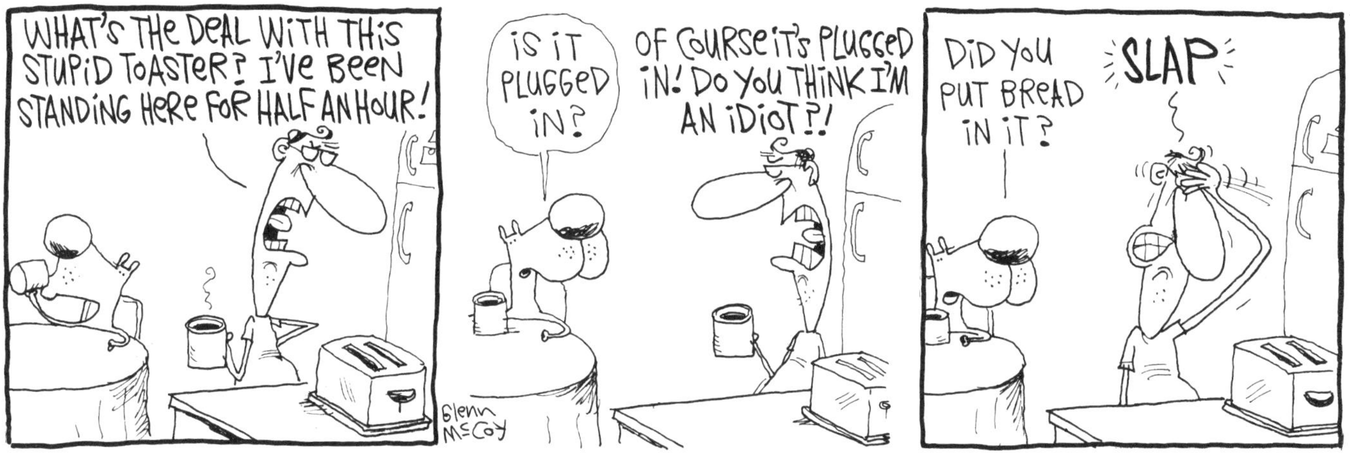
WHAT'S THE DEAL WITH THIS STUPID TOASTER? I'VE BEEN STANDING HERE FOR HALF AN HOUR!
Glenn McCoy
IS IT PLUGGED IN?
OF COURSE IT'S PLUGGED IN! DO YOU THINK I'M AN IDIOT?!
DID YOU PUT BREAD IN IT?
SLAP

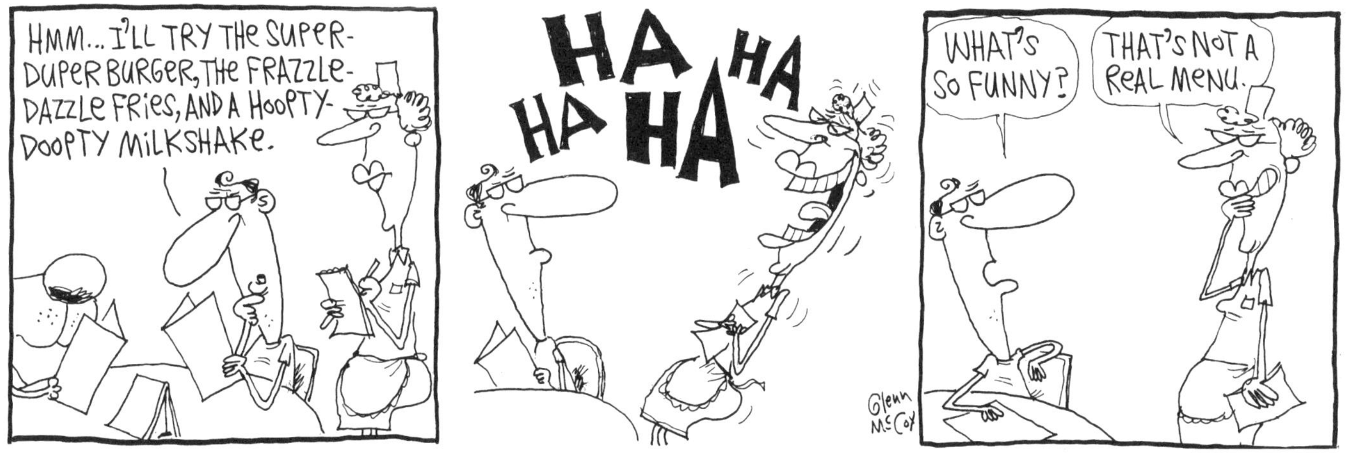
HMM... I'LL TRY THE SUPER-DUPER BURGER, THE FRAZZLE-DAZZLE FRIES, AND A HOOPTY-DOOPTY MILKSHAKE.
HA HA HA HA HA
WHAT'S SO FUNNY?
THAT'S NOT A REAL MENU.
Glenn McCoy

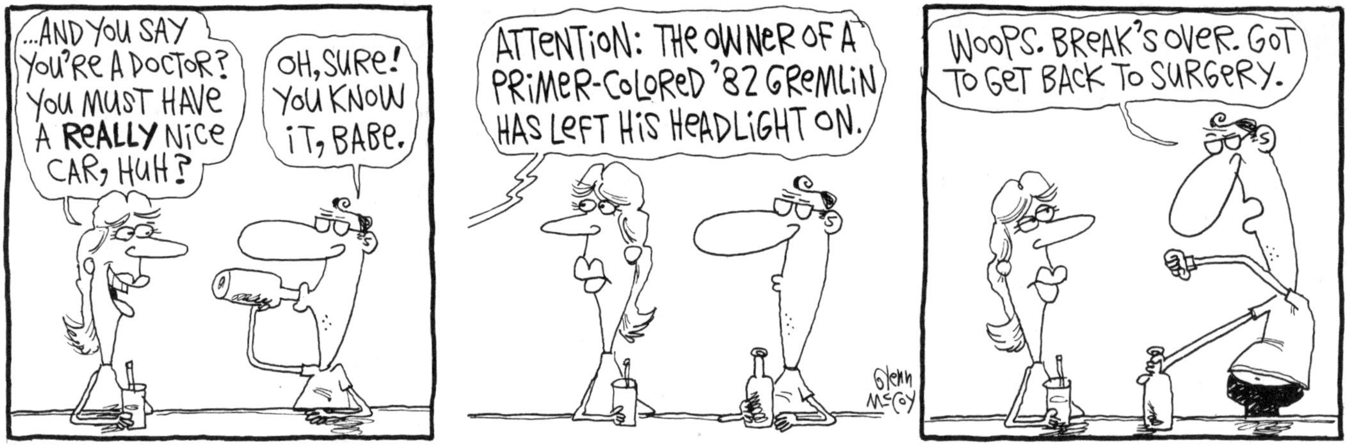
...AND YOU SAY YOU'RE A DOCTOR? YOU MUST HAVE A **REALLY** NICE CAR, HUH?
OH, SURE! YOU KNOW IT, BABE.
ATTENTION: THE OWNER OF A PRIMER-COLORED '82 GREMLIN HAS LEFT HIS HEADLIGHT ON.
Glenn McCoy
WOOPS. BREAK'S OVER. GOT TO GET BACK TO SURGERY.

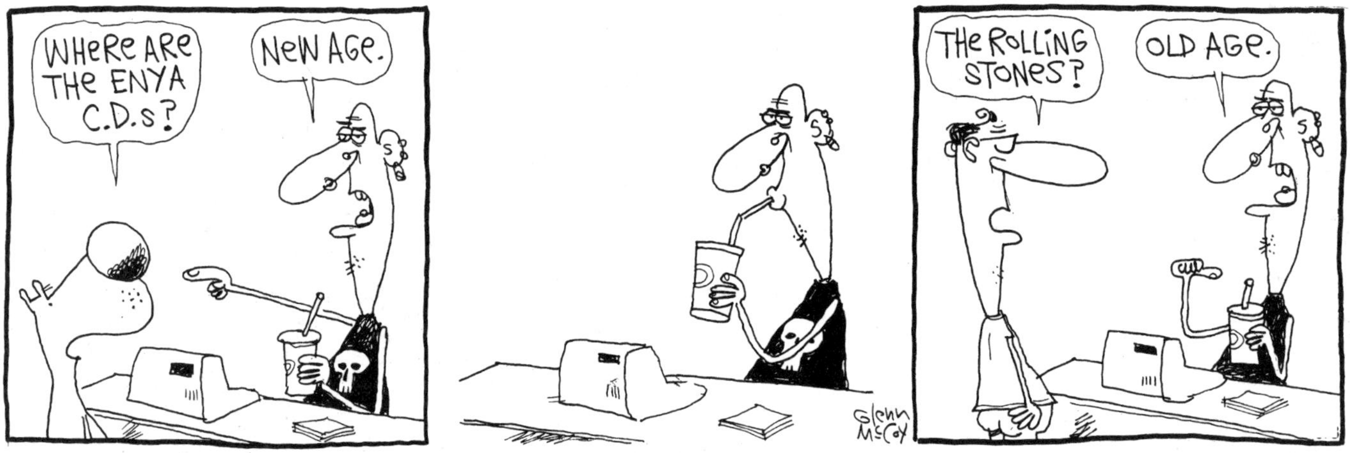
WHERE ARE THE ENYA C.D.s?
NEW AGE.
Glenn McCoy
THE ROLLING STONES?
OLD AGE.

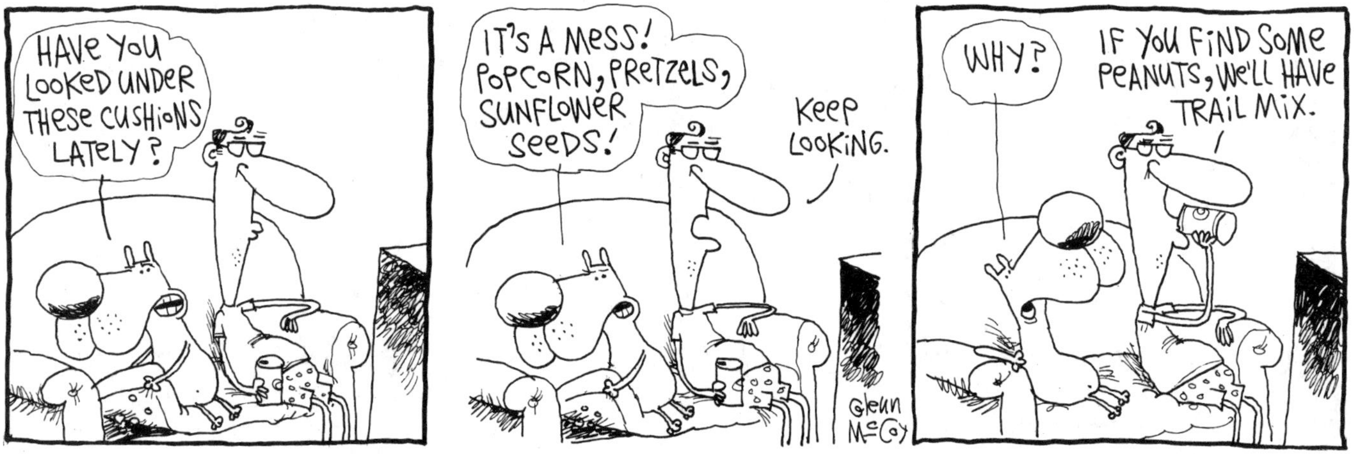
HAVE YOU LOOKED UNDER THESE CUSHIONS LATELY?
IT'S A MESS! POPCORN, PRETZELS, SUNFLOWER SEEDS!
KEEP LOOKING.
Glenn McCoy
WHY?
IF YOU FIND SOME PEANUTS, WE'LL HAVE TRAIL MIX.

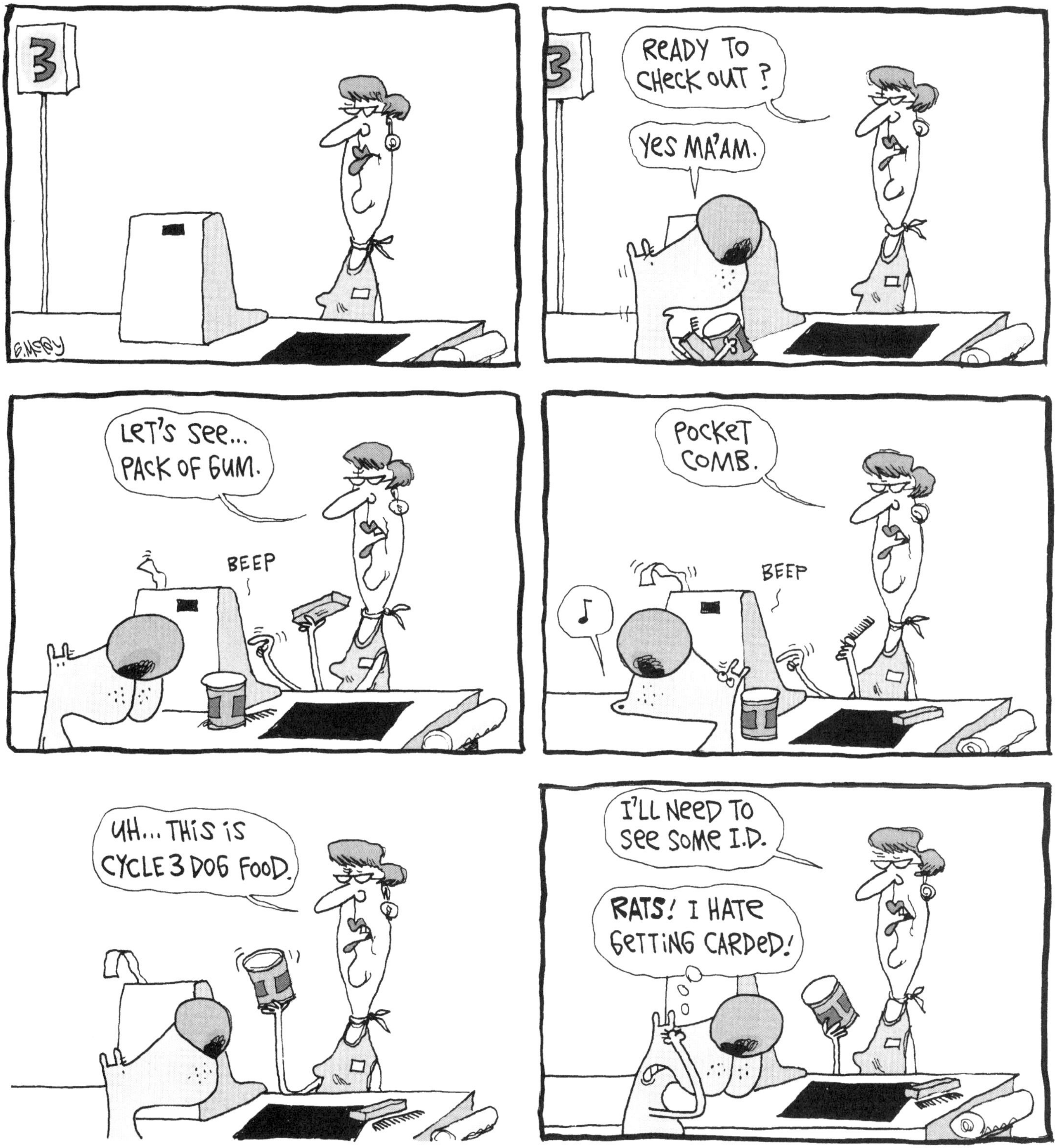
READY TO CHECK OUT ?
YES MA'AM.
LET'S SEE... PACK OF GUM.
BEEP
POCKET COMB.
BEEP
UH... THIS IS CYCLE 3 DOG FOOD.
I'LL NEED TO SEE SOME I.D.
RATS! I HATE GETTING CARDED!

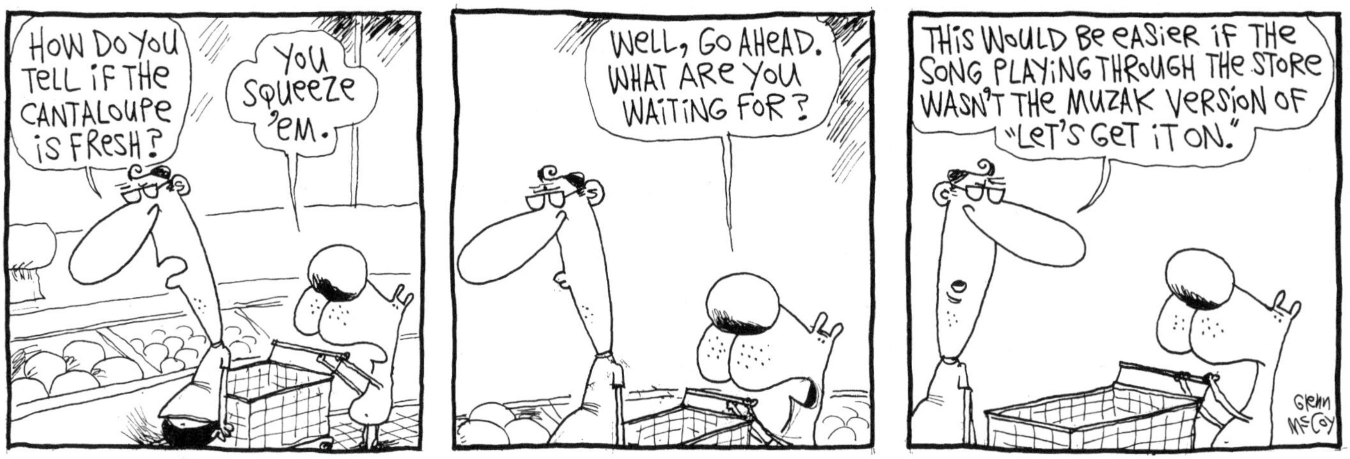
HOW DO YOU TELL IF THE CANTALOUPE IS FRESH?
YOU SQUEEZE 'EM.
WELL, GO AHEAD. WHAT ARE YOU WAITING FOR?
THIS WOULD BE EASIER IF THE SONG PLAYING THROUGH THE STORE WASN'T THE MUZAK VERSION OF "LET'S GET IT ON."
GLENN McCOY

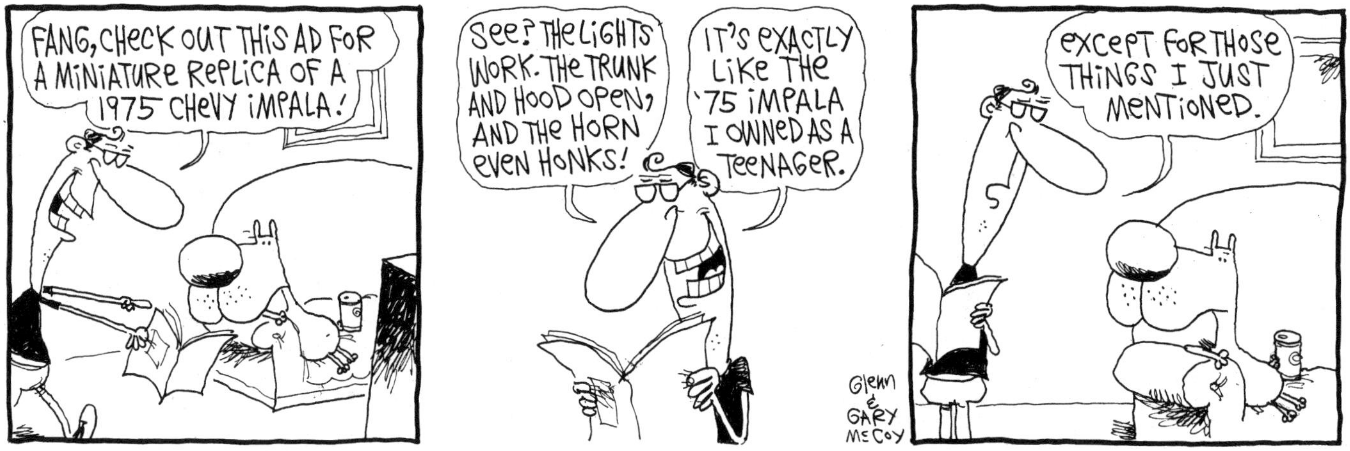
FANG, CHECK OUT THIS AD FOR A MINIATURE REPLICA OF A 1975 CHEVY IMPALA!
SEE? THE LIGHTS WORK. THE TRUNK AND HOOD OPEN, AND THE HORN EVEN HONKS!
IT'S EXACTLY LIKE THE '75 IMPALA I OWNED AS A TEENAGER.
GLENN & GARY McCOY
EXCEPT FOR THOSE THINGS I JUST MENTIONED.

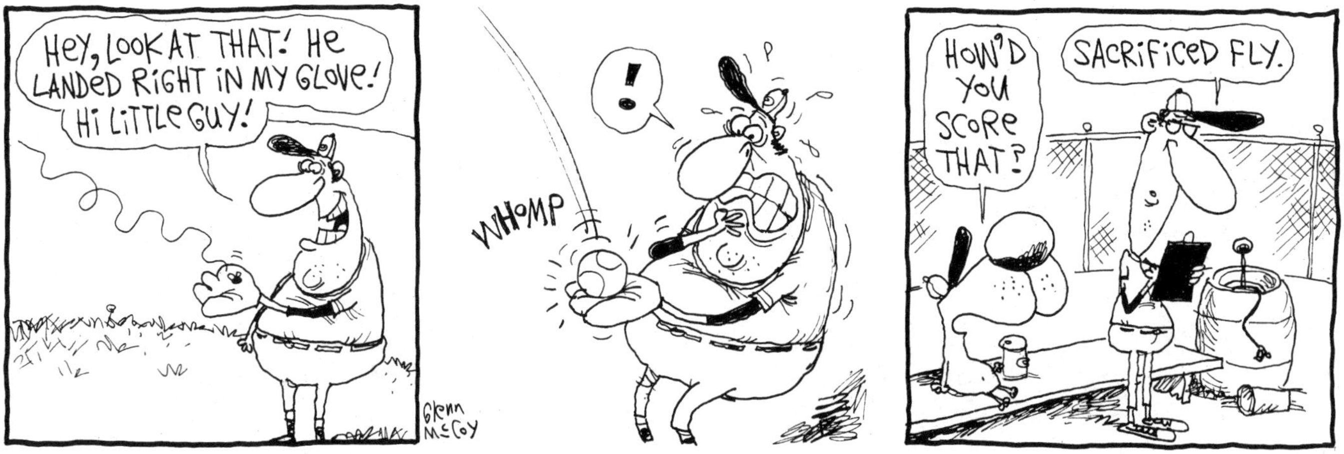
HEY, LOOK AT THAT! HE LANDED RIGHT IN MY GLOVE! HI LITTLE GUY!
GLENN McCOY
!
WHOMP
HOW'D YOU SCORE THAT?
SACRIFICED FLY.

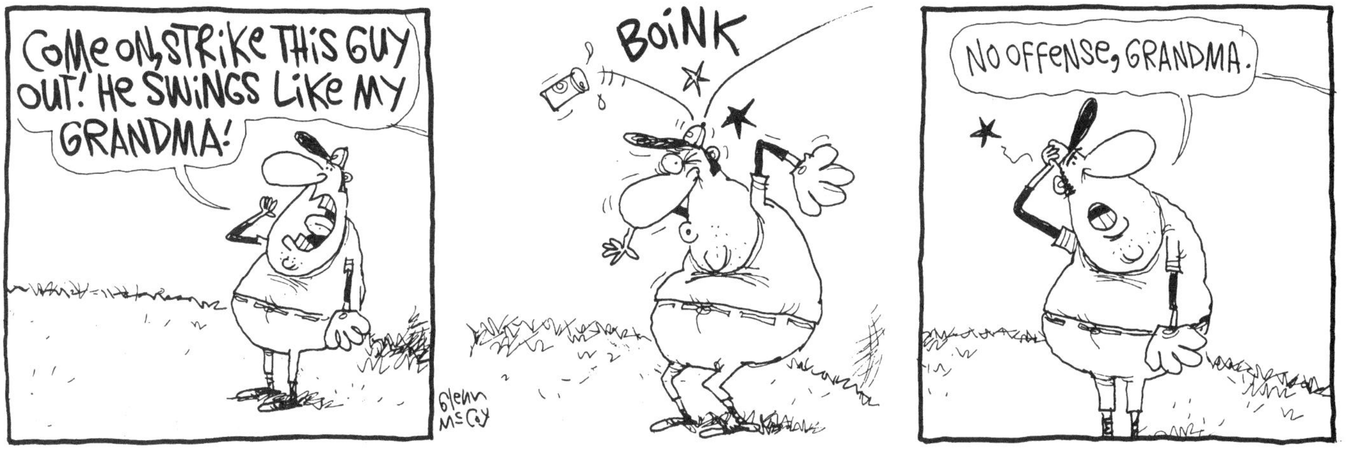
COME ON, STRIKE THIS GUY OUT! HE SWINGS LIKE MY GRANDMA!
BOINK
Glenn McCoy
NO OFFENSE, GRANDMA.

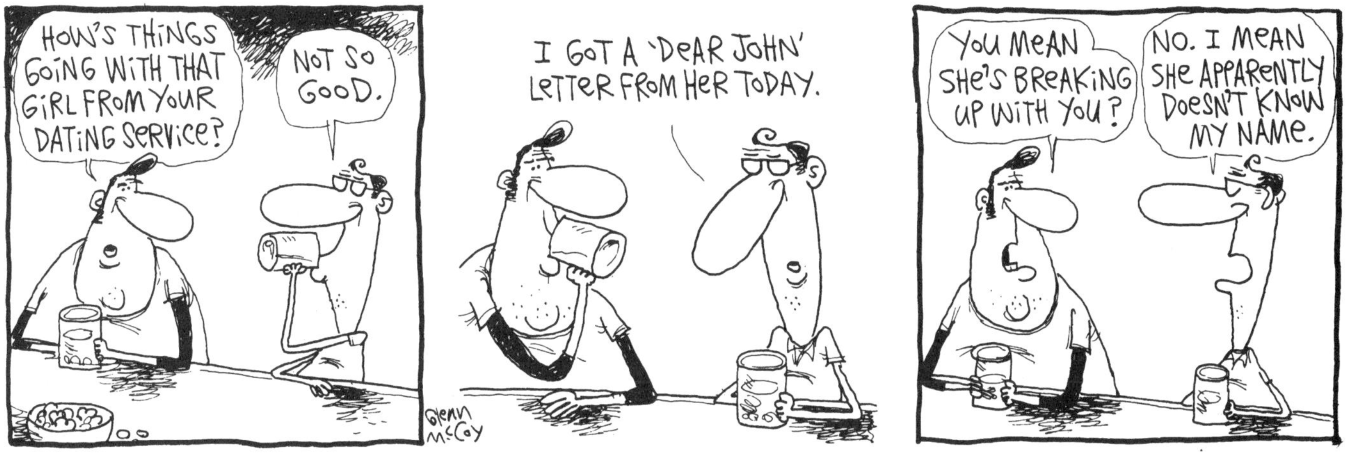
HOW'S THINGS GOING WITH THAT GIRL FROM YOUR DATING SERVICE?
NOT SO GOOD.
Glenn McCoy
I GOT A 'DEAR JOHN' LETTER FROM HER TODAY.
YOU MEAN SHE'S BREAKING UP WITH YOU?
NO. I MEAN SHE APPARENTLY DOESN'T KNOW MY NAME.

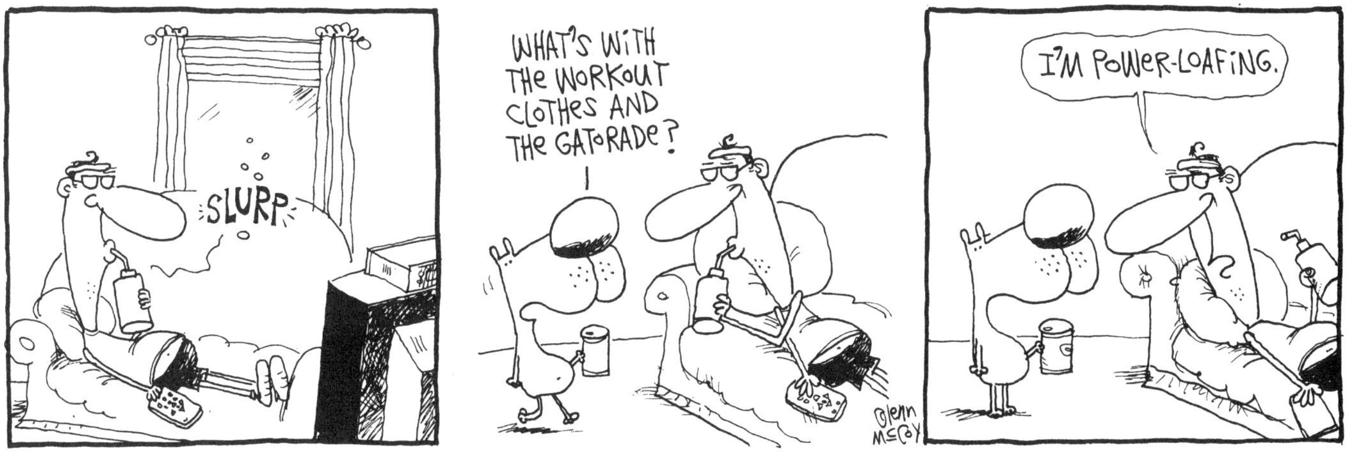
SLURP
WHAT'S WITH THE WORKOUT CLOTHES AND THE GATORADE?
Glenn McCoy
I'M POWER-LOAFING.

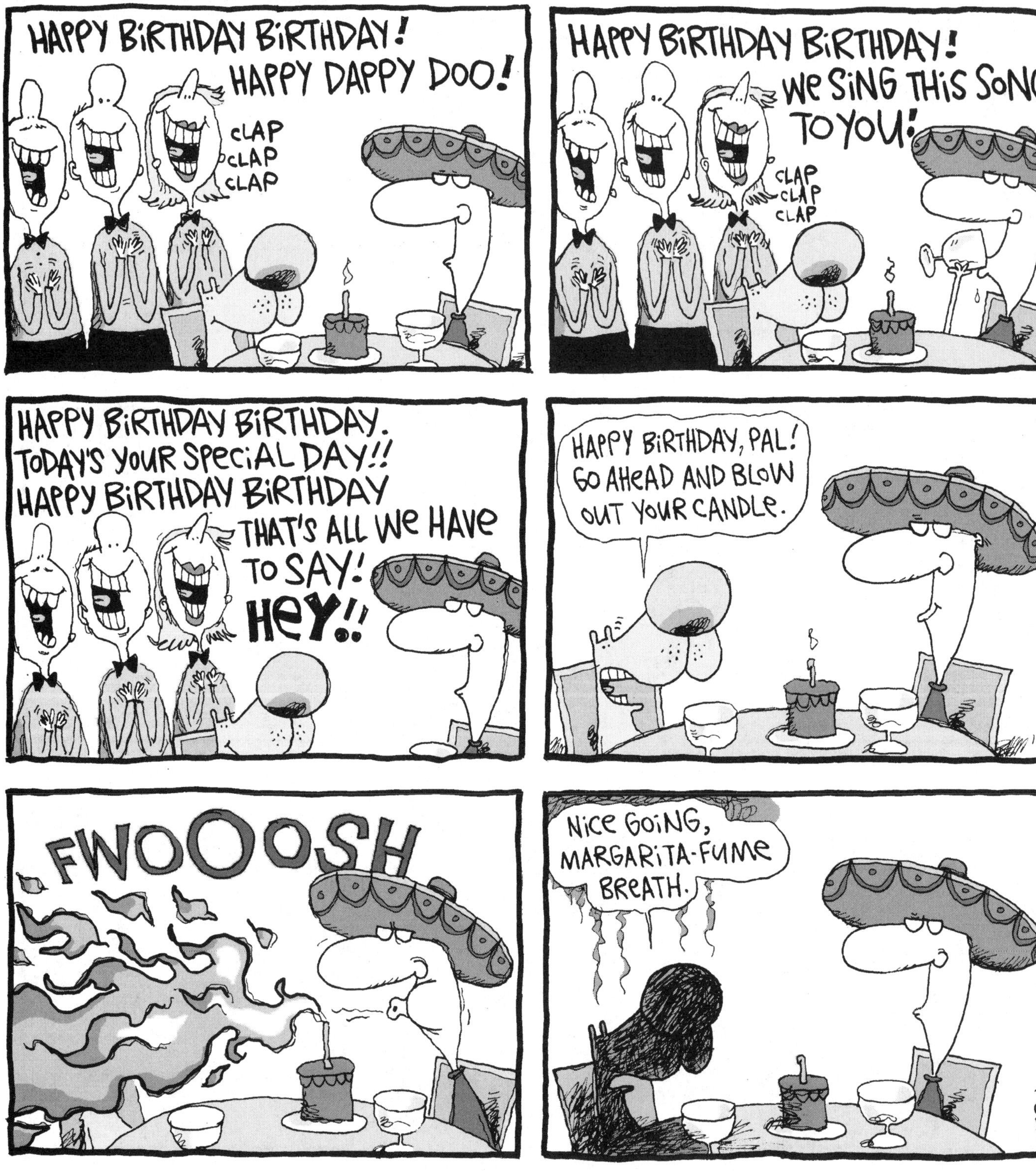
HAPPY BiRTHDAY BiRTHDAY!
HAPPY DAPPY DOO!
CLAP CLAP CLAP
HAPPY BiRTHDAY BiRTHDAY!
We SiNG THIS SONG TO YOU!
CLAP CLAP CLAP
HAPPY BiRTHDAY BiRTHDAY.
TODAY'S YOUR SPeCiAL DAY!!
HAPPY BiRTHDAY BiRTHDAY
THAT'S ALL We HAVe TO SAY!
HeY!!
HAPPY BiRTHDAY, PAL! GO AHeAD AND BLOW OUT YOUR CANDLe.
FWOOOSH
NiCe GOiNG, MARGARiTA-FUMe BReATH.

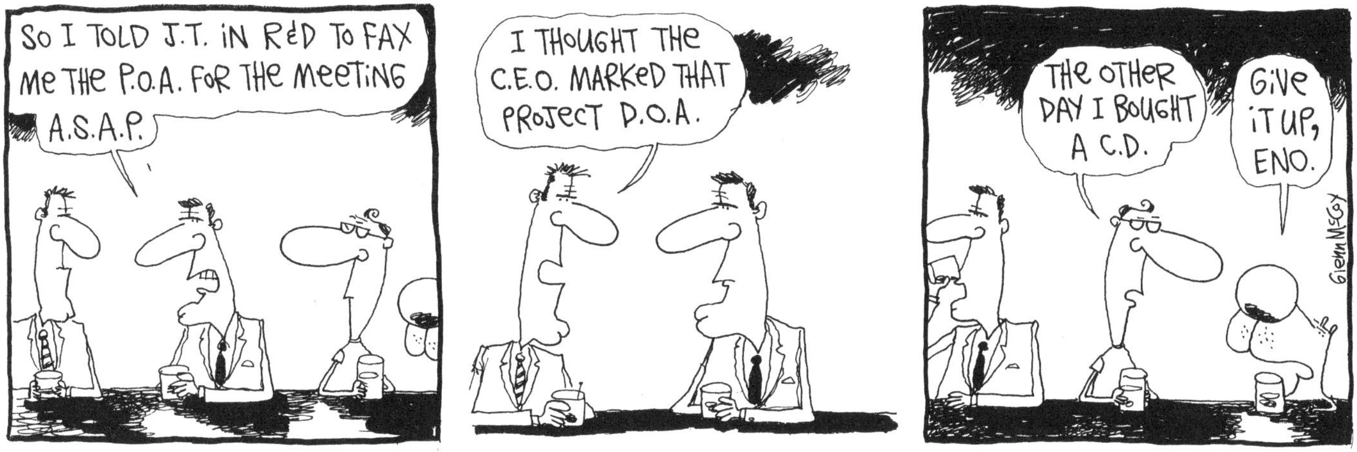
SO I TOLD J.T. IN R&D TO FAX ME THE P.O.A. FOR THE MEETING A.S.A.P.
I THOUGHT THE C.E.O. MARKED THAT PROJECT D.O.A.
THE OTHER DAY I BOUGHT A C.D.
GIVE IT UP, ENO.
GLENN McCOY

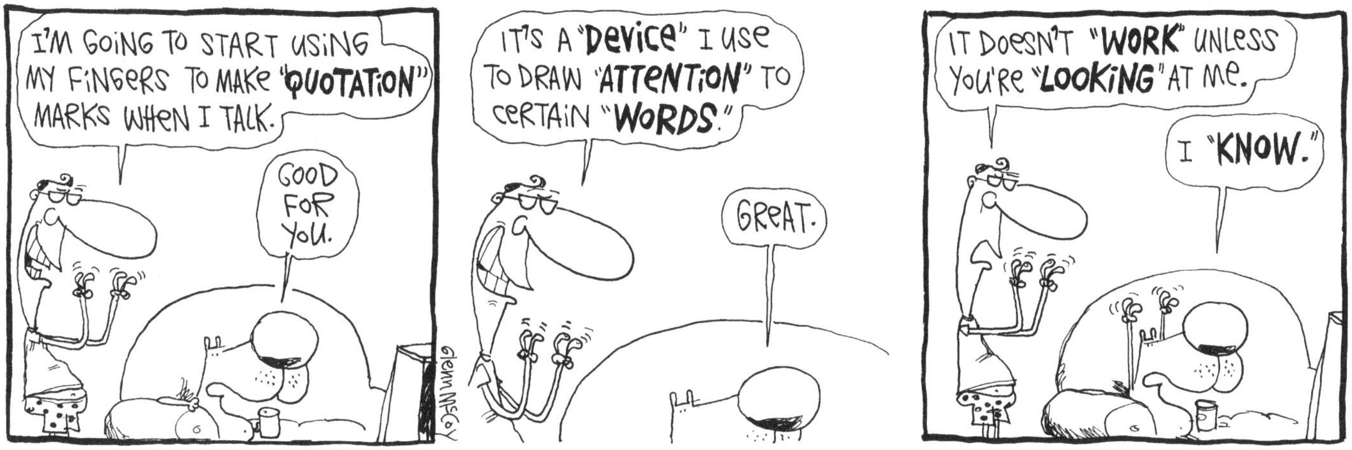
I'M GOING TO START USING MY FINGERS TO MAKE "QUOTATION" MARKS WHEN I TALK.
GOOD FOR YOU.
GLENN McCOY
IT'S A "DEVICE" I USE TO DRAW "ATTENTION" TO CERTAIN "WORDS."
GREAT.
IT DOESN'T "WORK" UNLESS YOU'RE "LOOKING" AT ME.
I "KNOW."

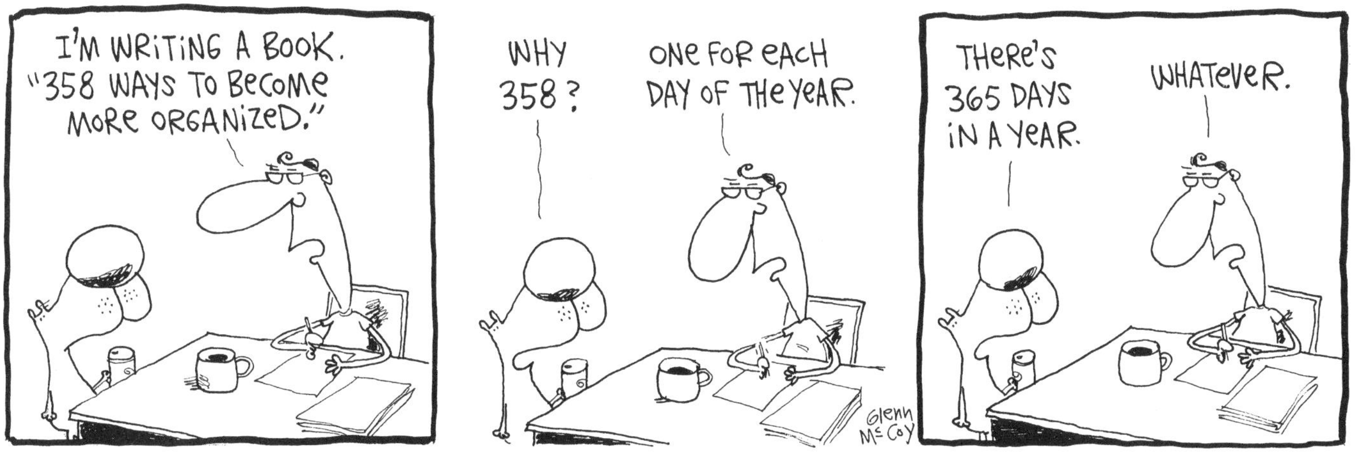
I'M WRITING A BOOK. "358 WAYS TO BECOME MORE ORGANIZED."
WHY 358?
ONE FOR EACH DAY OF THE YEAR.
GLENN McCOY
THERE'S 365 DAYS IN A YEAR.
WHATEVER.

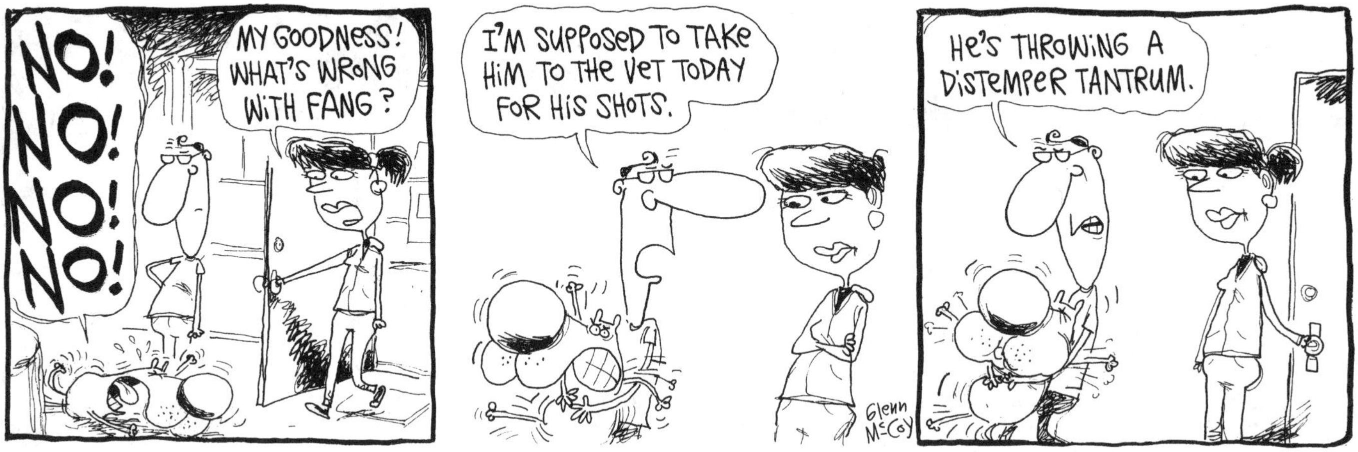
NO! NO! NO! NO!
MY GOODNESS! WHAT'S WRONG WITH FANG?
I'M SUPPOSED TO TAKE HIM TO THE VET TODAY FOR HIS SHOTS.
HE'S THROWING A DISTEMPER TANTRUM.
Glenn McCoy

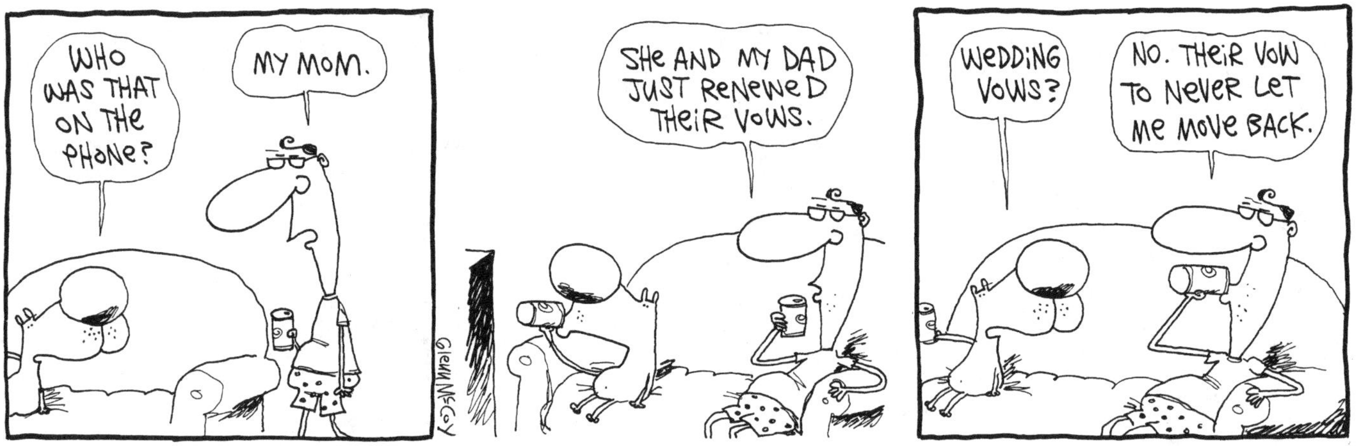
WHO WAS THAT ON THE PHONE?
MY MOM.
SHE AND MY DAD JUST RENEWED THEIR VOWS.
WEDDING VOWS?
NO. THEIR VOW TO NEVER LET ME MOVE BACK.
Glenn McCoy

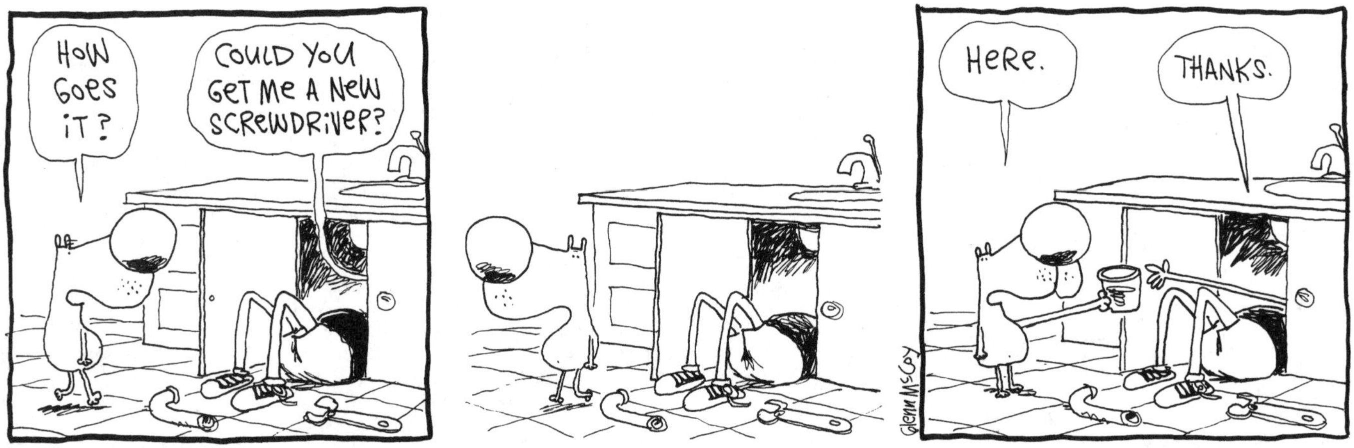
HOW GOES IT?
COULD YOU GET ME A NEW SCREWDRIVER?
HERE.
THANKS.
Glenn McCoy

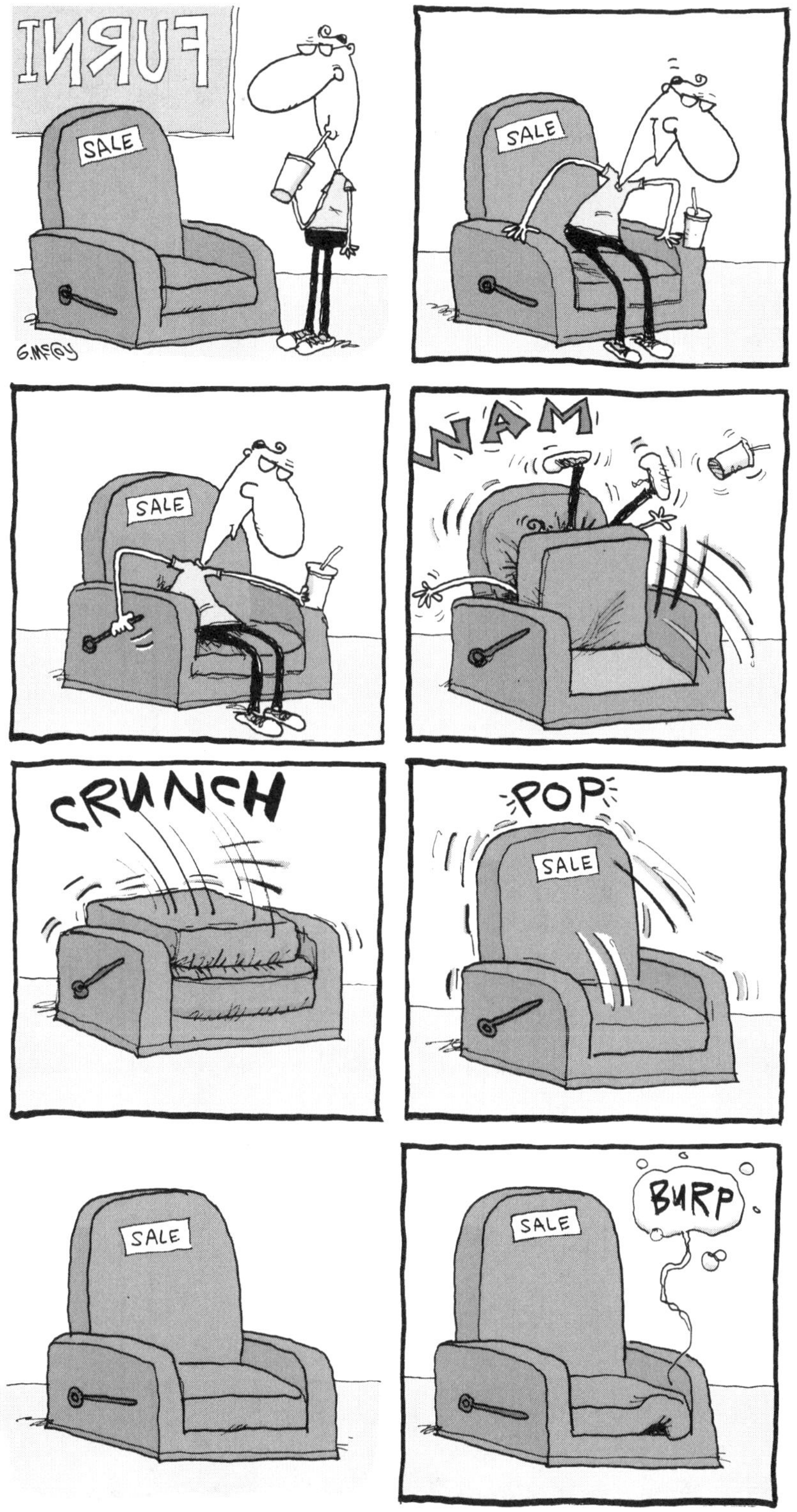
FURNI
SALE
SALE
SALE
WAM
CRUNCH
POP
SALE
SALE
SALE
BURP

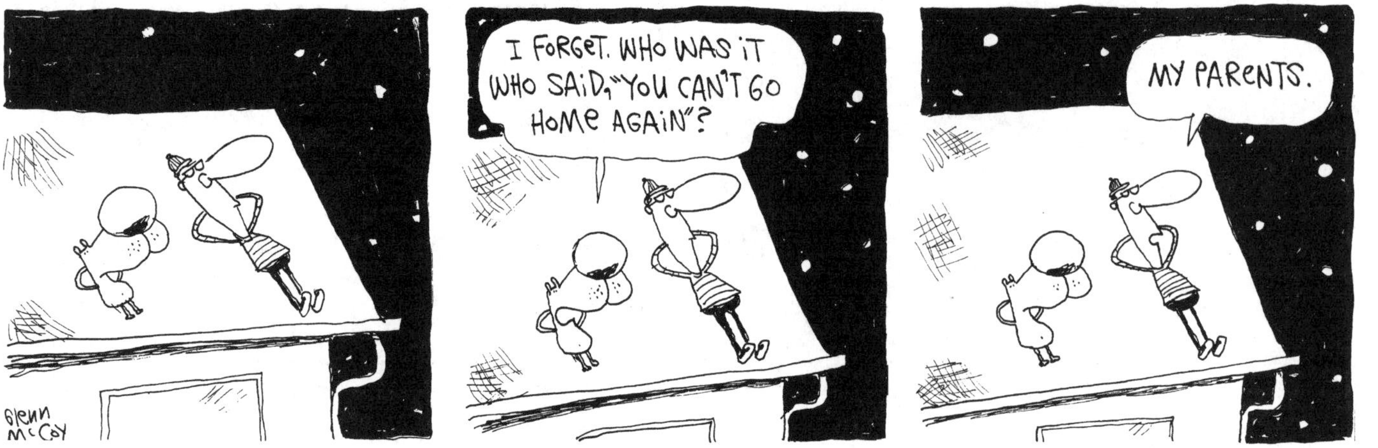
Glenn McCoy
I FORGET. WHO WAS IT WHO SAID, "YOU CAN'T GO HOME AGAIN"?
MY PARENTS.

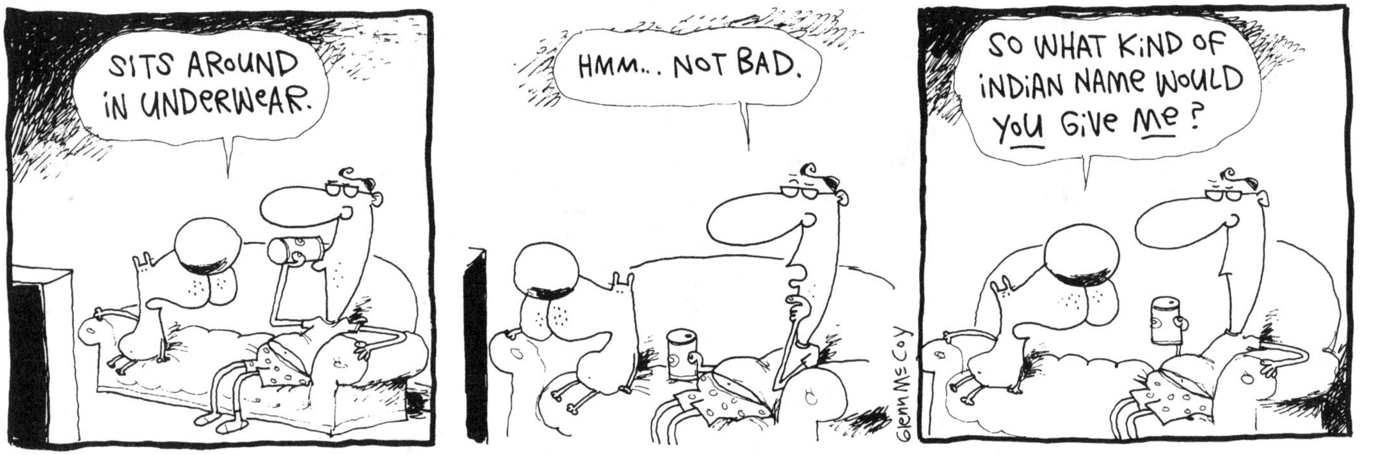
SITS AROUND IN UNDERWEAR.
HMM... NOT BAD.
Glenn McCoy
SO WHAT KIND OF INDIAN NAME WOULD YOU GIVE ME?

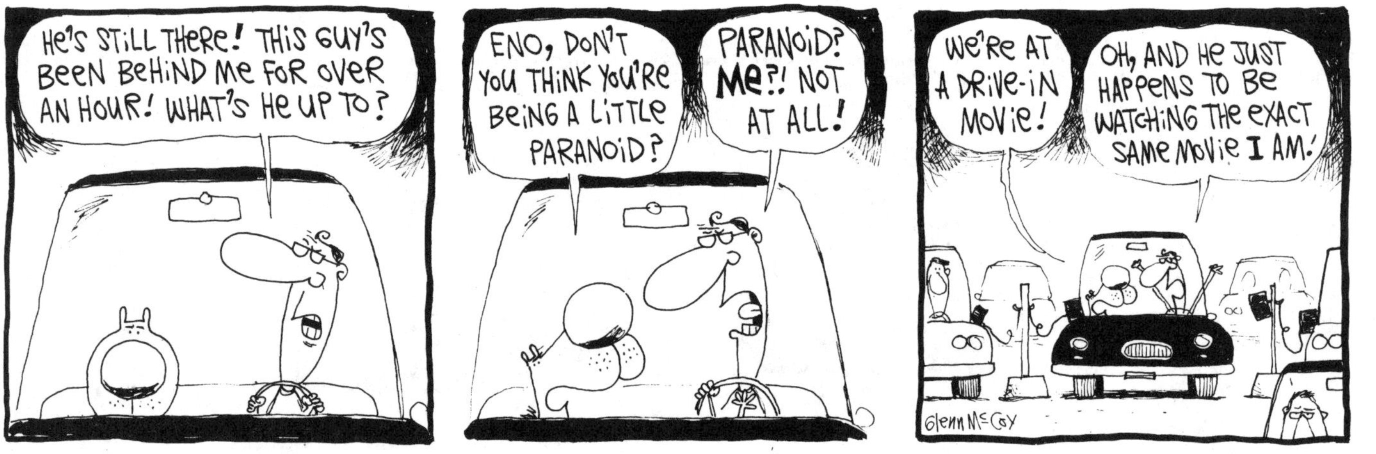
HE'S STILL THERE! THIS GUY'S BEEN BEHIND ME FOR OVER AN HOUR! WHAT'S HE UP TO?
ENO, DON'T YOU THINK YOU'RE BEING A LITTLE PARANOID?
PARANOID? ME?! NOT AT ALL!
WE'RE AT A DRIVE-IN MOVIE!
OH, AND HE JUST HAPPENS TO BE WATCHING THE EXACT SAME MOVIE I AM!
Glenn McCoy

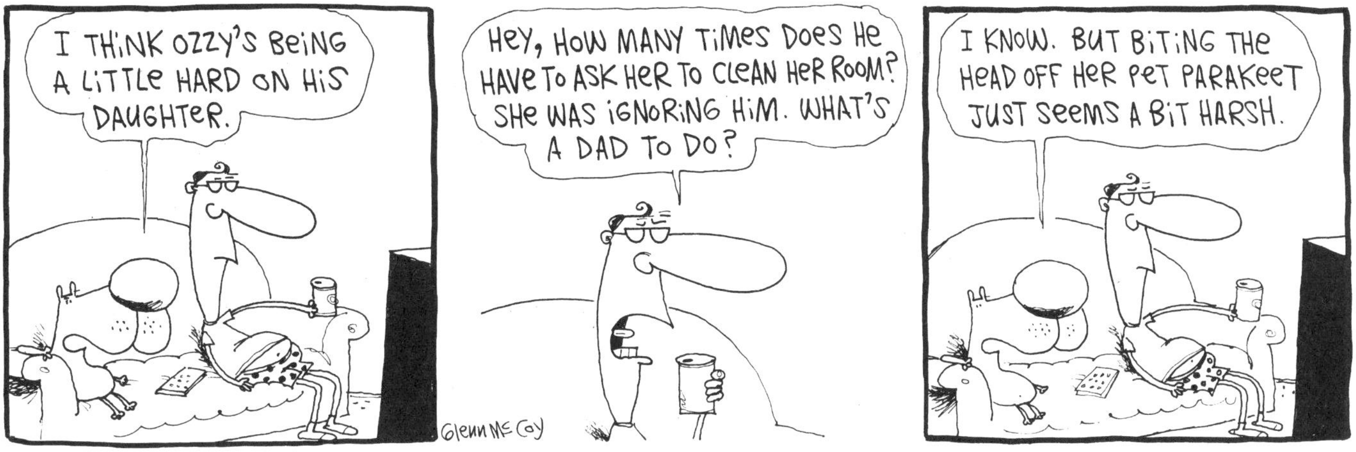
I THINK OZZY'S BEING A LITTLE HARD ON HIS DAUGHTER.
HEY, HOW MANY TIMES DOES HE HAVE TO ASK HER TO CLEAN HER ROOM? SHE WAS IGNORING HIM. WHAT'S A DAD TO DO?
I KNOW. BUT BITING THE HEAD OFF HER PET PARAKEET JUST SEEMS A BIT HARSH.
GLENN MCCOY

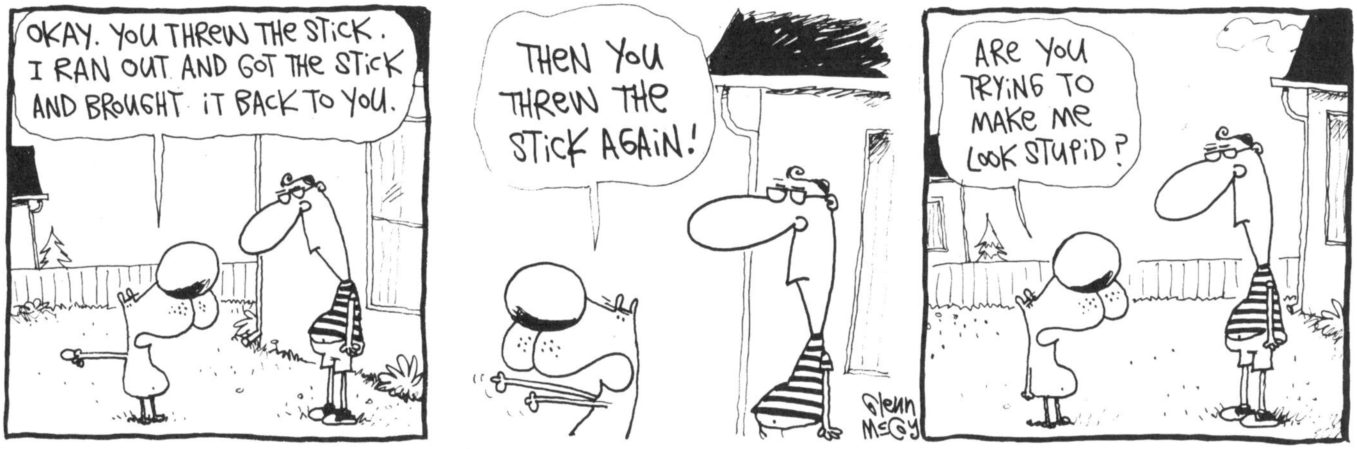
OKAY. YOU THREW THE STICK. I RAN OUT AND GOT THE STICK AND BROUGHT IT BACK TO YOU.
THEN YOU THREW THE STICK AGAIN!
ARE YOU TRYING TO MAKE ME LOOK STUPID?
GLENN MCCOY

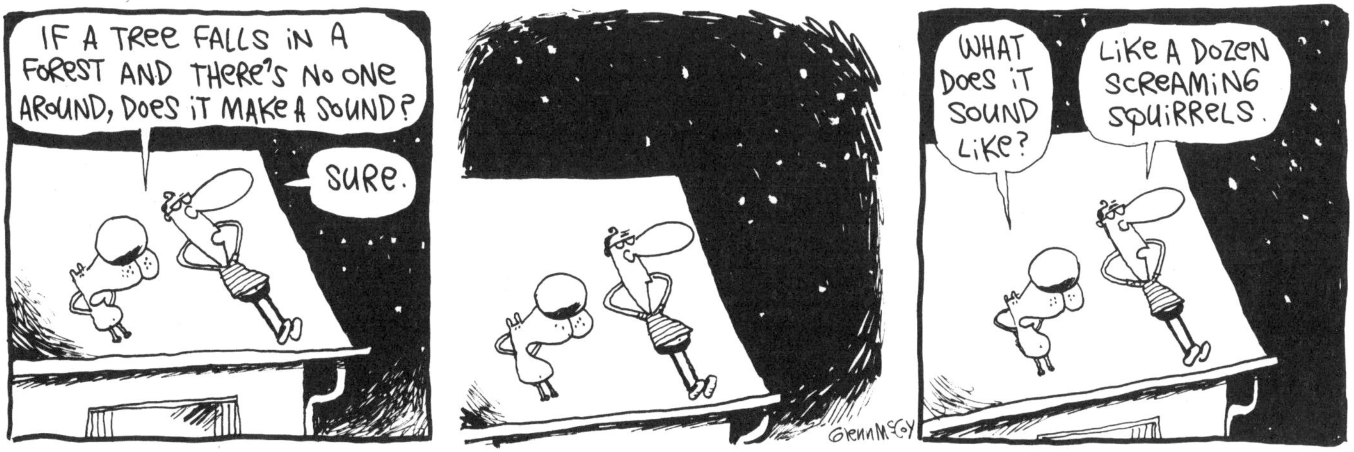
IF A TREE FALLS IN A FOREST AND THERE'S NO ONE AROUND, DOES IT MAKE A SOUND?
SURE.
WHAT DOES IT SOUND LIKE?
LIKE A DOZEN SCREAMING SQUIRRELS.
GLENN MCCOY

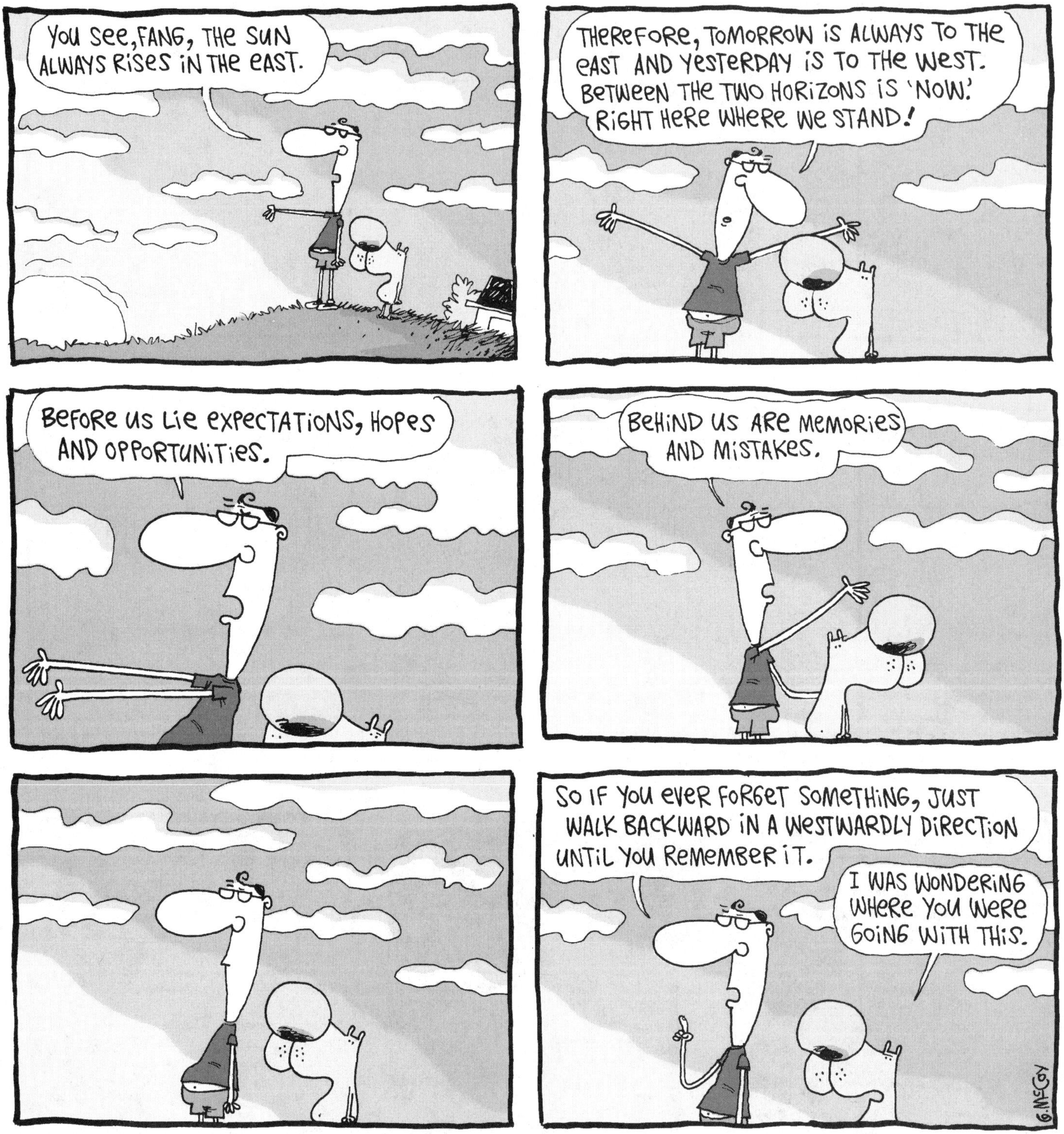
YOU SEE, FANG, THE SUN ALWAYS RISES IN THE EAST.
THEREFORE, TOMORROW IS ALWAYS TO THE EAST AND YESTERDAY IS TO THE WEST. BETWEEN THE TWO HORIZONS IS 'NOW.' RIGHT HERE WHERE WE STAND!
BEFORE US LIE EXPECTATIONS, HOPES AND OPPORTUNITIES.
BEHIND US ARE MEMORIES AND MISTAKES.
SO IF YOU EVER FORGET SOMETHING, JUST WALK BACKWARD IN A WESTWARDLY DIRECTION UNTIL YOU REMEMBER IT.
I WAS WONDERING WHERE YOU WERE GOING WITH THIS.
G. McCOY

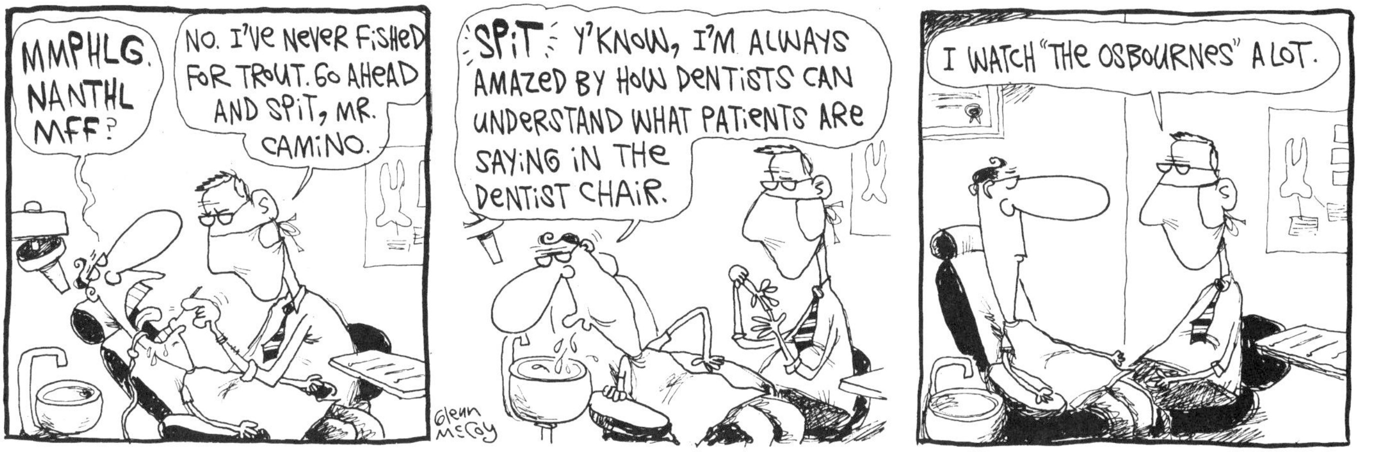
MMPHLG. NANTHL MFF?
NO. I'VE NEVER FISHED FOR TROUT. GO AHEAD AND SPIT, MR. CAMINO.
SPIT
Y'KNOW, I'M ALWAYS AMAZED BY HOW DENTISTS CAN UNDERSTAND WHAT PATIENTS ARE SAYING IN THE DENTIST CHAIR.
I WATCH "THE OSBOURNES" A LOT.
Glenn McCoy

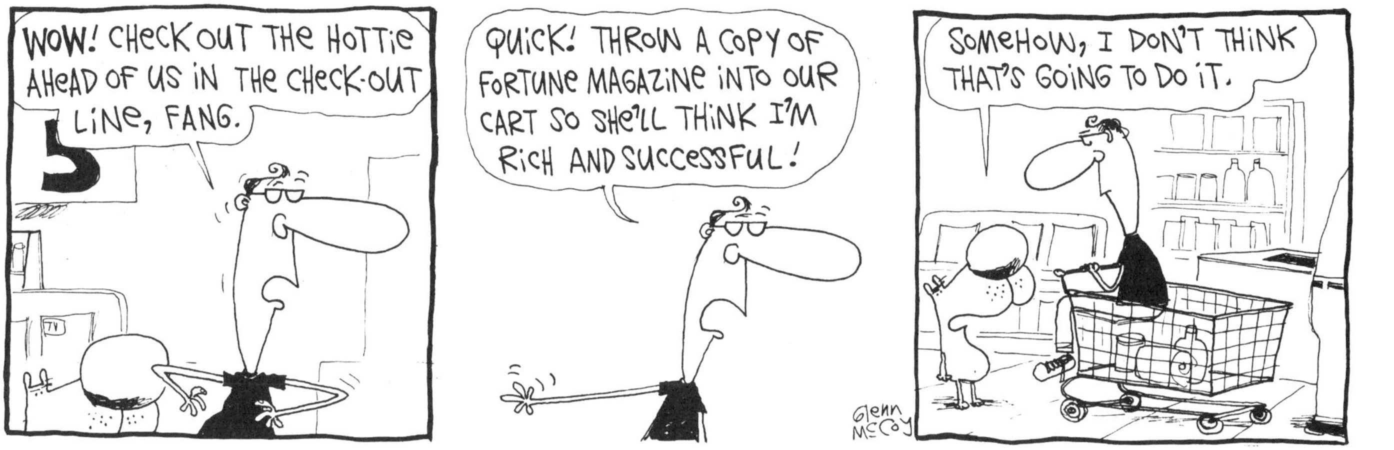
WOW! CHECK OUT THE HOTTIE AHEAD OF US IN THE CHECK-OUT LINE, FANG.
QUICK! THROW A COPY OF FORTUNE MAGAZINE INTO OUR CART SO SHE'LL THINK I'M RICH AND SUCCESSFUL!
SOMEHOW, I DON'T THINK THAT'S GOING TO DO IT.
Glenn McCoy

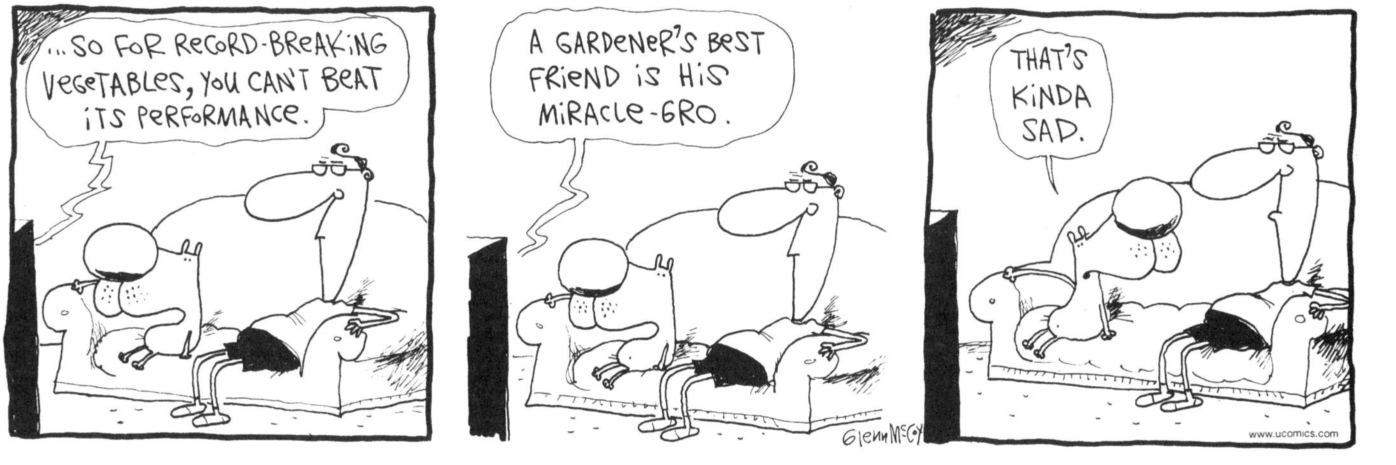
...SO FOR RECORD-BREAKING VEGETABLES, YOU CAN'T BEAT ITS PERFORMANCE.
A GARDENER'S BEST FRIEND IS HIS MIRACLE-GRO.
THAT'S KINDA SAD.
Glenn McCoy
www.ucomics.com

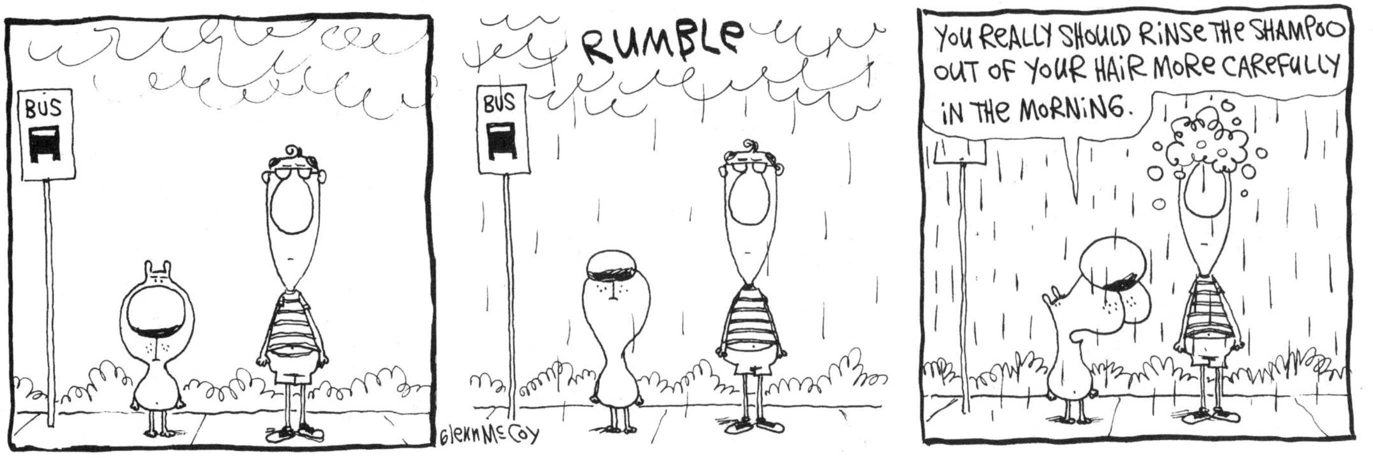
BUS
RUMBLE
BUS
GLENN McCOY
YOU REALLY SHOULD RINSE THE SHAMPOO OUT OF YOUR HAIR MORE CAREFULLY IN THE MORNING.

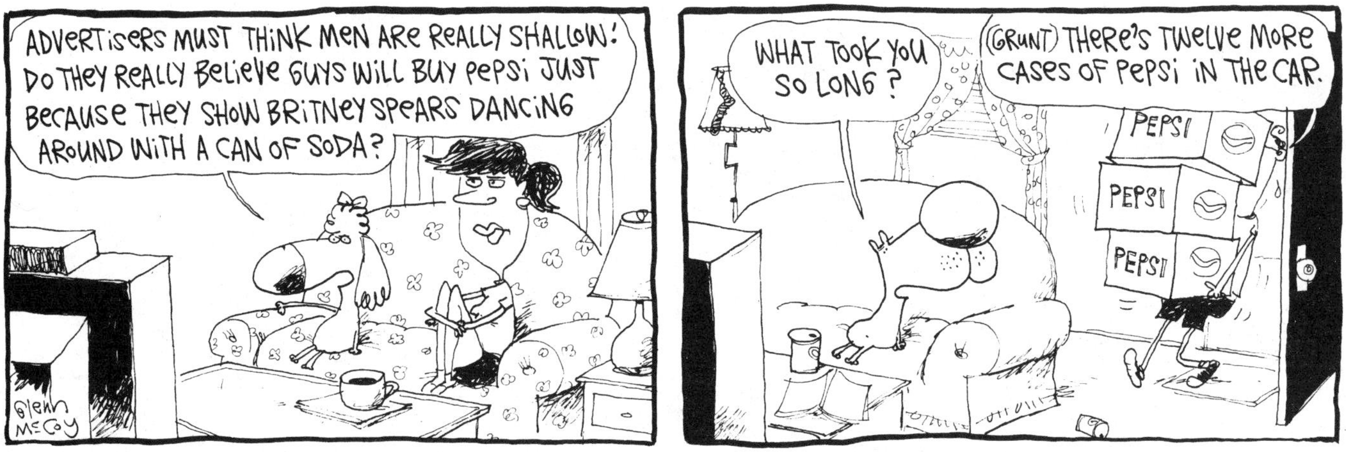
ADVERTISERS MUST THINK MEN ARE REALLY SHALLOW! DO THEY REALLY BELIEVE GUYS WILL BUY PEPSI JUST BECAUSE THEY SHOW BRITNEY SPEARS DANCING AROUND WITH A CAN OF SODA?
GLENN McCOY
WHAT TOOK YOU SO LONG?
(GRUNT) THERE'S TWELVE MORE CASES OF PEPSI IN THE CAR.
PEPSI
PEPSI
PEPSI

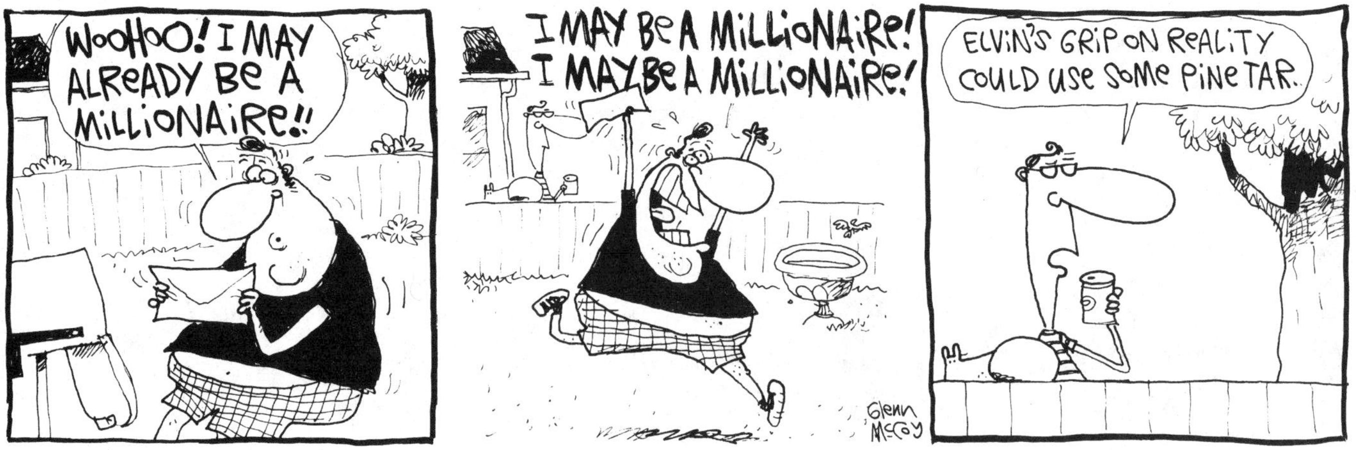
WOOHOO! I MAY ALREADY BE A MILLIONAIRE!!
I MAY BE A MILLIONAIRE! I MAY BE A MILLIONAIRE!
GLENN McCOY
ELVIN'S GRIP ON REALITY COULD USE SOME PINE TAR.

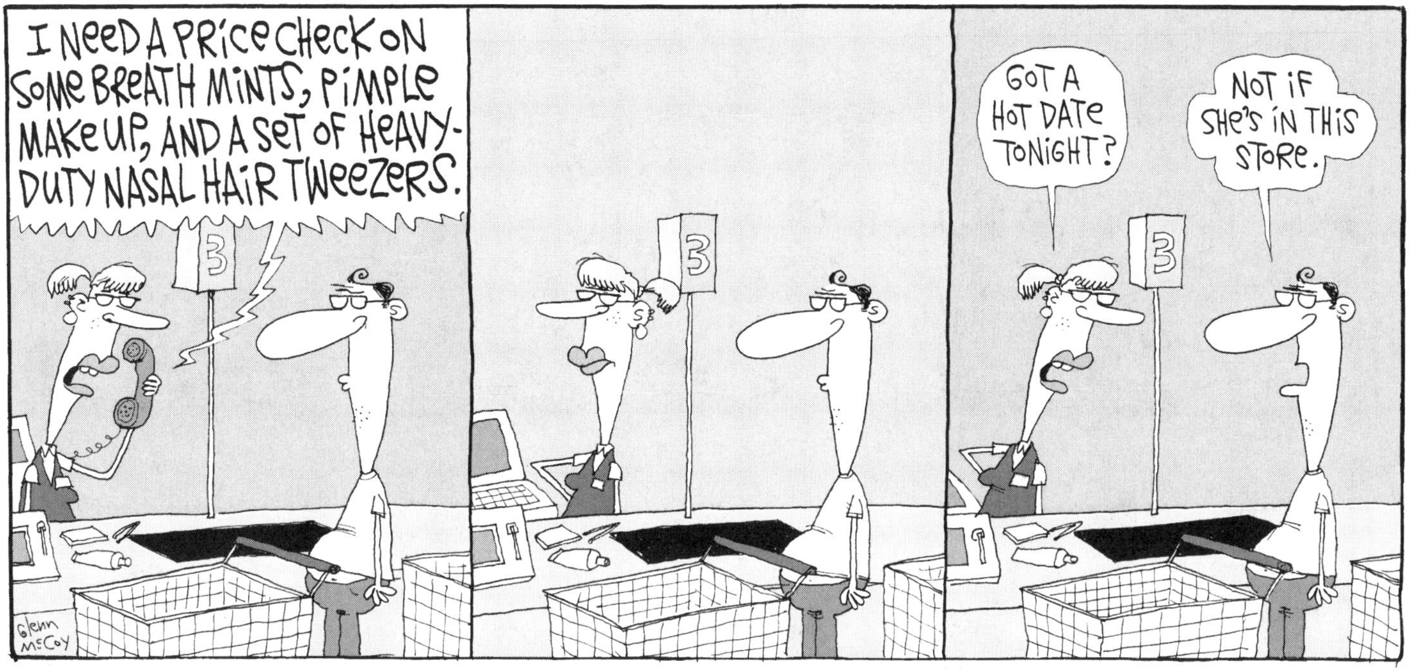
I NEED A PRICE CHECK ON SOME BREATH MINTS, PIMPLE MAKEUP, AND A SET OF HEAVY-DUTY NASAL HAIR TWEEZERS.
GOT A HOT DATE TONIGHT?
NOT IF SHE'S IN THIS STORE.
Glenn McCoy

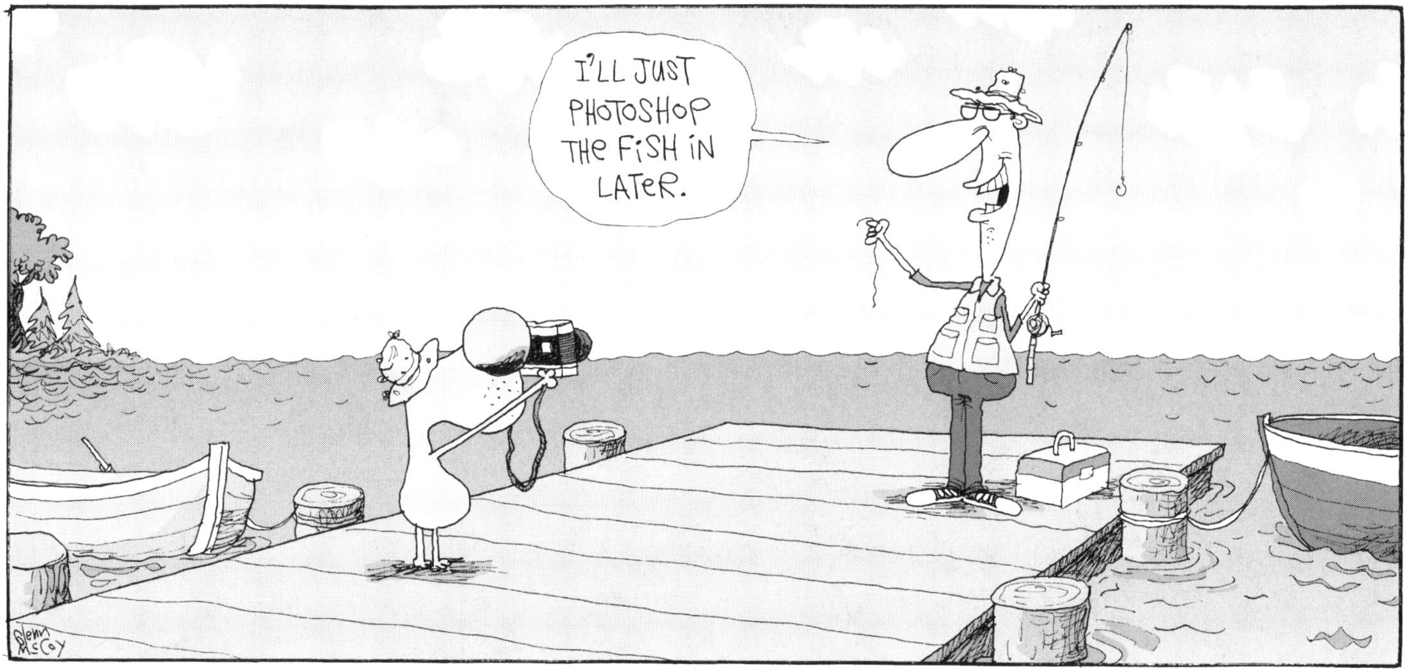
I'LL JUST PHOTOSHOP THE FISH IN LATER.
Glenn McCoy

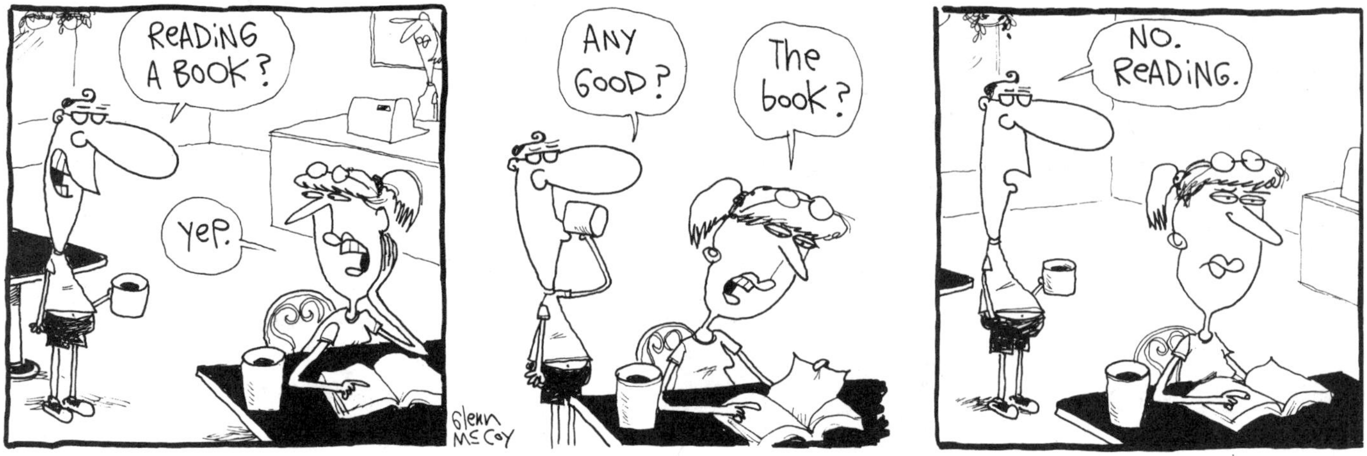
READING A BOOK?
YEP.
Glenn McCoy
ANY GOOD?
The book?
NO. READING.

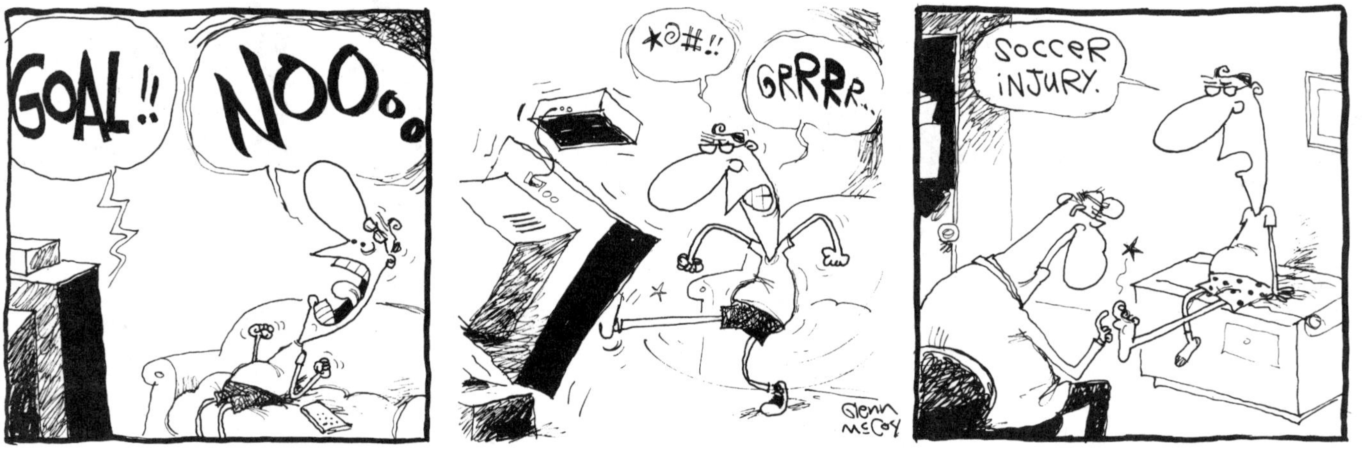
GOAL!!
NOOooo
*@#!!
GRRRR..
Glenn McCoy
SOCCER INJURY.

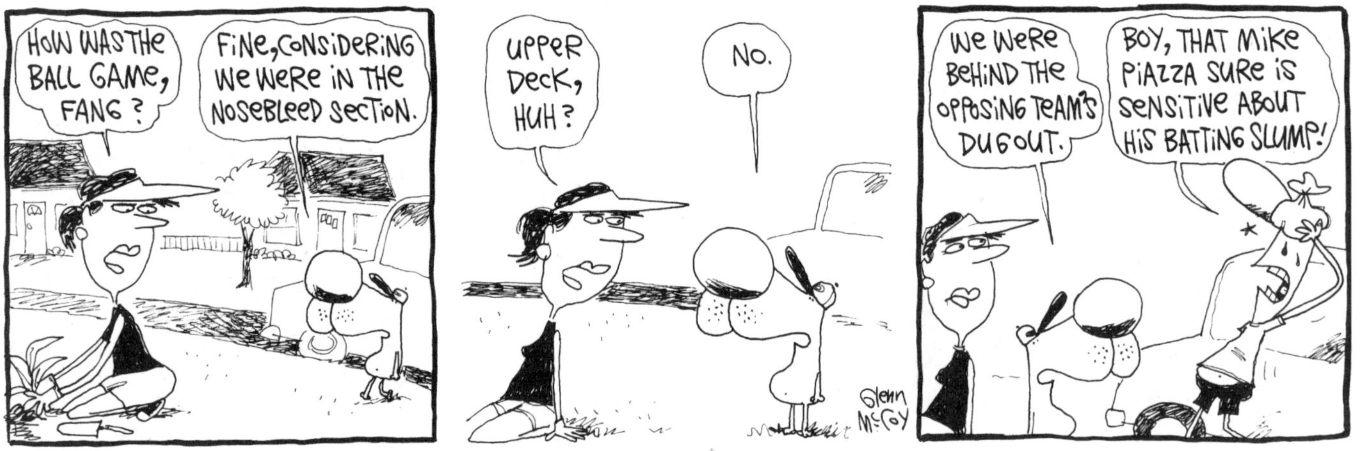
HOW WAS THE BALL GAME, FANG?
FINE, CONSIDERING WE WERE IN THE NOSEBLEED SECTION.
UPPER DECK, HUH?
NO.
Glenn McCoy
WE WERE BEHIND THE OPPOSING TEAM'S DUGOUT.
BOY, THAT MIKE PIAZZA SURE IS SENSITIVE ABOUT HIS BATTING SLUMP!

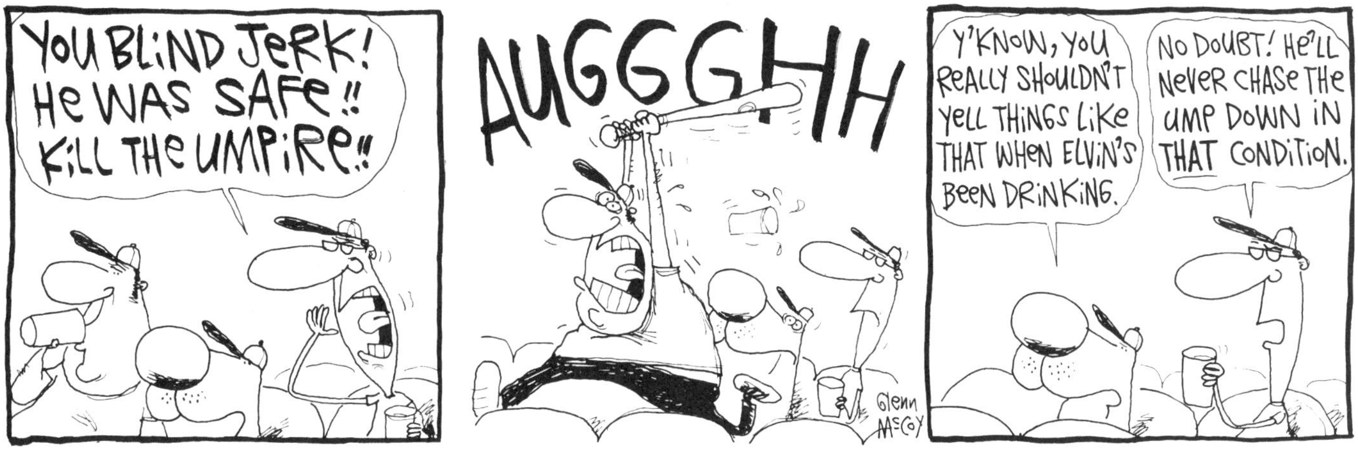
YOU BLIND JERK! HE WAS SAFE!! KILL THE UMPIRE!!
AUGGGHH
Glenn McCoy
Y'KNOW, YOU REALLY SHOULDN'T YELL THINGS LIKE THAT WHEN ELVIN'S BEEN DRINKING.
NO DOUBT! HE'LL NEVER CHASE THE UMP DOWN IN THAT CONDITION.

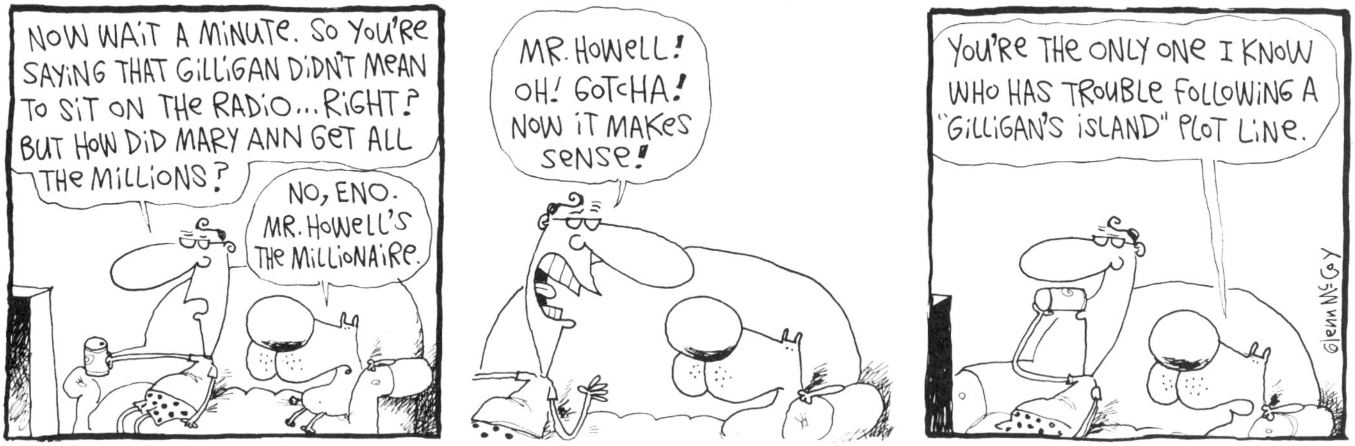
NOW WAIT A MINUTE. SO YOU'RE SAYING THAT GILLIGAN DIDN'T MEAN TO SIT ON THE RADIO... RIGHT? BUT HOW DID MARY ANN GET ALL THE MILLIONS?
NO, ENO. MR. HOWELL'S THE MILLIONAIRE.
MR. HOWELL! OH! GOTCHA! NOW IT MAKES SENSE!
YOU'RE THE ONLY ONE I KNOW WHO HAS TROUBLE FOLLOWING A "GILLIGAN'S ISLAND" PLOT LINE.
Glenn McCoy

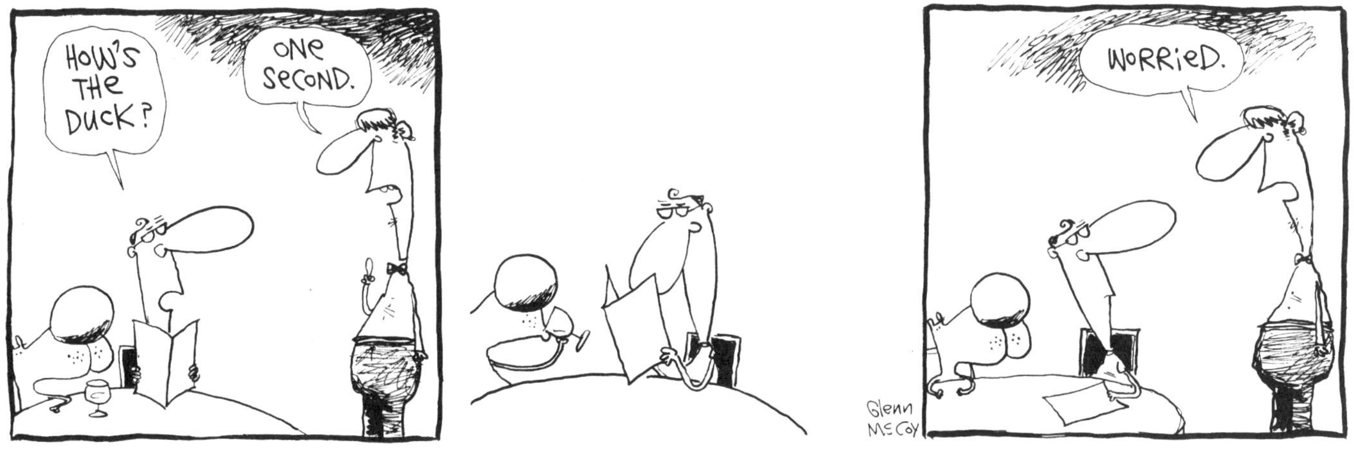
HOW'S THE DUCK?
ONE SECOND.
Glenn McCoy
WORRIED.

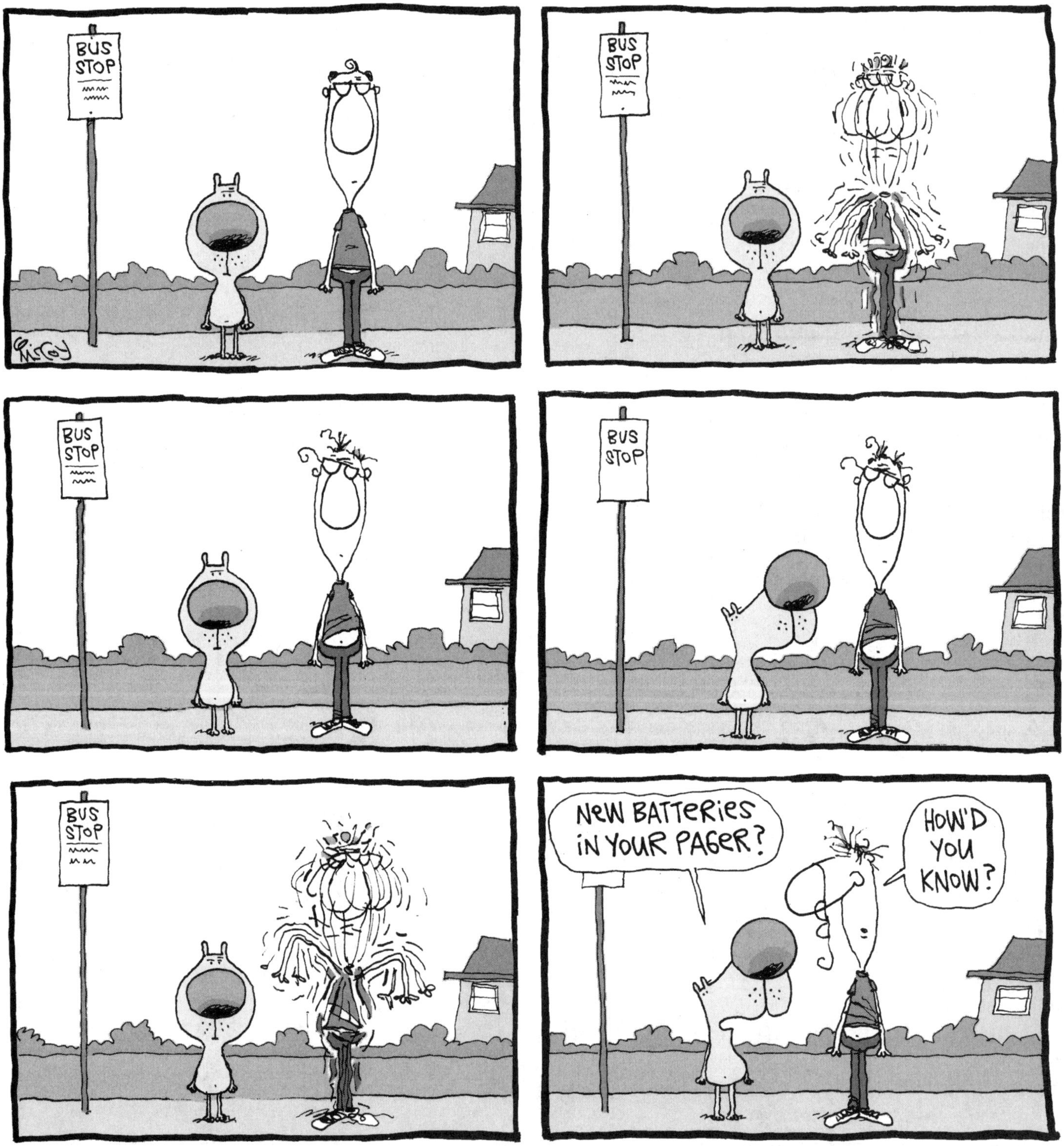
BUS STOP
BUS STOP
BUS STOP
BUS STOP
BUS STOP
NEW BATTERIES IN YOUR PAGER?
HOW'D YOU KNOW?

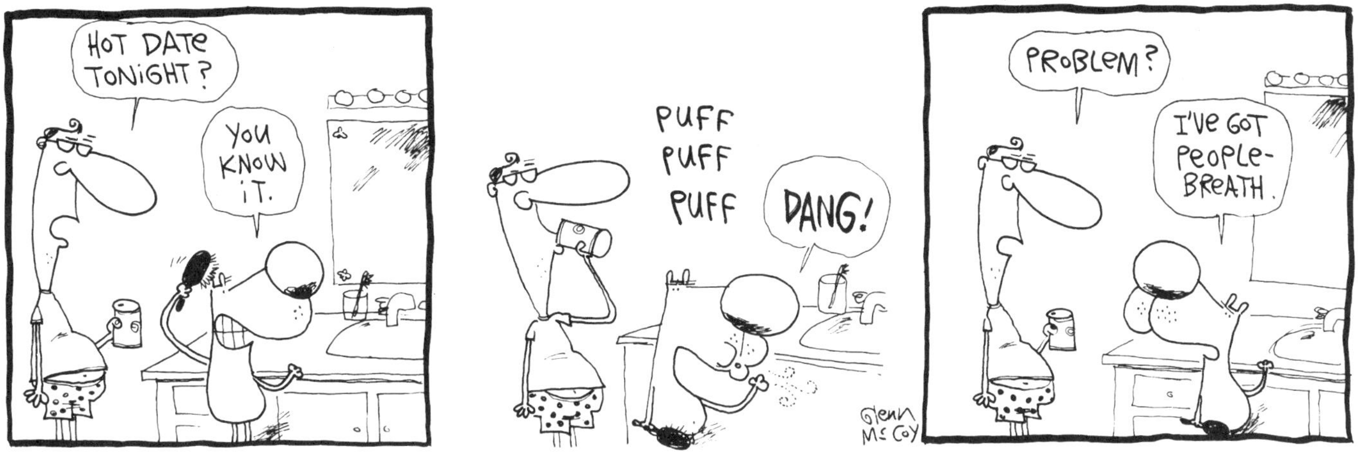
HOT DATE TONIGHT?
YOU KNOW IT.
PUFF PUFF PUFF
DANG!
Glenn McCoy
PROBLEM?
I'VE GOT PEOPLE-BREATH.

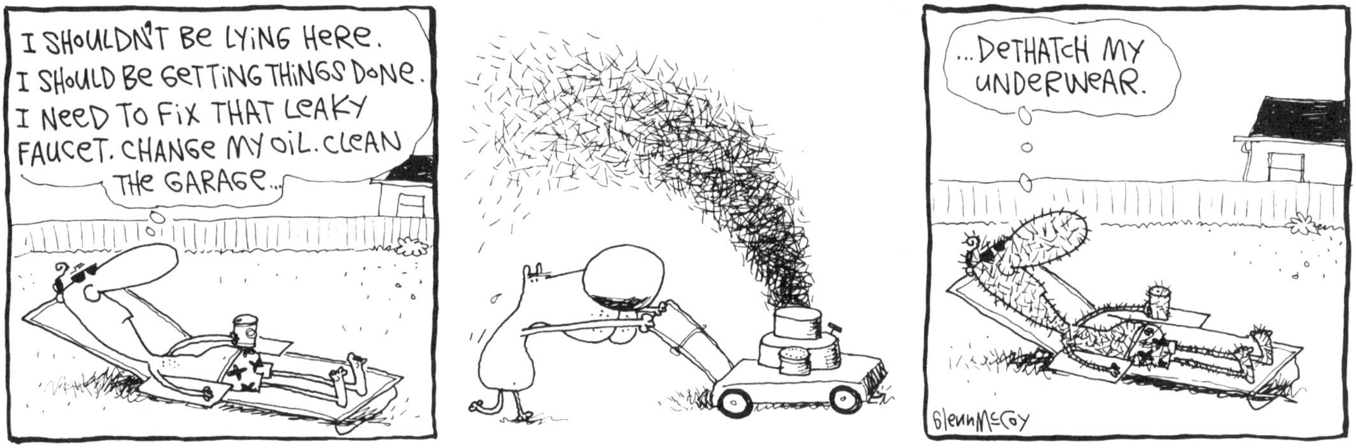
I SHOULDN'T BE LYING HERE. I SHOULD BE GETTING THINGS DONE. I NEED TO FIX THAT LEAKY FAUCET. CHANGE MY OIL. CLEAN THE GARAGE...
...DETHATCH MY UNDERWEAR.
GlennMcCoy

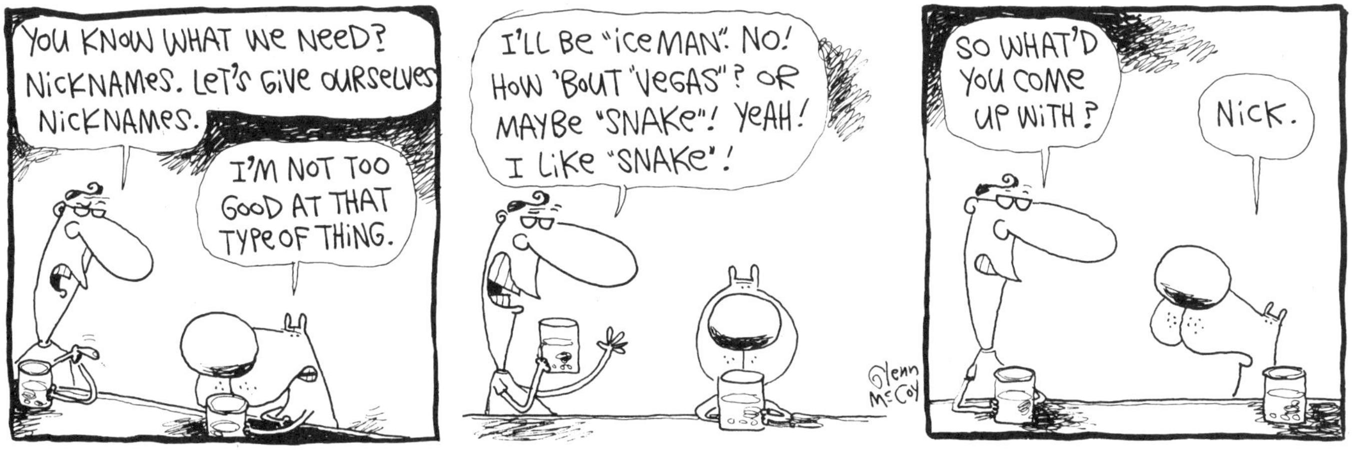
YOU KNOW WHAT WE NEED? NICKNAMES. LET'S GIVE OURSELVES NICKNAMES.
I'M NOT TOO GOOD AT THAT TYPE OF THING.
I'LL BE "ICEMAN". NO! HOW 'BOUT "VEGAS"? OR MAYBE "SNAKE"! YEAH! I LIKE "SNAKE"!
Glenn McCoy
SO WHAT'D YOU COME UP WITH?
NICK.

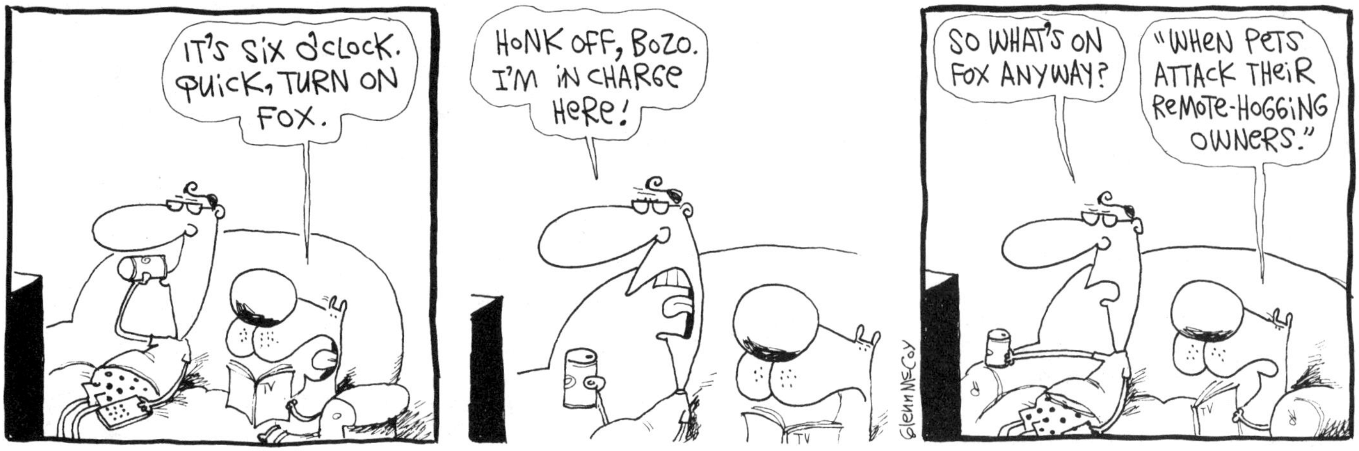
IT'S SIX O'CLOCK. QUICK, TURN ON FOX.
HONK OFF, BOZO. I'M IN CHARGE HERE!
SO WHAT'S ON FOX ANYWAY?
"WHEN PETS ATTACK THEIR REMOTE-HOGGING OWNERS."
GLENN McCOY

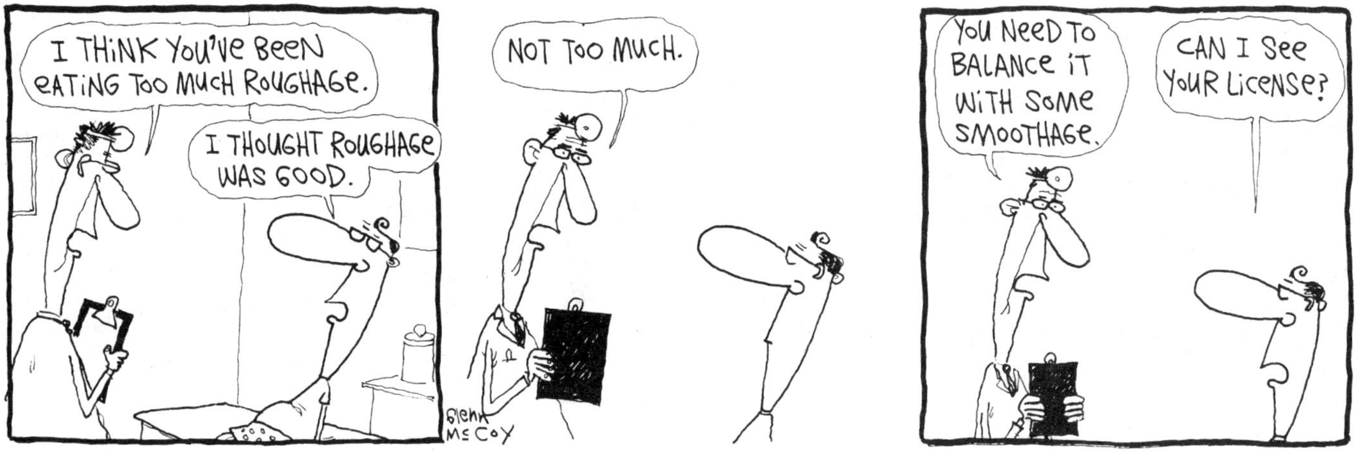
I THINK YOU'VE BEEN EATING TOO MUCH ROUGHAGE.
I THOUGHT ROUGHAGE WAS GOOD.
NOT TOO MUCH.
YOU NEED TO BALANCE IT WITH SOME SMOOTHAGE.
CAN I SEE YOUR LICENSE?
GLENN McCOY

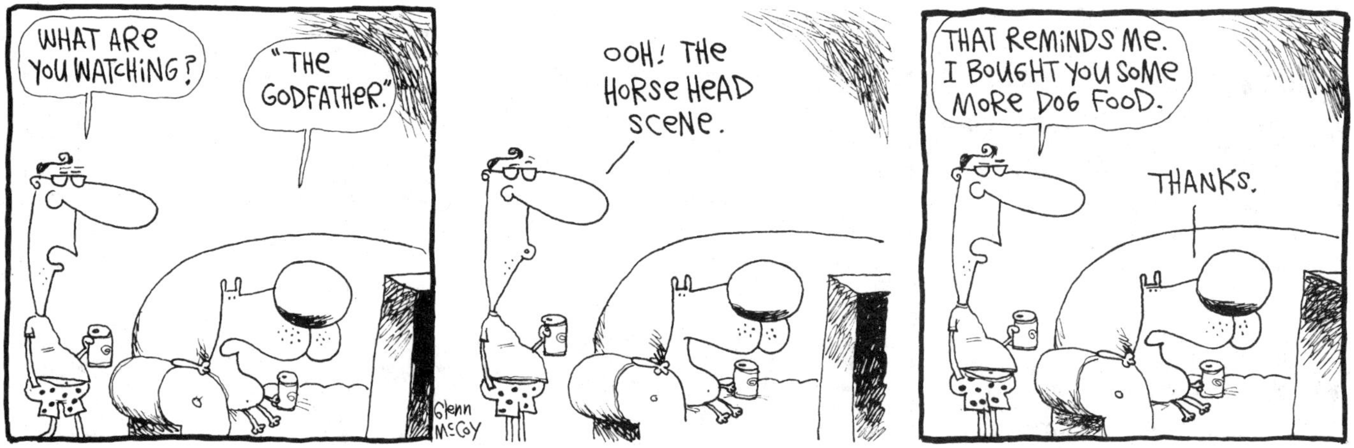
WHAT ARE YOU WATCHING?
"THE GODFATHER."
OOH! THE HORSE HEAD SCENE.
THAT REMINDS ME. I BOUGHT YOU SOME MORE DOG FOOD.
THANKS.
GLENN McCOY

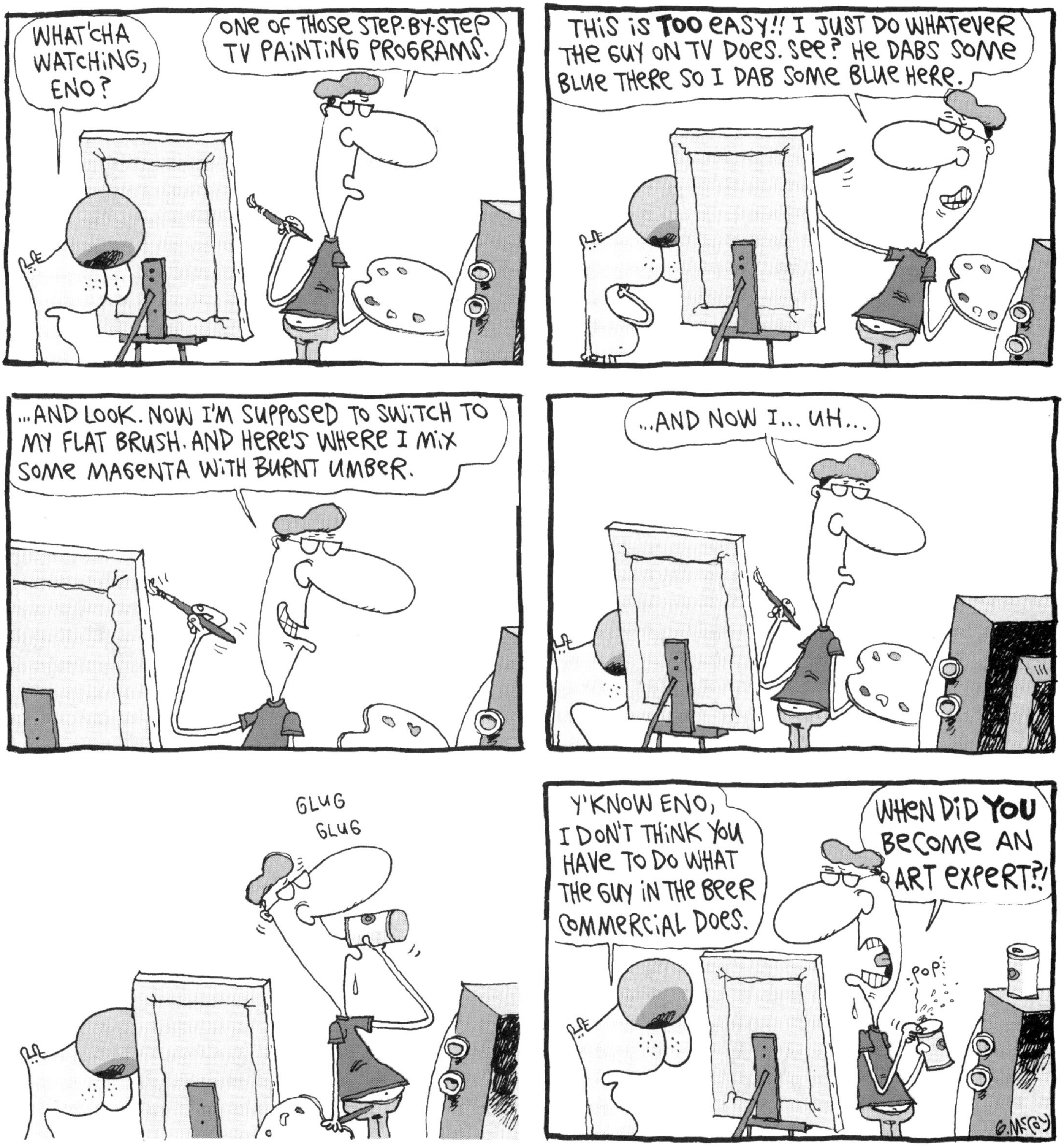
WHAT'CHA WATCHING, ENO?
ONE OF THOSE STEP-BY-STEP TV PAINTING PROGRAMS.
THIS IS **TOO** EASY!! I JUST DO WHATEVER THE GUY ON TV DOES. SEE? HE DABS SOME BLUE THERE SO I DAB SOME BLUE HERE.
...AND LOOK. NOW I'M SUPPOSED TO SWITCH TO MY FLAT BRUSH. AND HERE'S WHERE I MIX SOME MAGENTA WITH BURNT UMBER.
...AND NOW I... UH...
GLUG
GLUG
Y'KNOW ENO, I DON'T THINK YOU HAVE TO DO WHAT THE GUY IN THE BEER COMMERCIAL DOES.
WHEN DID **YOU** BECOME AN ART EXPERT?!
POP
G. MCCOY

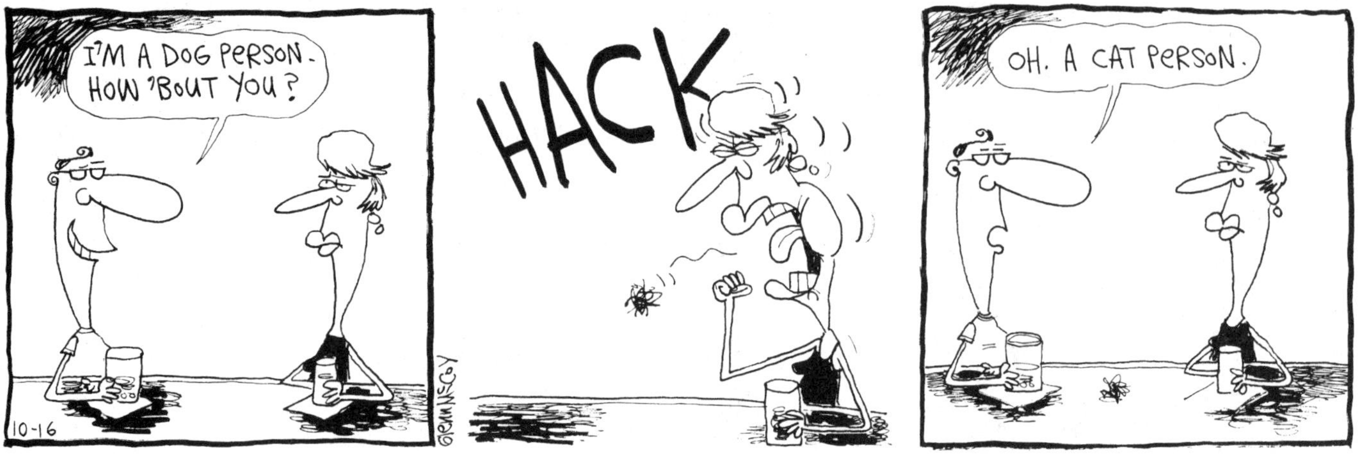
I'M A DOG PERSON. HOW 'BOUT YOU?
10-16
GLENN McCOY
HACK
OH. A CAT PERSON.

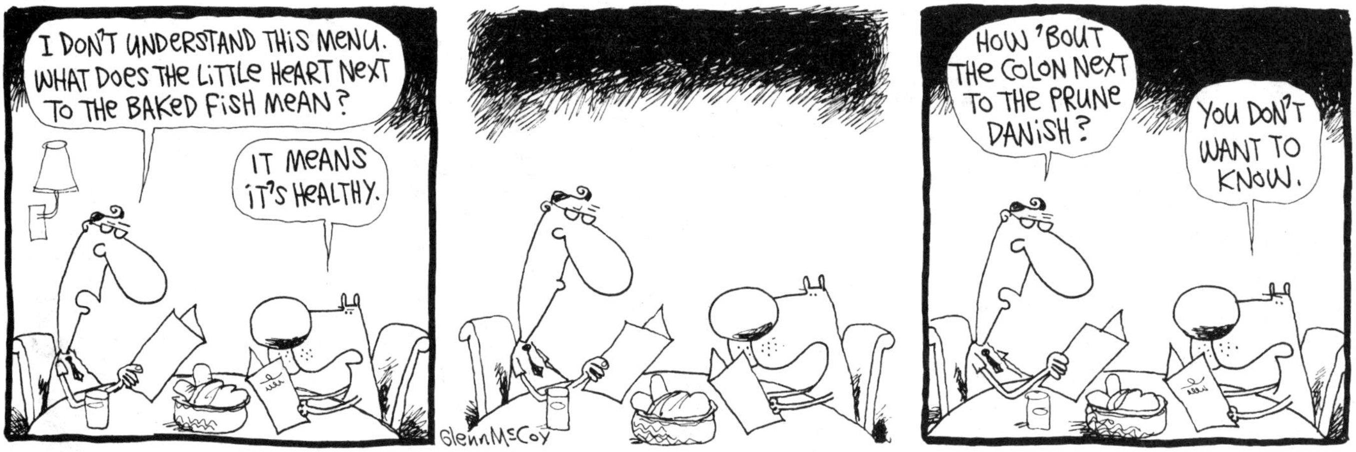
I DON'T UNDERSTAND THIS MENU. WHAT DOES THE LITTLE HEART NEXT TO THE BAKED FISH MEAN?
IT MEANS IT'S HEALTHY.
GLENN McCOY
HOW 'BOUT THE COLON NEXT TO THE PRUNE DANISH?
YOU DON'T WANT TO KNOW.

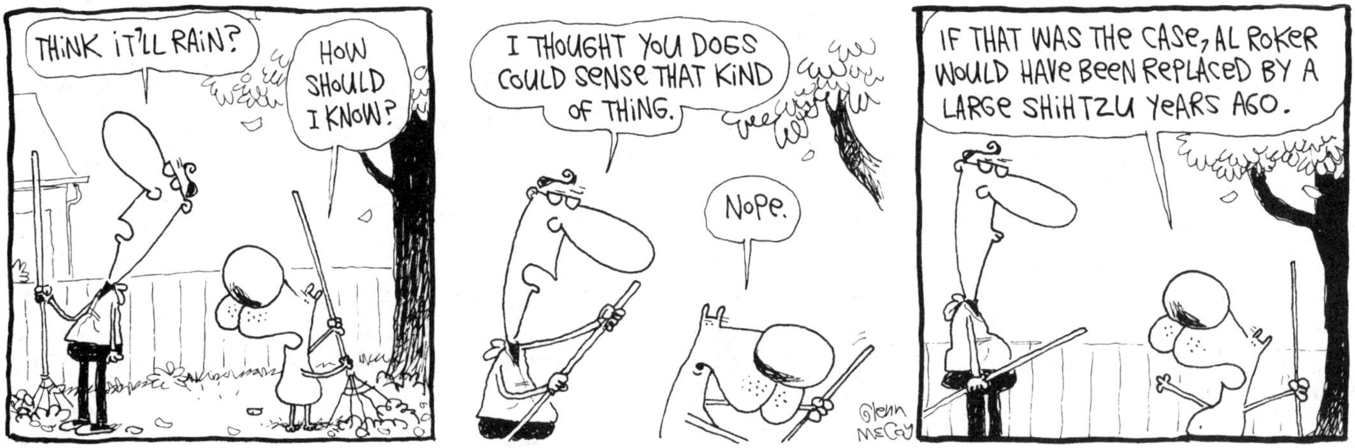
THINK IT'LL RAIN?
HOW SHOULD I KNOW?
I THOUGHT YOU DOGS COULD SENSE THAT KIND OF THING.
NOPE.
GLENN McCOY
IF THAT WAS THE CASE, AL ROKER WOULD HAVE BEEN REPLACED BY A LARGE SHIHTZU YEARS AGO.

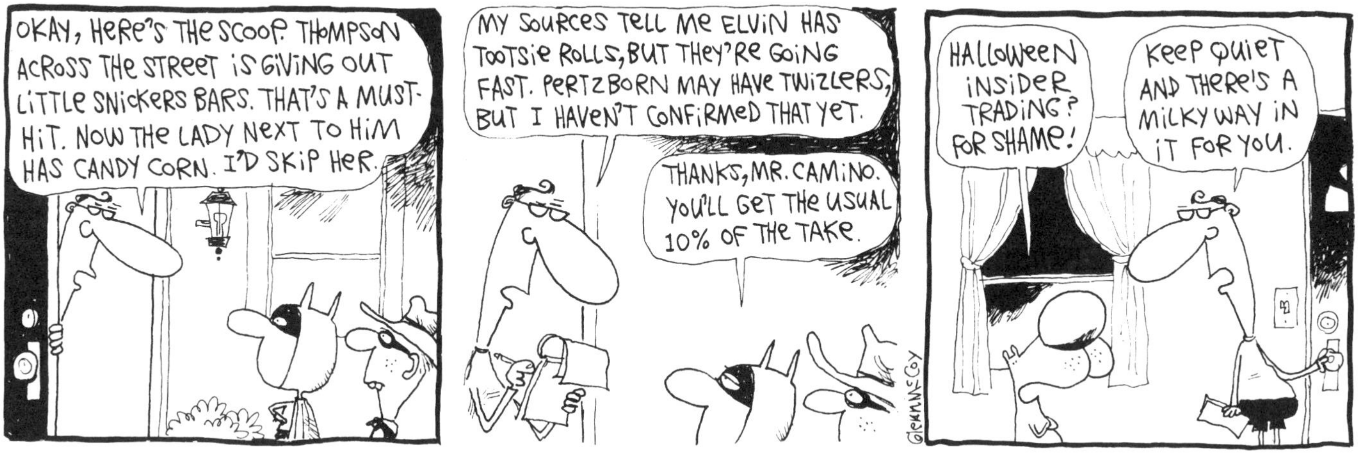
OKAY, HERE'S THE SCOOP. THOMPSON ACROSS THE STREET IS GIVING OUT LITTLE SNICKERS BARS. THAT'S A MUST-HIT. NOW THE LADY NEXT TO HIM HAS CANDY CORN. I'D SKIP HER.
MY SOURCES TELL ME ELVIN HAS TOOTSIE ROLLS, BUT THEY'RE GOING FAST. PERTZBORN MAY HAVE TWIZLERS, BUT I HAVEN'T CONFIRMED THAT YET.
THANKS, MR. CAMINO. YOU'LL GET THE USUAL 10% OF THE TAKE.
HALLOWEEN INSIDER TRADING? FOR SHAME!
KEEP QUIET AND THERE'S A MILKY WAY IN IT FOR YOU.

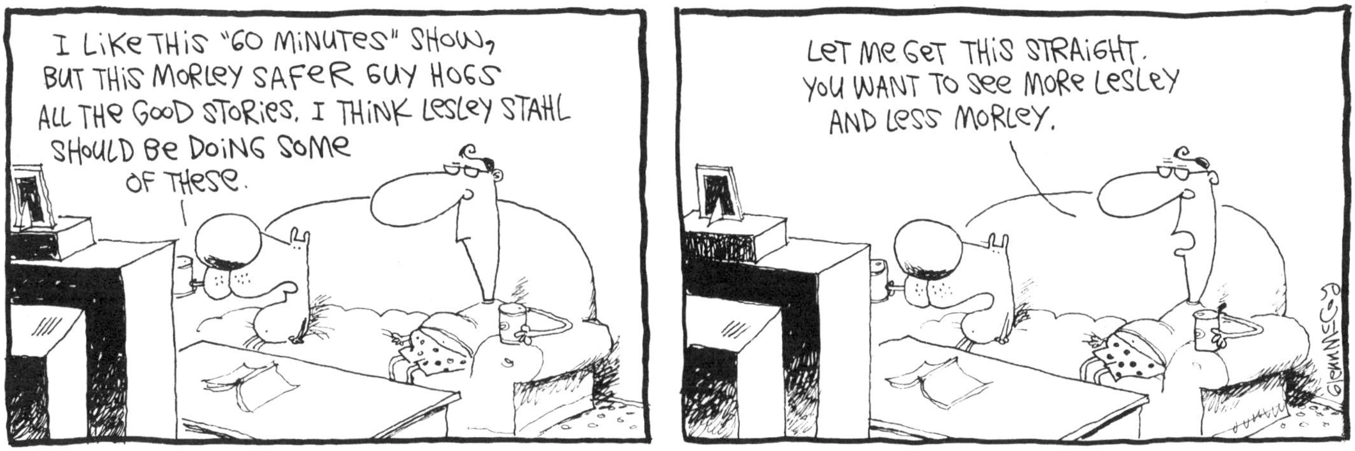
I LIKE THIS "60 MINUTES" SHOW, BUT THIS MORLEY SAFER GUY HOGS ALL THE GOOD STORIES. I THINK LESLEY STAHL SHOULD BE DOING SOME OF THESE.
LET ME GET THIS STRAIGHT. YOU WANT TO SEE MORE LESLEY AND LESS MORLEY.

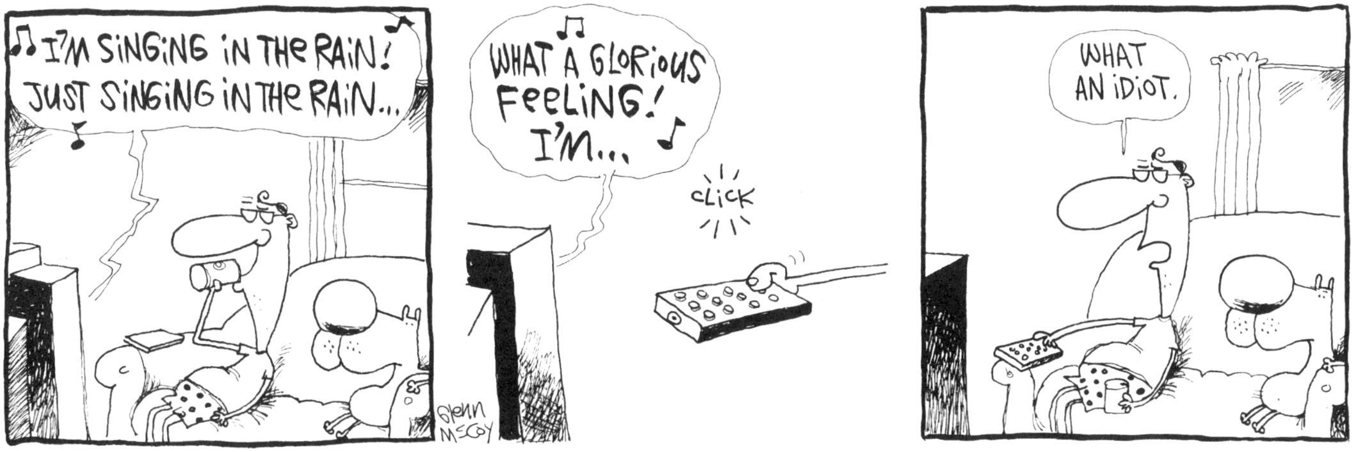
I'M SINGING IN THE RAIN! JUST SINGING IN THE RAIN...
WHAT A GLORIOUS FEELING! I'M...
CLICK
WHAT AN IDIOT.
Glenn McCoy

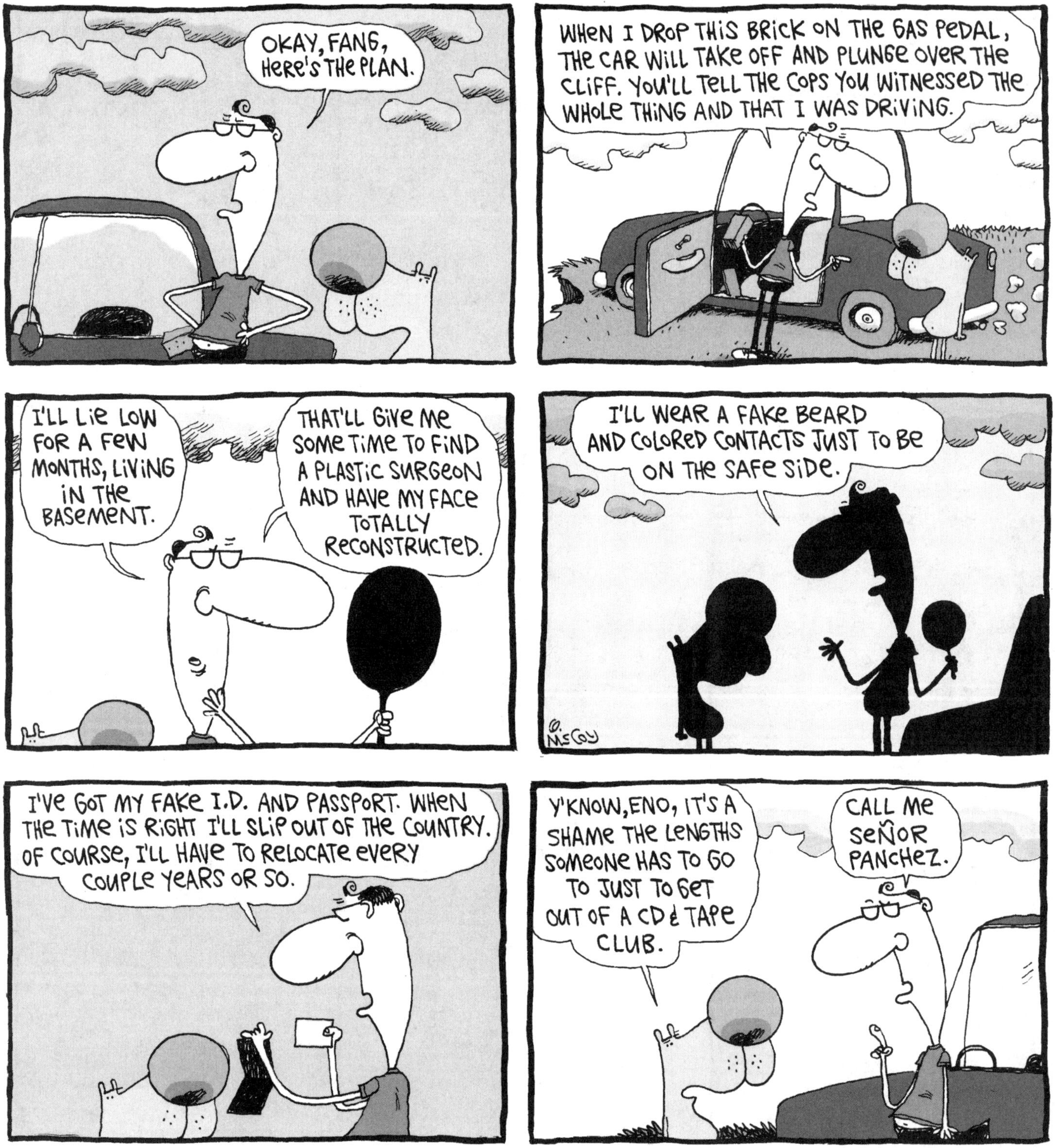
OKAY, FANG, HERE'S THE PLAN.
WHEN I DROP THIS BRICK ON THE GAS PEDAL, THE CAR WILL TAKE OFF AND PLUNGE OVER THE CLIFF. YOU'LL TELL THE COPS YOU WITNESSED THE WHOLE THING AND THAT I WAS DRIVING.
I'LL LIE LOW FOR A FEW MONTHS, LIVING IN THE BASEMENT.
THAT'LL GIVE ME SOME TIME TO FIND A PLASTIC SURGEON AND HAVE MY FACE TOTALLY RECONSTRUCTED.
I'LL WEAR A FAKE BEARD AND COLORED CONTACTS JUST TO BE ON THE SAFE SIDE.
McCoy
I'VE GOT MY FAKE I.D. AND PASSPORT. WHEN THE TIME IS RIGHT I'LL SLIP OUT OF THE COUNTRY. OF COURSE, I'LL HAVE TO RELOCATE EVERY COUPLE YEARS OR SO.
Y'KNOW, ENO, IT'S A SHAME THE LENGTHS SOMEONE HAS TO GO TO JUST TO GET OUT OF A CD & TAPE CLUB.
CALL ME SEÑOR PANCHEZ.

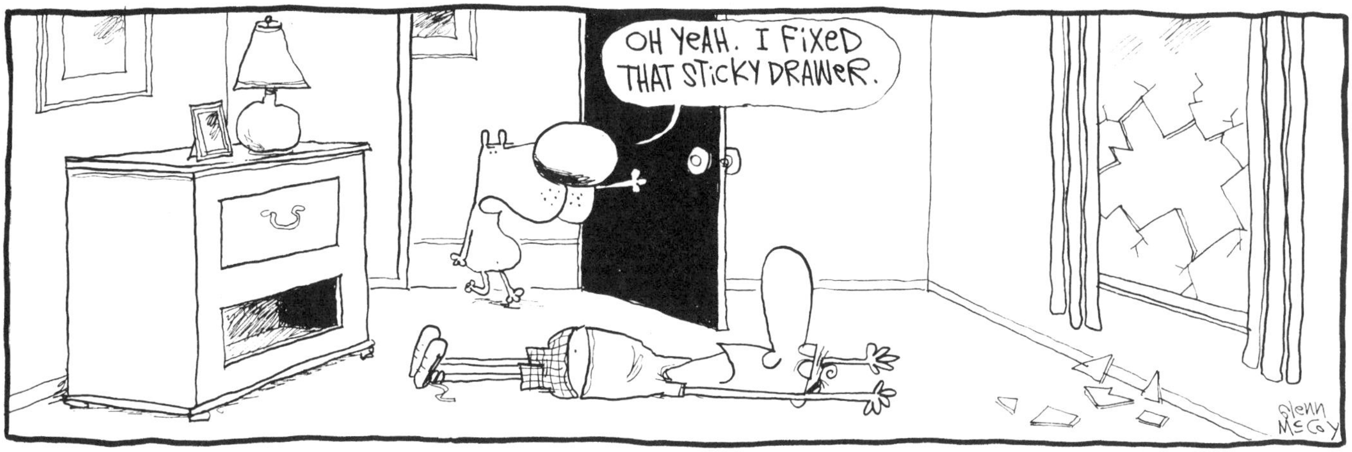
OH YEAH. I FIXED THAT STICKY DRAWER.
Glenn McCoy

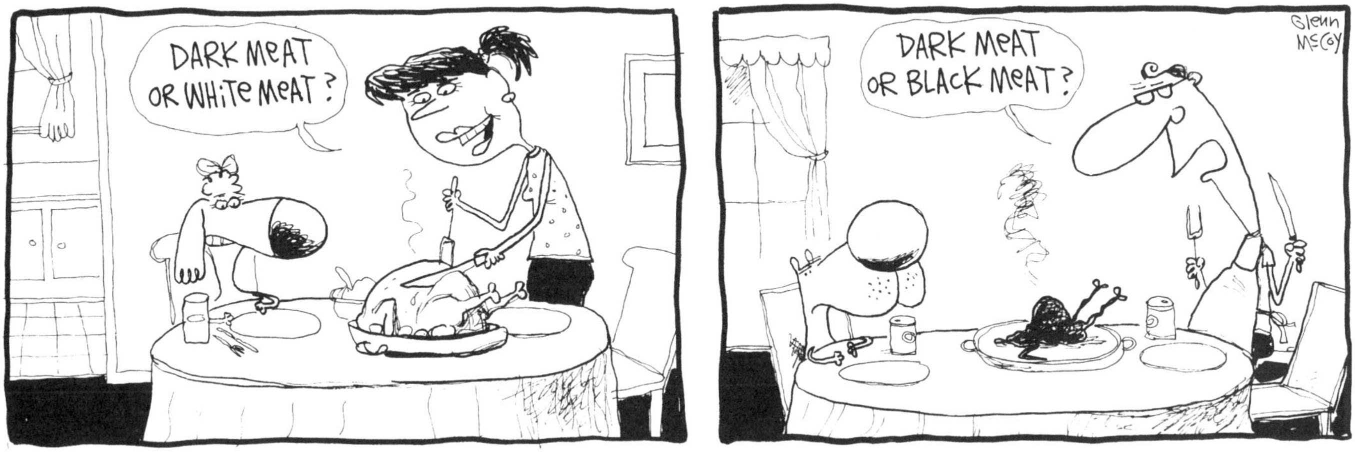
DARK MEAT OR WHITE MEAT?
DARK MEAT OR BLACK MEAT?
Glenn McCoy

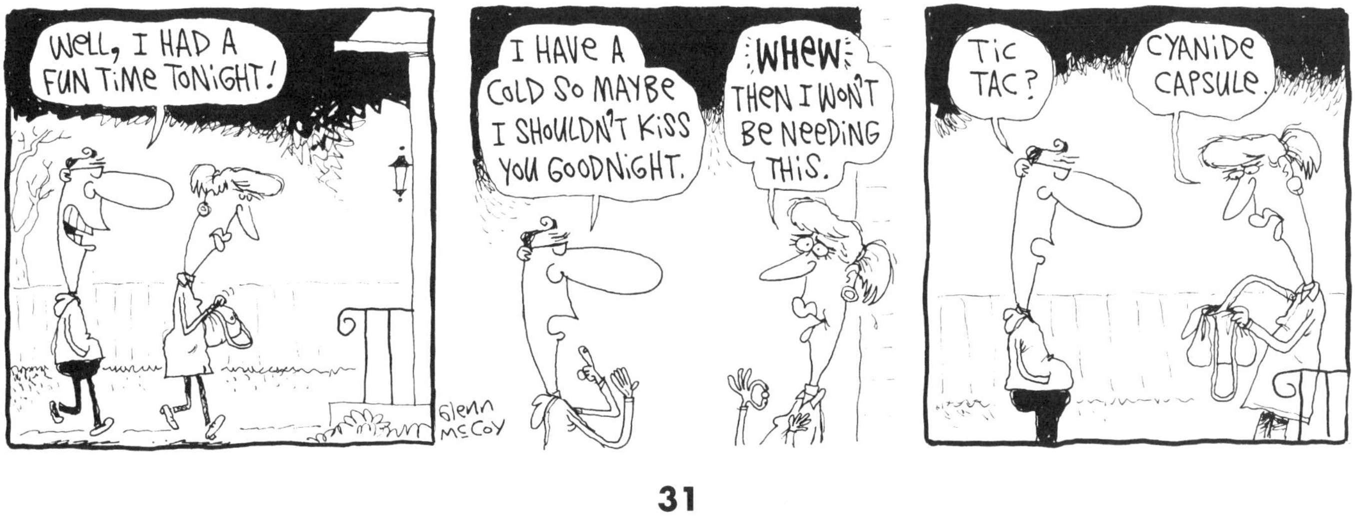
WELL, I HAD A FUN TIME TONIGHT!
Glenn McCoy
I HAVE A COLD SO MAYBE I SHOULDN'T KISS YOU GOODNIGHT.
WHEW
THEN I WON'T BE NEEDING THIS.
TIC TAC?
CYANIDE CAPSULE.

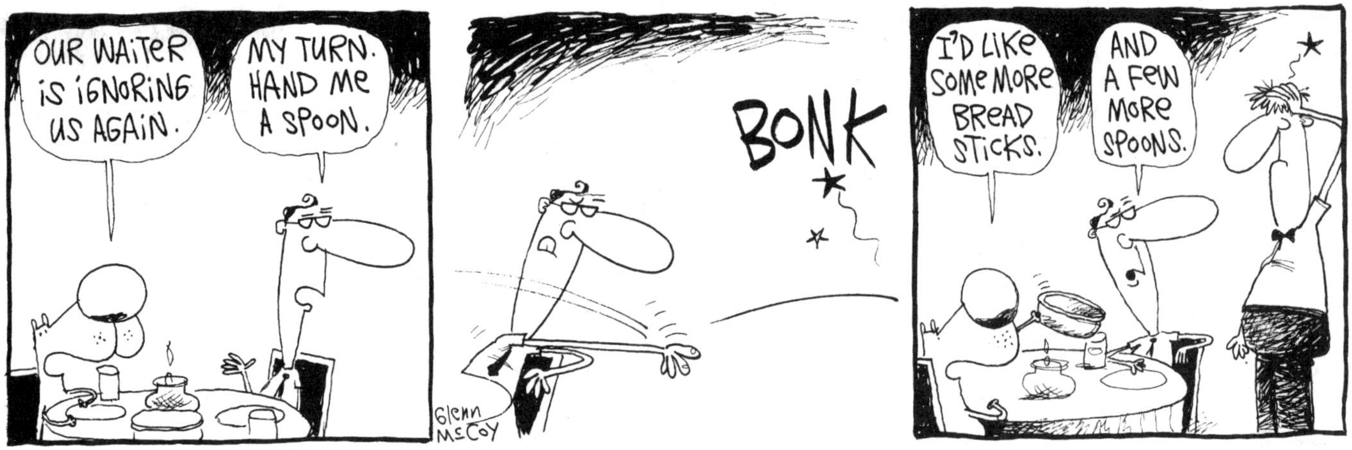
OUR WAITER IS IGNORING US AGAIN.
MY TURN. HAND ME A SPOON.
BONK
GLENN McCOY
I'D LIKE SOME MORE BREAD STICKS.
AND A FEW MORE SPOONS.

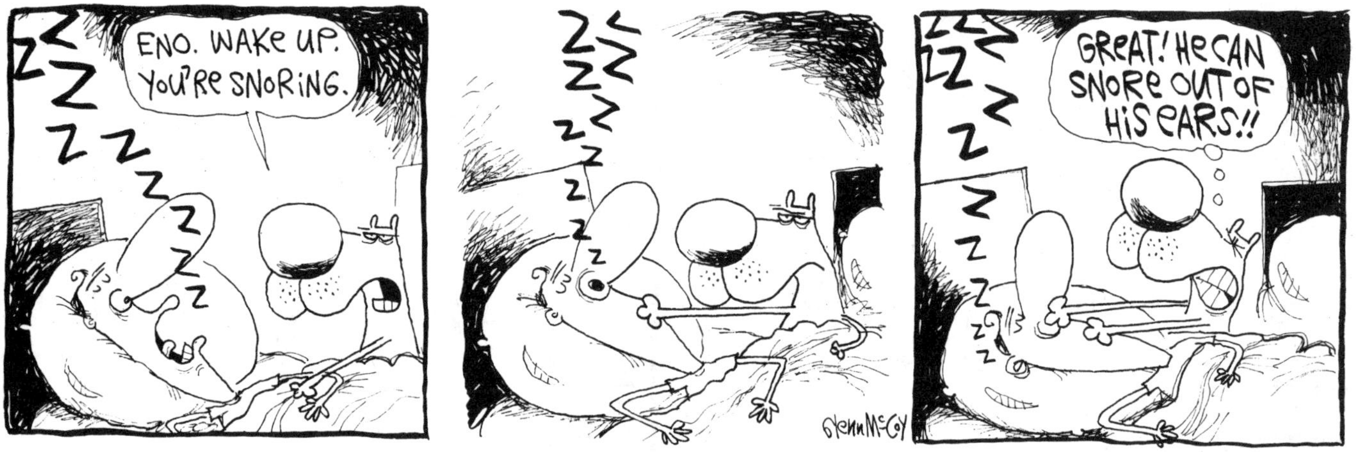
ZZZ
ENO. WAKE UP. YOU'RE SNORING.
GLENN McCOY
GREAT! HE CAN SNORE OUT OF HIS EARS!!

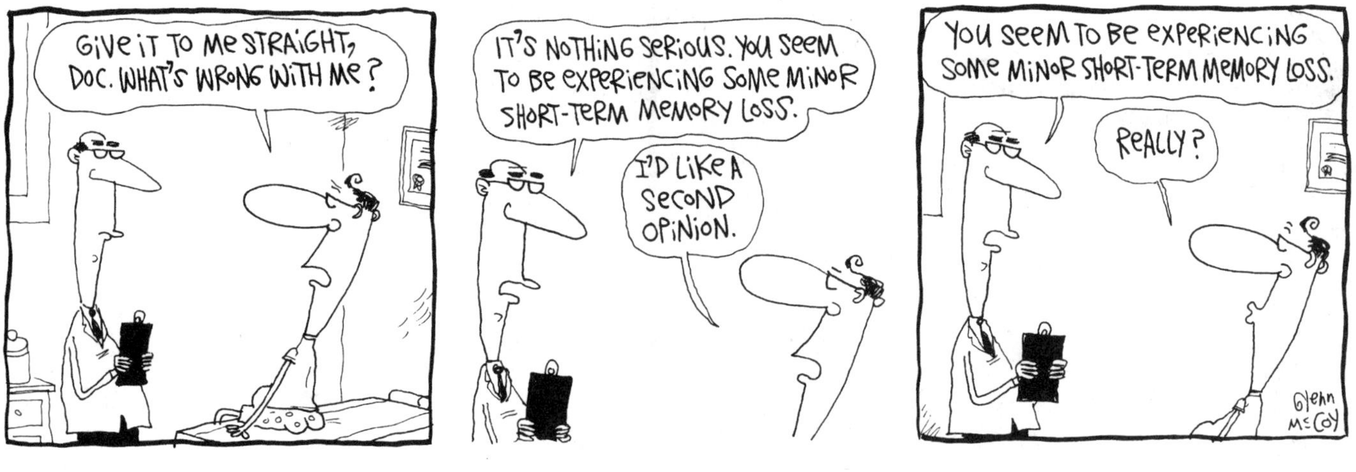
GIVE IT TO ME STRAIGHT, DOC. WHAT'S WRONG WITH ME?
IT'S NOTHING SERIOUS. YOU SEEM TO BE EXPERIENCING SOME MINOR SHORT-TERM MEMORY LOSS.
I'D LIKE A SECOND OPINION.
YOU SEEM TO BE EXPERIENCING SOME MINOR SHORT-TERM MEMORY LOSS.
REALLY?
GLENN McCOY

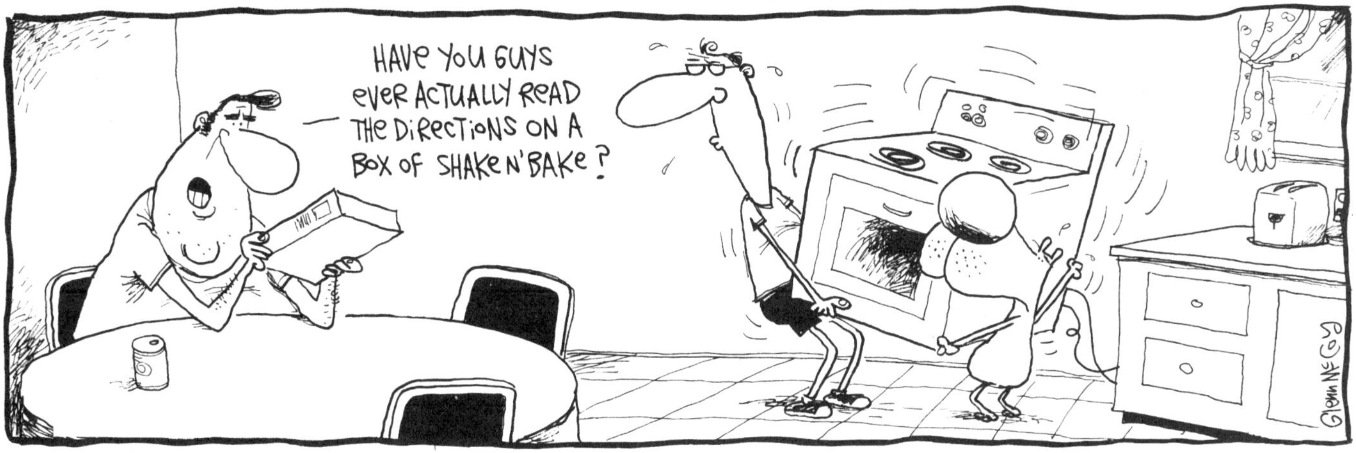
HAVE YOU GUYS EVER ACTUALLY READ THE DIRECTIONS ON A BOX OF SHAKE N'BAKE?
Glenn McCoy

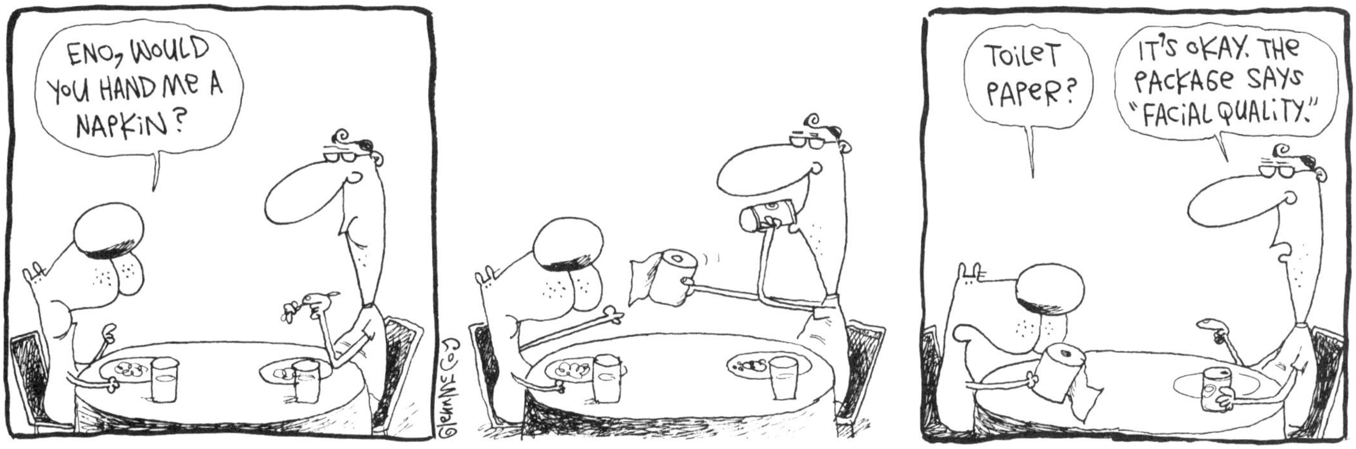
ENO, WOULD YOU HAND ME A NAPKIN?
Glenn McCoy
TOILET PAPER?
IT'S OKAY. THE PACKAGE SAYS "FACIAL QUALITY."

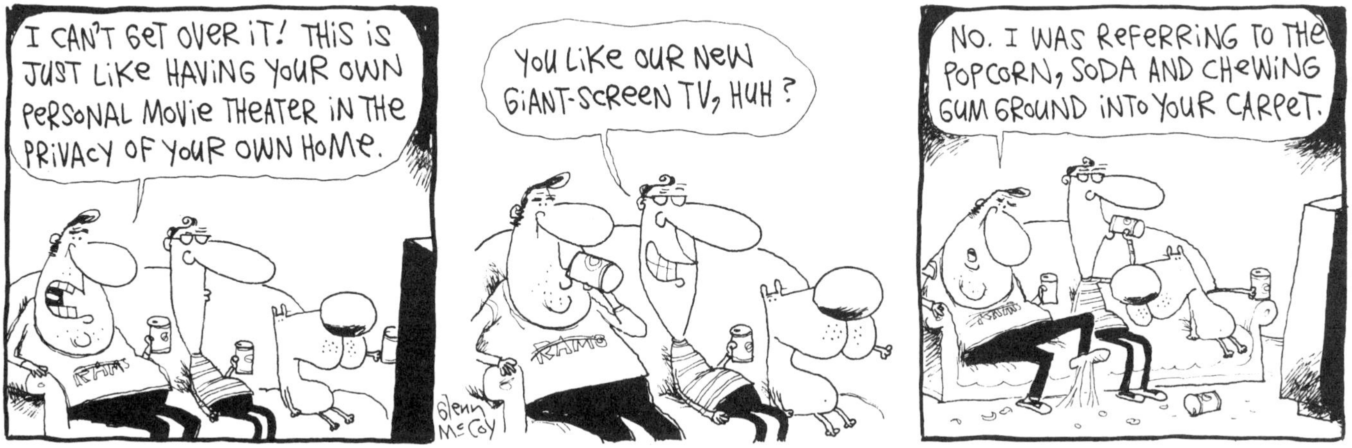
I CAN'T GET OVER IT! THIS IS JUST LIKE HAVING YOUR OWN PERSONAL MOVIE THEATER IN THE PRIVACY OF YOUR OWN HOME.
RAMS
Glenn McCoy
YOU LIKE OUR NEW GIANT-SCREEN TV, HUH?
RAMS
NO. I WAS REFERRING TO THE POPCORN, SODA AND CHEWING GUM GROUND INTO YOUR CARPET.

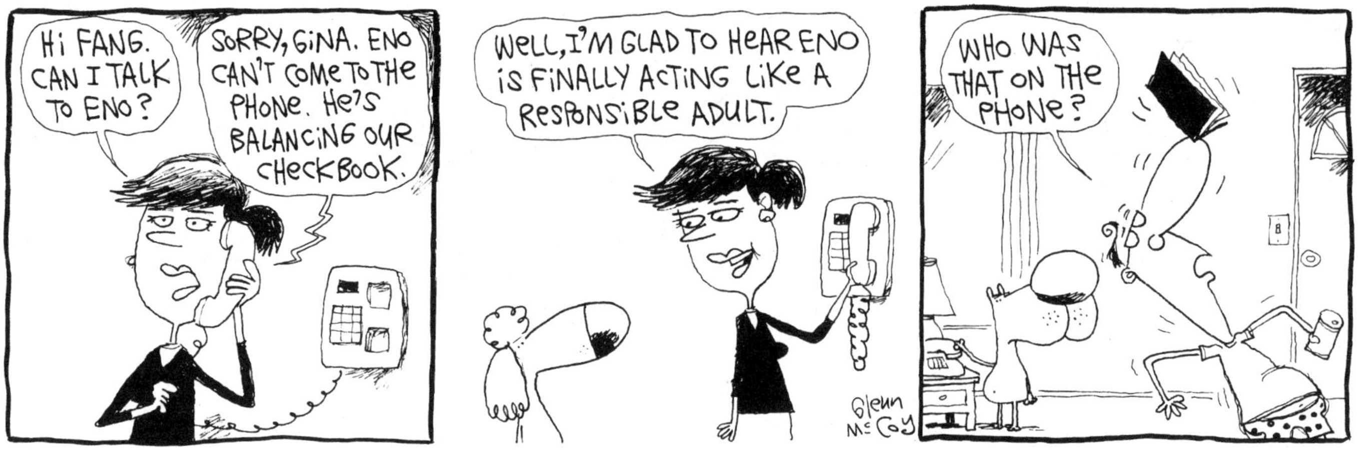
Hi FANG. CAN I TALK TO ENO?
SORRY, GINA. ENO CAN'T COME TO THE PHONE. He'S BALANCING OUR CHECKBOOK.
WELL, I'M GLAD TO HEAR ENO IS FINALLY ACTING LIKE A RESPONSIBLE ADULT.
Glenn McCoy
WHO WAS THAT ON THE PHONE?

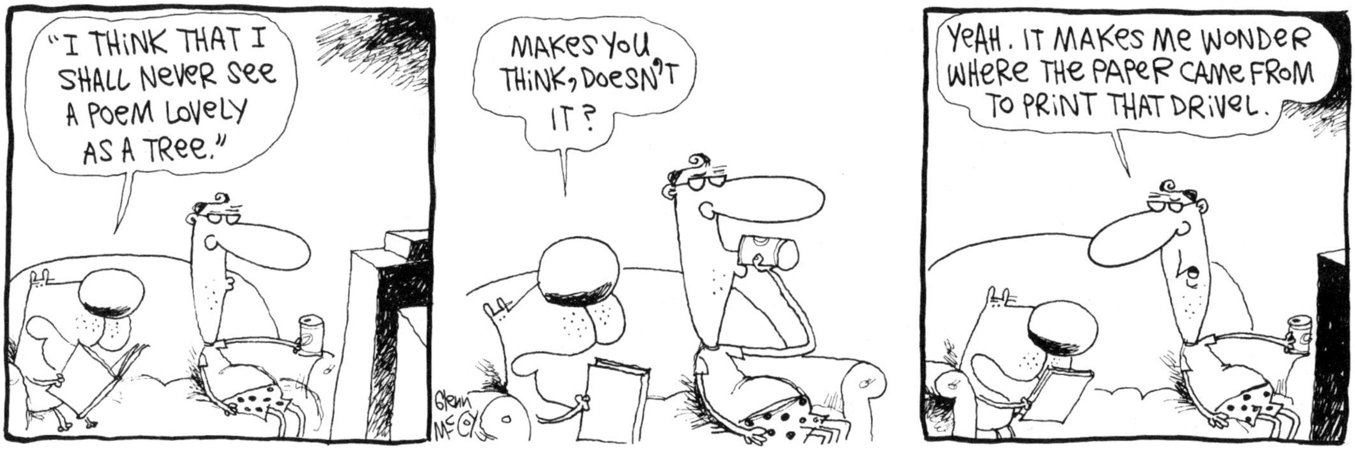
"I THINK THAT I SHALL NEVER SEE A POEM LOVELY AS A TREE."
MAKES YOU THINK, DOESN'T IT?
Glenn McCoy
YEAH. IT MAKES ME WONDER WHERE THE PAPER CAME FROM TO PRINT THAT DRIVEL.

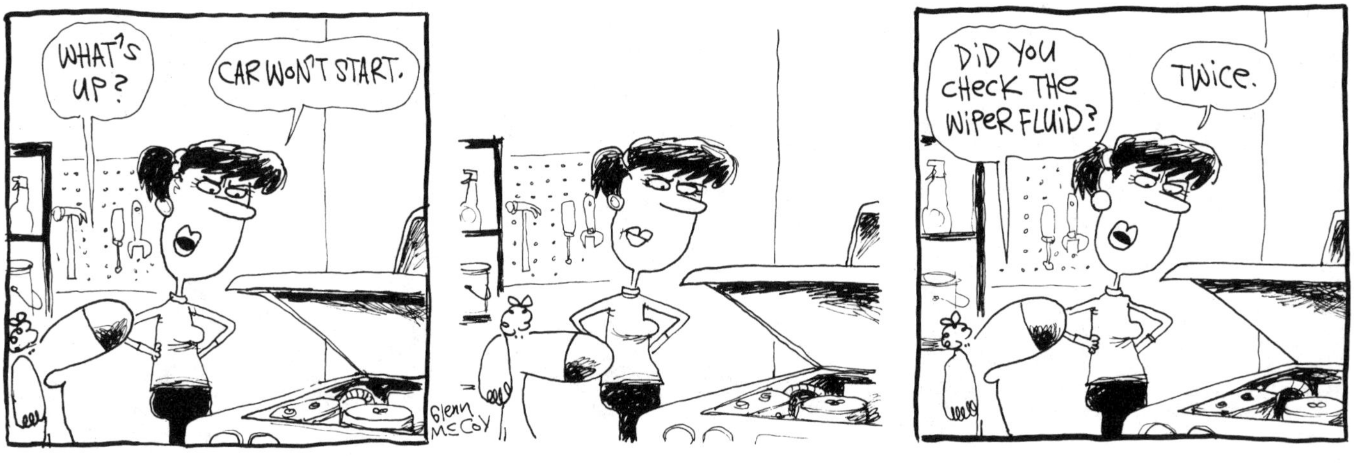
WHAT'S UP?
CAR WON'T START.
Glenn McCoy
DID YOU CHECK THE WIPER FLUID?
TWICE.

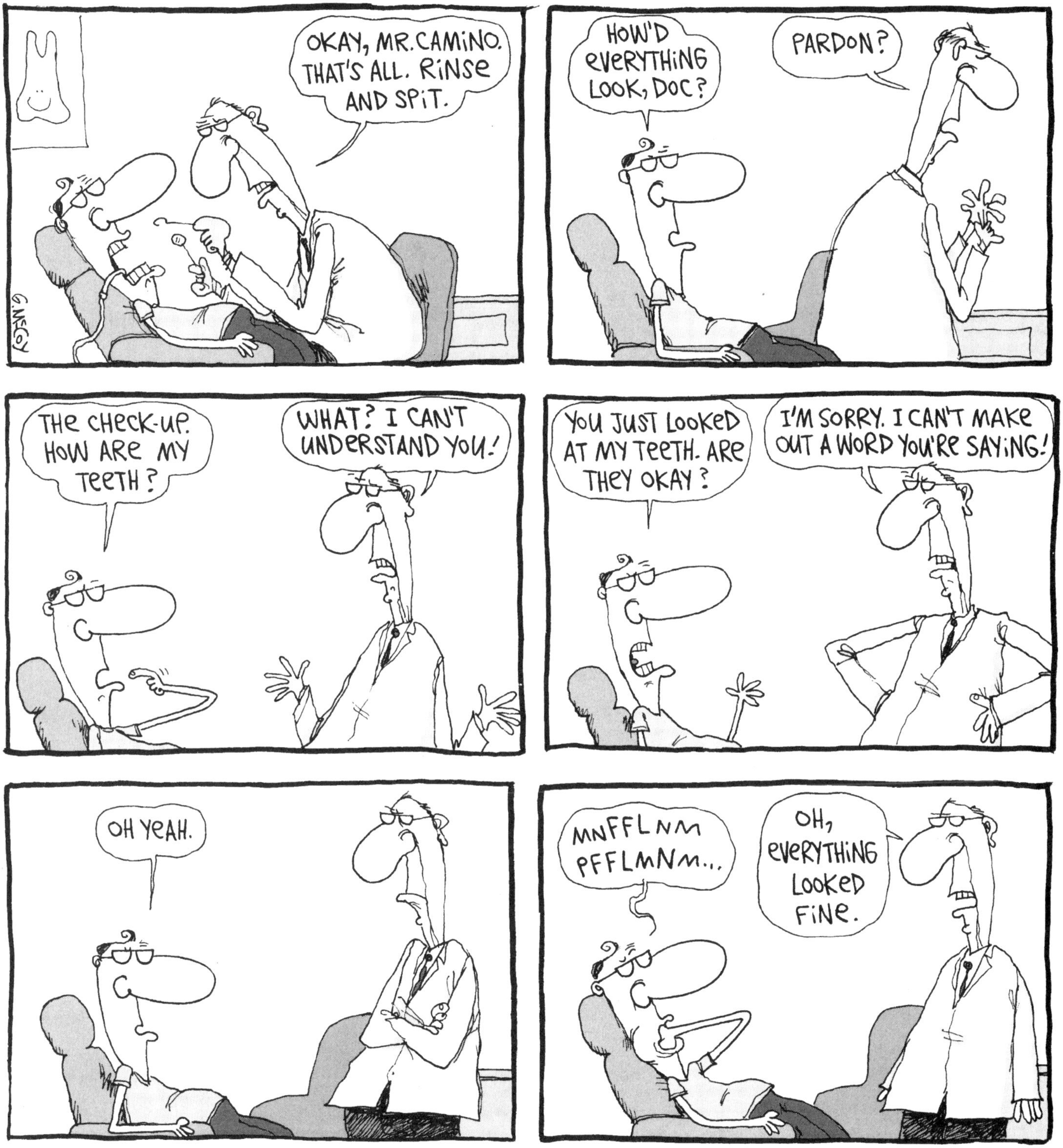
G. McCOY
OKAY, MR. CAMINO. THAT'S ALL. RINSE AND SPIT.
HOW'D EVERYTHING LOOK, DOC?
PARDON?
THE CHECK-UP. HOW ARE MY TEETH?
WHAT? I CAN'T UNDERSTAND YOU!
YOU JUST LOOKED AT MY TEETH. ARE THEY OKAY?
I'M SORRY. I CAN'T MAKE OUT A WORD YOU'RE SAYING!
OH YEAH.
MNFFLNM PFFLMNM...
OH, EVERYTHING LOOKED FINE.

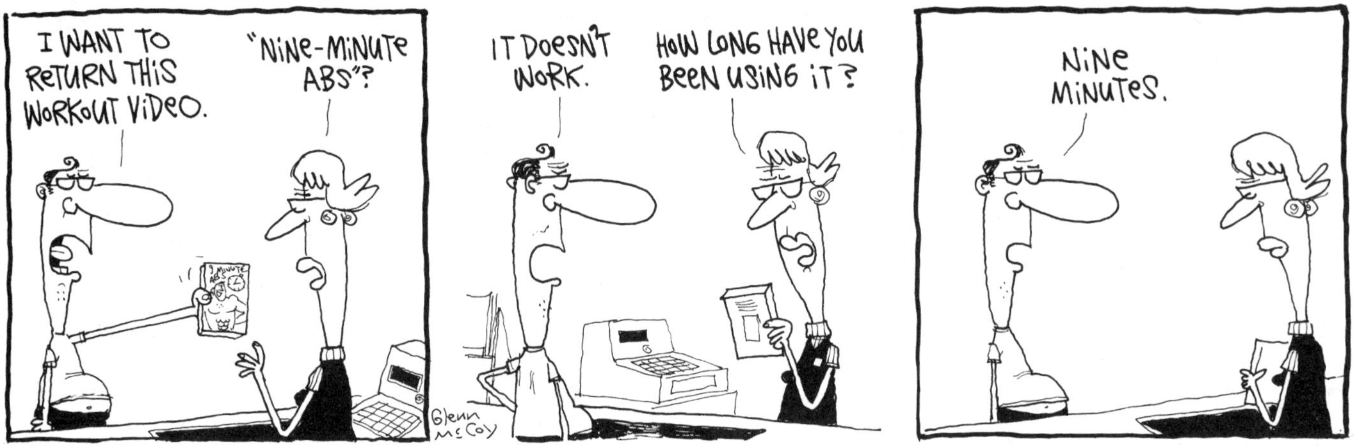
I WANT TO RETURN THIS WORKOUT VIDEO.
"NINE-MINUTE ABS"?
Glenn McCoy
IT DOESN'T WORK.
HOW LONG HAVE YOU BEEN USING IT?
NINE MINUTES.

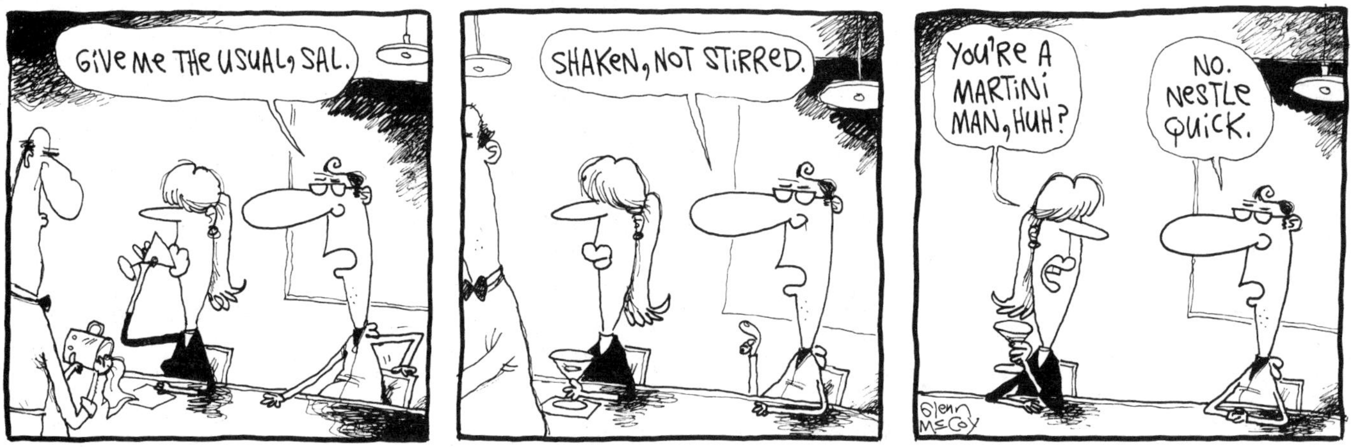
GIVE ME THE USUAL, SAL.
SHAKEN, NOT STIRRED.
YOU'RE A MARTINI MAN, HUH?
NO. NESTLE QUICK.
Glenn McCoy

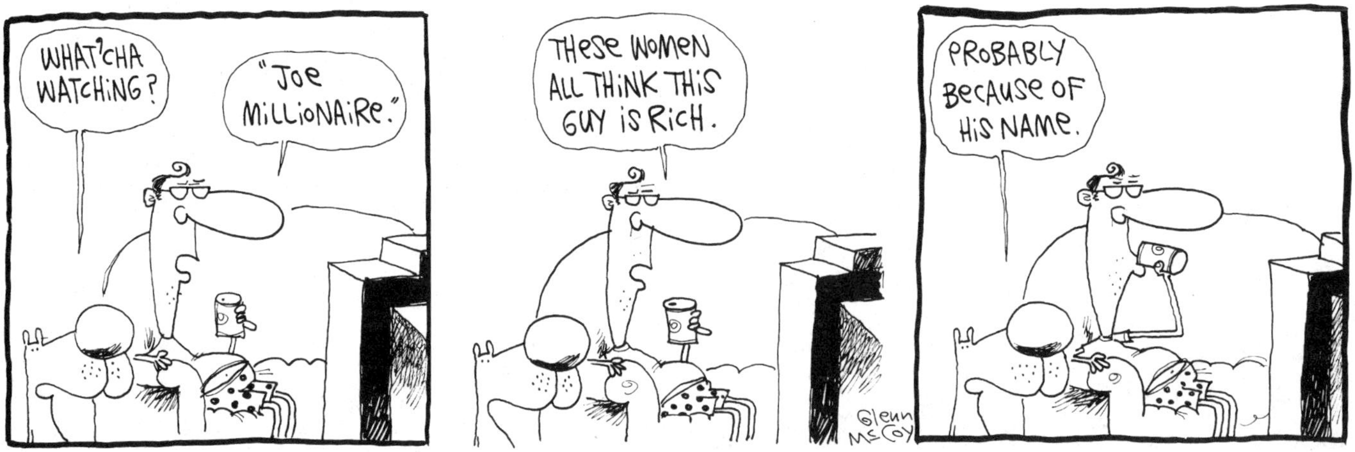
WHAT'CHA WATCHING?
"JOE MILLIONAIRE."
THESE WOMEN ALL THINK THIS GUY IS RICH.
Glenn McCoy
PROBABLY BECAUSE OF HIS NAME.

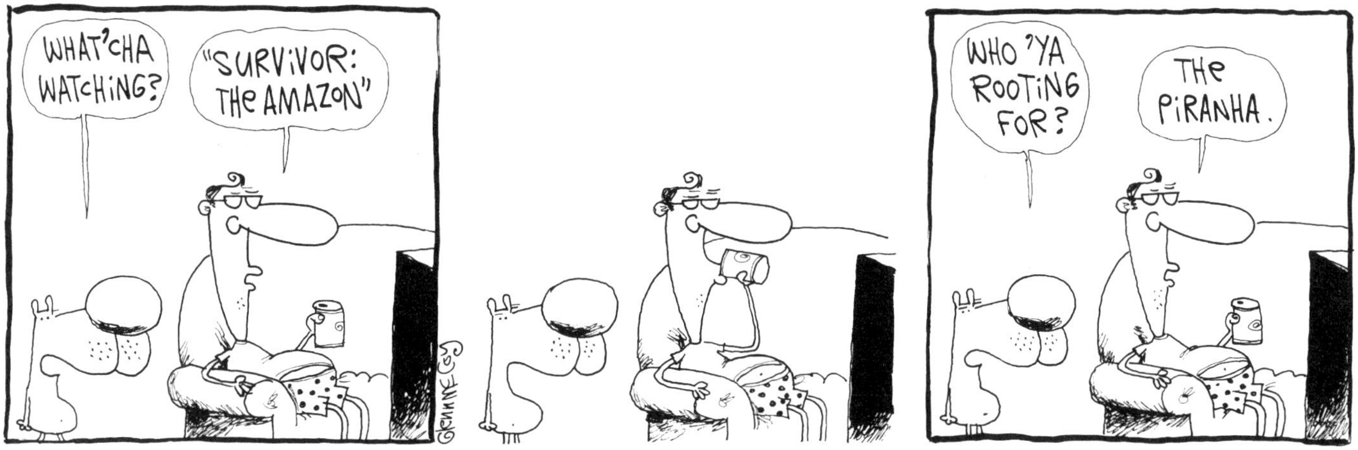
WHAT'CHA WATCHING?
"SURVIVOR: THE AMAZON"
WHO 'YA ROOTING FOR?
THE PIRANHA.

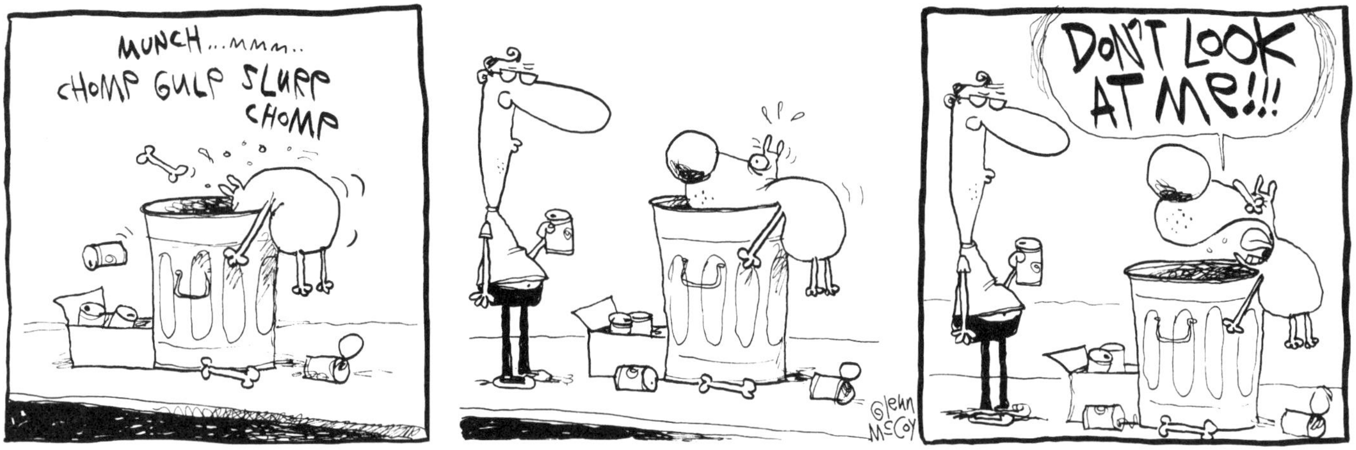
MUNCH...MMM..
CHOMP GULP SLURP CHOMP
DON'T LOOK AT ME!!!
Glenn McCoy

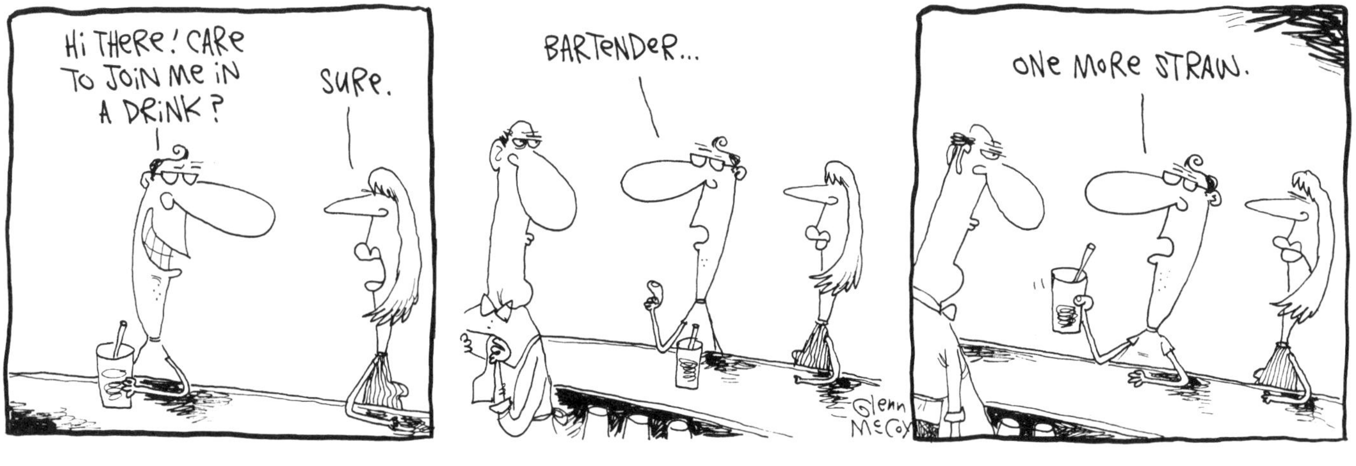
Hi THERE! CARE TO JOIN ME IN A DRINK?
SURE.
BARTENDER...
Glenn McCoy
ONE MORE STRAW.

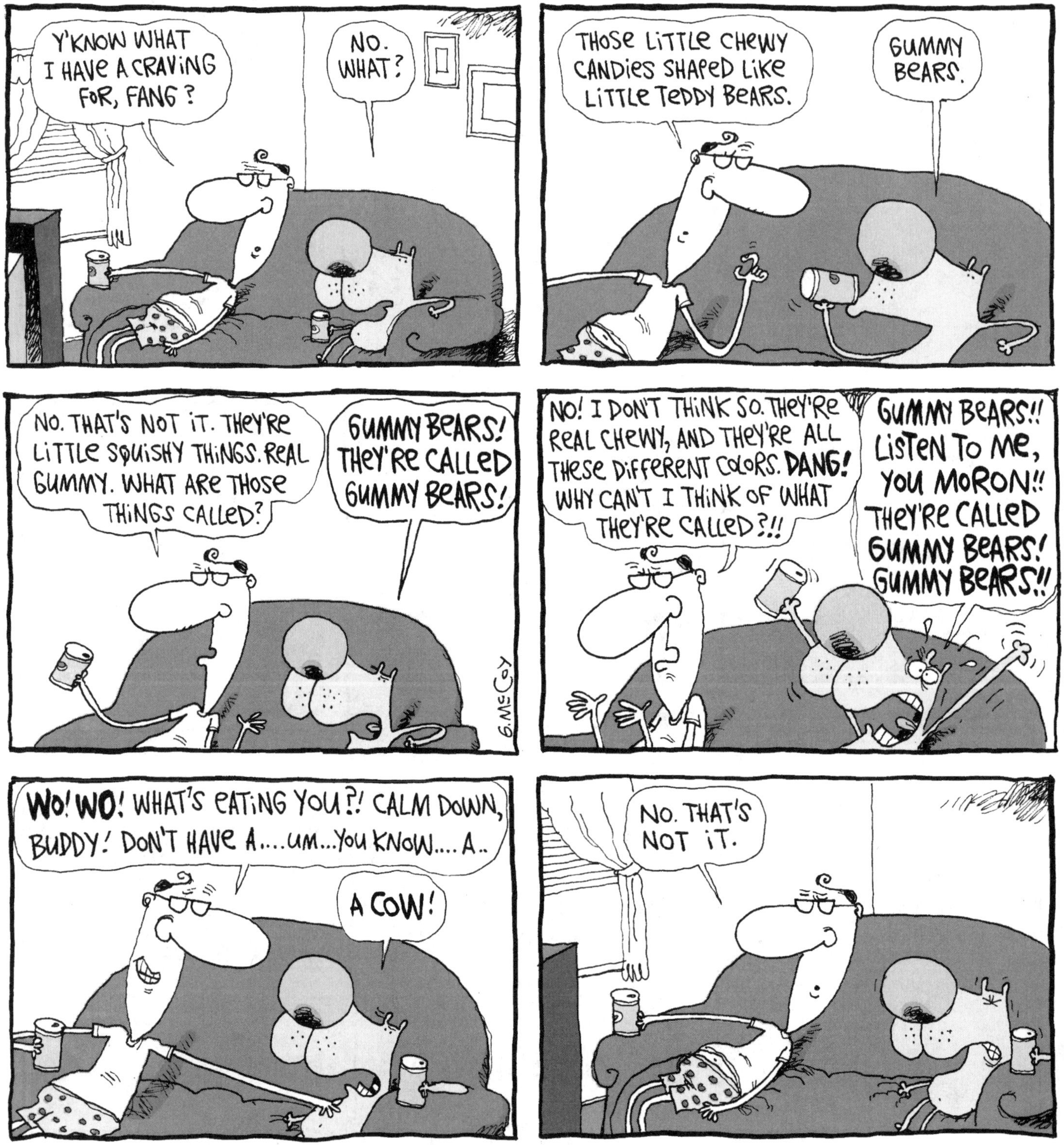

Y'KNOW WHAT I HAVE A CRAVING FOR, FANG?
NO. WHAT?
THOSE LITTLE CHEWY CANDIES SHAPED LIKE LITTLE TEDDY BEARS.
GUMMY BEARS.
NO. THAT'S NOT IT. THEY'RE LITTLE SQUISHY THINGS. REAL GUMMY. WHAT ARE THOSE THINGS CALLED?
GUMMY BEARS! THEY'RE CALLED GUMMY BEARS!
G. McCOY
NO! I DON'T THINK SO. THEY'RE REAL CHEWY, AND THEY'RE ALL THESE DIFFERENT COLORS. DANG! WHY CAN'T I THINK OF WHAT THEY'RE CALLED?!!
GUMMY BEARS!! LISTEN TO ME, YOU MORON!! THEY'RE CALLED GUMMY BEARS! GUMMY BEARS!!
WO! WO! WHAT'S EATING YOU?! CALM DOWN, BUDDY! DON'T HAVE A....UM...YOU KNOW.... A..
A COW!
NO. THAT'S NOT IT.

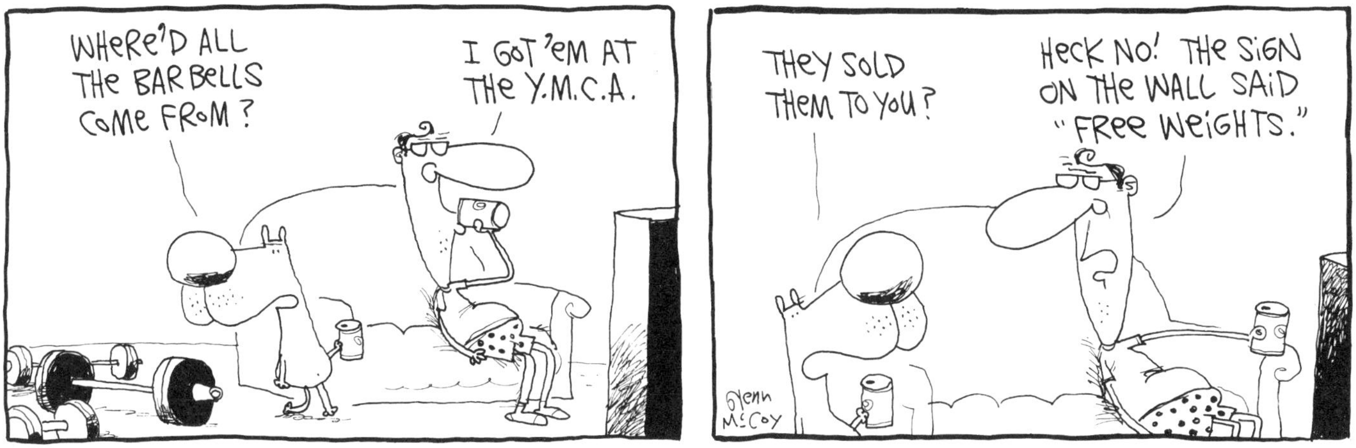
WHERE'D ALL THE BARBELLS COME FROM?
I GOT 'EM AT THE Y.M.C.A.
THEY SOLD THEM TO YOU?
HECK NO! THE SIGN ON THE WALL SAID "FREE WEIGHTS."
Glenn McCoy

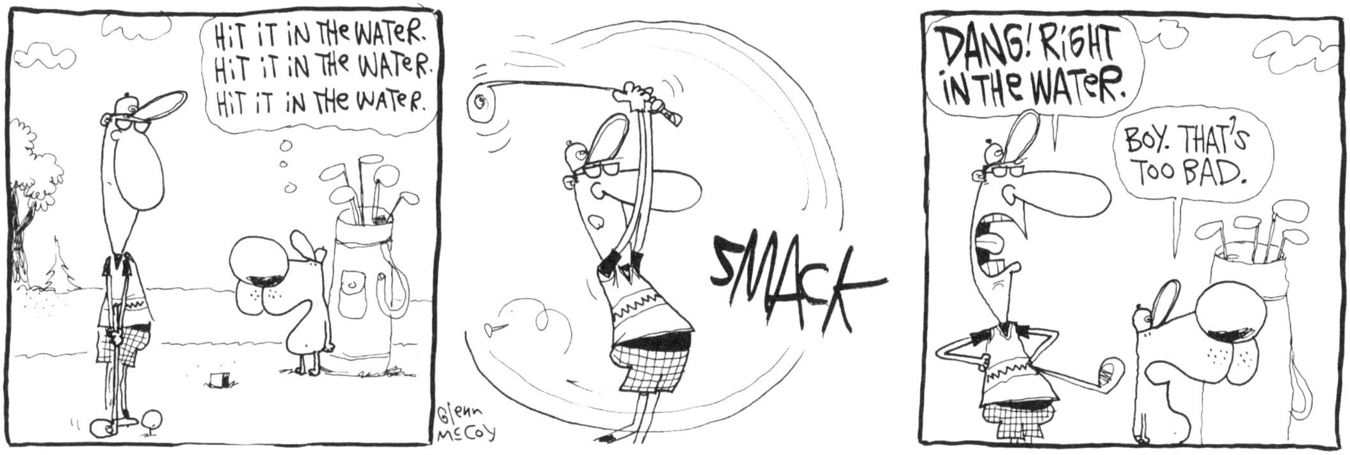
HIT IT IN THE WATER. HIT IT IN THE WATER. HIT IT IN THE WATER.
Glenn McCoy
SMACK
DANG! RIGHT IN THE WATER.
BOY. THAT'S TOO BAD.

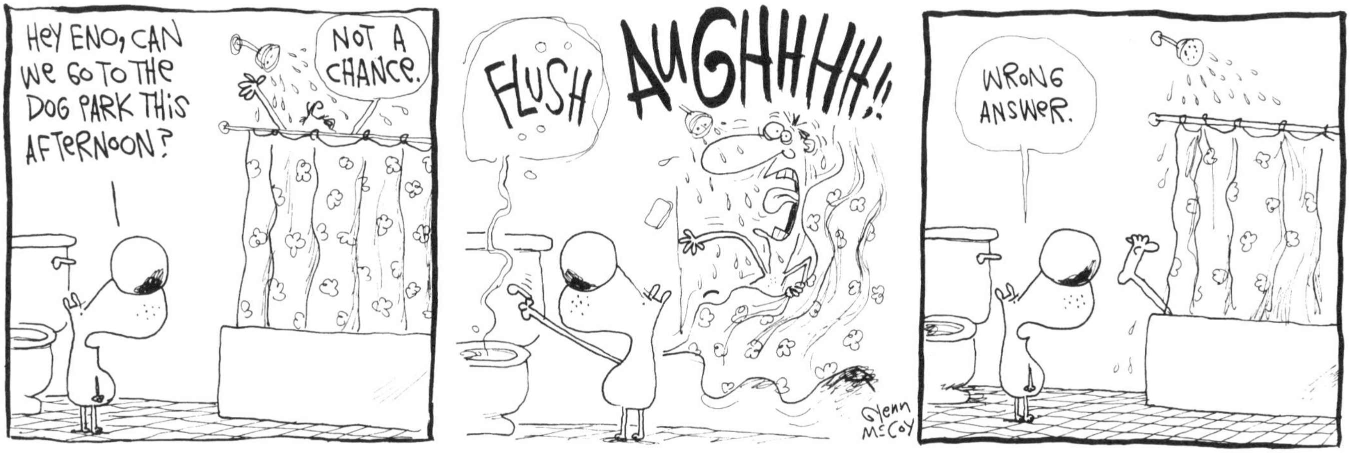
HEY ENO, CAN WE GO TO THE DOG PARK THIS AFTERNOON?
NOT A CHANCE.
FLUSH
AUGHHHH!!
Glenn McCoy
WRONG ANSWER.

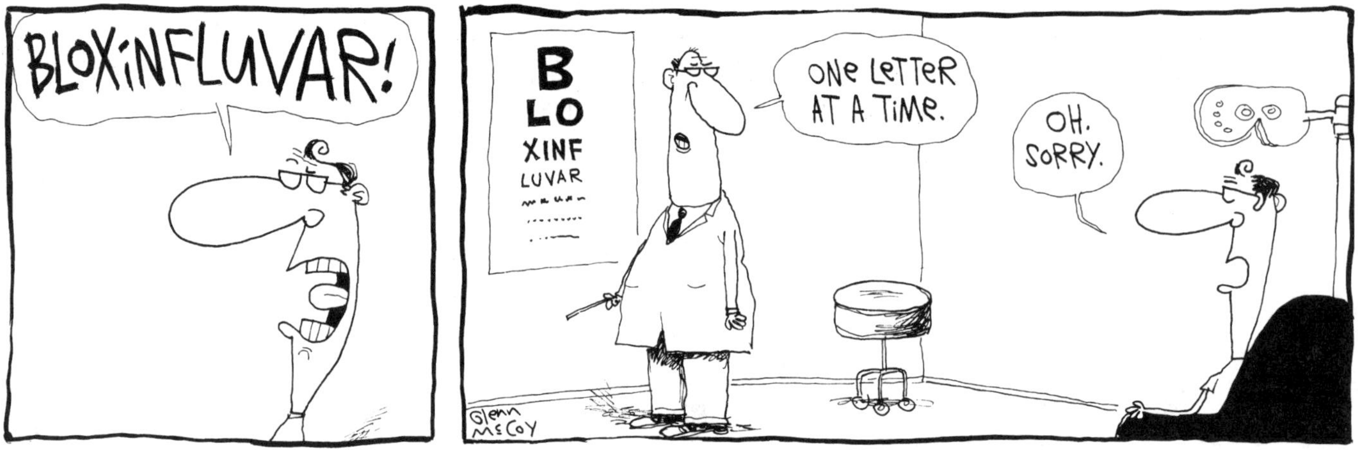
BLOXINFLUVAR!
B
LO
XINF
LUVAR
ONE LETTER AT A TIME.
OH. SORRY.
Glenn McCoy

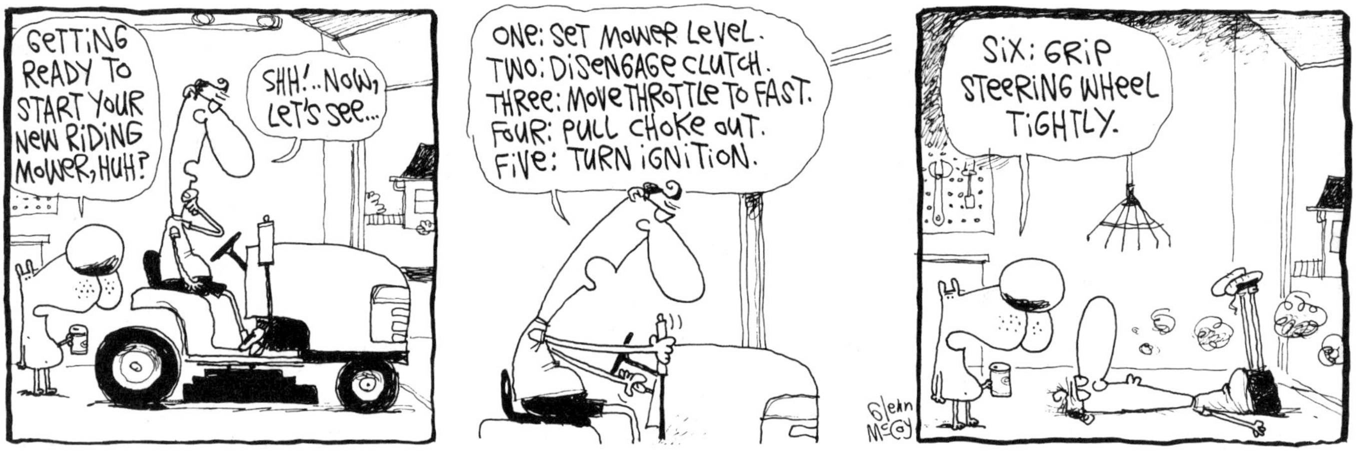
GETTING READY TO START YOUR NEW RIDING MOWER, HUH?
SHH!..NOW, LET'S SEE...
ONE: SET MOWER LEVEL.
TWO: DISENGAGE CLUTCH.
THREE: MOVE THROTTLE TO FAST.
FOUR: PULL CHOKE OUT.
FIVE: TURN IGNITION.
SIX: GRIP STEERING WHEEL TIGHTLY.
Glenn McCoy

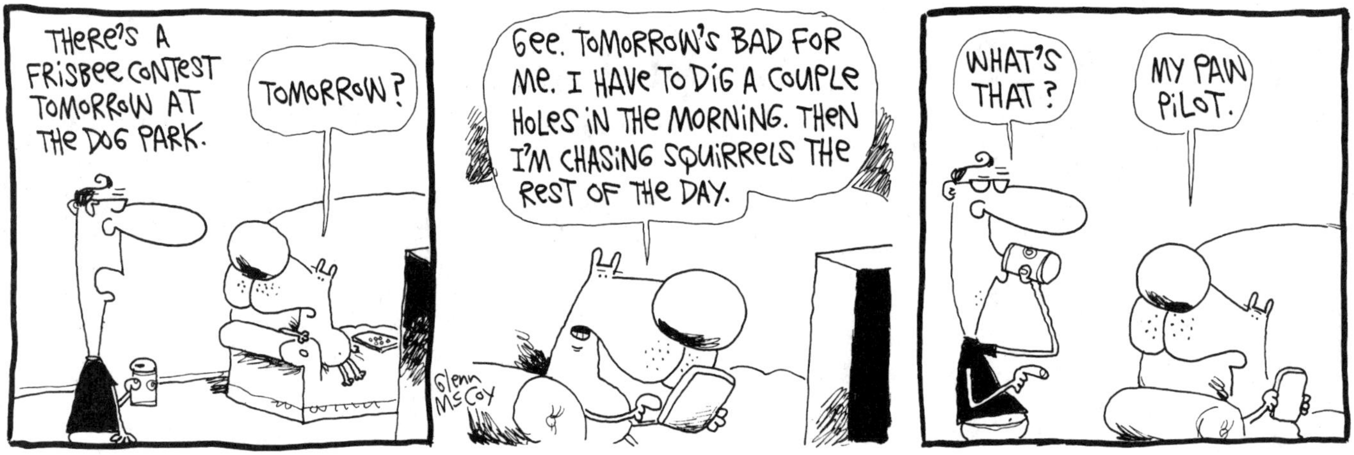
THERE'S A FRISBEE CONTEST TOMORROW AT THE DOG PARK.
TOMORROW?
GEE. TOMORROW'S BAD FOR ME. I HAVE TO DIG A COUPLE HOLES IN THE MORNING. THEN I'M CHASING SQUIRRELS THE REST OF THE DAY.
Glenn McCoy
WHAT'S THAT?
MY PAW PILOT.

HOLD STILL, GINA. I'LL TAKE YOUR PICTURE.
NO! WAIT!
MY HAIR'S A MESS! WHERE'S MY MAKEUP!!
AUGHHH!!
HOLD STILL, ENO. I'LL TAKE YOUR PICTURE!
NO. WAIT.
OKAY. GO AHEAD.
G.McCOY

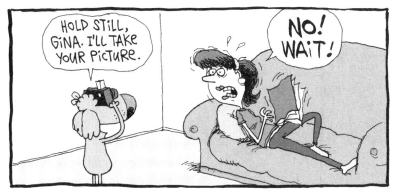

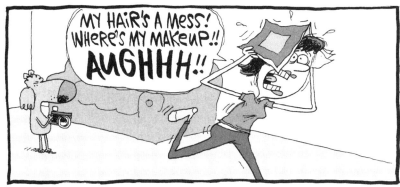

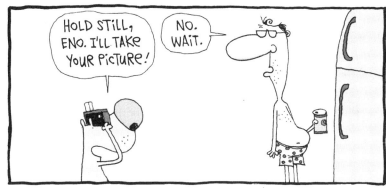

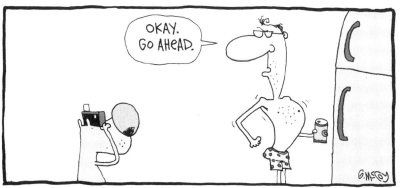

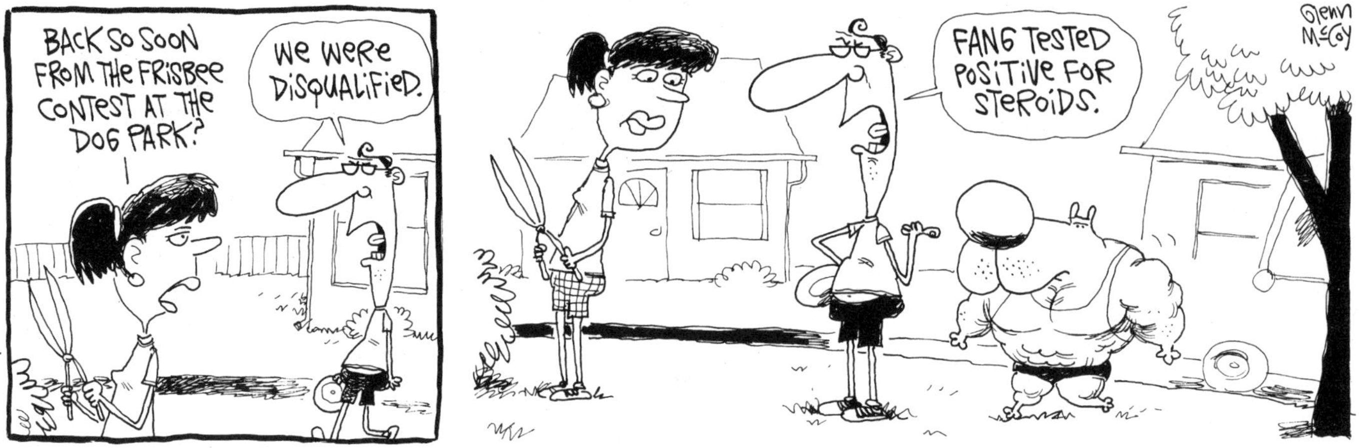
BACK SO SOON FROM THE FRISBEE CONTEST AT THE DOG PARK?
WE WERE DISQUALIFIED.
FANG TESTED POSITIVE FOR STEROIDS.
Glenn McCoy

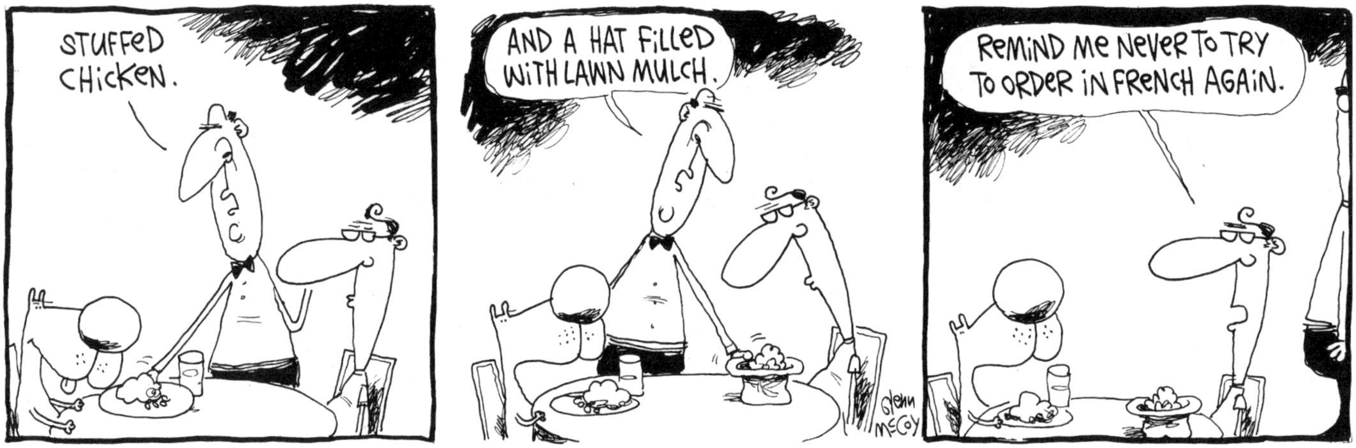
STUFFED CHICKEN.
AND A HAT FILLED WITH LAWN MULCH.
Glenn McCoy
REMIND ME NEVER TO TRY TO ORDER IN FRENCH AGAIN.

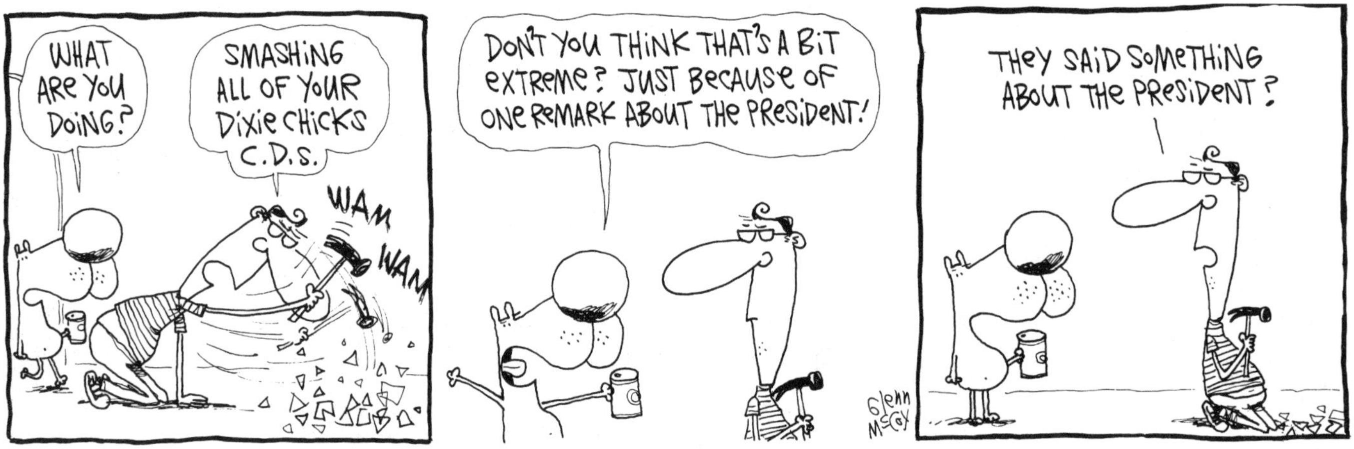
WHAT ARE YOU DOING?
SMASHING ALL OF YOUR DIXIE CHICKS C.D.S.
WAM
WAM
DON'T YOU THINK THAT'S A BIT EXTREME? JUST BECAUSE OF ONE REMARK ABOUT THE PRESIDENT!
Glenn McCoy
THEY SAID SOMETHING ABOUT THE PRESIDENT?

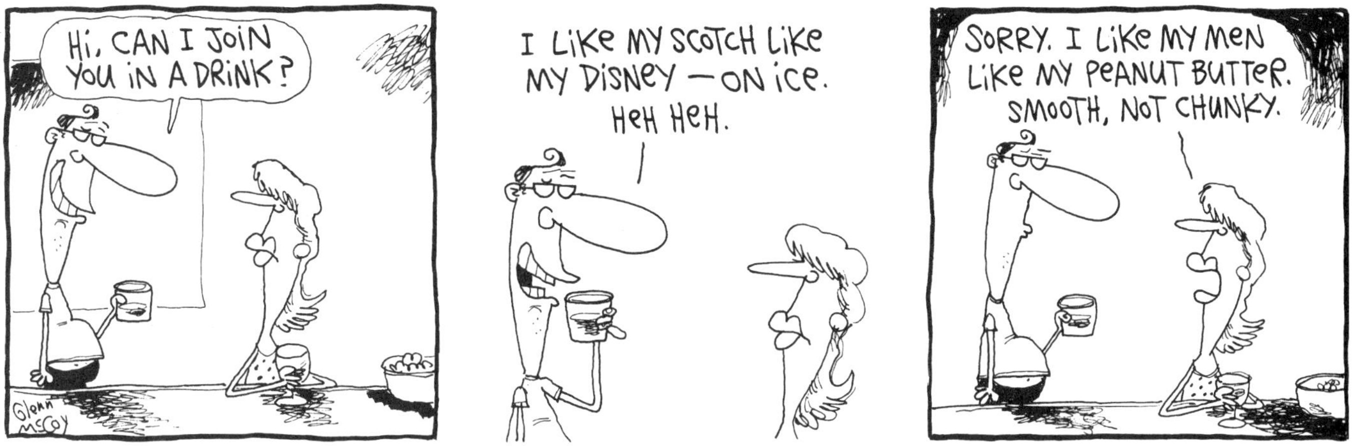
Hi, CAN I JOIN YOU IN A DRINK?
Glenn McCoy
I LIKE MY SCOTCH LIKE MY DISNEY — ON ICE. HEH HEH.
SORRY. I LIKE MY MEN LIKE MY PEANUT BUTTER. SMOOTH, NOT CHUNKY.

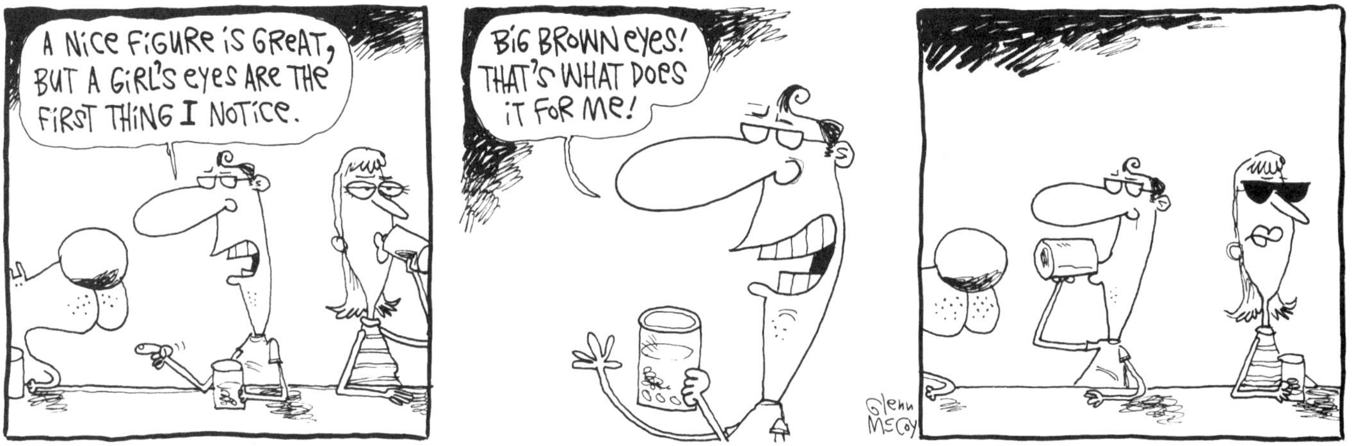
A NICE FIGURE IS GREAT, BUT A GIRL'S EYES ARE THE FIRST THING I NOTICE.
BIG BROWN EYES! THAT'S WHAT DOES IT FOR ME!
Glenn McCoy

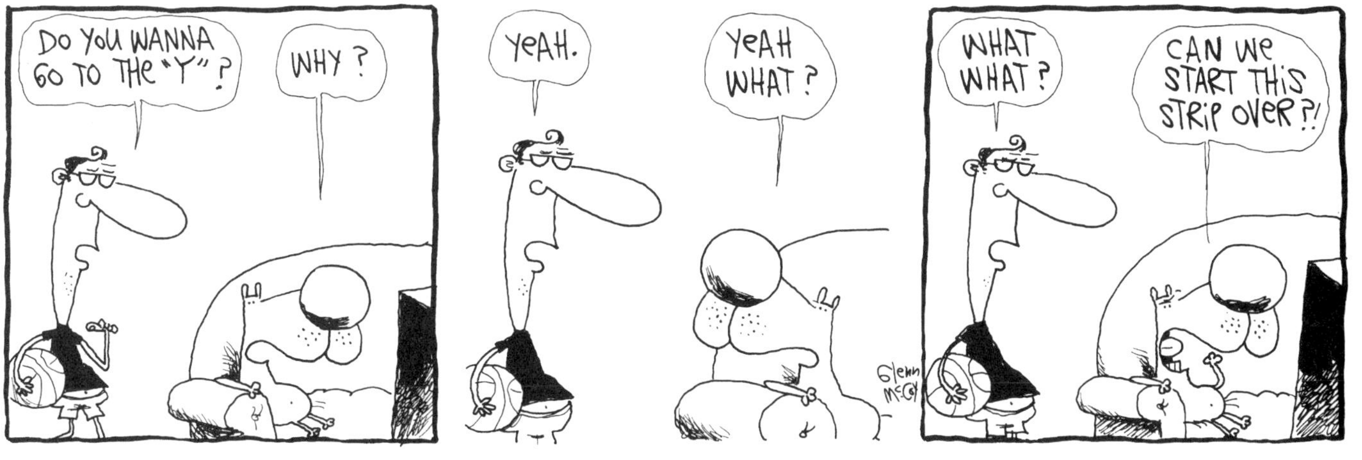
DO YOU WANNA GO TO THE "Y"?
WHY?
YEAH.
YEAH WHAT?
Glenn McCoy
WHAT WHAT?
CAN WE START THIS STRIP OVER?!

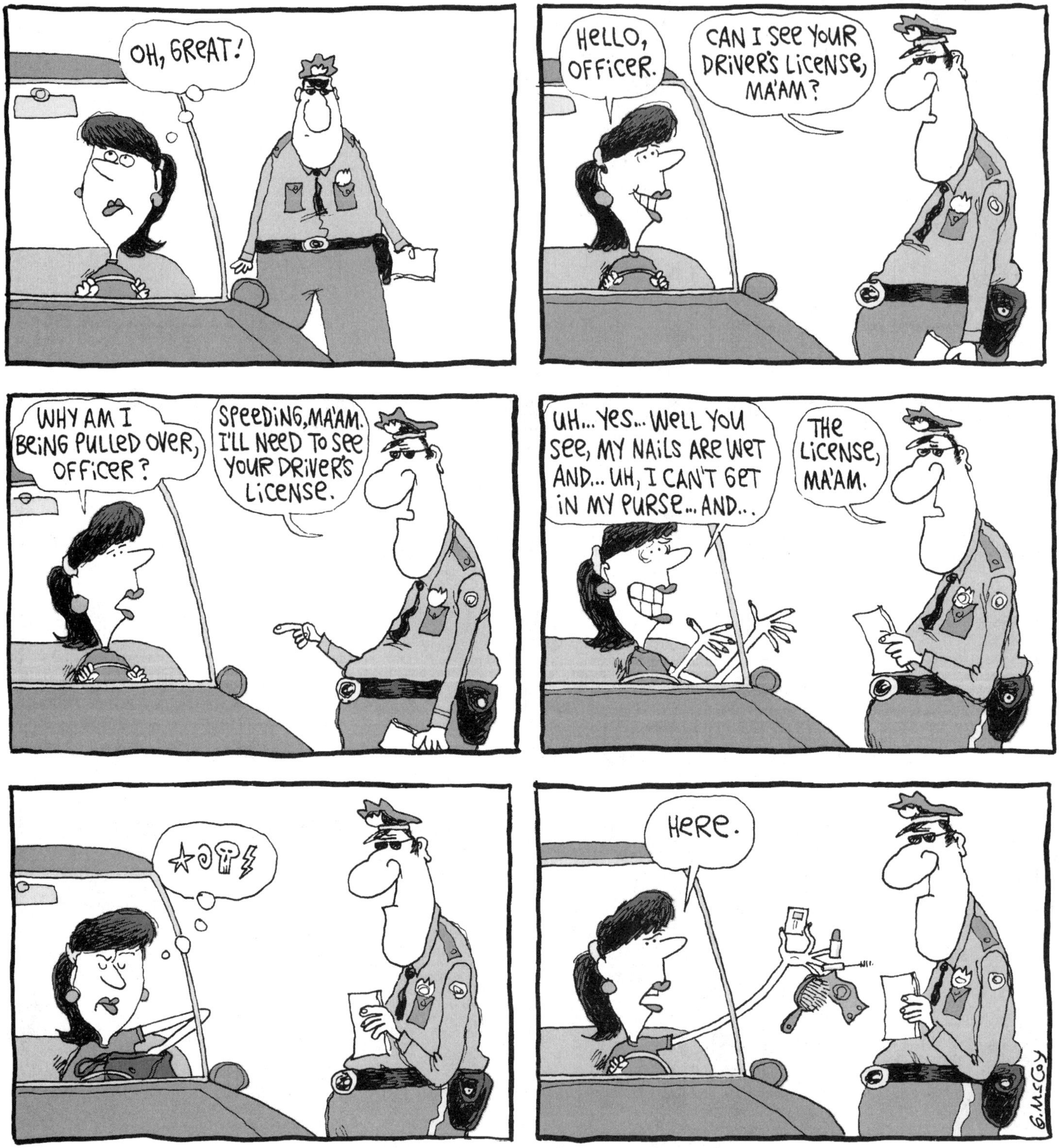
OH, GREAT!
HELLO, OFFICER.
CAN I SEE YOUR DRIVER'S LICENSE, MA'AM?
WHY AM I BEING PULLED OVER, OFFICER?
SPEEDING, MA'AM. I'LL NEED TO SEE YOUR DRIVER'S LICENSE.
UH... YES... WELL YOU SEE, MY NAILS ARE WET AND... UH, I CAN'T GET IN MY PURSE... AND...
THE LICENSE, MA'AM.
HERE.

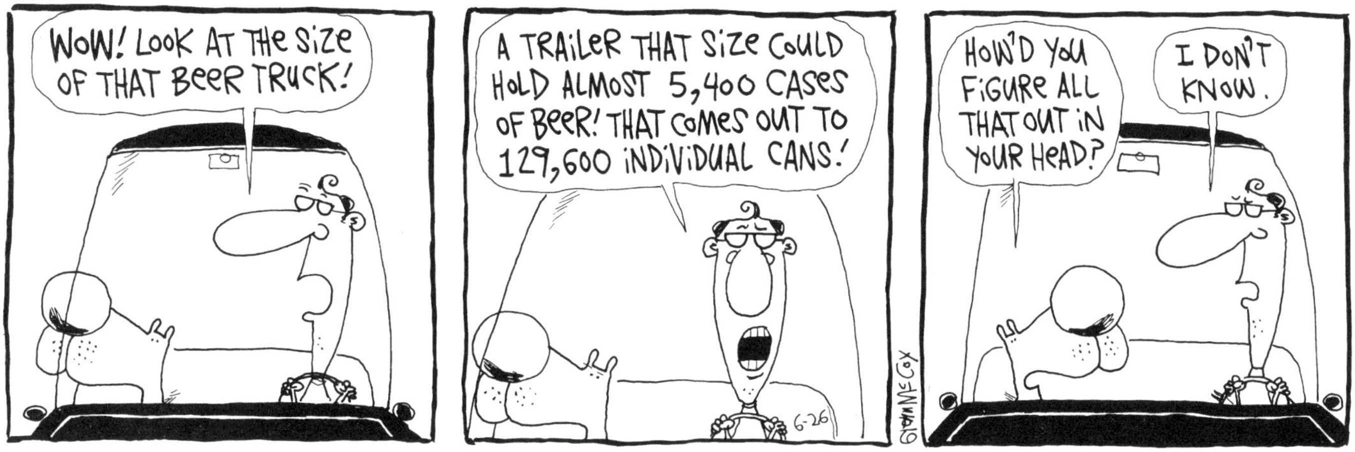
WOW! LOOK AT THE SIZE OF THAT BEER TRUCK!
A TRAILER THAT SIZE COULD HOLD ALMOST 5,400 CASES OF BEER! THAT COMES OUT TO 129,600 INDIVIDUAL CANS!
6-26
HOW'D YOU FIGURE ALL THAT OUT IN YOUR HEAD?
I DON'T KNOW.
Glenn McCoy

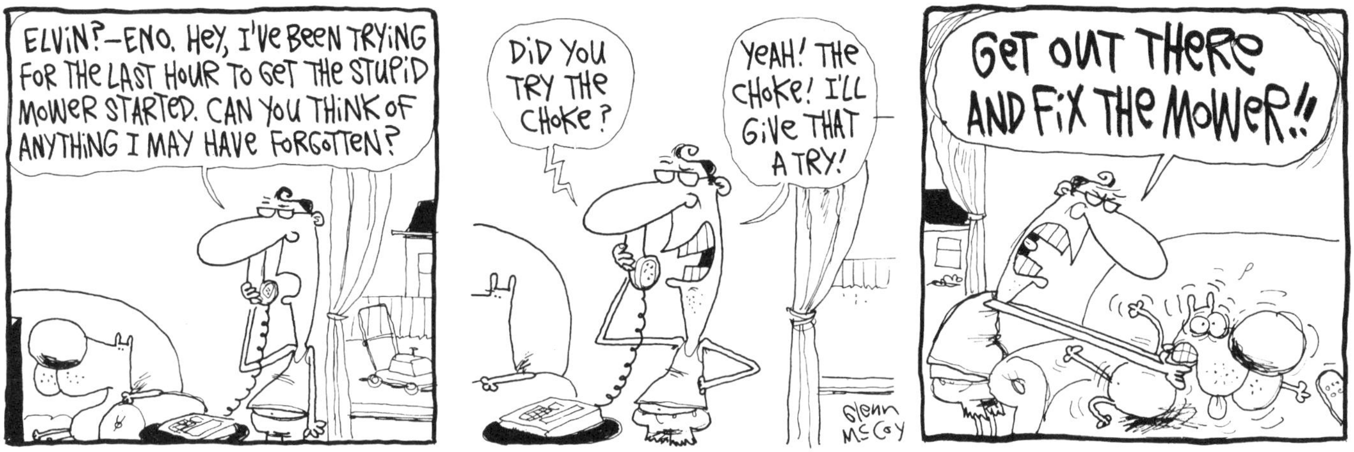
ELVIN?—ENO. HEY, I'VE BEEN TRYING FOR THE LAST HOUR TO GET THE STUPID MOWER STARTED. CAN YOU THINK OF ANYTHING I MAY HAVE FORGOTTEN?
DID YOU TRY THE CHOKE?
YEAH! THE CHOKE! I'LL GIVE THAT A TRY!
Glenn McCoy
GET OUT THERE AND FIX THE MOWER!!

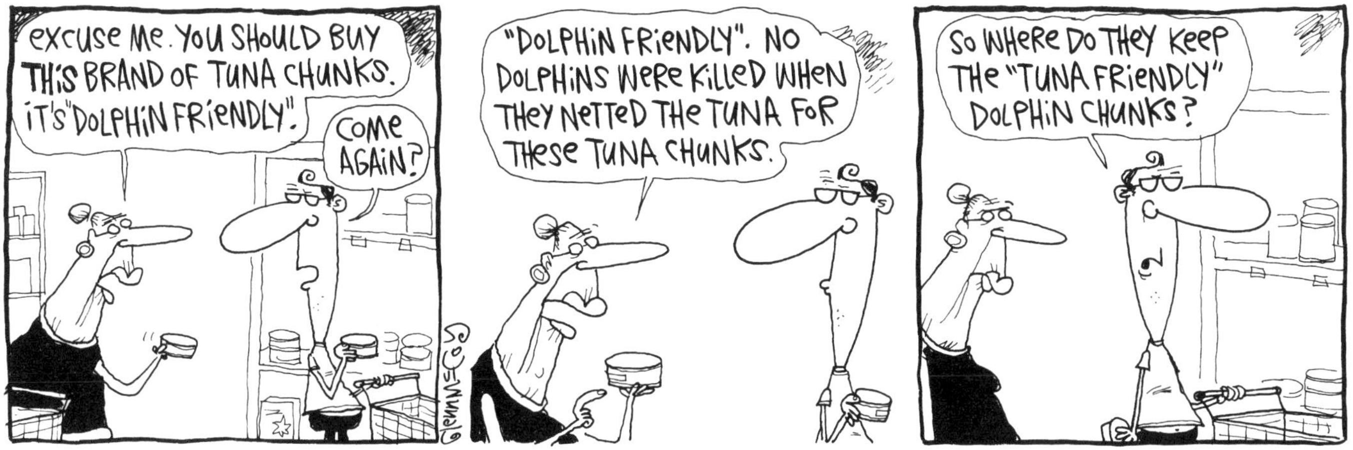
EXCUSE ME. YOU SHOULD BUY THIS BRAND OF TUNA CHUNKS. IT'S "DOLPHIN FRIENDLY".
COME AGAIN?
Glenn McCoy
"DOLPHIN FRIENDLY". NO DOLPHINS WERE KILLED WHEN THEY NETTED THE TUNA FOR THESE TUNA CHUNKS.
SO WHERE DO THEY KEEP THE "TUNA FRIENDLY" DOLPHIN CHUNKS?

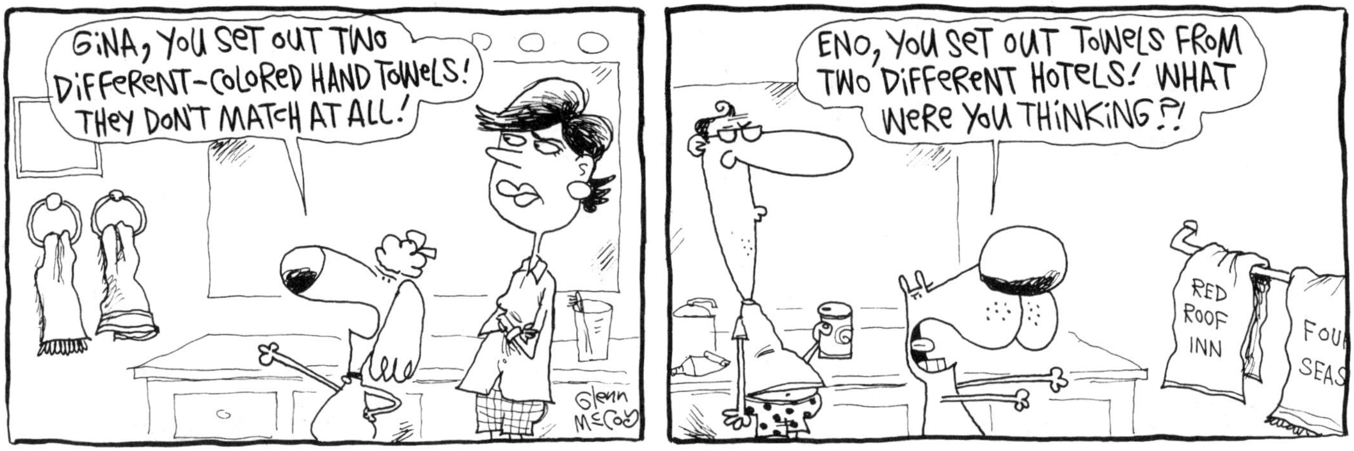
GINA, YOU SET OUT TWO DIFFERENT-COLORED HAND TOWELS! THEY DON'T MATCH AT ALL!
Glenn McCoy
ENO, YOU SET OUT TOWELS FROM TWO DIFFERENT HOTELS! WHAT WERE YOU THINKING?!
RED ROOF INN

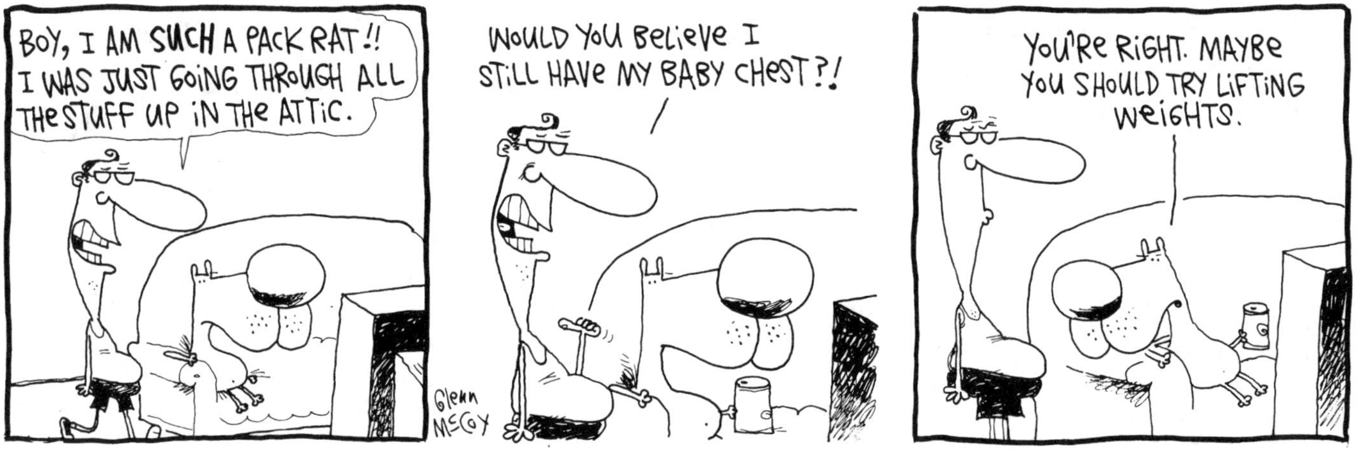
BOY, I AM SUCH A PACK RAT!! I WAS JUST GOING THROUGH ALL THE STUFF UP IN THE ATTIC.
Glenn McCoy
WOULD YOU BELIEVE I STILL HAVE MY BABY CHEST?!
YOU'RE RIGHT. MAYBE YOU SHOULD TRY LIFTING WEIGHTS.

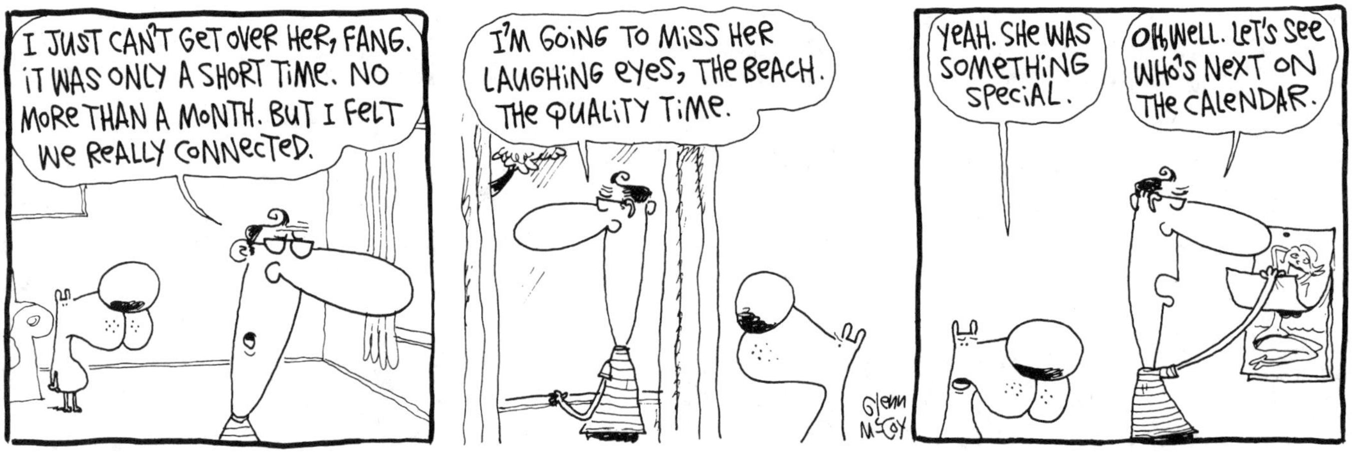
I JUST CAN'T GET OVER HER, FANG. IT WAS ONLY A SHORT TIME. NO MORE THAN A MONTH. BUT I FELT WE REALLY CONNECTED.
I'M GOING TO MISS HER LAUGHING EYES, THE BEACH. THE QUALITY TIME.
Glenn McCoy
YEAH. SHE WAS SOMETHING SPECIAL.
OH, WELL. LET'S SEE WHO'S NEXT ON THE CALENDAR.

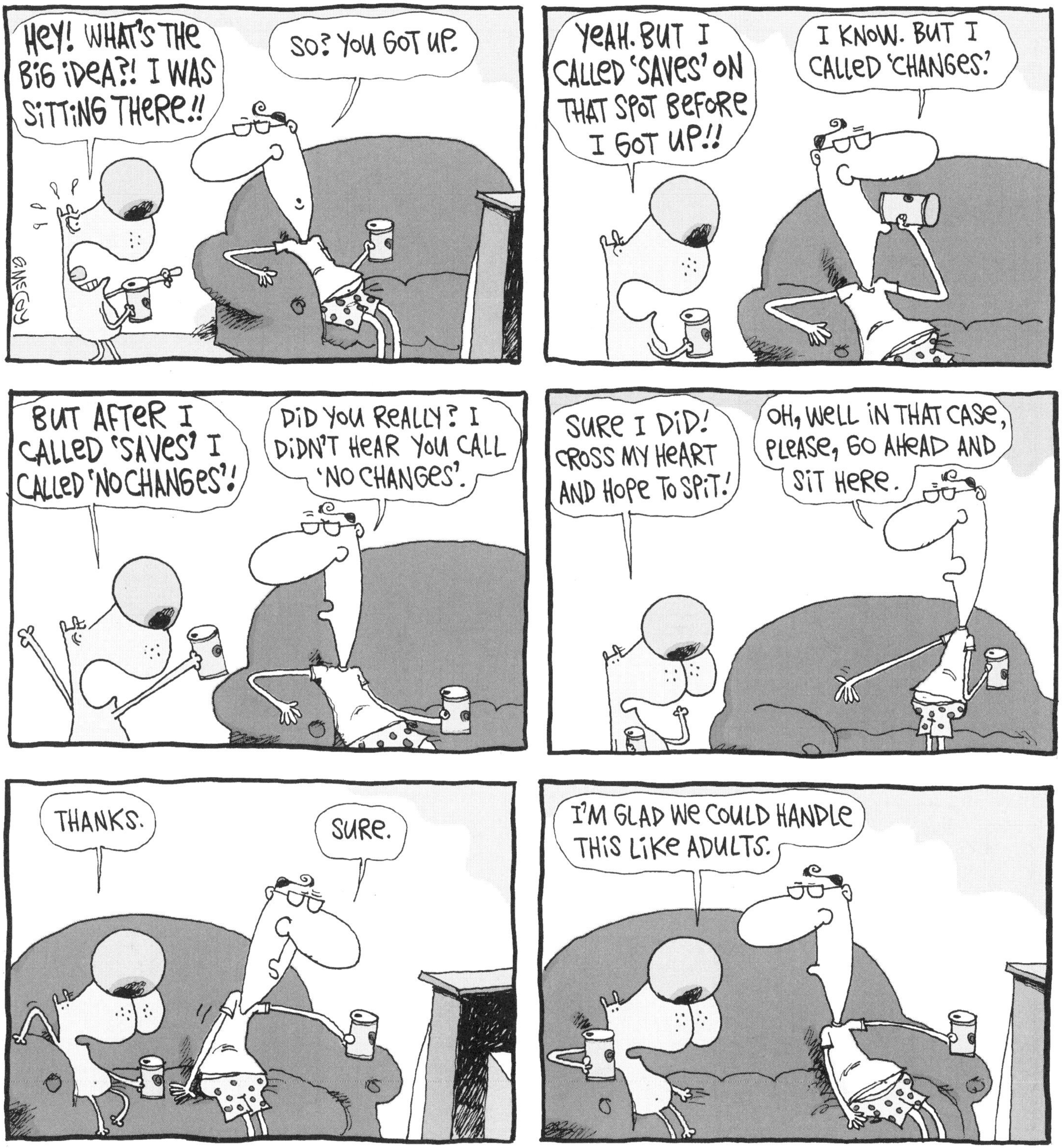
HEY! WHAT'S THE BIG IDEA?! I WAS SITTING THERE!!
SO? YOU GOT UP.
YEAH. BUT I CALLED 'SAVES' ON THAT SPOT BEFORE I GOT UP!!
I KNOW. BUT I CALLED 'CHANGES.'
BUT AFTER I CALLED 'SAVES' I CALLED 'NO CHANGES'!
DID YOU REALLY? I DIDN'T HEAR YOU CALL 'NO CHANGES'.
SURE I DID! CROSS MY HEART AND HOPE TO SPIT!
OH, WELL IN THAT CASE, PLEASE, GO AHEAD AND SIT HERE.
THANKS.
SURE.
I'M GLAD WE COULD HANDLE THIS LIKE ADULTS.

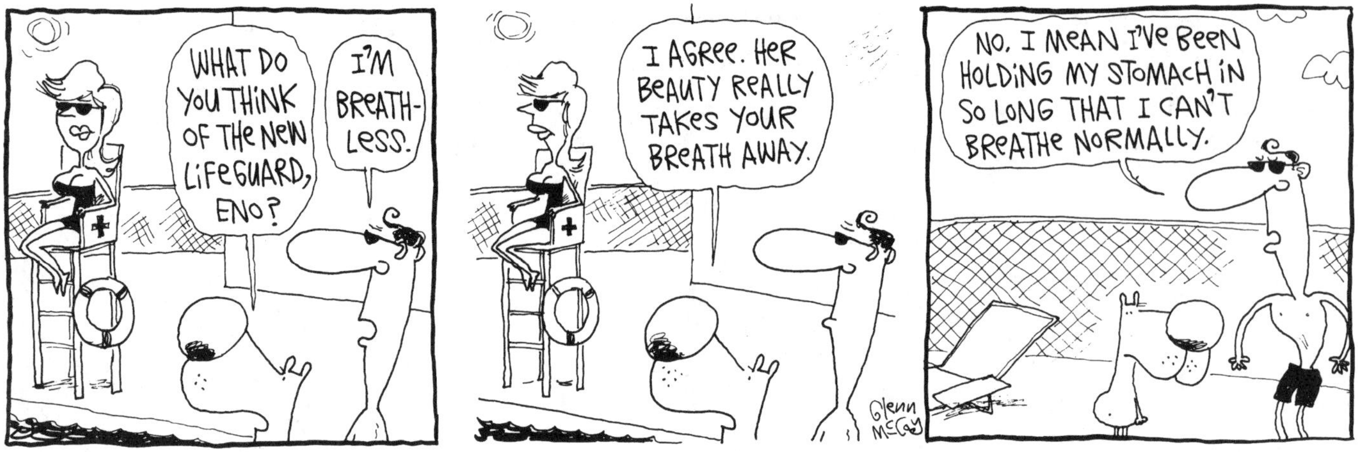
WHAT DO YOU THINK OF THE NEW LIFEGUARD, ENO?
I'M BREATH-LESS.
I AGREE. HER BEAUTY REALLY TAKES YOUR BREATH AWAY.
Glenn McCoy
NO, I MEAN I'VE BEEN HOLDING MY STOMACH IN SO LONG THAT I CAN'T BREATHE NORMALLY.

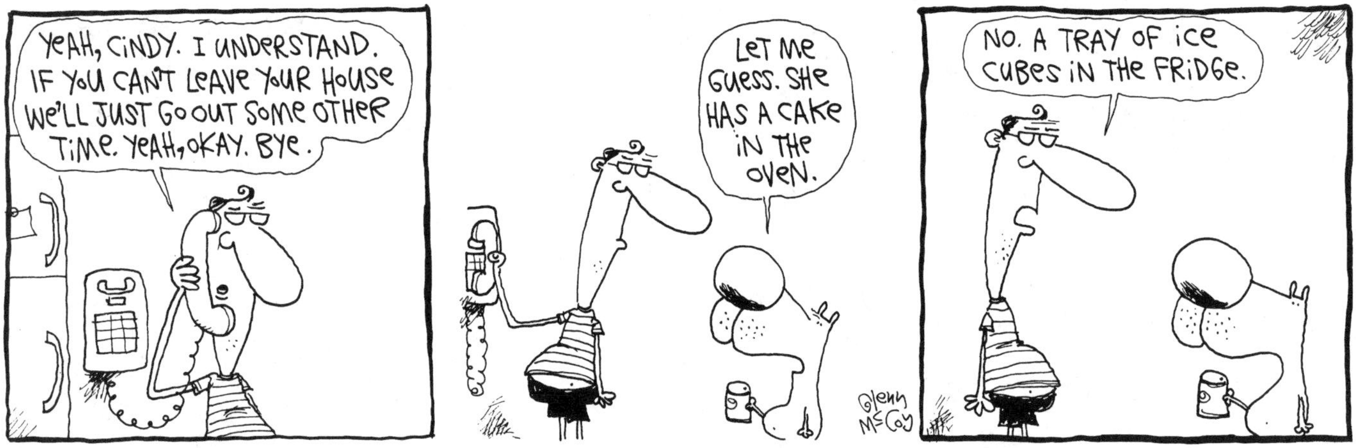
YEAH, CINDY. I UNDERSTAND. IF YOU CAN'T LEAVE YOUR HOUSE WE'LL JUST GO OUT SOME OTHER TIME. YEAH, OKAY. BYE.
LET ME GUESS. SHE HAS A CAKE IN THE OVEN.
Glenn McCoy
NO. A TRAY OF ICE CUBES IN THE FRIDGE.

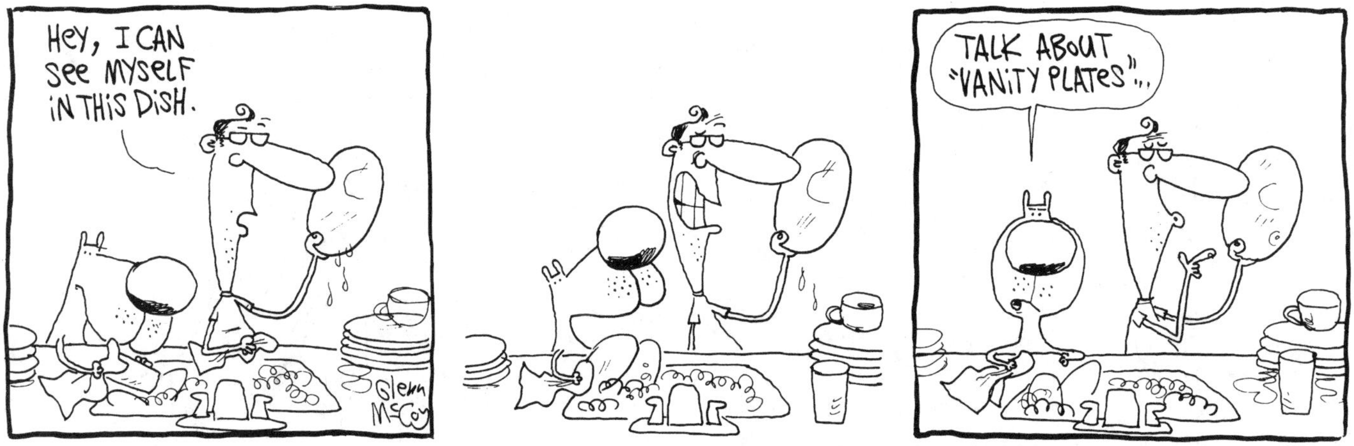
HEY, I CAN SEE MYSELF IN THIS DISH.
Glenn McCoy
TALK ABOUT "VANITY PLATES"...

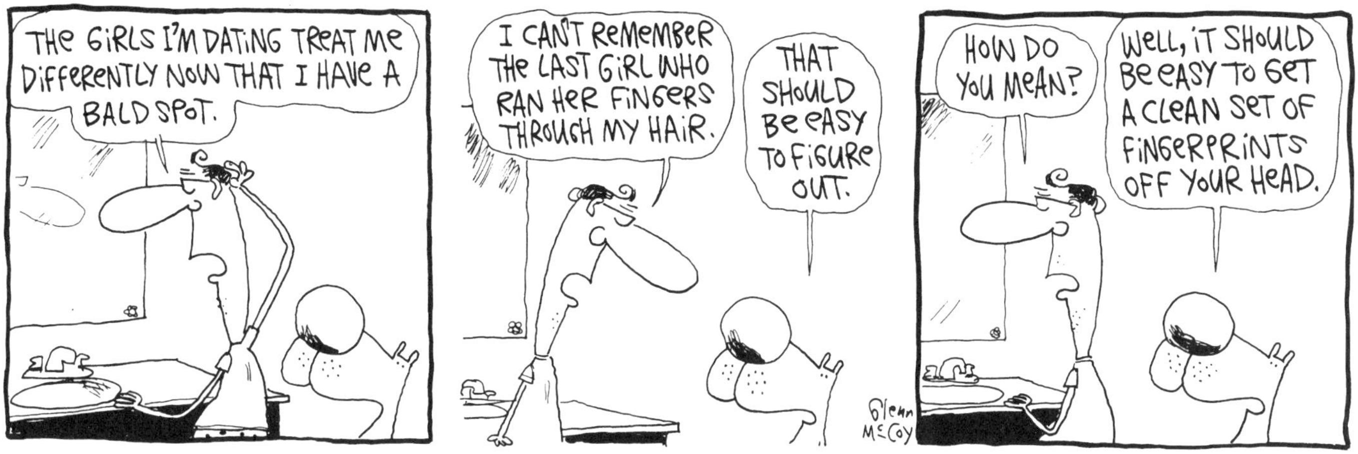
THE GIRLS I'M DATING TREAT ME DIFFERENTLY NOW THAT I HAVE A BALD SPOT.
I CAN'T REMEMBER THE LAST GIRL WHO RAN HER FINGERS THROUGH MY HAIR.
THAT SHOULD BE EASY TO FIGURE OUT.
HOW DO YOU MEAN?
WELL, IT SHOULD BE EASY TO GET A CLEAN SET OF FINGERPRINTS OFF YOUR HEAD.
Glenn McCoy

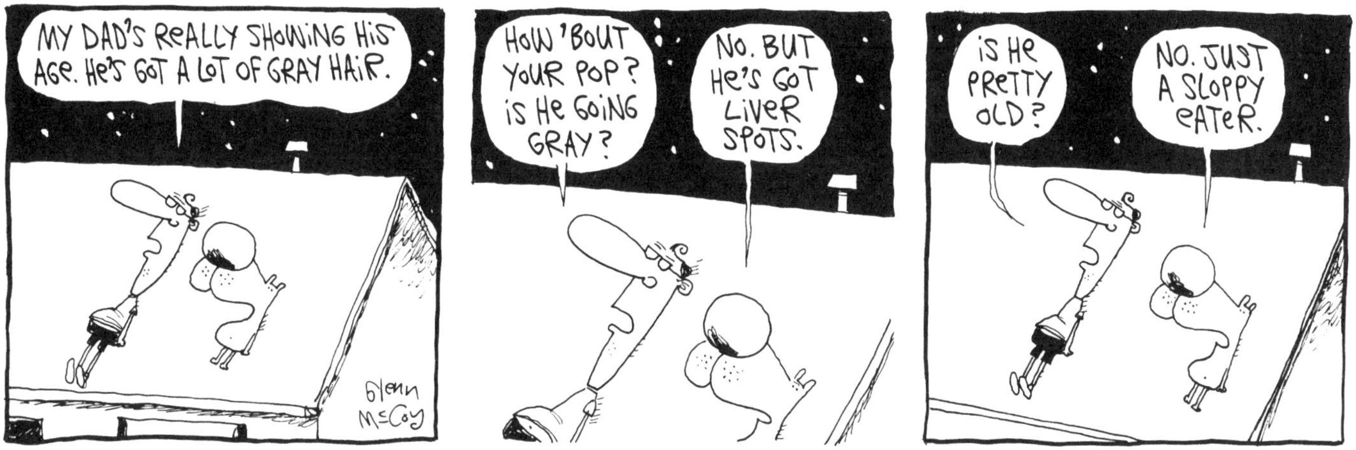
MY DAD'S REALLY SHOWING HIS AGE. HE'S GOT A LOT OF GRAY HAIR.
Glenn McCoy
HOW 'BOUT YOUR POP? IS HE GOING GRAY?
NO. BUT HE'S GOT LIVER SPOTS.
IS HE PRETTY OLD?
NO. JUST A SLOPPY EATER.

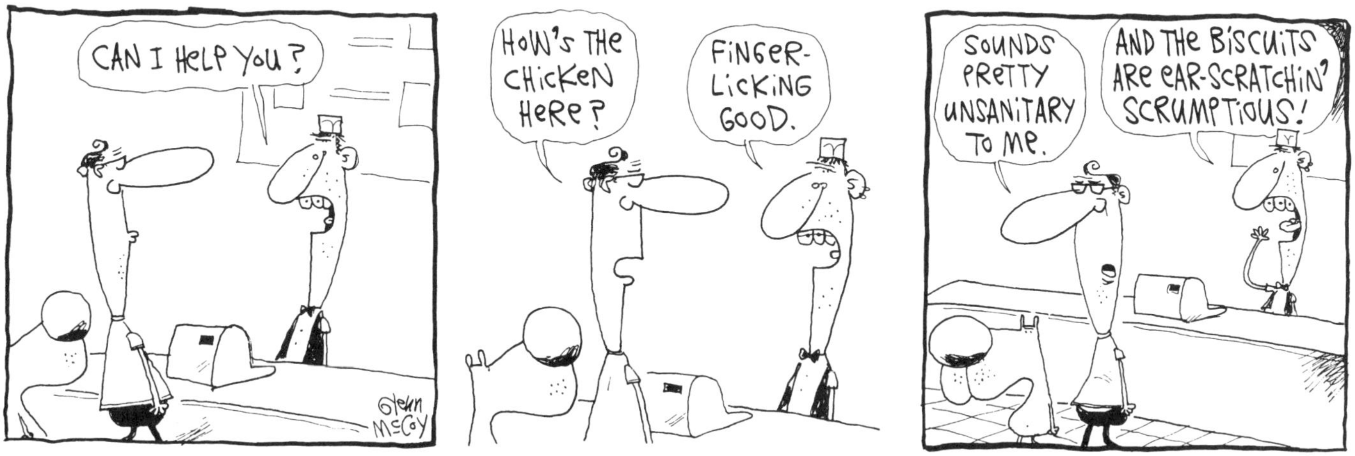
CAN I HELP YOU?
Glenn McCoy
HOW'S THE CHICKEN HERE?
FINGER-LICKING GOOD.
SOUNDS PRETTY UNSANITARY TO ME.
AND THE BISCUITS ARE EAR-SCRATCHIN' SCRUMPTIOUS!

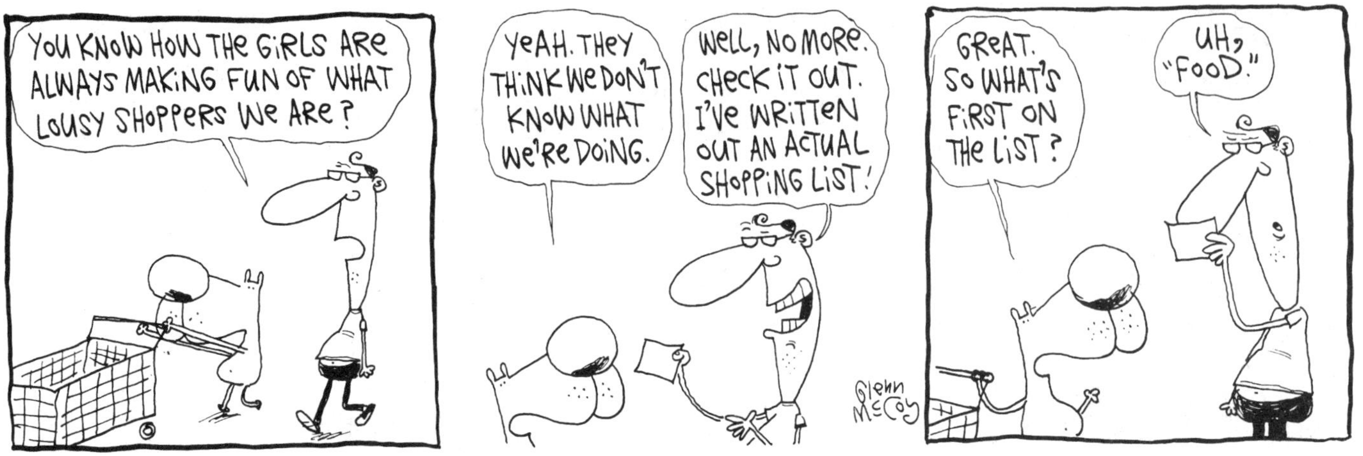
YOU KNOW HOW THE GIRLS ARE ALWAYS MAKING FUN OF WHAT LOUSY SHOPPERS WE ARE?
YEAH. THEY THINK WE DON'T KNOW WHAT WE'RE DOING.
WELL, NO MORE. CHECK IT OUT. I'VE WRITTEN OUT AN ACTUAL SHOPPING LIST!
GREAT. SO WHAT'S FIRST ON THE LIST?
UH, "FOOD."
Glenn McCoy

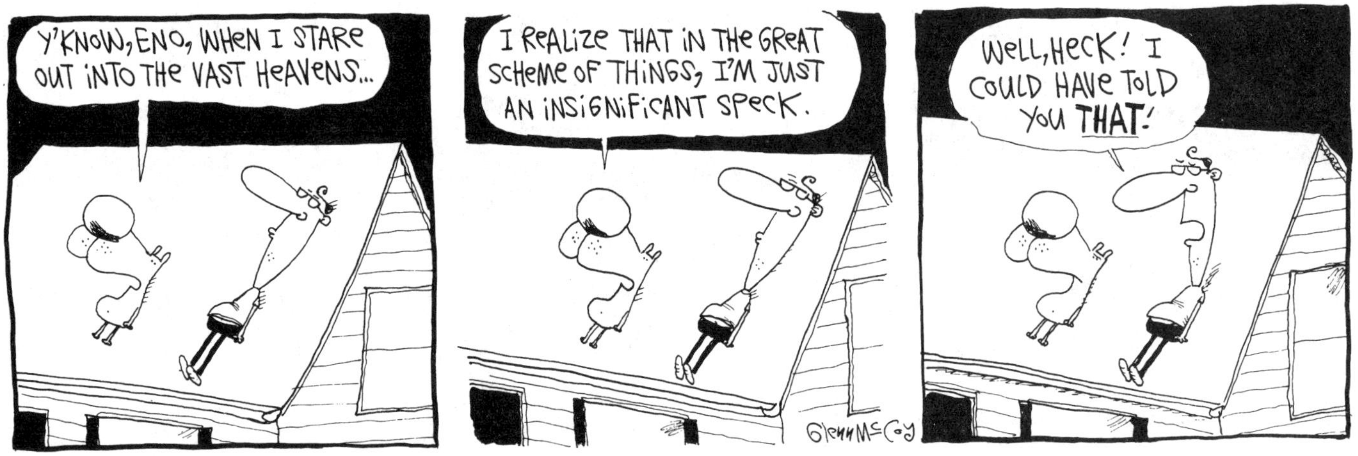
Y'KNOW, ENO, WHEN I STARE OUT INTO THE VAST HEAVENS...
I REALIZE THAT IN THE GREAT SCHEME OF THINGS, I'M JUST AN INSIGNIFICANT SPECK.
WELL, HECK! I COULD HAVE TOLD YOU THAT!
Glenn McCoy

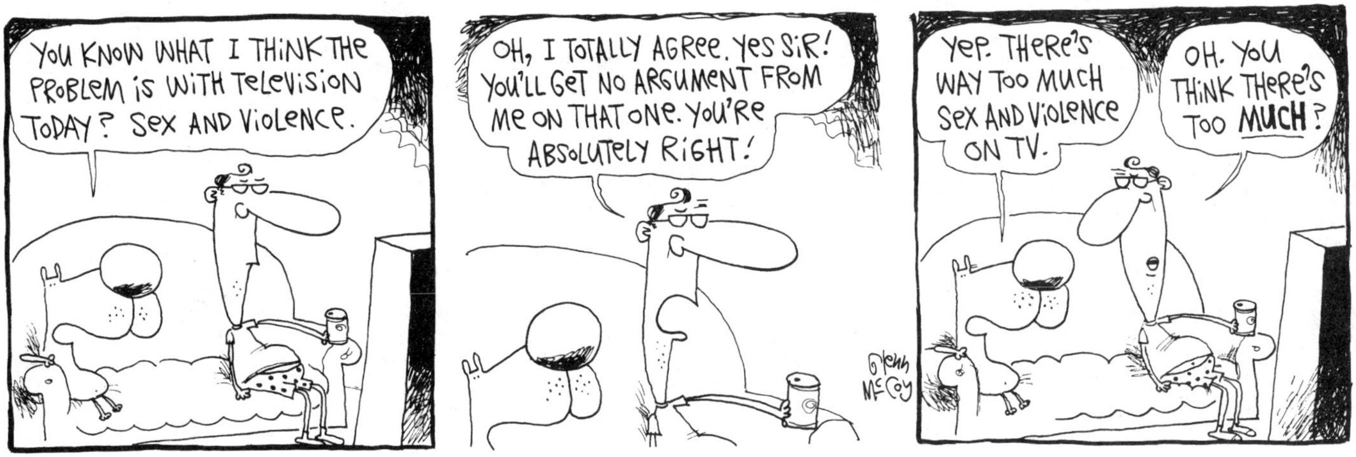
YOU KNOW WHAT I THINK THE PROBLEM IS WITH TELEVISION TODAY? SEX AND VIOLENCE.
OH, I TOTALLY AGREE. YES SIR! YOU'LL GET NO ARGUMENT FROM ME ON THAT ONE. YOU'RE ABSOLUTELY RIGHT!
YEP. THERE'S WAY TOO MUCH SEX AND VIOLENCE ON TV.
OH. YOU THINK THERE'S TOO MUCH?
Glenn McCoy

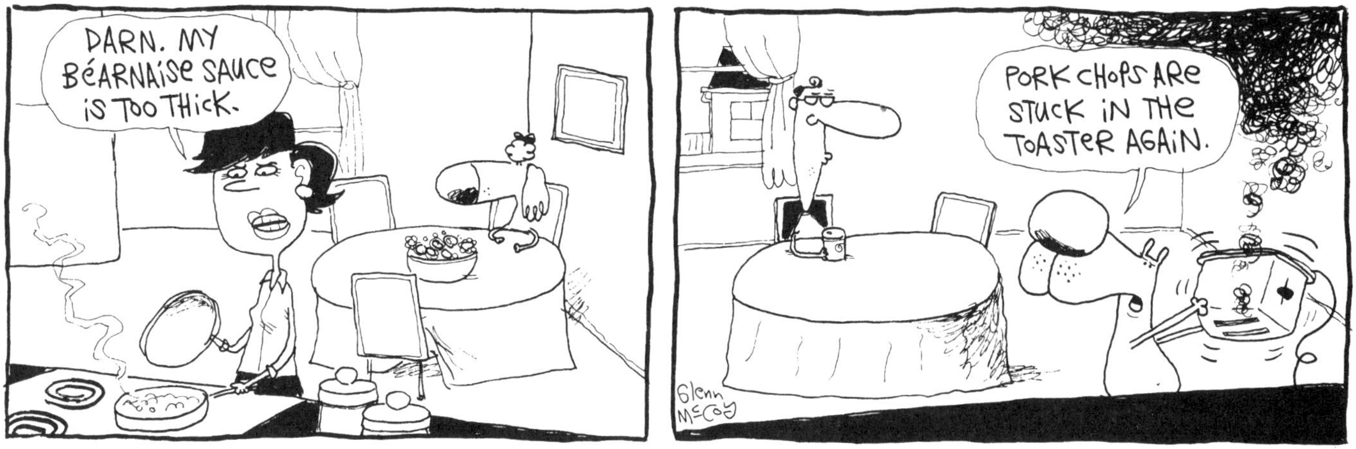
DARN. MY BÉARNAISE SAUCE IS TOO THICK.
PORK CHOPS ARE STUCK IN THE TOASTER AGAIN.
Glenn McCoy

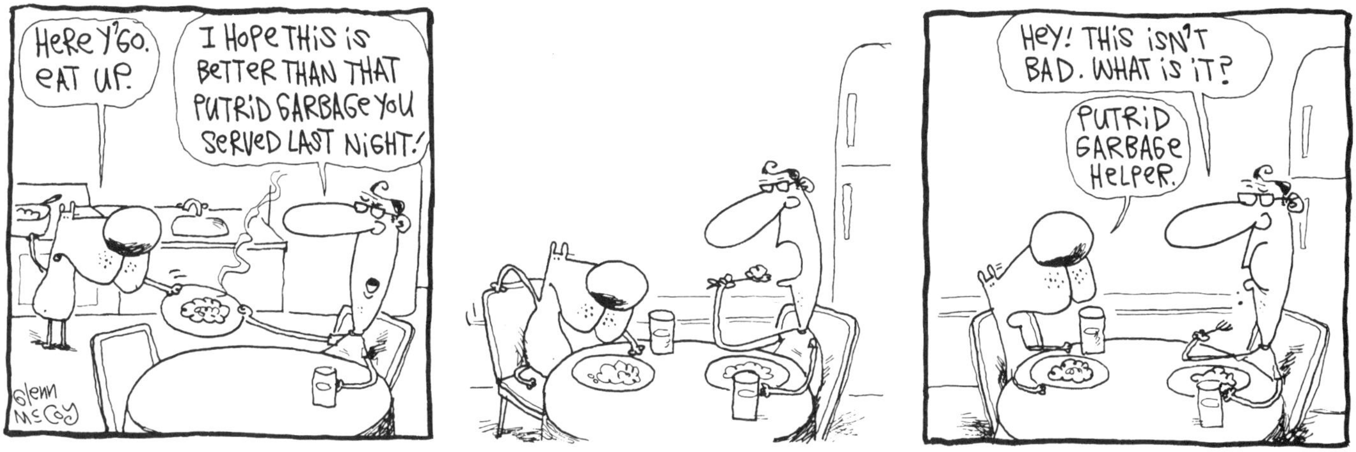
HERE Y'GO. EAT UP.
I HOPE THIS IS BETTER THAN THAT PUTRID GARBAGE YOU SERVED LAST NIGHT!
Glenn McCoy
HEY! THIS ISN'T BAD. WHAT IS IT?
PUTRID GARBAGE HELPER.

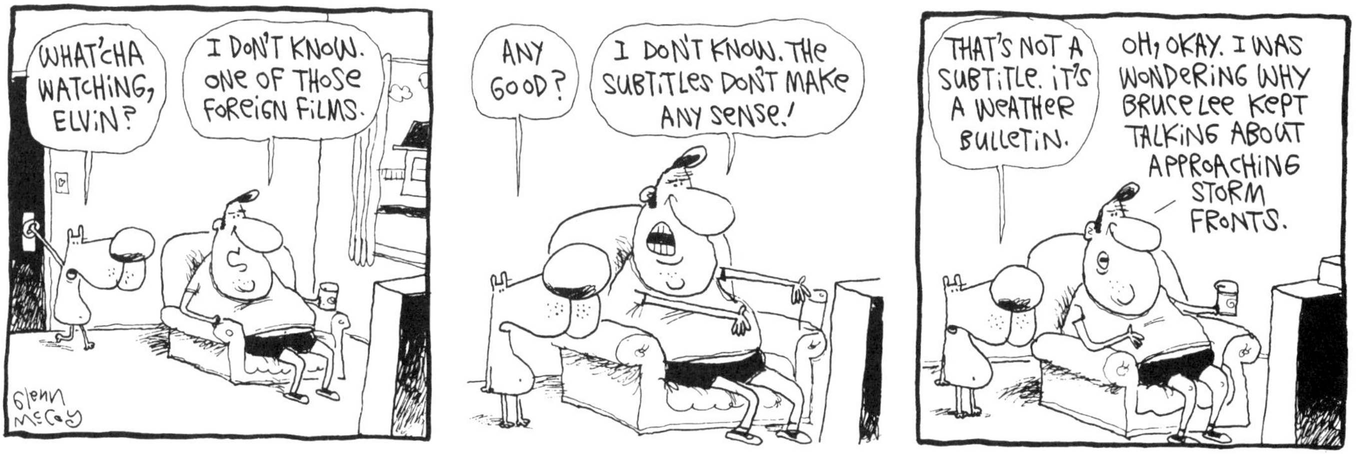
WHAT'CHA WATCHING, ELVIN?
I DON'T KNOW. ONE OF THOSE FOREIGN FILMS.
Glenn McCoy
ANY GOOD?
I DON'T KNOW. THE SUBTITLES DON'T MAKE ANY SENSE!
THAT'S NOT A SUBTITLE. IT'S A WEATHER BULLETIN.
OH, OKAY. I WAS WONDERING WHY BRUCE LEE KEPT TALKING ABOUT APPROACHING STORM FRONTS.

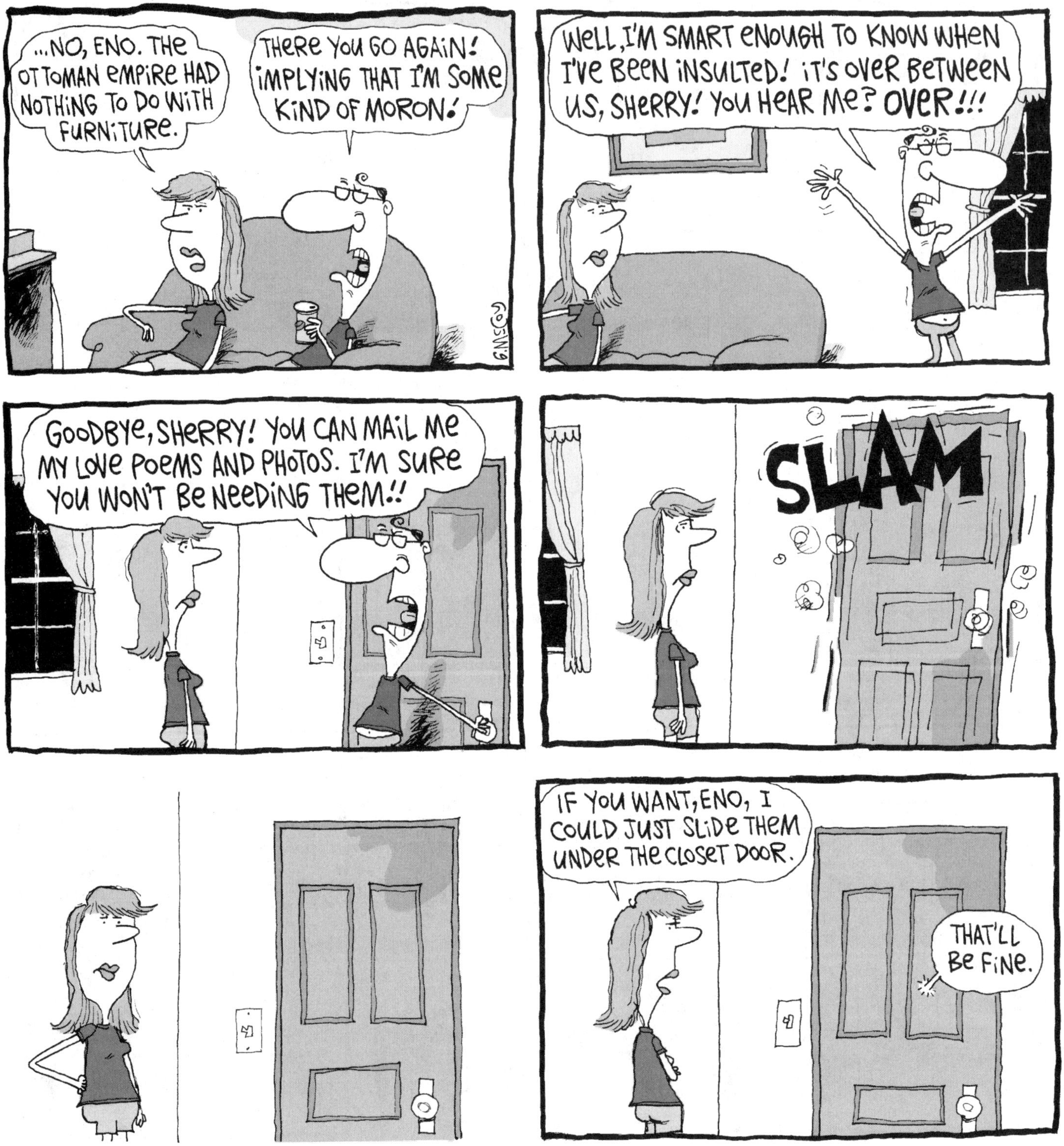
...NO, ENO. THE OTTOMAN EMPIRE HAD NOTHING TO DO WITH FURNITURE.
THERE YOU GO AGAIN! IMPLYING THAT I'M SOME KIND OF MORON!
G.McCOY
WELL, I'M SMART ENOUGH TO KNOW WHEN I'VE BEEN INSULTED! IT'S OVER BETWEEN US, SHERRY! YOU HEAR ME? OVER!!!
GOODBYE, SHERRY! YOU CAN MAIL ME MY LOVE POEMS AND PHOTOS. I'M SURE YOU WON'T BE NEEDING THEM!!
SLAM
IF YOU WANT, ENO, I COULD JUST SLIDE THEM UNDER THE CLOSET DOOR.
THAT'LL BE FINE.

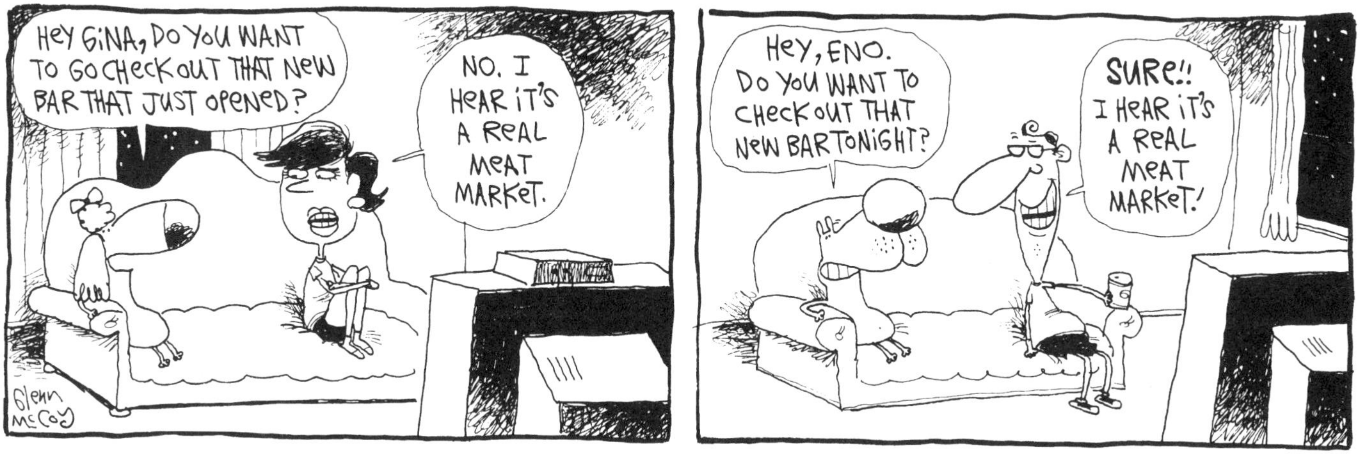
HEY GINA, DO YOU WANT TO GO CHECK OUT THAT NEW BAR THAT JUST OPENED?
NO. I HEAR IT'S A REAL MEAT MARKET.
HEY, ENO. DO YOU WANT TO CHECK OUT THAT NEW BAR TONIGHT?
SURE!! I HEAR IT'S A REAL MEAT MARKET!
Glenn McCoy

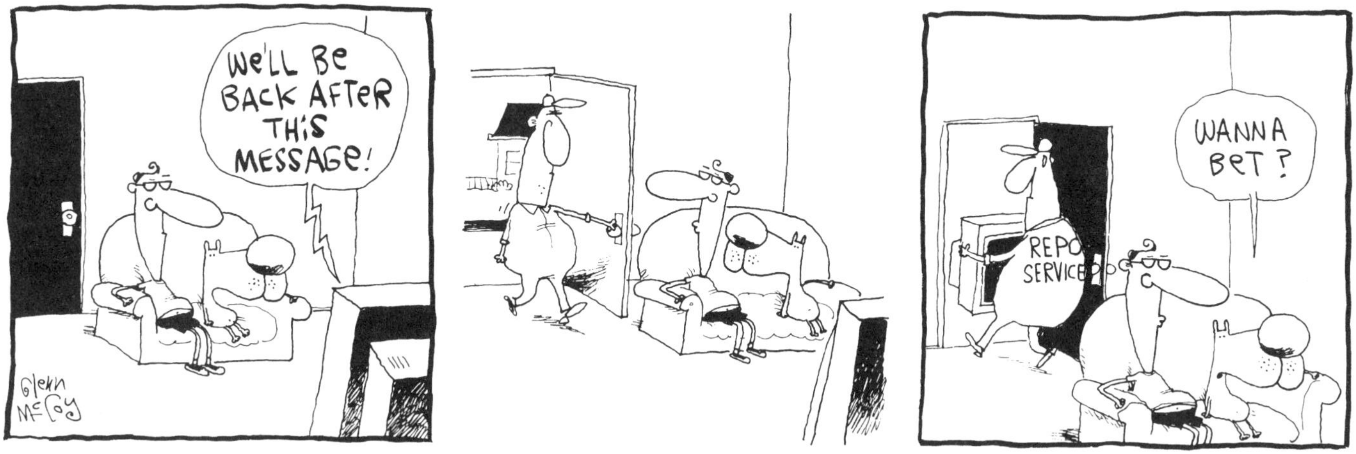
WE'LL BE BACK AFTER THIS MESSAGE!
REPO SERVICE
WANNA BET?
Glenn McCoy

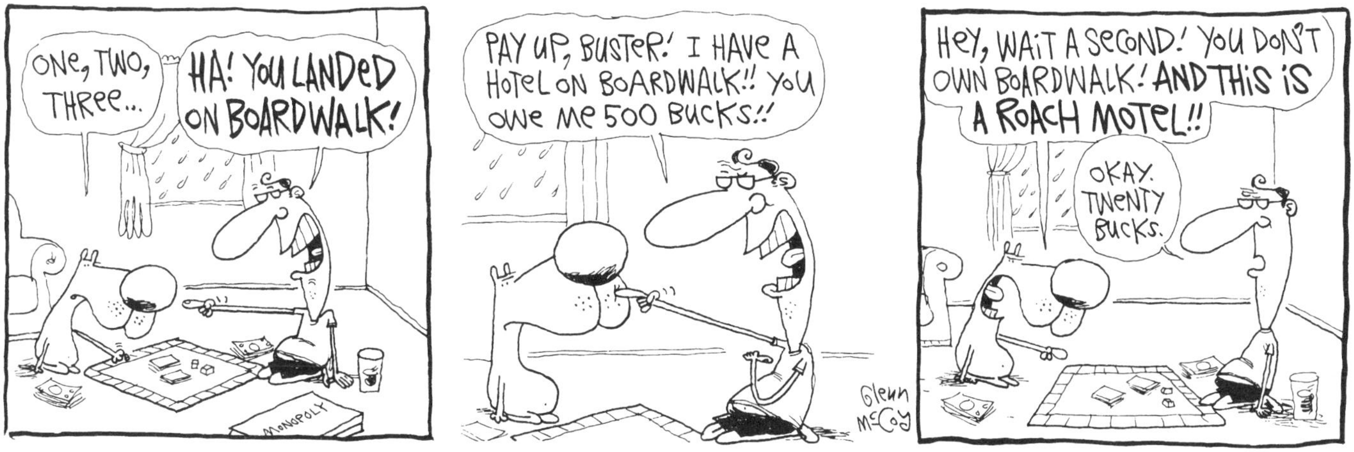
ONE, TWO, THREE...
HA! YOU LANDED ON BOARDWALK!
MONOPOLY
PAY UP, BUSTER! I HAVE A HOTEL ON BOARDWALK!! YOU OWE ME 500 BUCKS!!
HEY, WAIT A SECOND! YOU DON'T OWN BOARDWALK! AND THIS IS A ROACH MOTEL!!
OKAY. TWENTY BUCKS.
Glenn McCoy

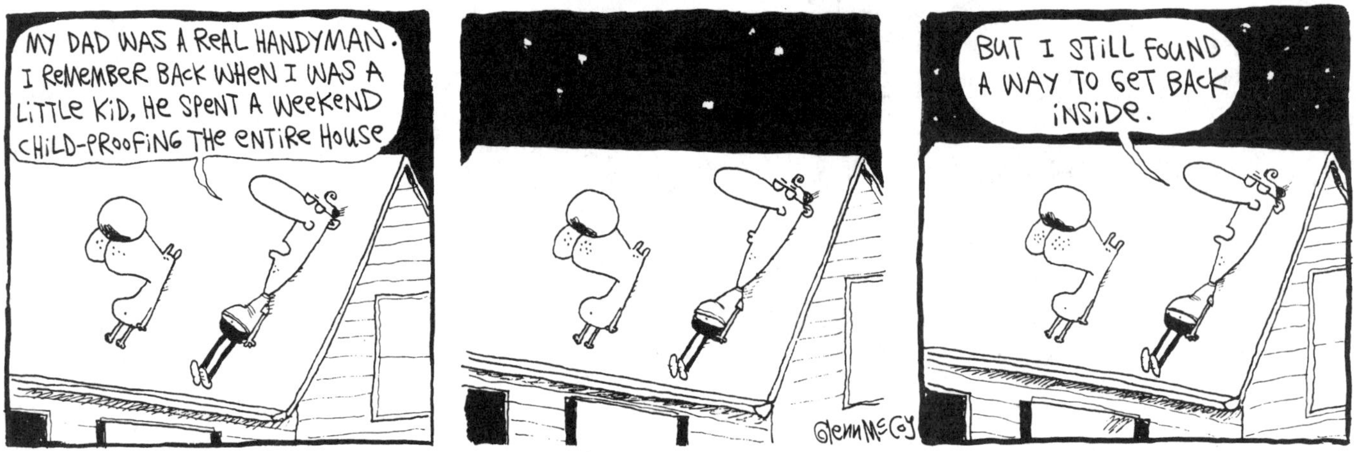
MY DAD WAS A REAL HANDYMAN. I REMEMBER BACK WHEN I WAS A LITTLE KID, HE SPENT A WEEKEND CHILD-PROOFING THE ENTIRE HOUSE
BUT I STILL FOUND A WAY TO GET BACK INSIDE.
GLENN McCOY

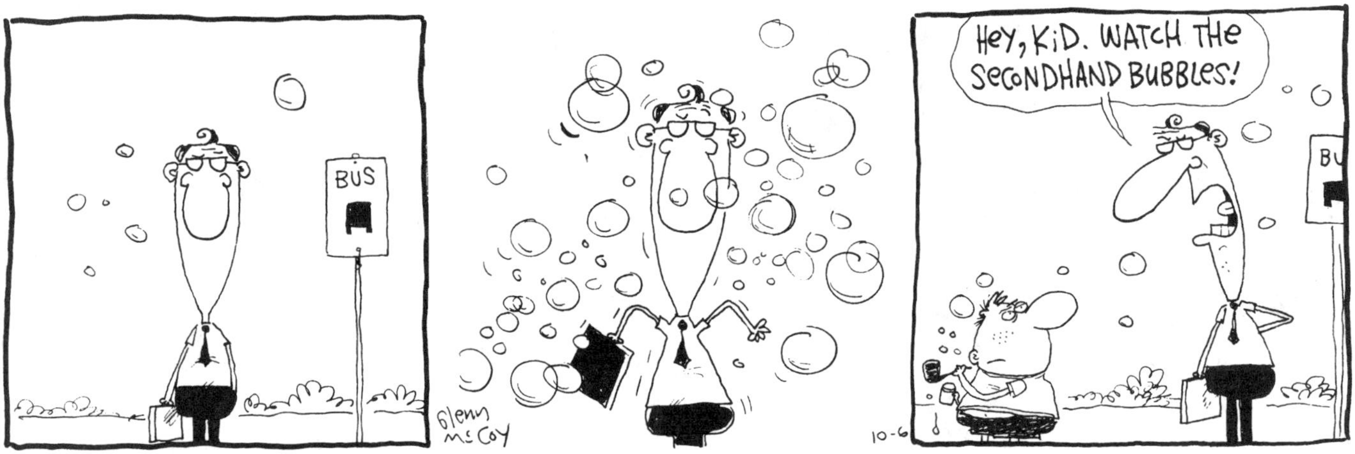
BUS
GLENN McCOY
HEY, KID. WATCH THE SECONDHAND BUBBLES!
10-6

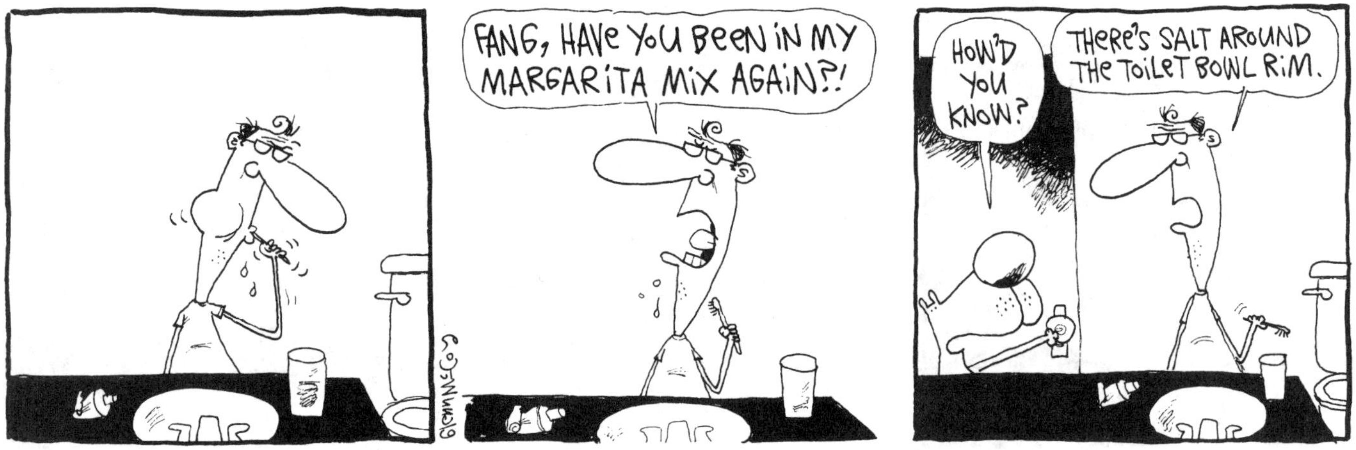
GLENN McCOY
FANG, HAVE YOU BEEN IN MY MARGARITA MIX AGAIN?!
HOW'D YOU KNOW?
THERE'S SALT AROUND THE TOILET BOWL RIM.

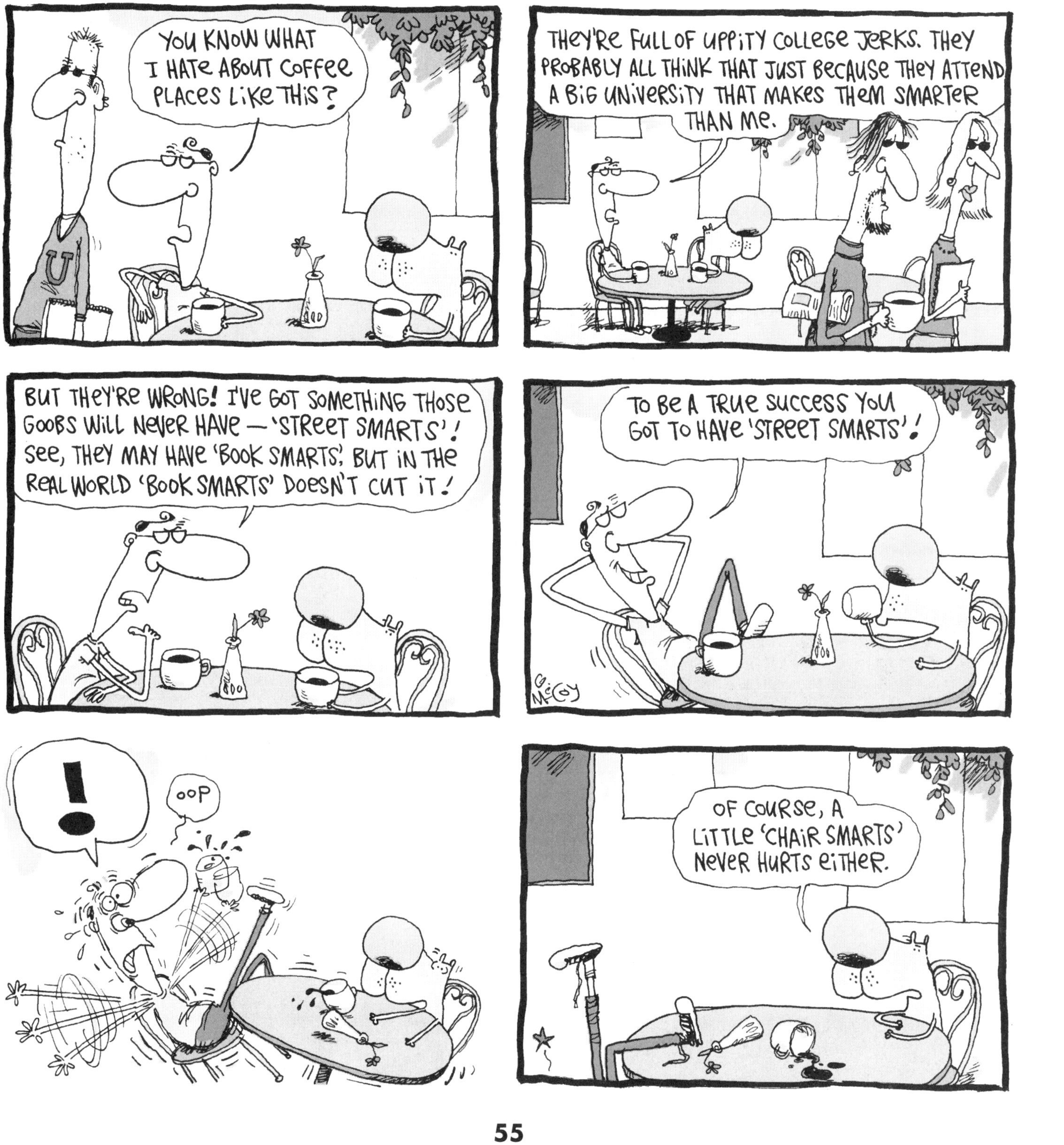
YOU KNOW WHAT I HATE ABOUT COFFEE PLACES LIKE THIS?
THEY'RE FULL OF UPPITY COLLEGE JERKS. THEY PROBABLY ALL THINK THAT JUST BECAUSE THEY ATTEND A BIG UNIVERSITY THAT MAKES THEM SMARTER THAN ME.
BUT THEY'RE WRONG! I'VE GOT SOMETHING THOSE GOOBS WILL NEVER HAVE — 'STREET SMARTS'! SEE, THEY MAY HAVE 'BOOK SMARTS,' BUT IN THE REAL WORLD 'BOOK SMARTS' DOESN'T CUT IT!
TO BE A TRUE SUCCESS YOU GOT TO HAVE 'STREET SMARTS'!
McCOY
!
OOP
OF COURSE, A LITTLE 'CHAIR SMARTS' NEVER HURTS EITHER.

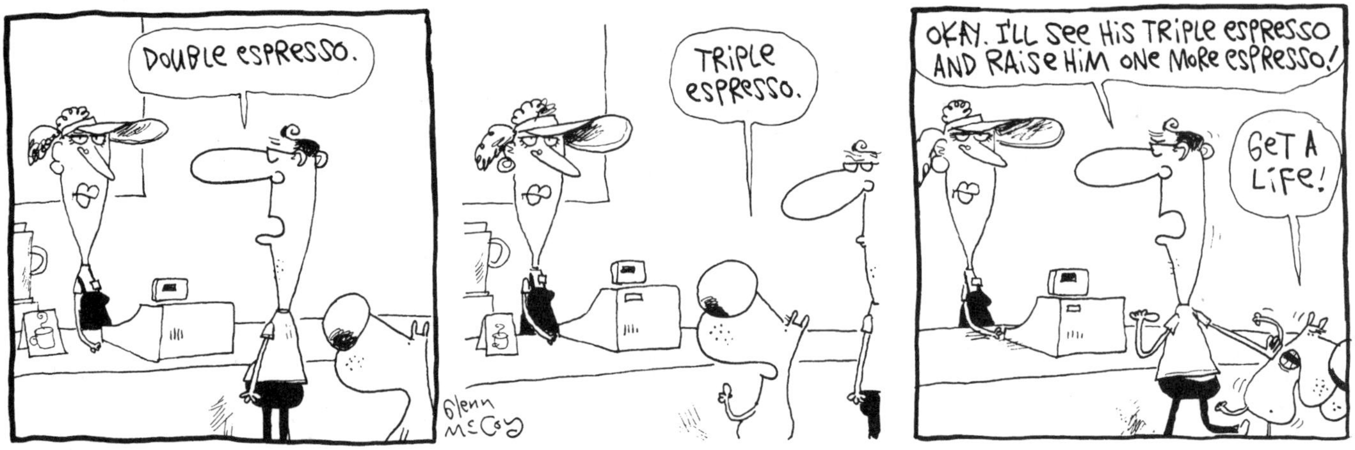
DOUBLE ESPRESSO.
Glenn McCoy
TRIPLE ESPRESSO.
OKAY. I'LL SEE HIS TRIPLE ESPRESSO AND RAISE HIM ONE MORE ESPRESSO!
GET A LIFE!

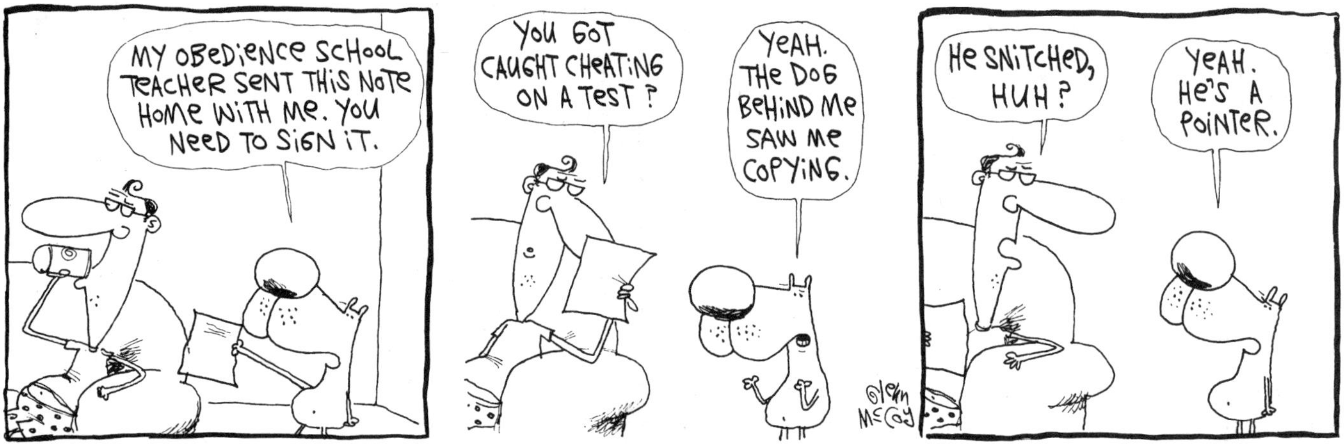
MY OBEDIENCE SCHOOL TEACHER SENT THIS NOTE HOME WITH ME. YOU NEED TO SIGN IT.
YOU GOT CAUGHT CHEATING ON A TEST?
YEAH. THE DOG BEHIND ME SAW ME COPYING.
Glenn McCoy
HE SNITCHED, HUH?
YEAH. HE'S A POINTER.

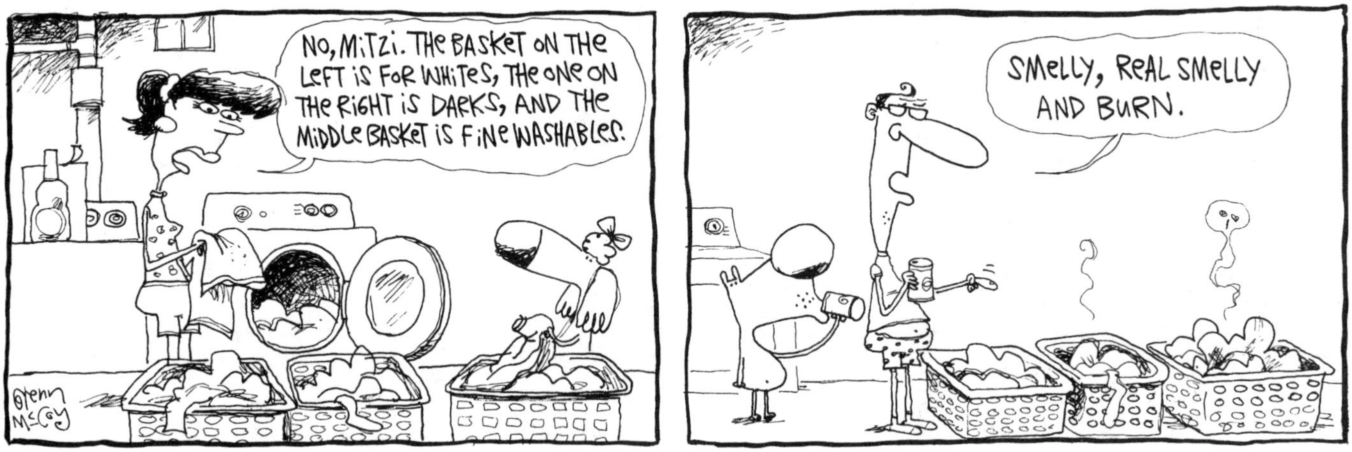
NO, MITZI. THE BASKET ON THE LEFT IS FOR WHITES, THE ONE ON THE RIGHT IS DARKS, AND THE MIDDLE BASKET IS FINE WASHABLES.
Glenn McCoy
SMELLY, REAL SMELLY AND BURN.

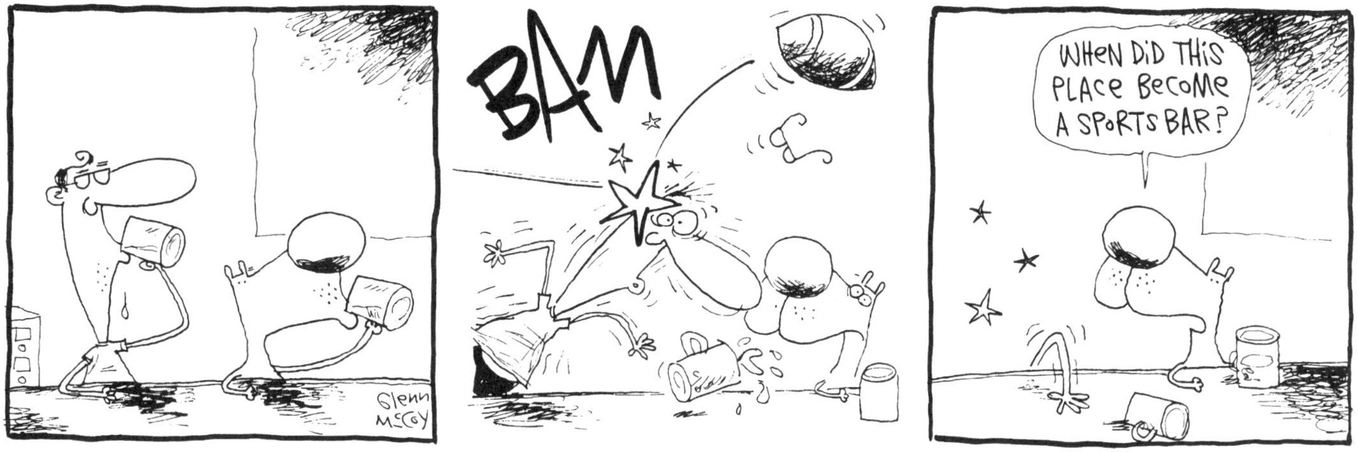
Glenn McCoy
BAM
WHEN DID THIS PLACE BECOME A SPORTS BAR?

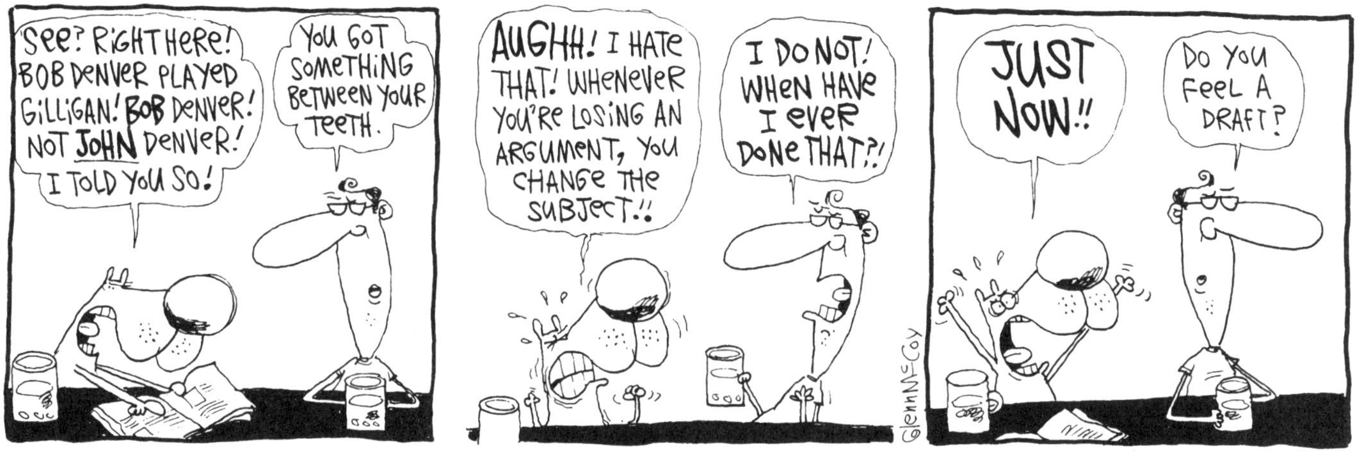
SEE? RIGHT HERE! BOB DENVER PLAYED GILLIGAN! BOB DENVER! NOT JOHN DENVER! I TOLD YOU SO!
YOU GOT SOMETHING BETWEEN YOUR TEETH.
AUGHH! I HATE THAT! WHENEVER YOU'RE LOSING AN ARGUMENT, YOU CHANGE THE SUBJECT!!
I DO NOT! WHEN HAVE I EVER DONE THAT?!
GlennMcCoy
JUST NOW!!
DO YOU FEEL A DRAFT?

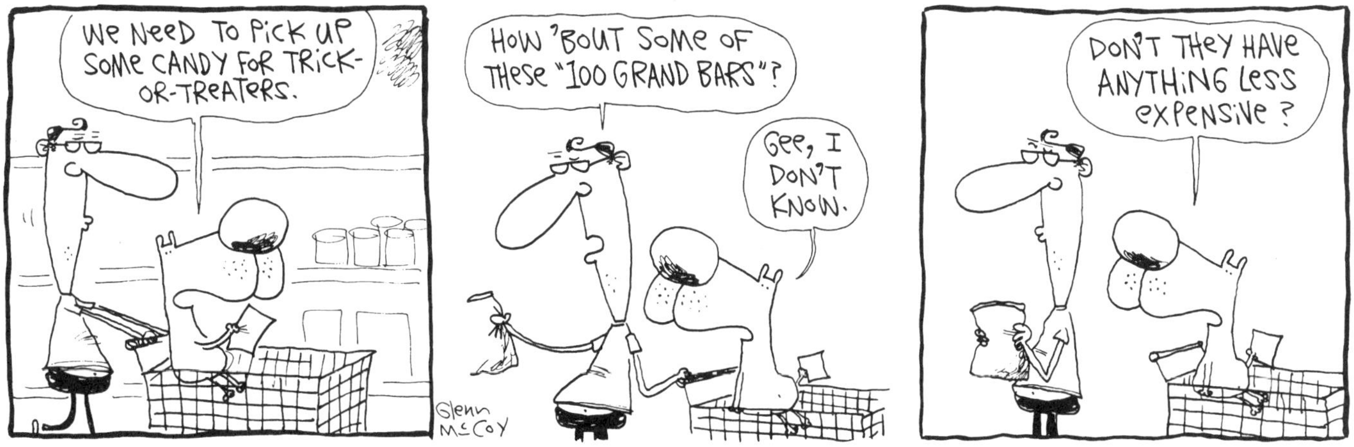
WE NEED TO PICK UP SOME CANDY FOR TRICK-OR-TREATERS.
Glenn McCoy
HOW 'BOUT SOME OF THESE "100 GRAND BARS"?
GEE, I DON'T KNOW.
DON'T THEY HAVE ANYTHING LESS EXPENSIVE?

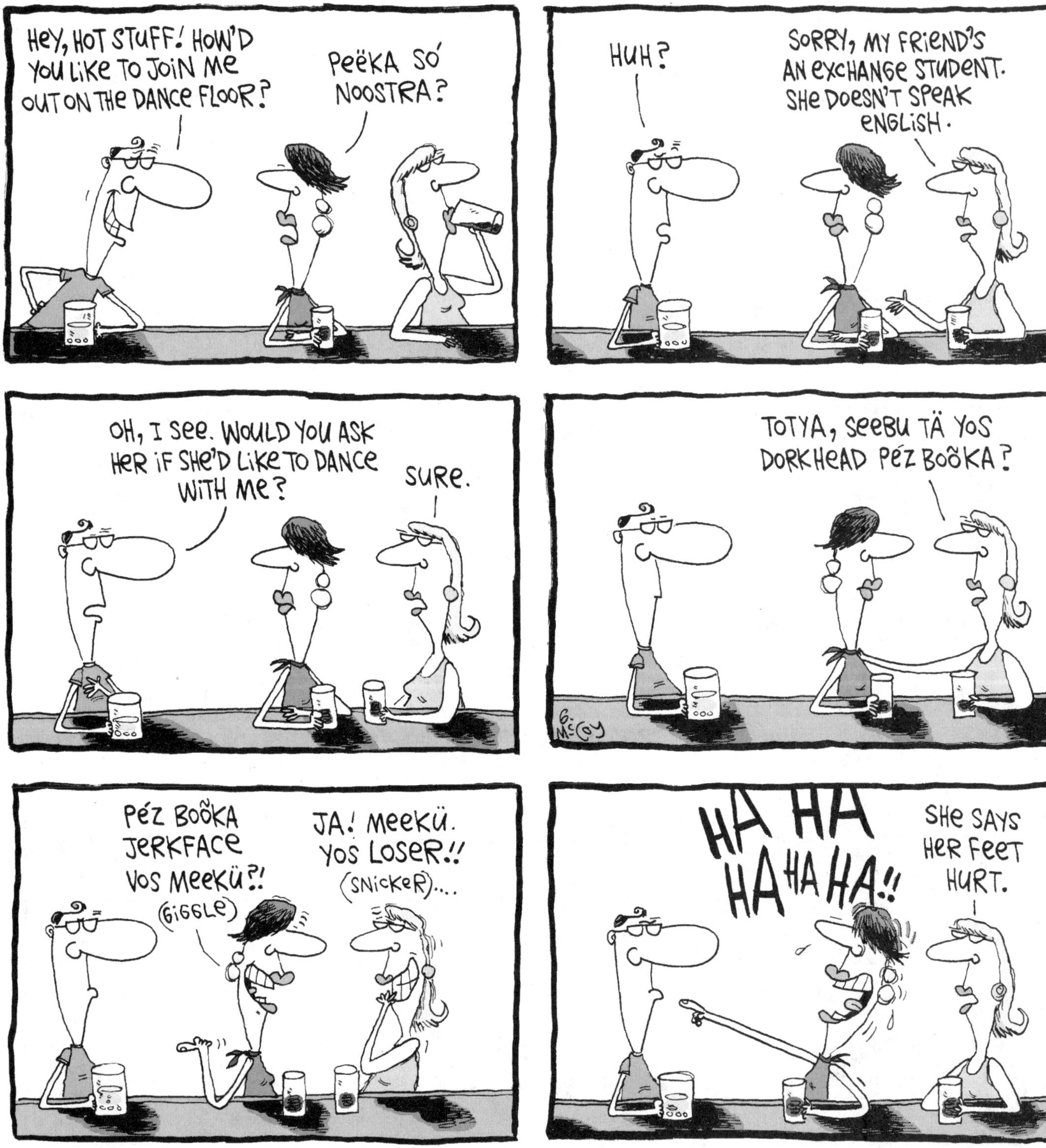
HEY, HOT STUFF! HOW'D YOU LIKE TO JOIN ME OUT ON THE DANCE FLOOR?
PEËKA SÓ NOOSTRA?
HUH?
SORRY, MY FRIEND'S AN EXCHANGE STUDENT. SHE DOESN'T SPEAK ENGLISH.
OH, I SEE. WOULD YOU ASK HER IF SHE'D LIKE TO DANCE WITH ME?
SURE.
TOTYA, SEEBU TÄ YOS DORKHEAD PÉZ BOÕKA?
PÉZ BOÕKA JERKFACE VOS MEEKÜ?!
(GIGGLE)
JA! MEEKÜ. YOS LOSER!!
(SNICKER)....
HA HA HA HA HA!!
SHE SAYS HER FEET HURT.

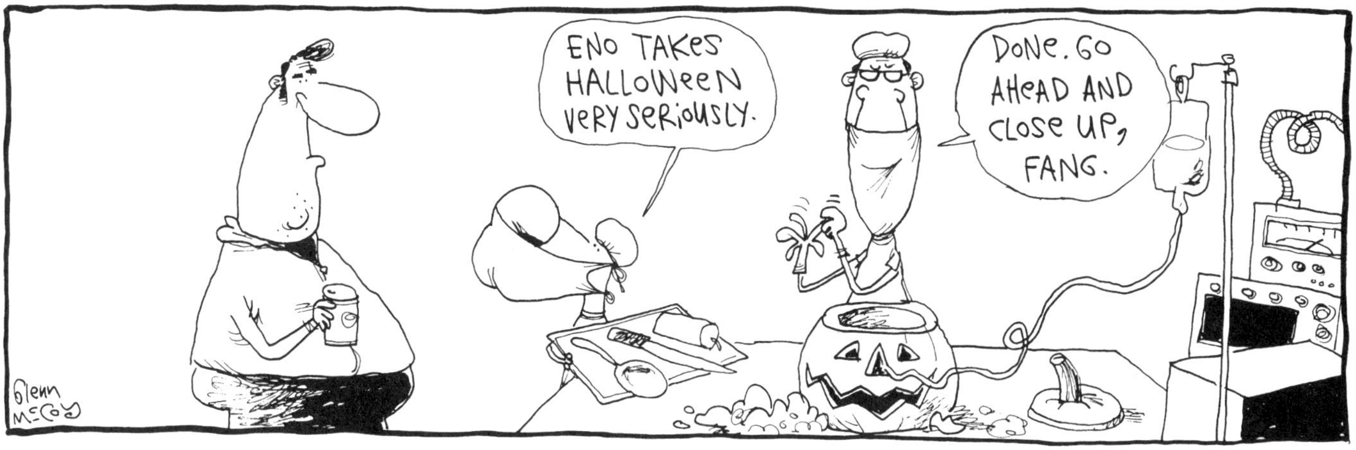
ENO TAKES HALLOWEEN VERY SERIOUSLY.
DONE. GO AHEAD AND CLOSE UP, FANG.
Glenn McCoy

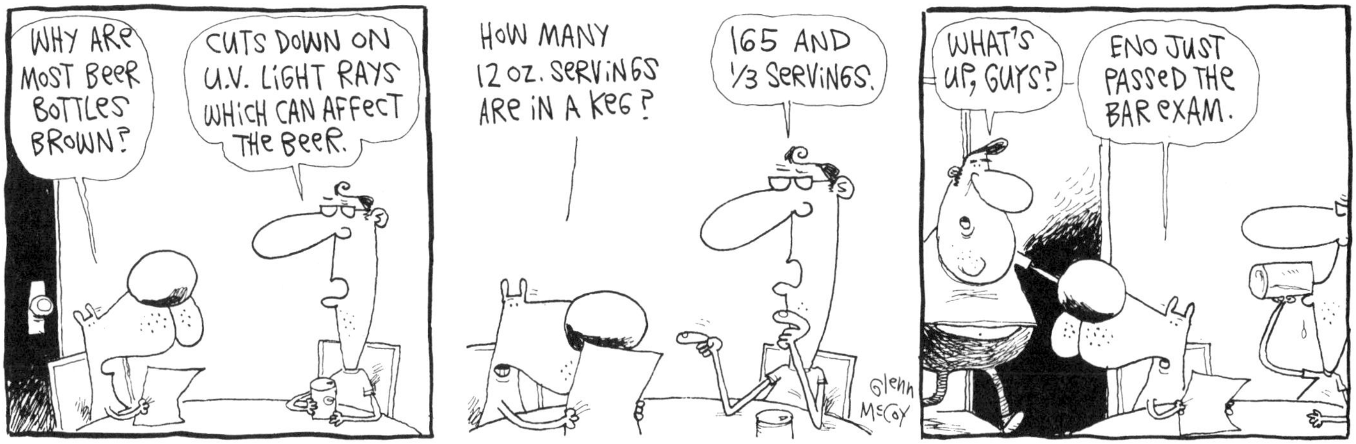
WHY ARE MOST BEER BOTTLES BROWN?
CUTS DOWN ON U.V. LIGHT RAYS WHICH CAN AFFECT THE BEER.
HOW MANY 12 OZ. SERVINGS ARE IN A KEG?
165 AND 1/3 SERVINGS.
Glenn McCoy
WHAT'S UP, GUYS?
ENO JUST PASSED THE BAR EXAM.

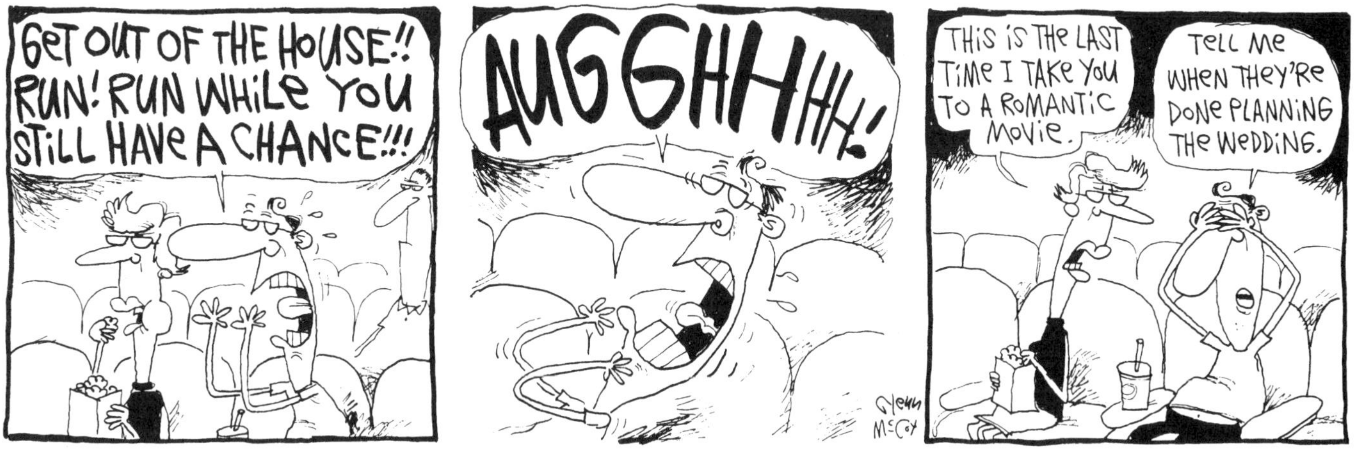
GET OUT OF THE HOUSE!! RUN! RUN WHILE YOU STILL HAVE A CHANCE!!!
AUGGHHHH!
Glenn McCoy
THIS IS THE LAST TIME I TAKE YOU TO A ROMANTIC MOVIE.
TELL ME WHEN THEY'RE DONE PLANNING THE WEDDING.

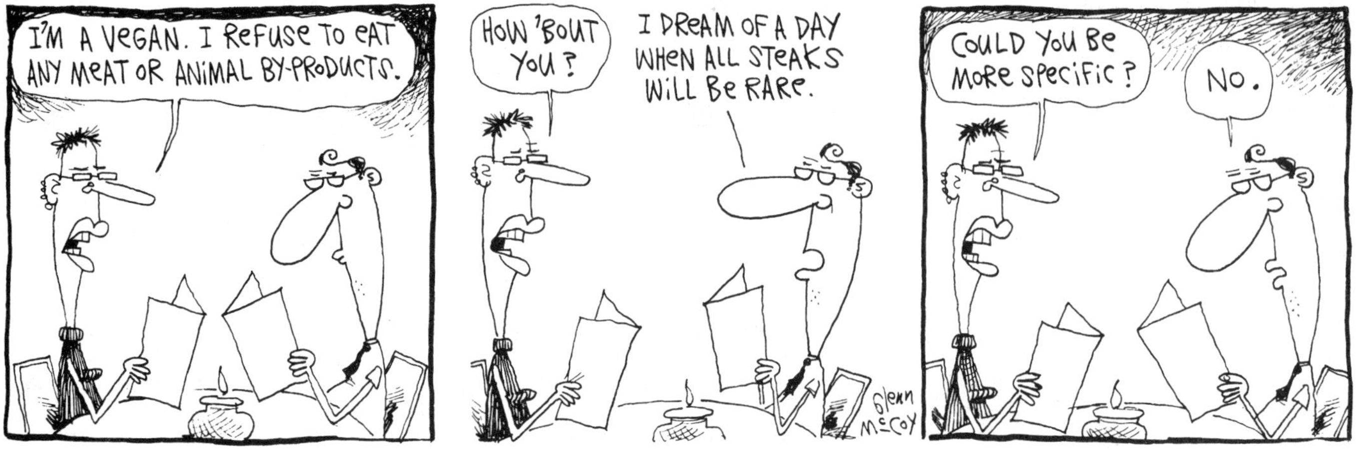
I'M A VEGAN. I REFUSE TO EAT ANY MEAT OR ANIMAL BY-PRODUCTS.
HOW 'BOUT YOU?
I DREAM OF A DAY WHEN ALL STEAKS WILL BE RARE.
Glenn McCoy
COULD YOU BE MORE SPECIFIC?
NO.

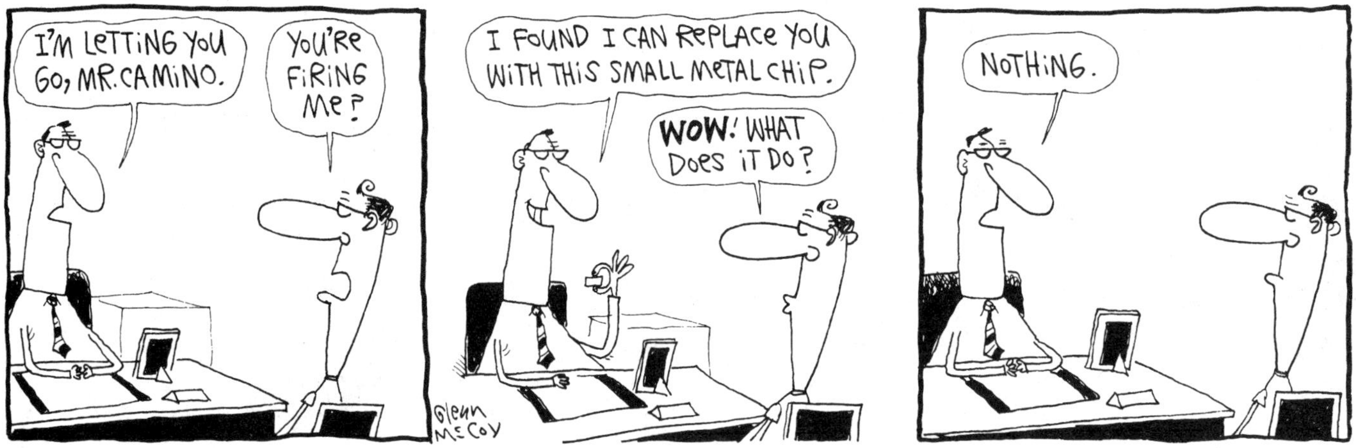
I'M LETTING YOU GO, MR. CAMINO.
YOU'RE FIRING ME?
Glenn McCoy
I FOUND I CAN REPLACE YOU WITH THIS SMALL METAL CHIP.
WOW! WHAT DOES IT DO?
NOTHING.

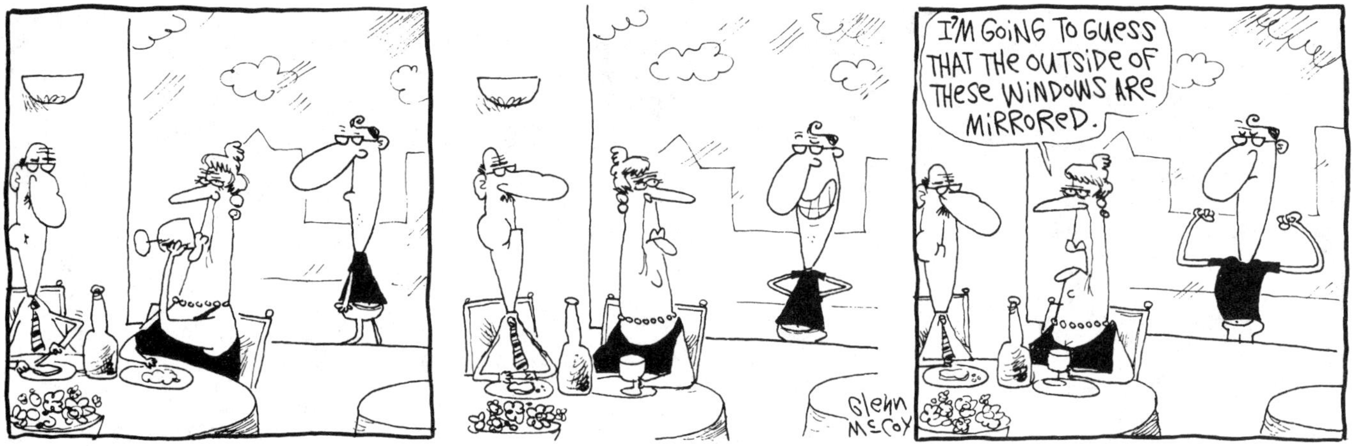
Glenn McCoy
I'M GOING TO GUESS THAT THE OUTSIDE OF THESE WINDOWS ARE MIRRORED.

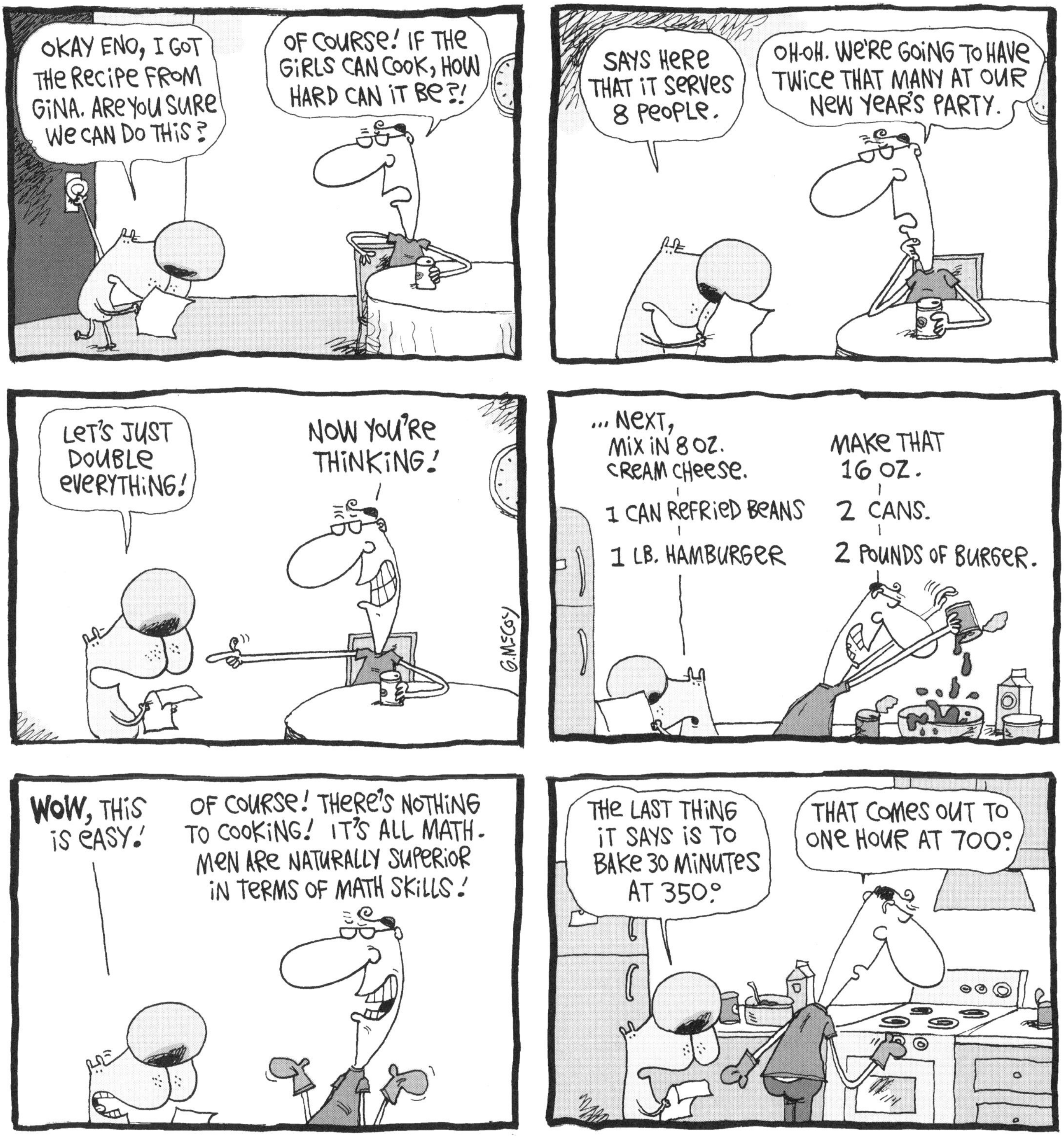
OKAY ENO, I GOT THE RECIPE FROM GINA. ARE YOU SURE WE CAN DO THIS?
OF COURSE! IF THE GIRLS CAN COOK, HOW HARD CAN IT BE?!
SAYS HERE THAT IT SERVES 8 PEOPLE.
OH-OH. WE'RE GOING TO HAVE TWICE THAT MANY AT OUR NEW YEAR'S PARTY.
LET'S JUST DOUBLE EVERYTHING!
NOW YOU'RE THINKING!
G. McCOY
... NEXT, MIX IN 8 OZ. CREAM CHEESE.
MAKE THAT 16 OZ.
1 CAN REFRIED BEANS
2 CANS.
1 LB. HAMBURGER
2 POUNDS OF BURGER.
WOW, THIS IS EASY!
OF COURSE! THERE'S NOTHING TO COOKING! IT'S ALL MATH. MEN ARE NATURALLY SUPERIOR IN TERMS OF MATH SKILLS!
THE LAST THING IT SAYS IS TO BAKE 30 MINUTES AT 350°
THAT COMES OUT TO ONE HOUR AT 700°

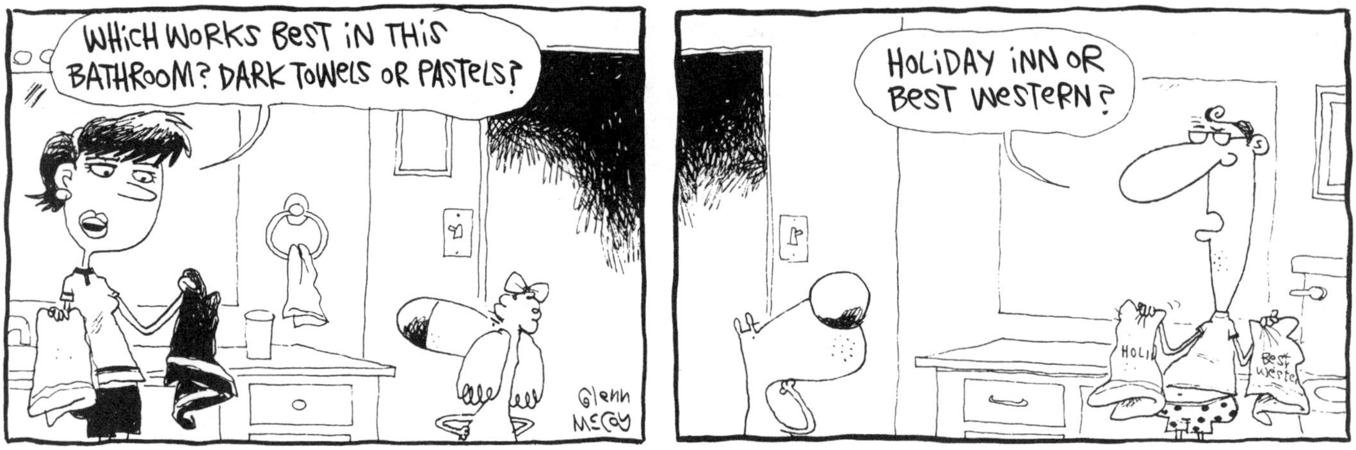
WHICH WORKS BEST IN THIS BATHROOM? DARK TOWELS OR PASTELS?
HOLIDAY INN OR BEST WESTERN?
Glenn McCoy

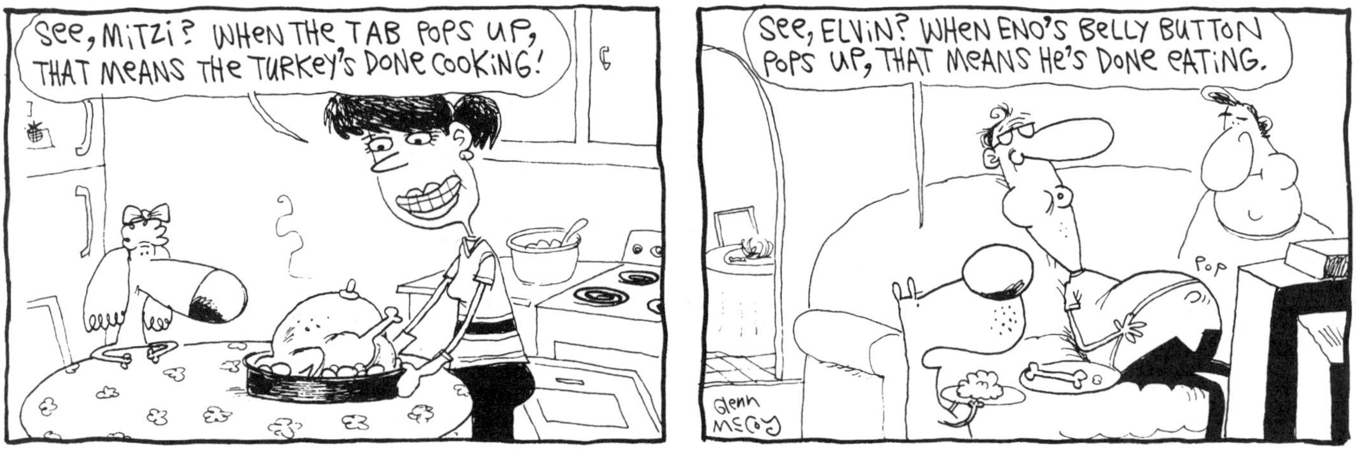
SEE, MITZI? WHEN THE TAB POPS UP, THAT MEANS THE TURKEY'S DONE COOKING!
SEE, ELVIN? WHEN ENO'S BELLY BUTTON POPS UP, THAT MEANS HE'S DONE EATING.
POP
Glenn McCoy

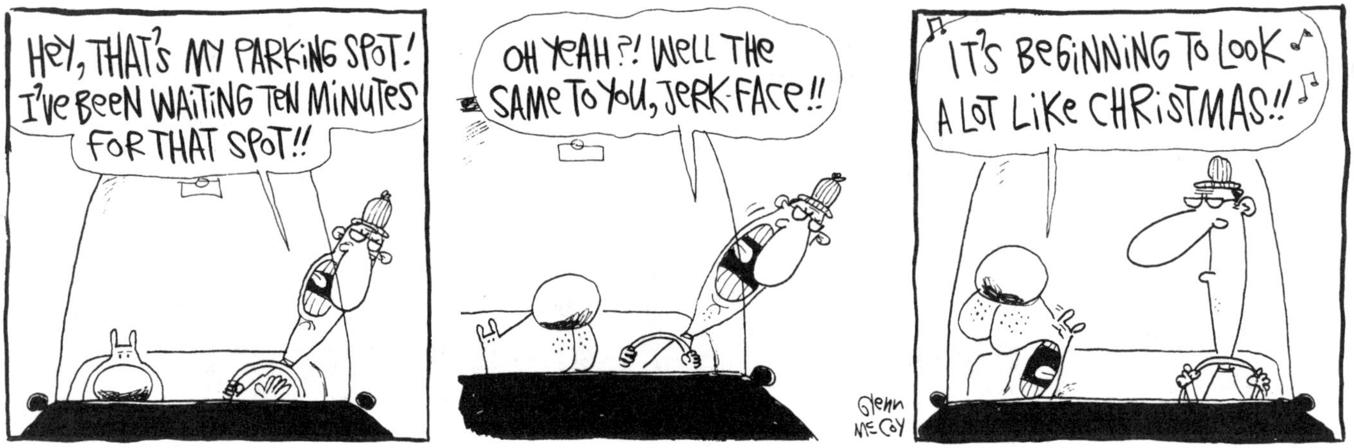
HEY, THAT'S MY PARKING SPOT! I'VE BEEN WAITING TEN MINUTES FOR THAT SPOT!!
OH YEAH?! WELL THE SAME TO YOU, JERK-FACE!!
IT'S BEGINNING TO LOOK A LOT LIKE CHRISTMAS!!
Glenn McCoy

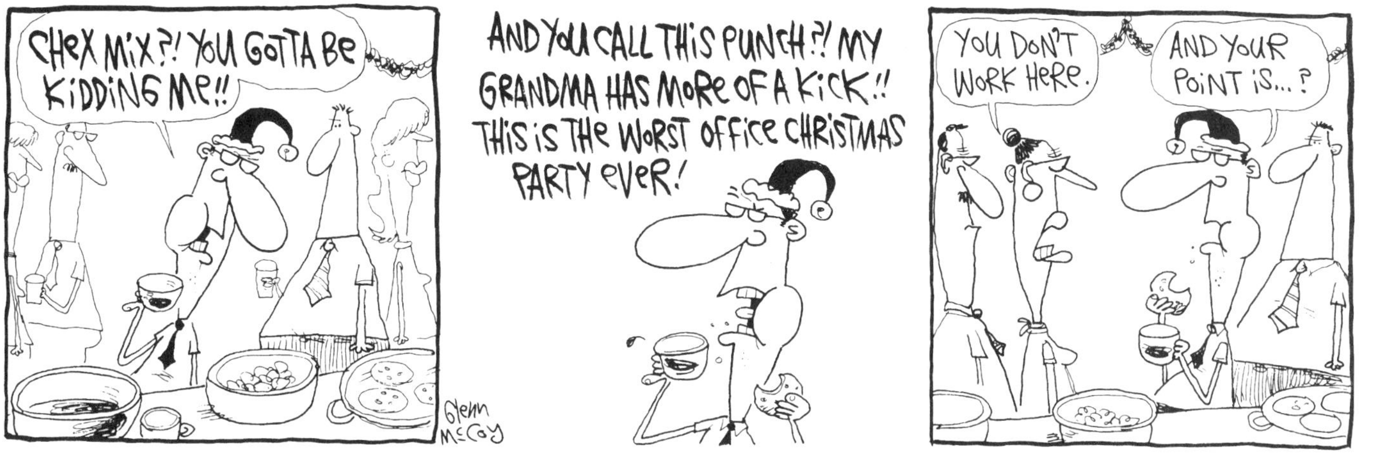
CHEX MIX?! YOU GOTTA BE KIDDING ME!!
AND YOU CALL THIS PUNCH?! MY GRANDMA HAS MORE OF A KICK!! THIS IS THE WORST OFFICE CHRISTMAS PARTY EVER!
YOU DON'T WORK HERE.
AND YOUR POINT IS...?
Glenn McCoy

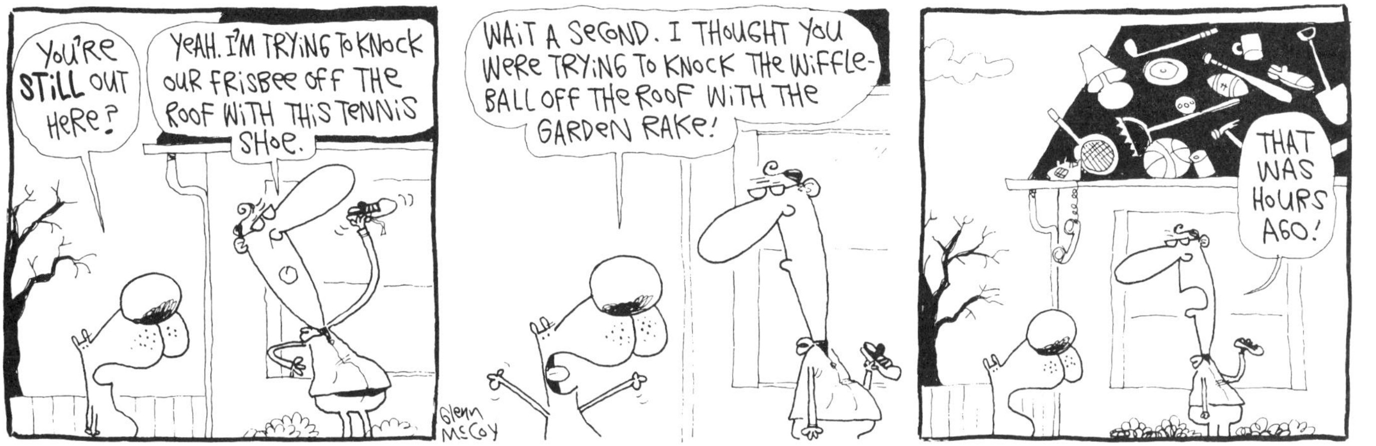
YOU'RE STILL OUT HERE?
YEAH. I'M TRYING TO KNOCK OUR FRISBEE OFF THE ROOF WITH THIS TENNIS SHOE.
WAIT A SECOND. I THOUGHT YOU WERE TRYING TO KNOCK THE WIFFLE-BALL OFF THE ROOF WITH THE GARDEN RAKE!
THAT WAS HOURS AGO!
Glenn McCoy

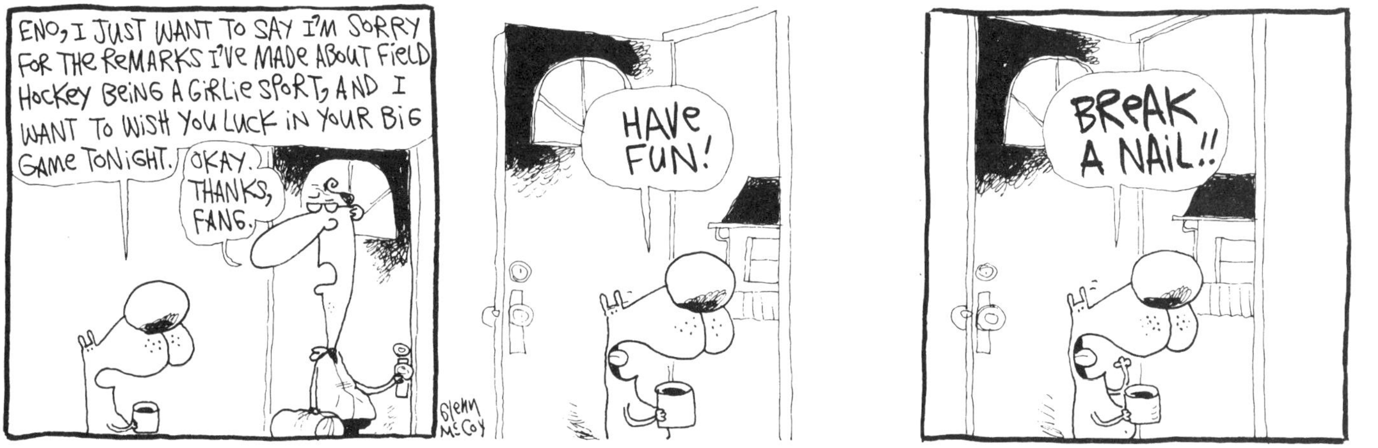
ENO, I JUST WANT TO SAY I'M SORRY FOR THE REMARKS I'VE MADE ABOUT FIELD HOCKEY BEING A GIRLIE SPORT, AND I WANT TO WISH YOU LUCK IN YOUR BIG GAME TONIGHT.
OKAY. THANKS, FANG.
HAVE FUN!
BREAK A NAIL!!
Glenn McCoy

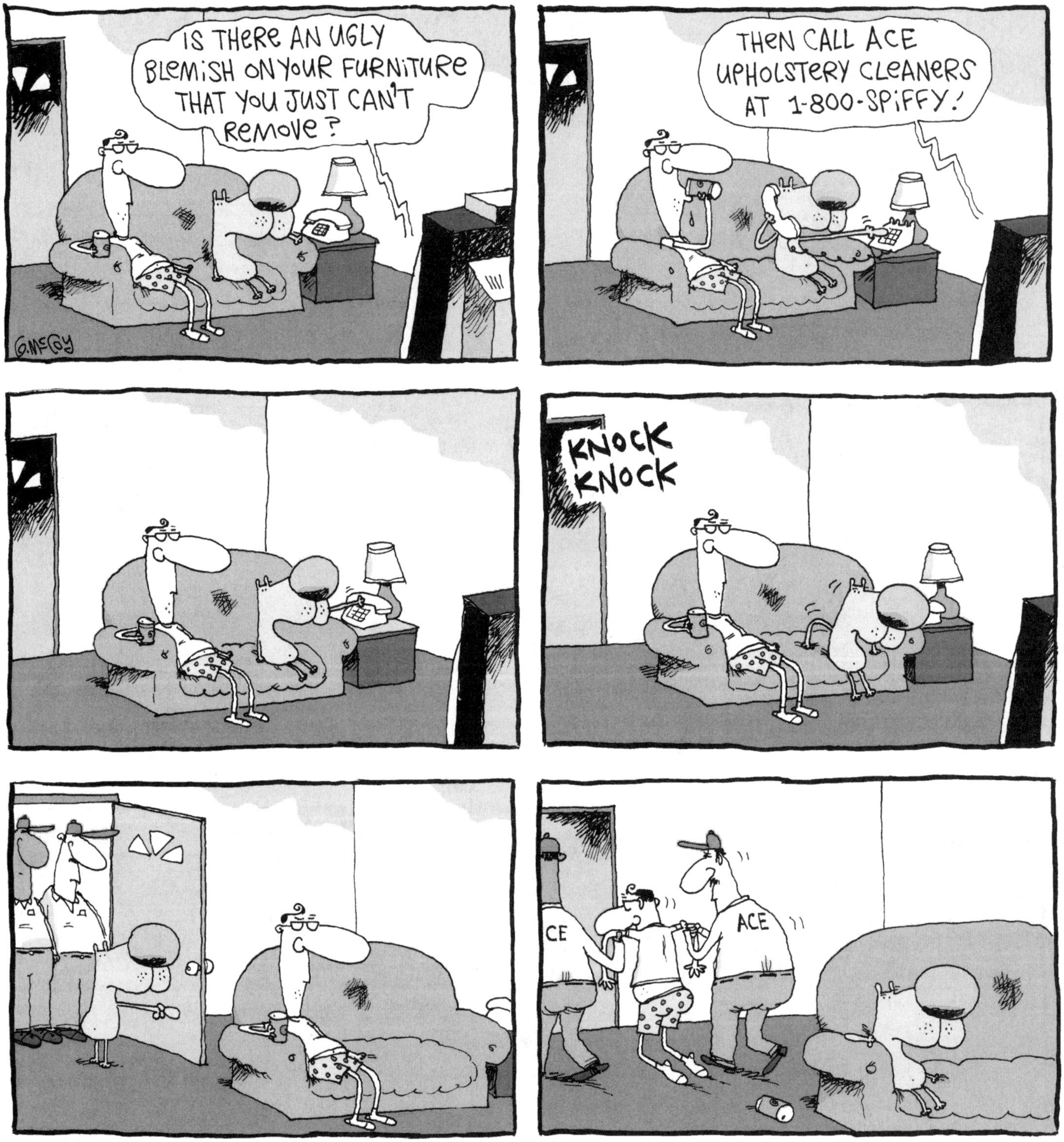
IS THERE AN UGLY BLEMISH ON YOUR FURNITURE THAT YOU JUST CAN'T REMOVE?
G. McCoy
THEN CALL ACE UPHOLSTERY CLEANERS AT 1-800-SPIFFY!
KNOCK KNOCK
CE
ACE

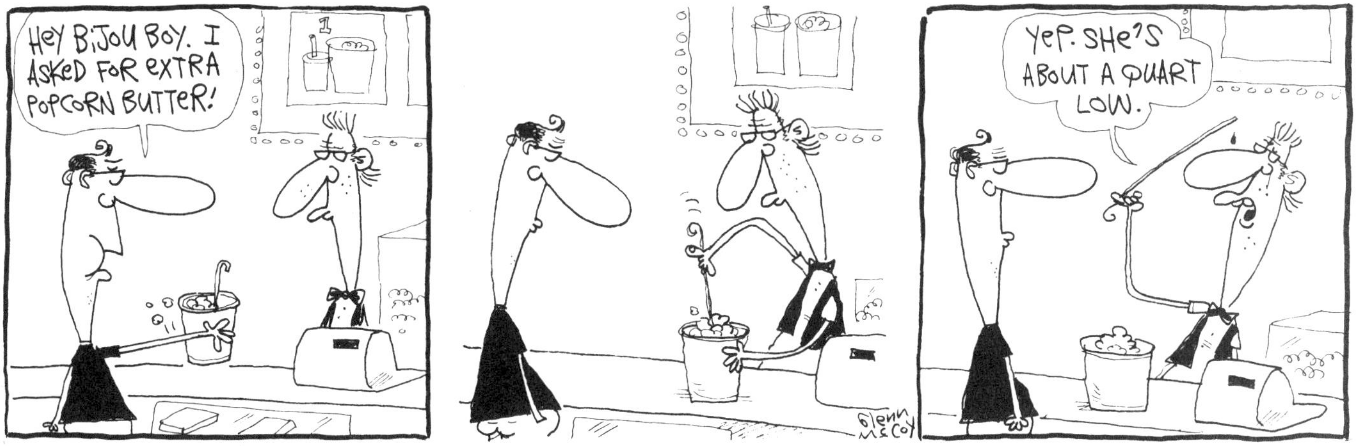
HEY BIJOU BOY. I ASKED FOR EXTRA POPCORN BUTTER!
YEP. SHE'S ABOUT A QUART LOW.
Glenn McCoy

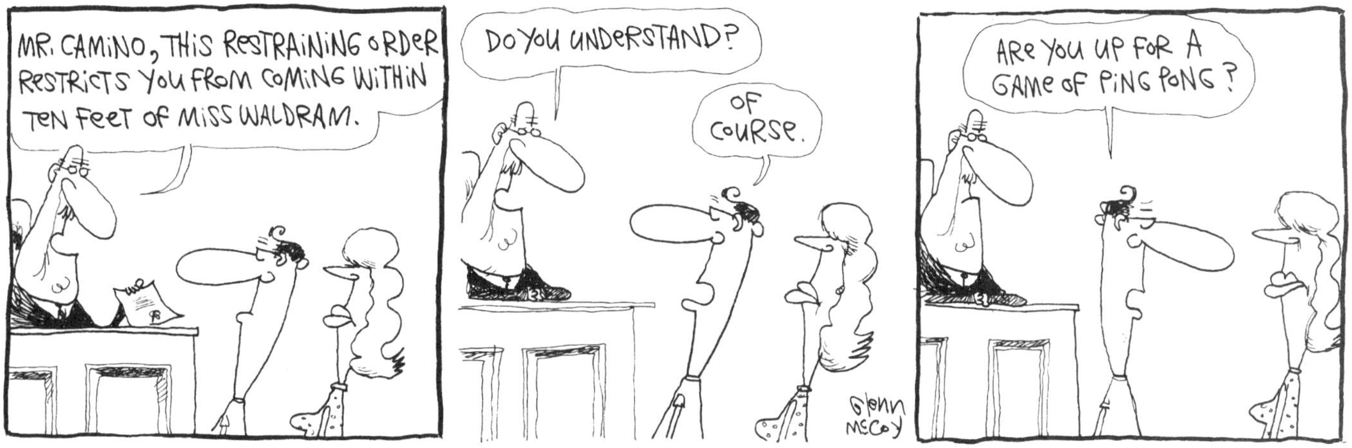
MR. CAMINO, THIS RESTRAINING ORDER RESTRICTS YOU FROM COMING WITHIN TEN FEET OF MISS WALDRAM.
DO YOU UNDERSTAND?
OF COURSE.
ARE YOU UP FOR A GAME OF PING PONG?
Glenn McCoy

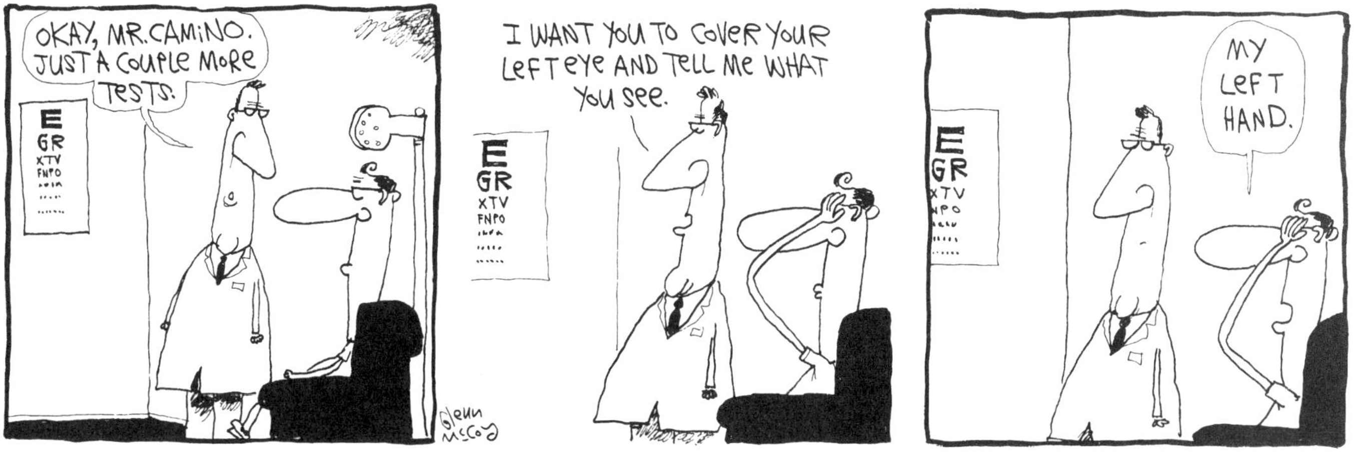
OKAY, MR. CAMINO. JUST A COUPLE MORE TESTS.
I WANT YOU TO COVER YOUR LEFT EYE AND TELL ME WHAT YOU SEE.
MY LEFT HAND.
Glenn McCoy

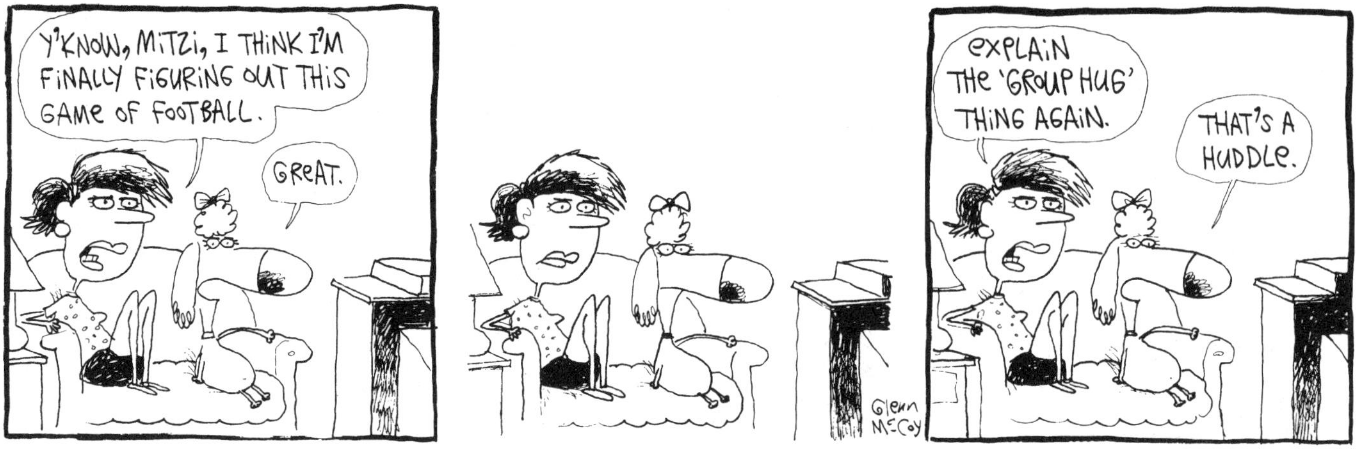
Y'KNOW, MITZI, I THINK I'M FINALLY FIGURING OUT THIS GAME OF FOOTBALL.
GREAT.
EXPLAIN THE 'GROUP HUG' THING AGAIN.
THAT'S A HUDDLE.
Glenn McCoy

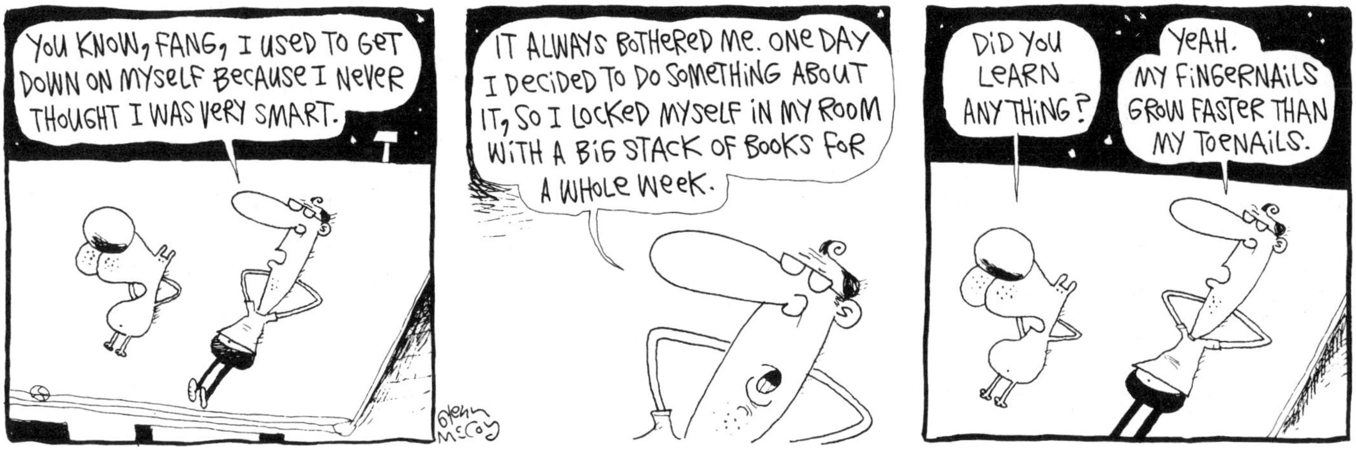
YOU KNOW, FANG, I USED TO GET DOWN ON MYSELF BECAUSE I NEVER THOUGHT I WAS VERY SMART.
IT ALWAYS BOTHERED ME. ONE DAY I DECIDED TO DO SOMETHING ABOUT IT, SO I LOCKED MYSELF IN MY ROOM WITH A BIG STACK OF BOOKS FOR A WHOLE WEEK.
DID YOU LEARN ANYTHING?
YEAH. MY FINGERNAILS GROW FASTER THAN MY TOENAILS.
Glenn McCoy

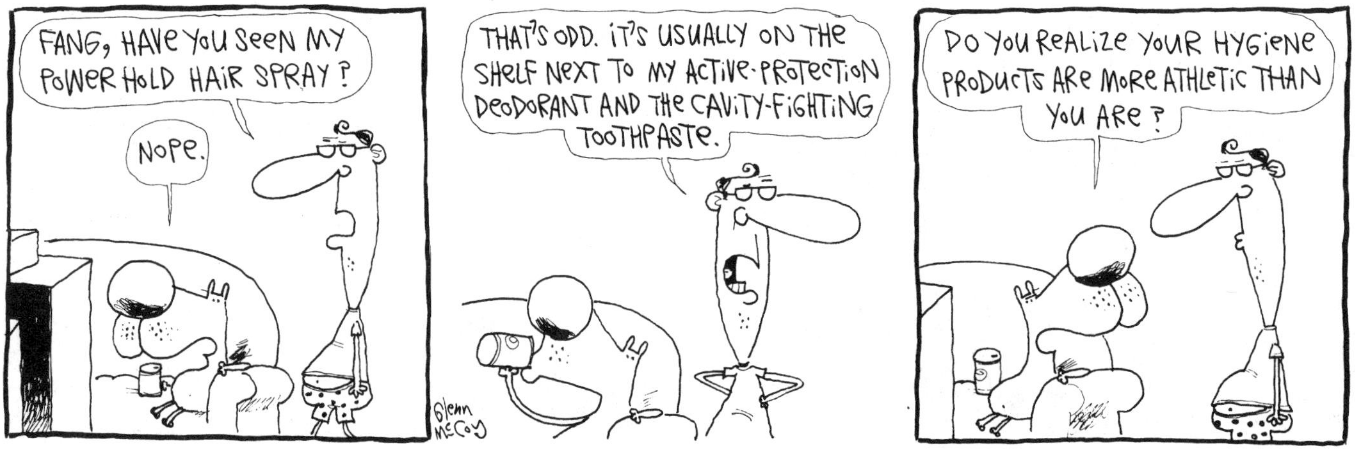
FANG, HAVE YOU SEEN MY POWER HOLD HAIR SPRAY?
NOPE.
THAT'S ODD. IT'S USUALLY ON THE SHELF NEXT TO MY ACTIVE-PROTECTION DEODORANT AND THE CAVITY-FIGHTING TOOTHPASTE.
DO YOU REALIZE YOUR HYGIENE PRODUCTS ARE MORE ATHLETIC THAN YOU ARE?
Glenn McCoy

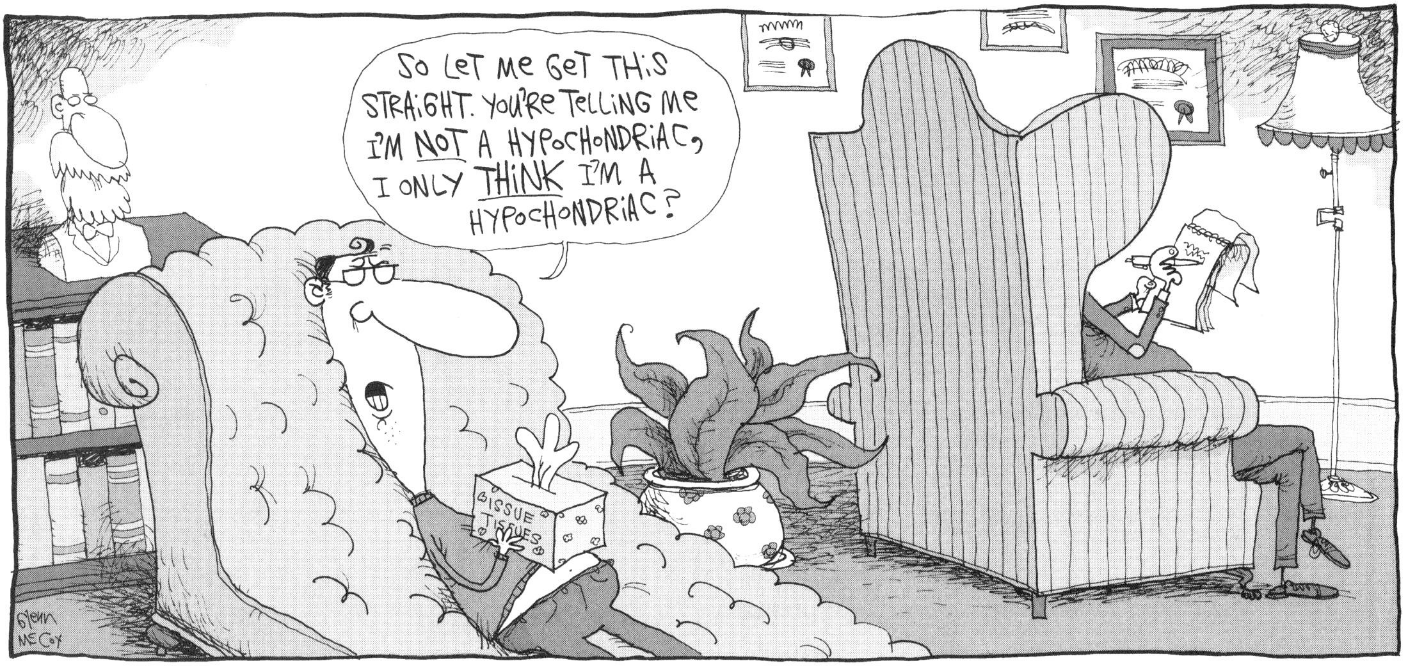
SO LET ME GET THIS STRAIGHT. YOU'RE TELLING ME I'M NOT A HYPOCHONDRIAC, I ONLY THINK I'M A HYPOCHONDRIAC?
TISSUE TISSUES
Glenn McCoy

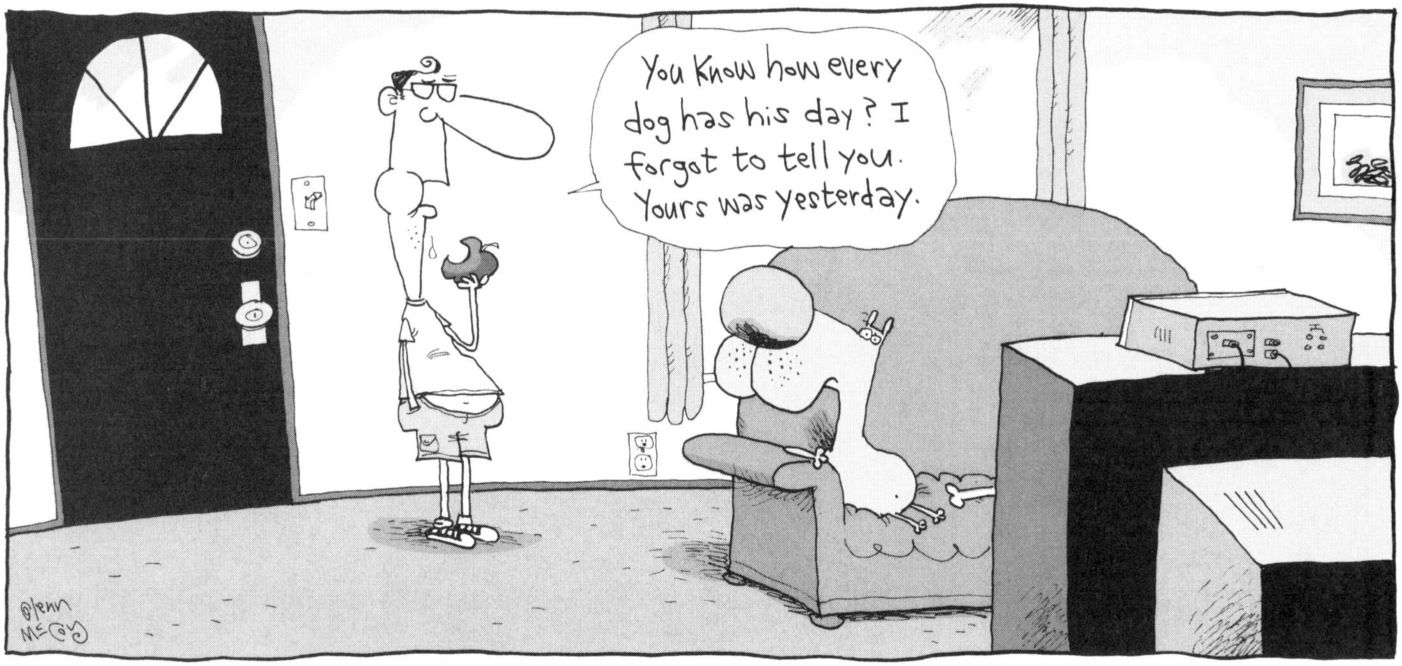
You know how every dog has his day? I forgot to tell you. Yours was yesterday.
Glenn McCoy

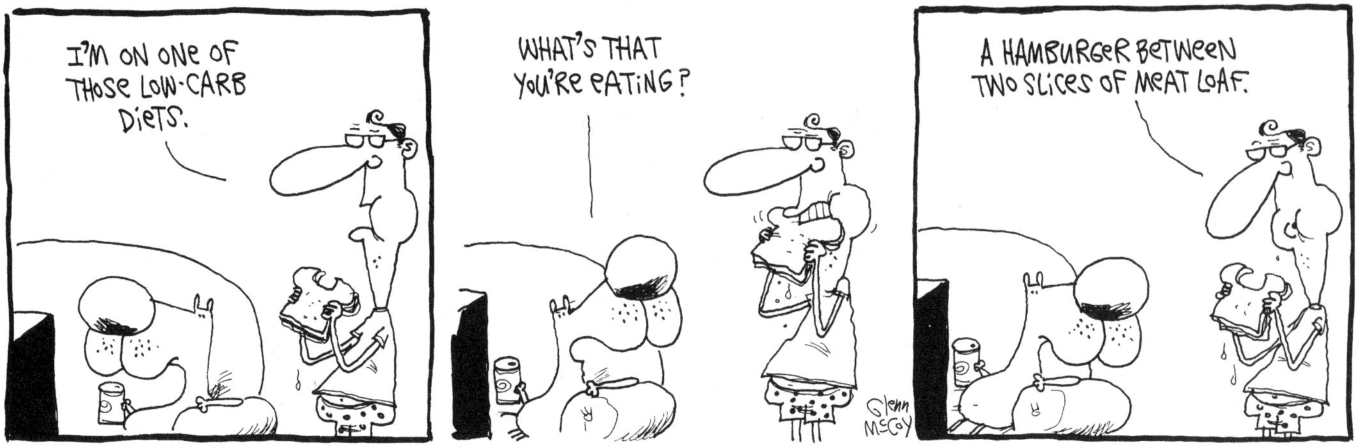
I'M ON ONE OF THOSE LOW-CARB DIETS.
WHAT'S THAT YOU'RE EATING?
A HAMBURGER BETWEEN TWO SLICES OF MEAT LOAF.
Glenn McCoy

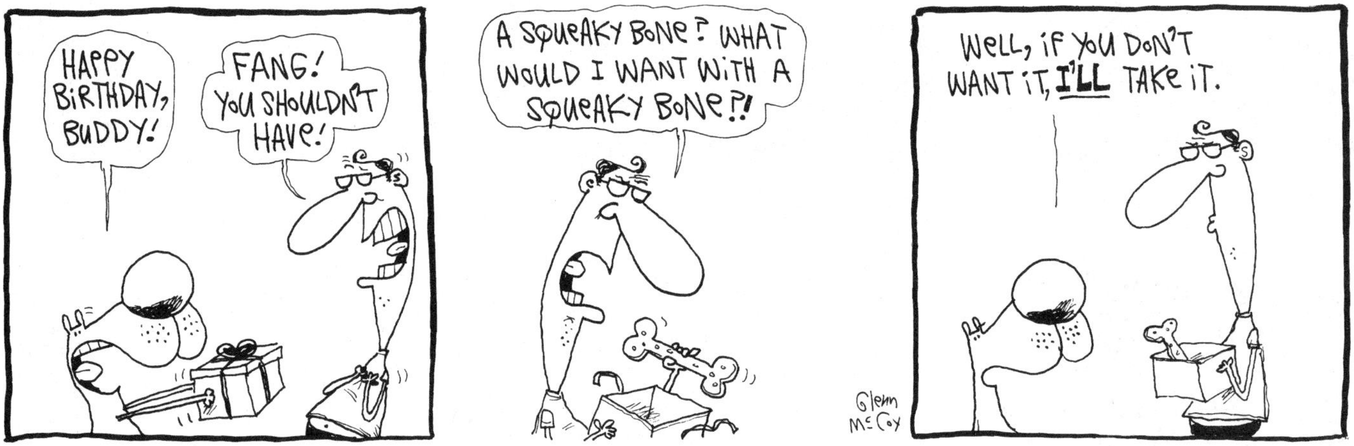
HAPPY BIRTHDAY, BUDDY!
FANG! YOU SHOULDN'T HAVE!
A SQUEAKY BONE?! WHAT WOULD I WANT WITH A SQUEAKY BONE?!
WELL, IF YOU DON'T WANT IT, I'LL TAKE IT.
Glenn McCoy

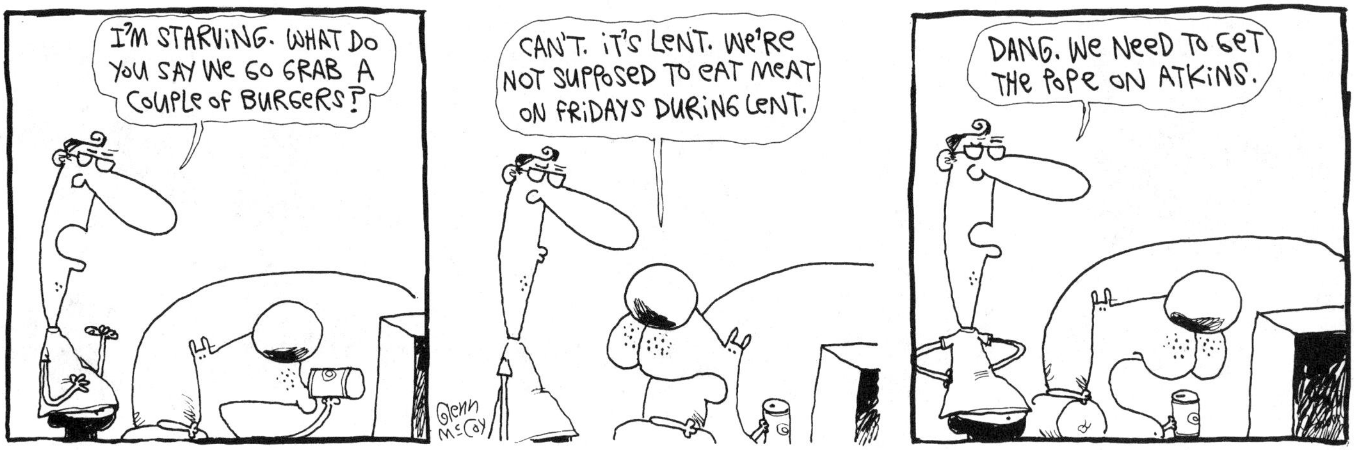
I'M STARVING. WHAT DO YOU SAY WE GO GRAB A COUPLE OF BURGERS?
CAN'T. IT'S LENT. WE'RE NOT SUPPOSED TO EAT MEAT ON FRIDAYS DURING LENT.
DANG. WE NEED TO GET THE POPE ON ATKINS.
Glenn McCoy

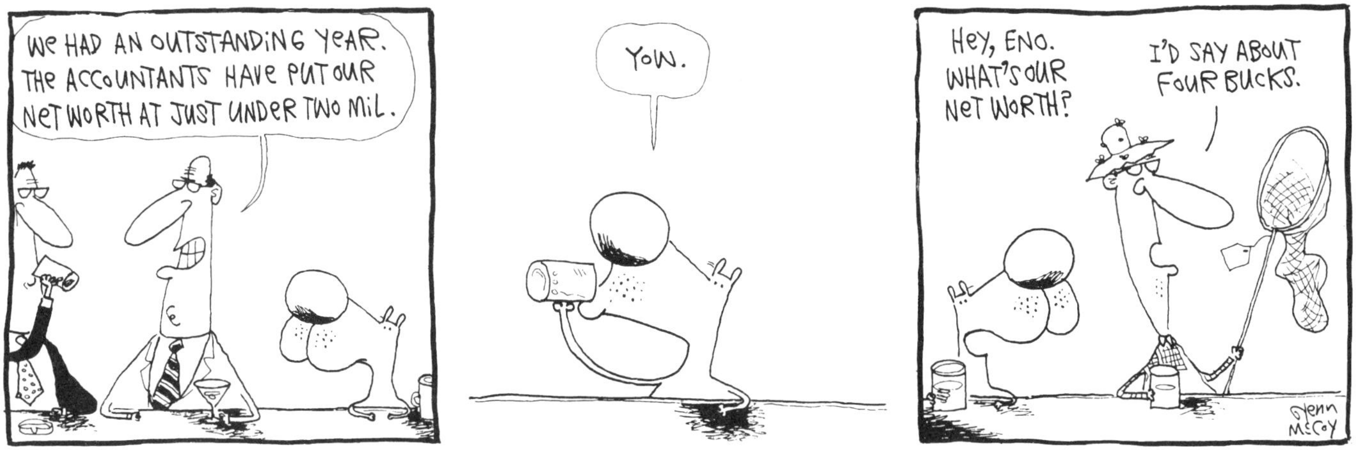
WE HAD AN OUTSTANDING YEAR. THE ACCOUNTANTS HAVE PUT OUR NET WORTH AT JUST UNDER TWO MIL.
YOW.
HEY, ENO. WHAT'S OUR NET WORTH?
I'D SAY ABOUT FOUR BUCKS.
Glenn McCoy

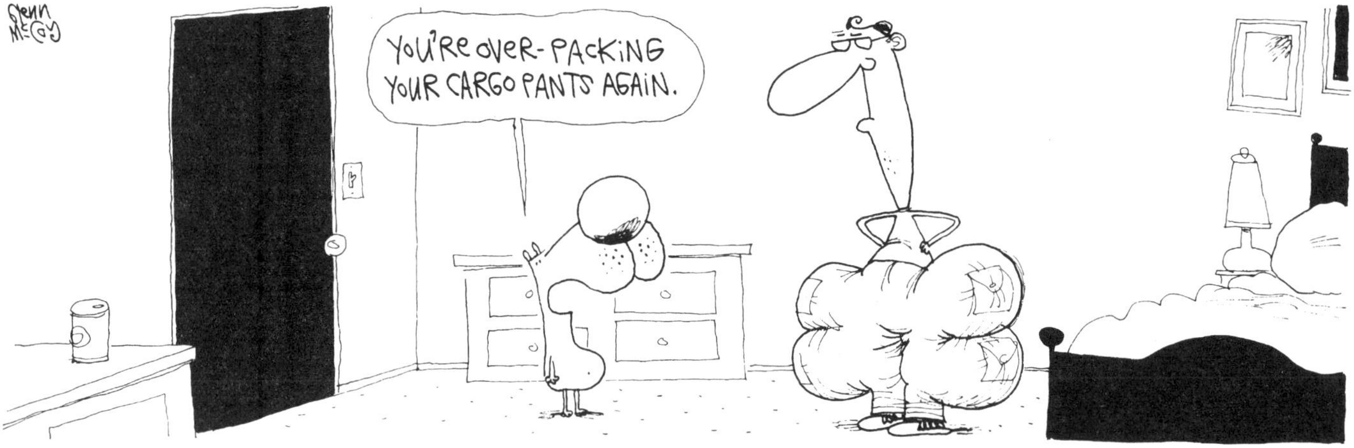
Glenn McCoy
YOU'RE OVER-PACKING YOUR CARGO PANTS AGAIN.

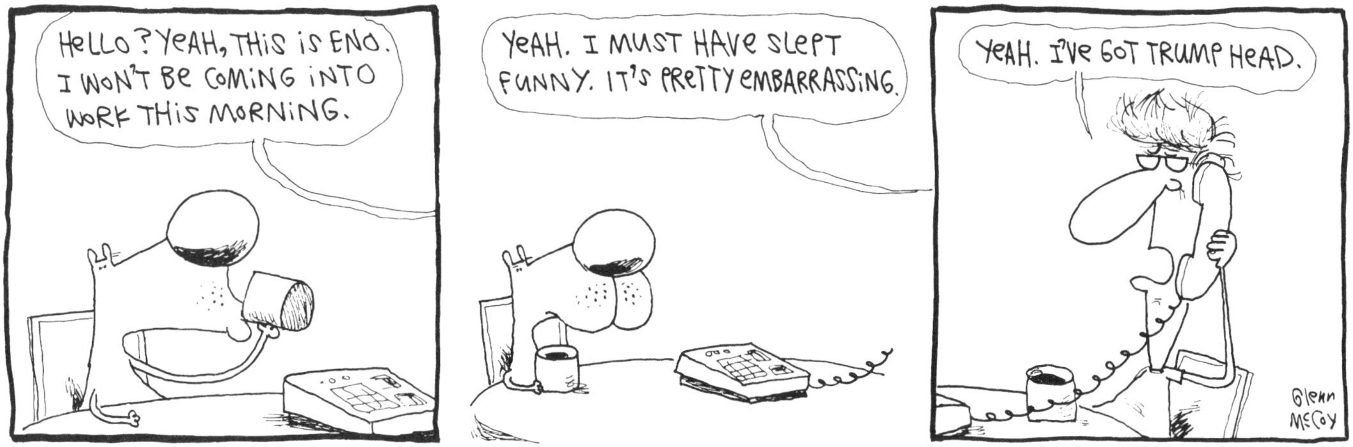
HELLO? YEAH, THIS IS ENO. I WON'T BE COMING INTO WORK THIS MORNING.
YEAH. I MUST HAVE SLEPT FUNNY. IT'S PRETTY EMBARRASSING.
YEAH. I'VE GOT TRUMP HEAD.
Glenn McCoy

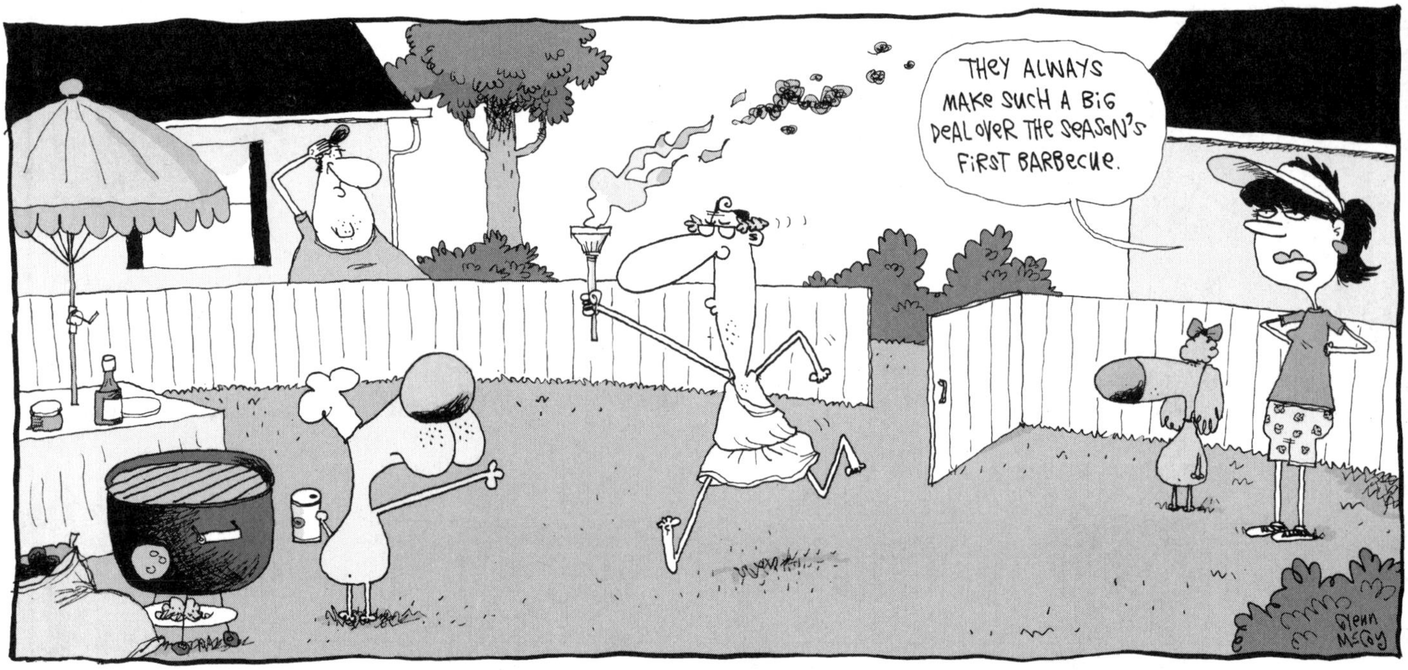
THEY ALWAYS MAKE SUCH A BIG DEAL OVER THE SEASON'S FIRST BARBECUE.
Glenn McCoy

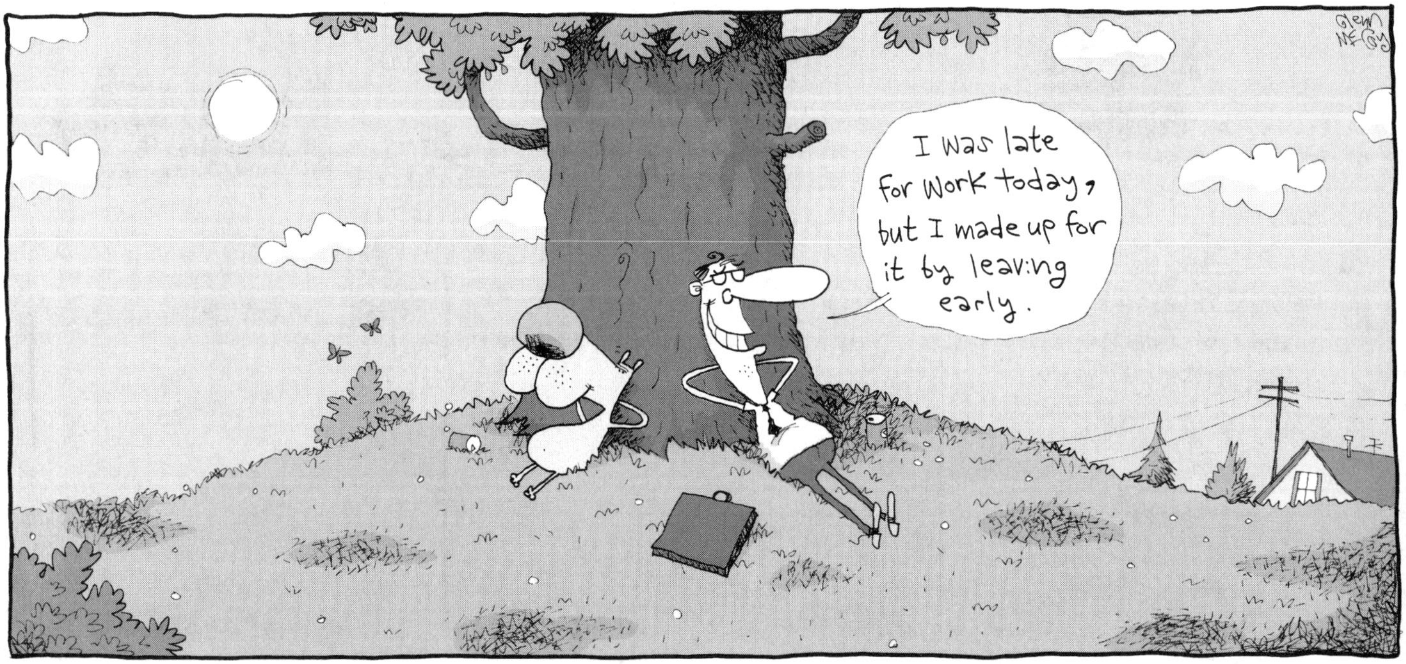
I was late for work today, but I made up for it by leaving early.
Glenn McCoy

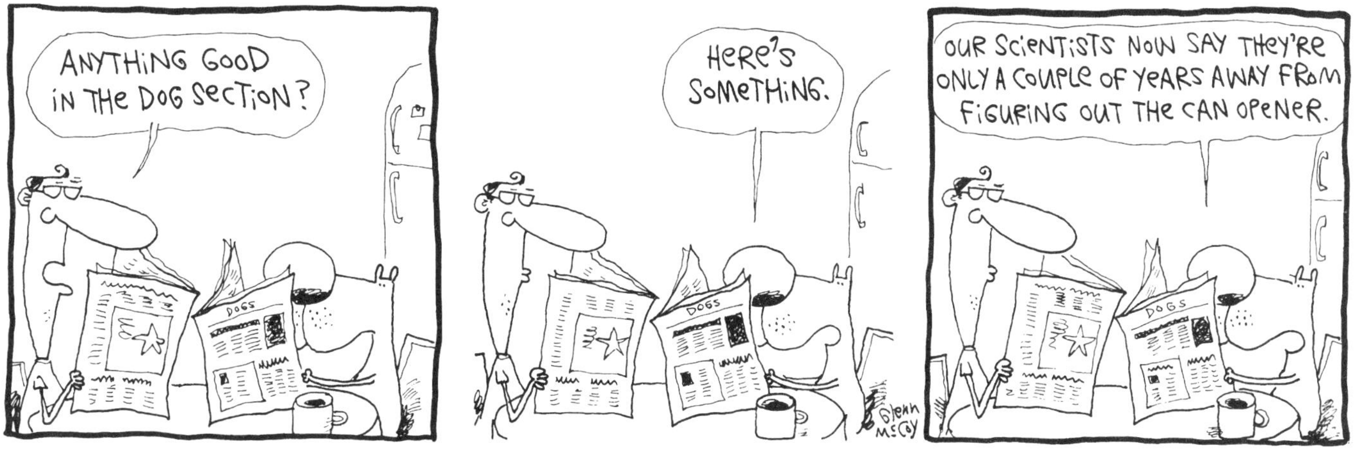
ANYTHING GOOD IN THE DOG SECTION?
DOGS
HERE'S SOMETHING.
Glenn McCoy
OUR SCIENTISTS NOW SAY THEY'RE ONLY A COUPLE OF YEARS AWAY FROM FIGURING OUT THE CAN OPENER.

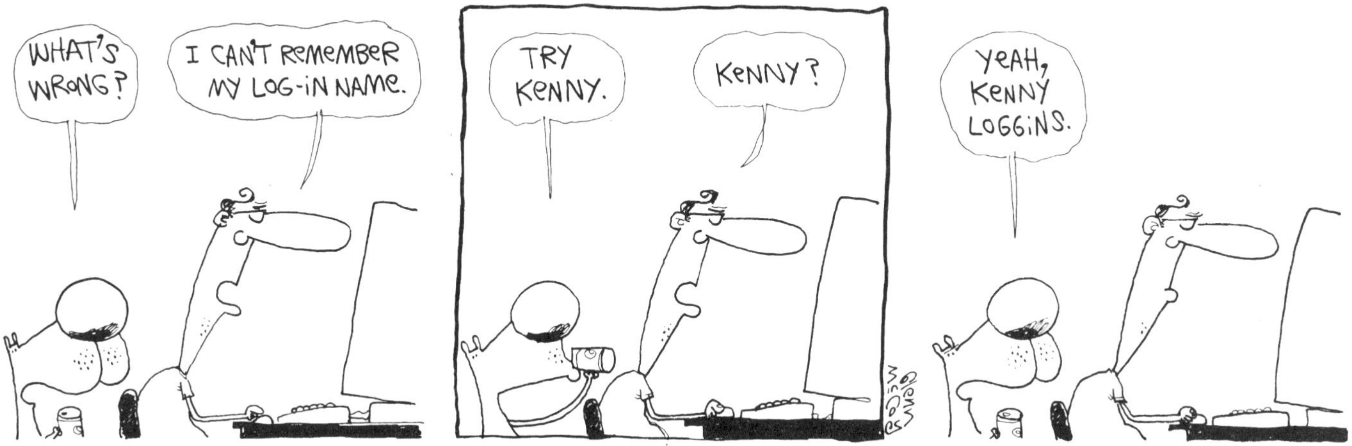
WHAT'S WRONG?
I CAN'T REMEMBER MY LOG-IN NAME.
TRY KENNY.
KENNY?
YEAH, KENNY LOGGINS.

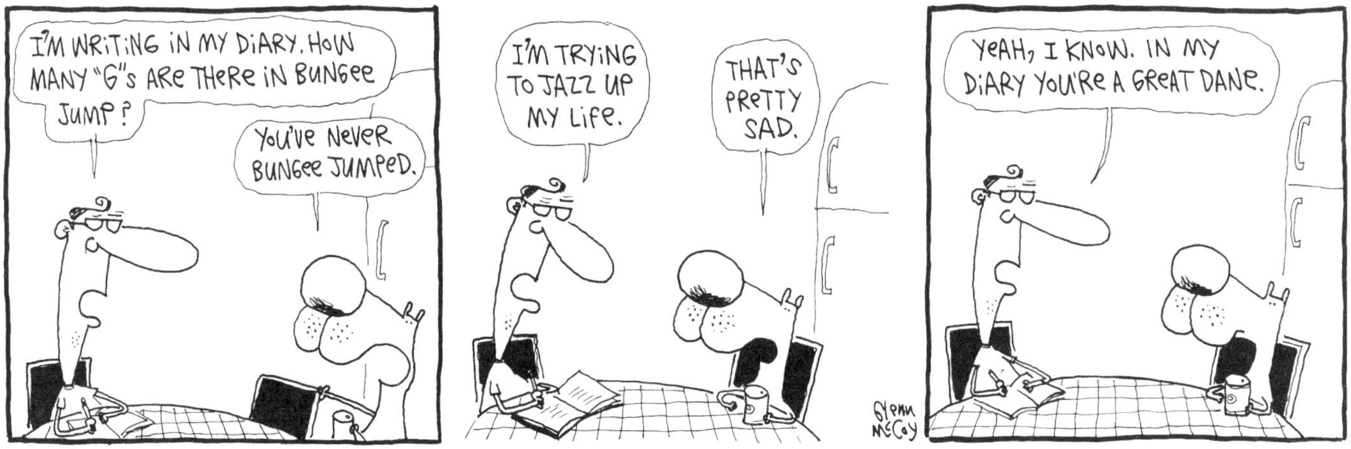
I'M WRITING IN MY DIARY. HOW MANY "G"S ARE THERE IN BUNGEE JUMP?
YOU'VE NEVER BUNGEE JUMPED.
I'M TRYING TO JAZZ UP MY LIFE.
THAT'S PRETTY SAD.
Glenn McCoy
YEAH, I KNOW. IN MY DIARY YOU'RE A GREAT DANE.

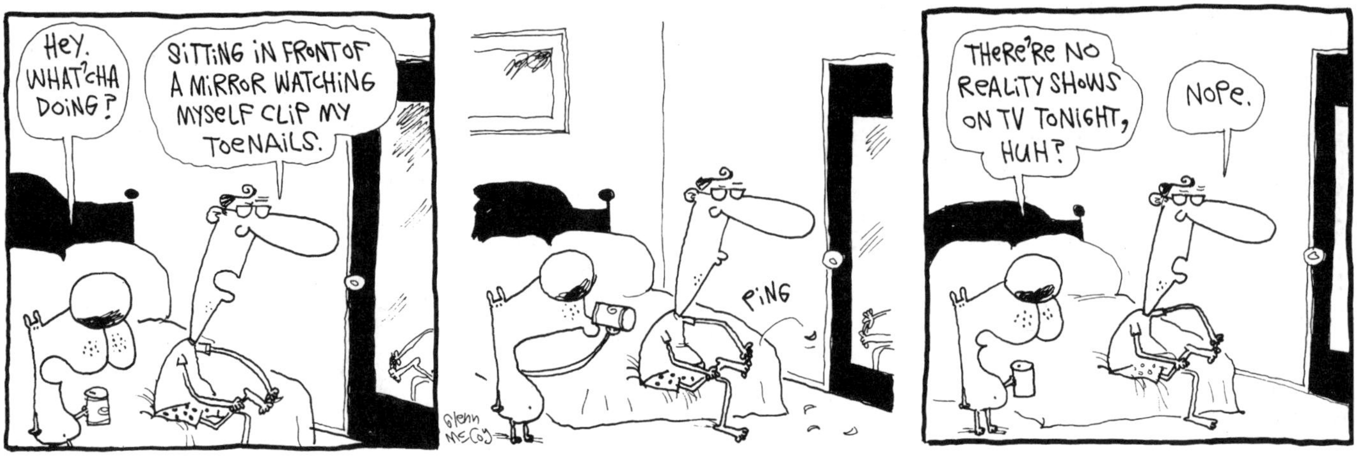
HEY. WHAT'CHA DOING?
SITTING IN FRONT OF A MIRROR WATCHING MYSELF CLIP MY TOENAILS.
PING
Glenn McCoy
THERE'RE NO REALITY SHOWS ON TV TONIGHT, HUH?
NOPE.

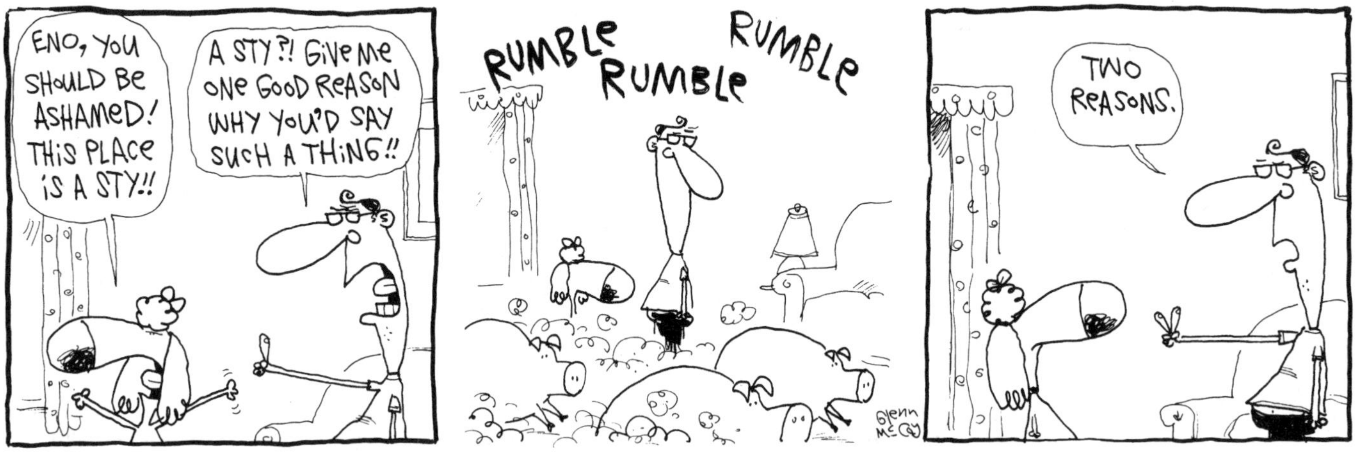
ENO, YOU SHOULD BE ASHAMED! THIS PLACE IS A STY!!
A STY?! GIVE ME ONE GOOD REASON WHY YOU'D SAY SUCH A THING!!
RUMBLE RUMBLE RUMBLE
Glenn McCoy
TWO REASONS.

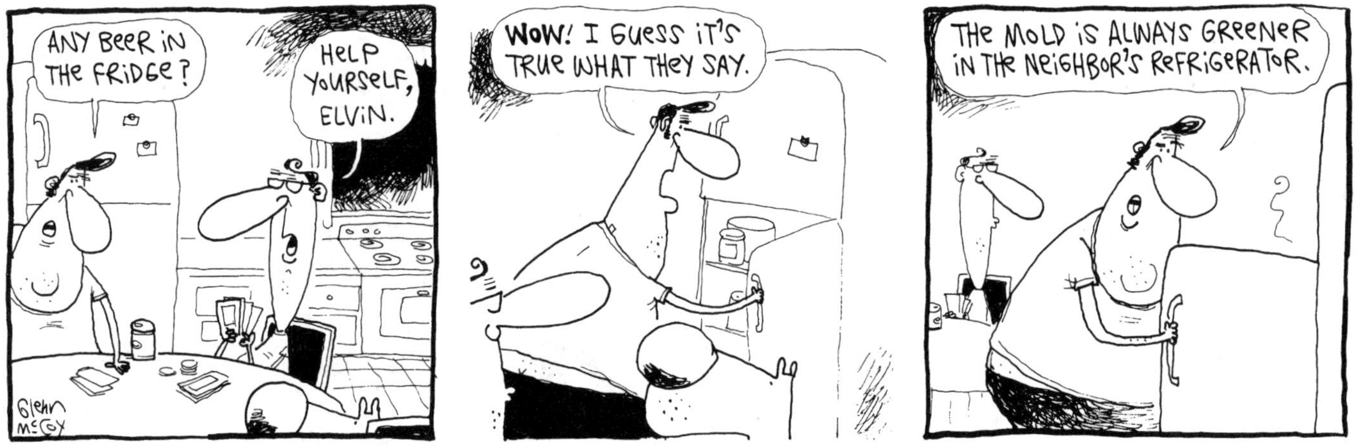
ANY BEER IN THE FRIDGE?
HELP YOURSELF, ELVIN.
Glenn McCoy
WOW! I GUESS IT'S TRUE WHAT THEY SAY.
THE MOLD IS ALWAYS GREENER IN THE NEIGHBOR'S REFRIGERATOR.

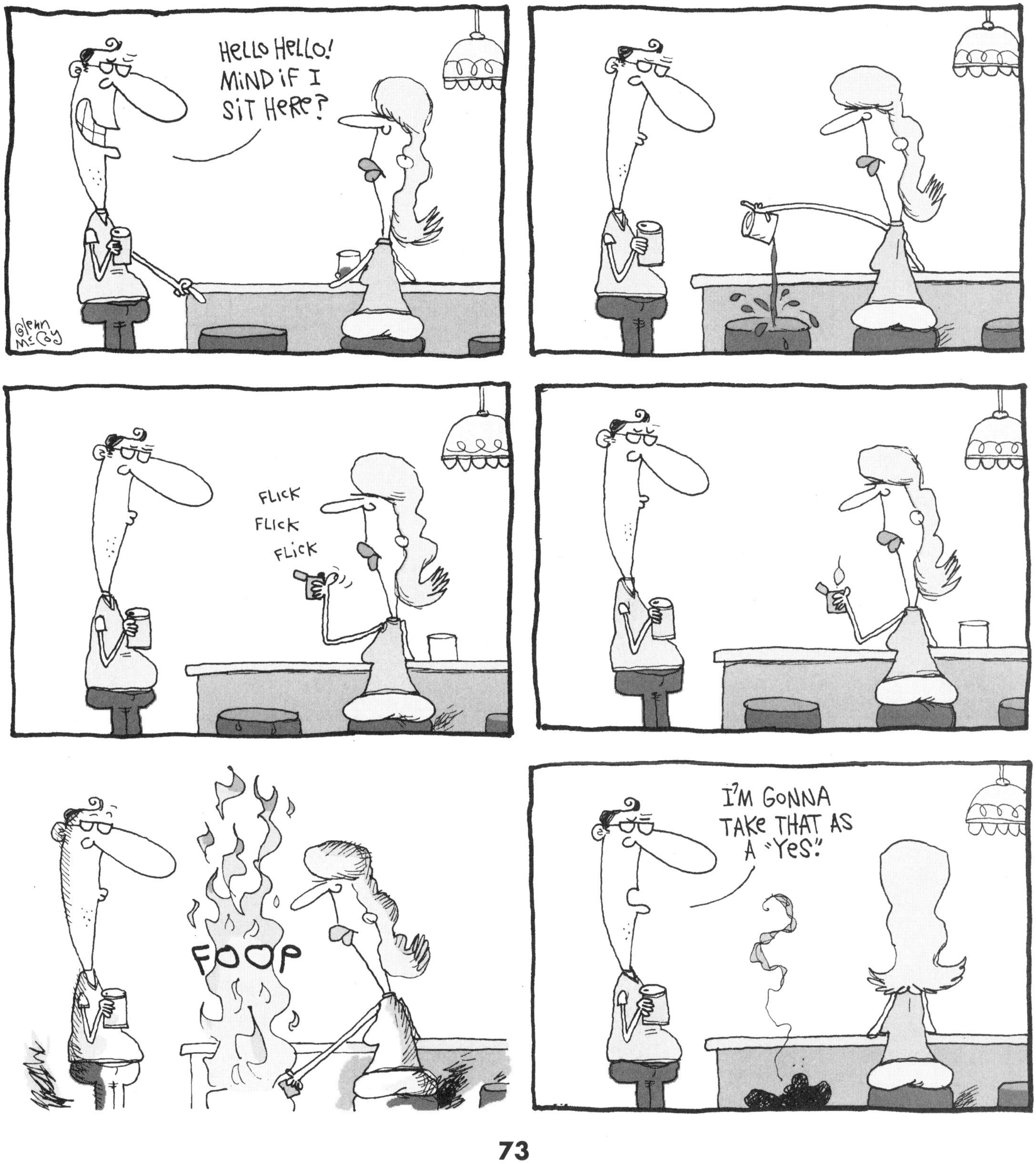
HELLO HELLO! MIND IF I SIT HERE?
FLICK
FLICK
FLICK
FOOP
I'M GONNA TAKE THAT AS A "YES."

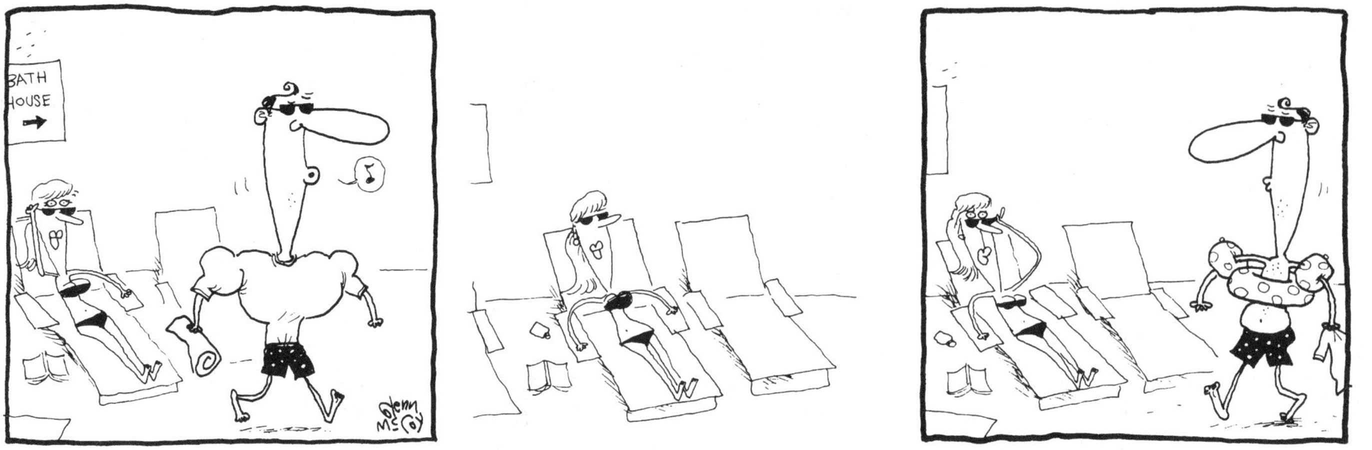
BATH
HOUSE
Glenn McCoy

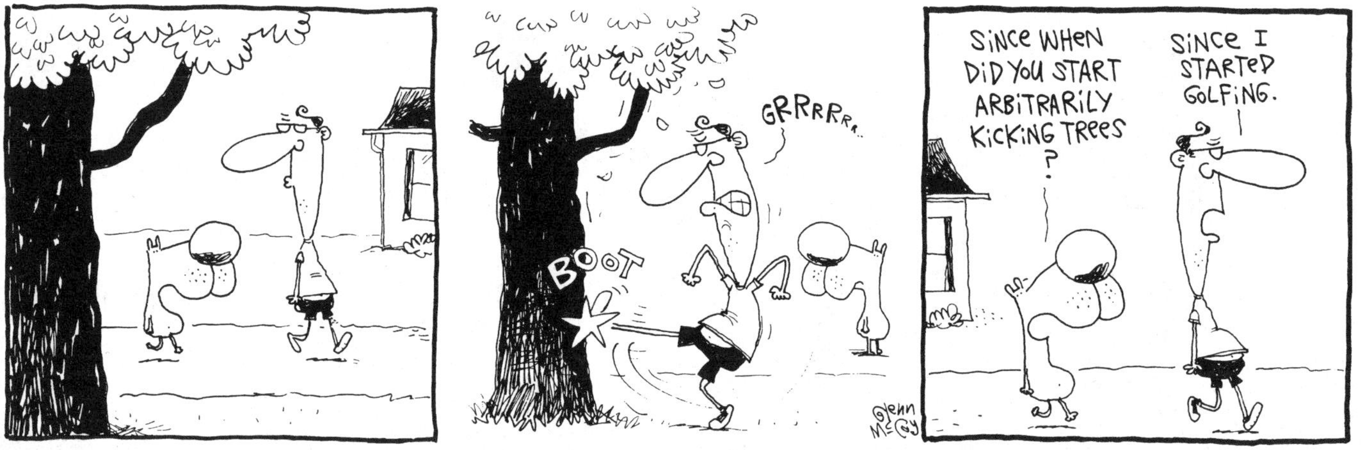
BOOT
GRRRRRRR
Glenn McCoy
SINCE WHEN DID YOU START ARBITRARILY KICKING TREES ?
SINCE I STARTED GOLFING.

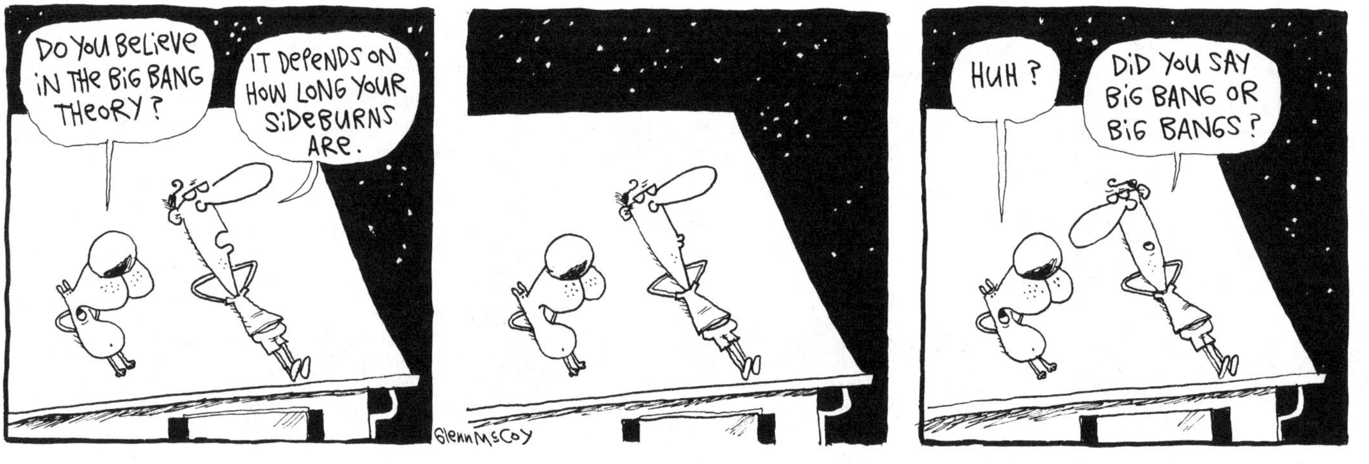
DO YOU BELIEVE IN THE BIG BANG THEORY ?
IT DEPENDS ON HOW LONG YOUR SIDEBURNS ARE.
Glenn McCoy
HUH ?
DID YOU SAY BIG BANG OR BIG BANGS ?

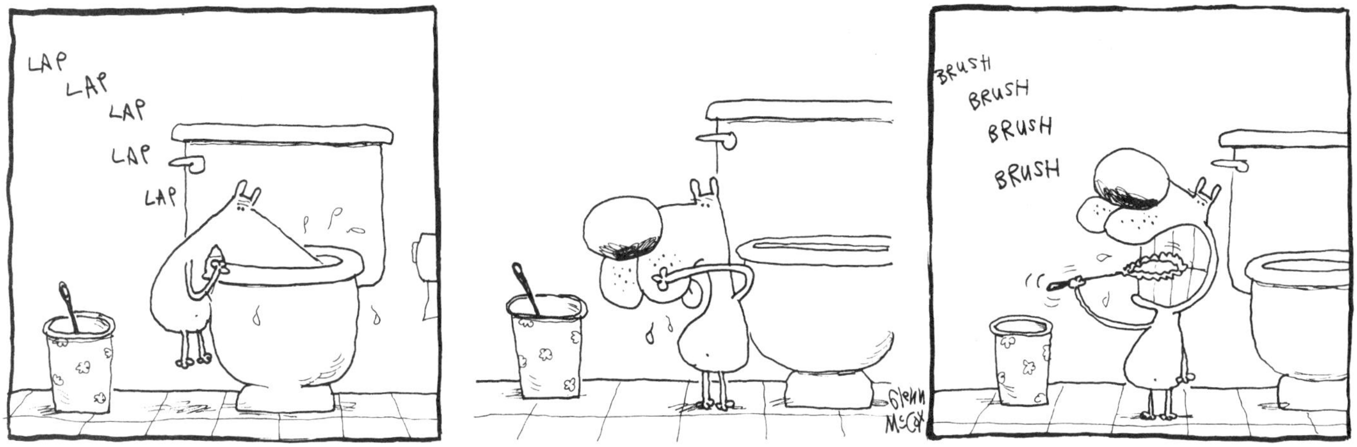
LAP
LAP
LAP
LAP
LAP
BRUSH
BRUSH
BRUSH
BRUSH
Glenn McCoy

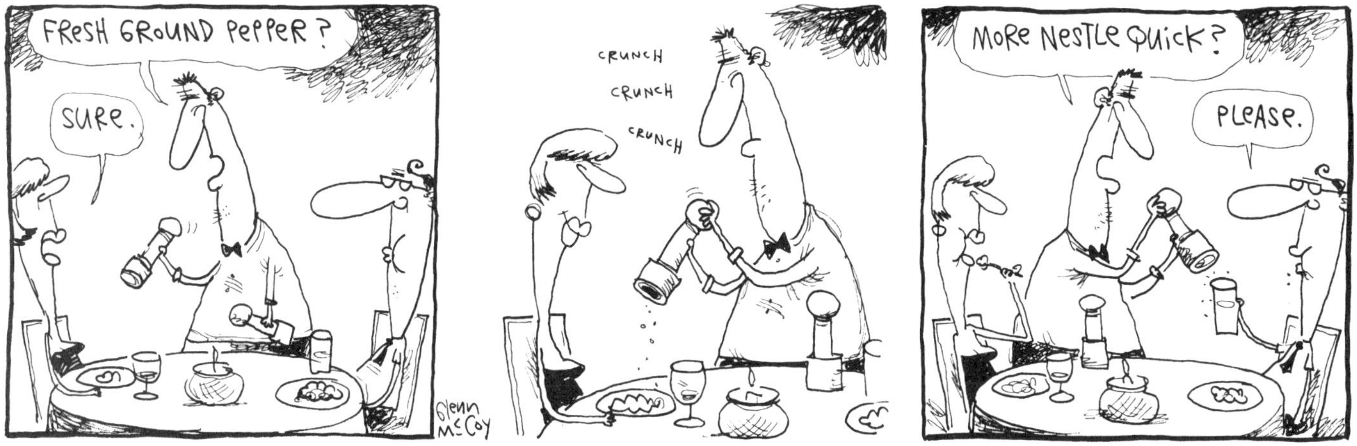
FRESH GROUND PEPPER?
SURE.
Glenn McCoy
CRUNCH
CRUNCH
CRUNCH
MORE NESTLE QUICK?
PLEASE.

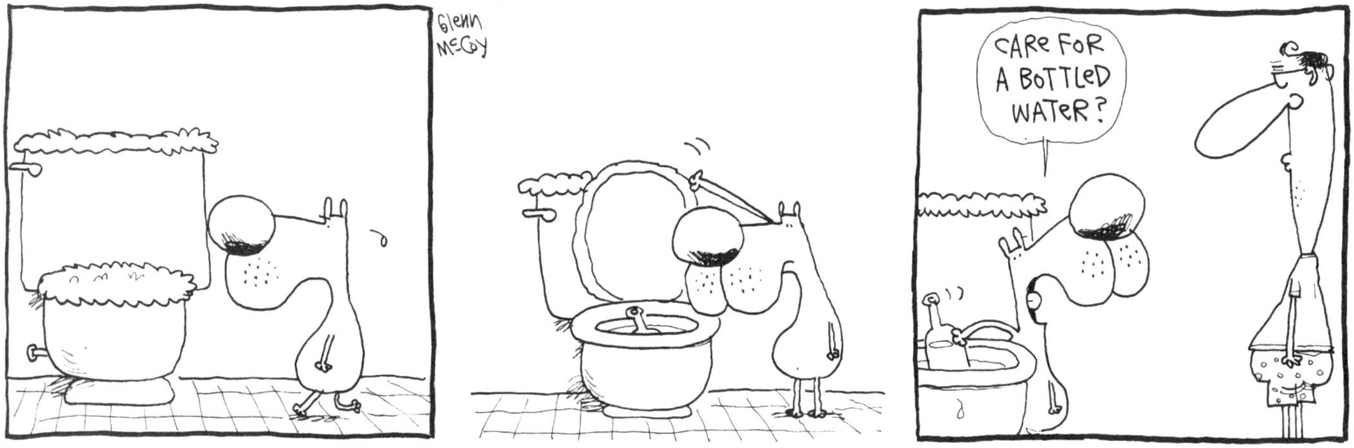
Glenn McCoy
CARE FOR A BOTTLED WATER?

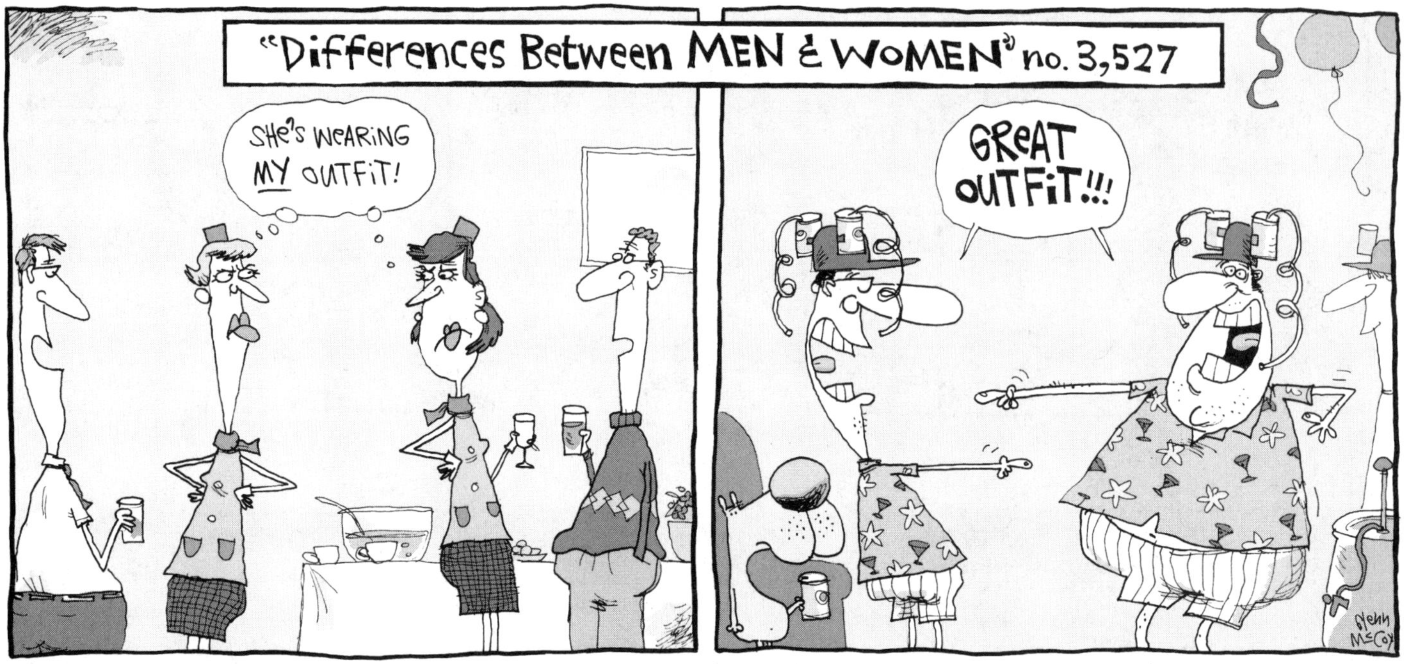
"Differences Between MEN & WOMEN" no. 3,527
SHE'S WEARING MY OUTFIT!
GREAT OUTFIT!!!

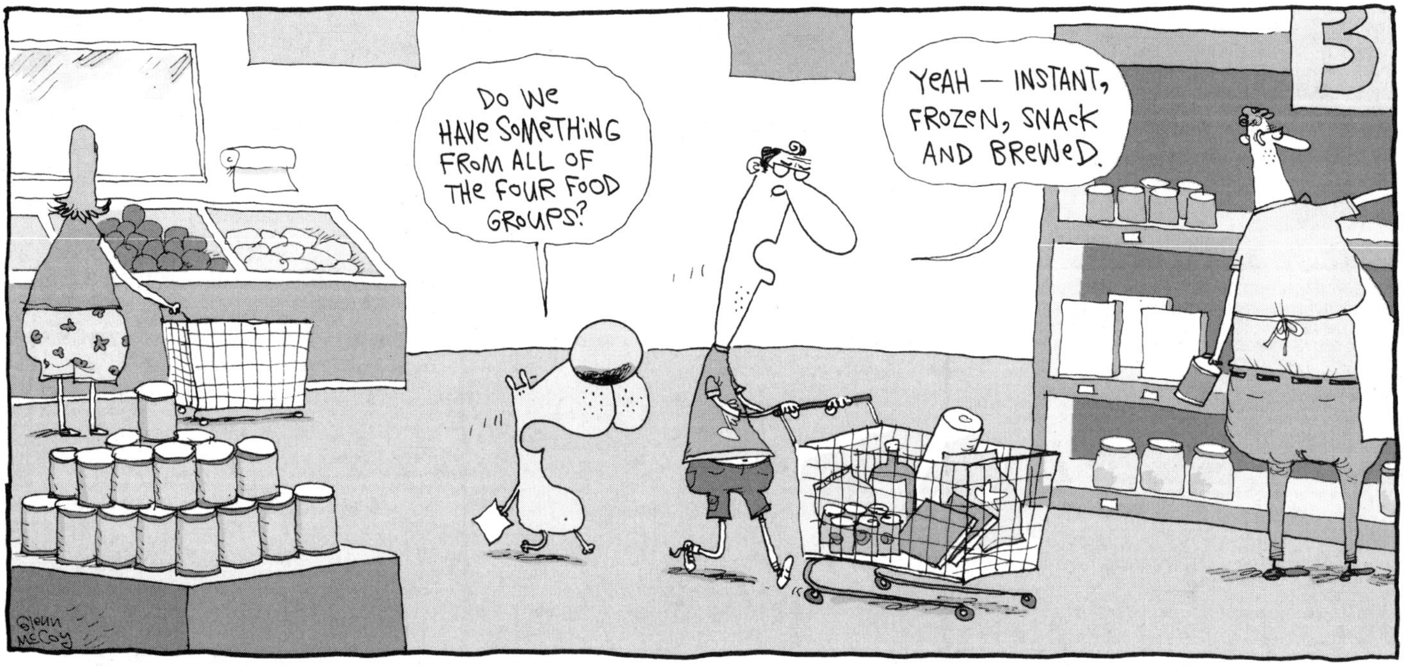
DO WE HAVE SOMETHING FROM ALL OF THE FOUR FOOD GROUPS?
YEAH — INSTANT, FROZEN, SNACK AND BREWED.

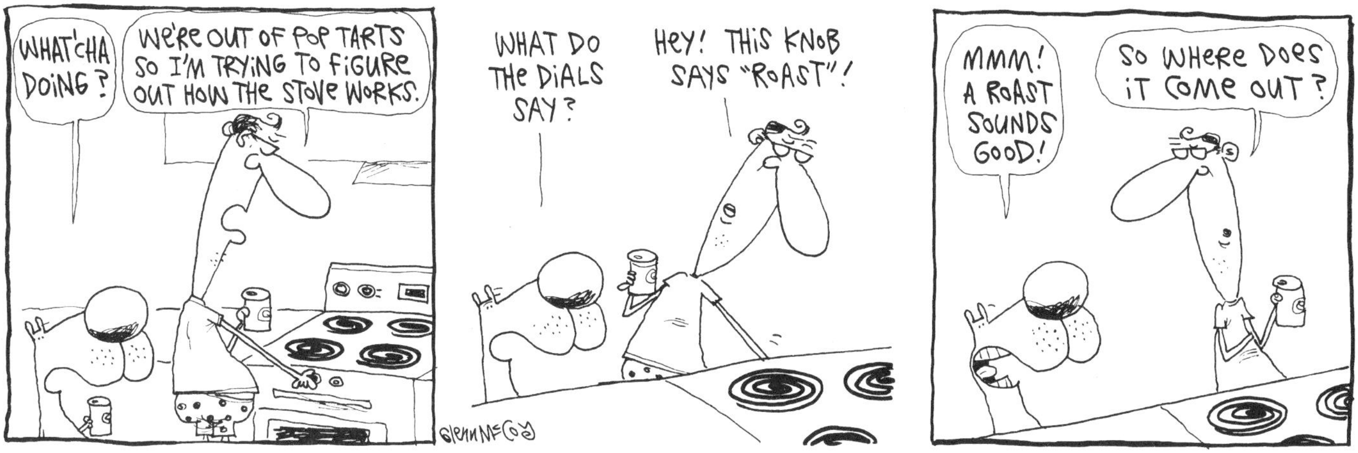
WHAT'CHA DOING?
WE'RE OUT OF POP TARTS SO I'M TRYING TO FIGURE OUT HOW THE STOVE WORKS.
WHAT DO THE DIALS SAY?
HEY! THIS KNOB SAYS "ROAST"!
MMM! A ROAST SOUNDS GOOD!
SO WHERE DOES IT COME OUT?
GLENN MCCOY

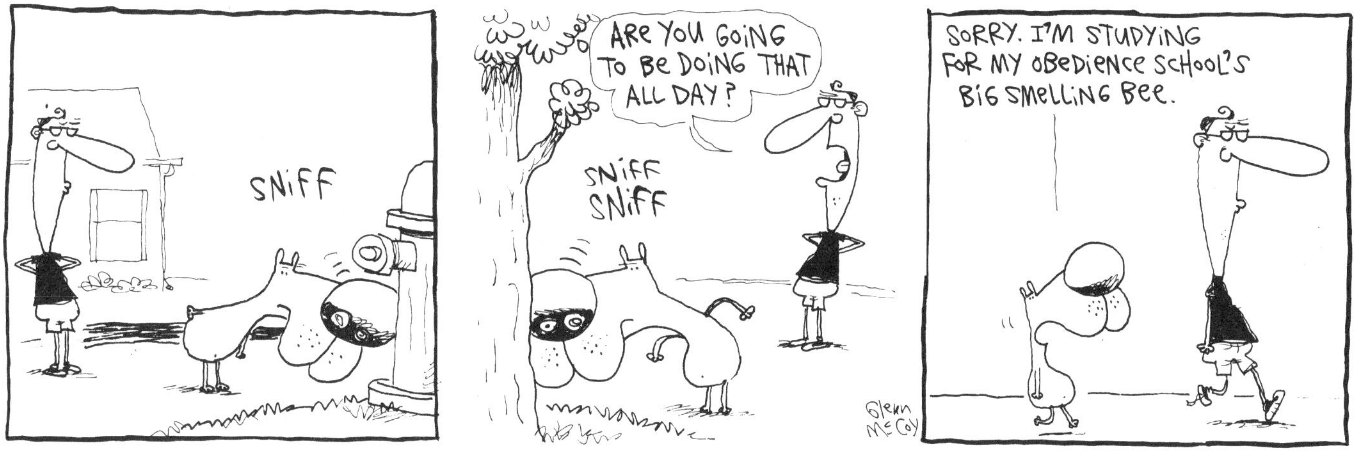
SNIFF
ARE YOU GOING TO BE DOING THAT ALL DAY?
SNIFF SNIFF
SORRY. I'M STUDYING FOR MY OBEDIENCE SCHOOL'S BIG SMELLING BEE.
GLENN MCCOY

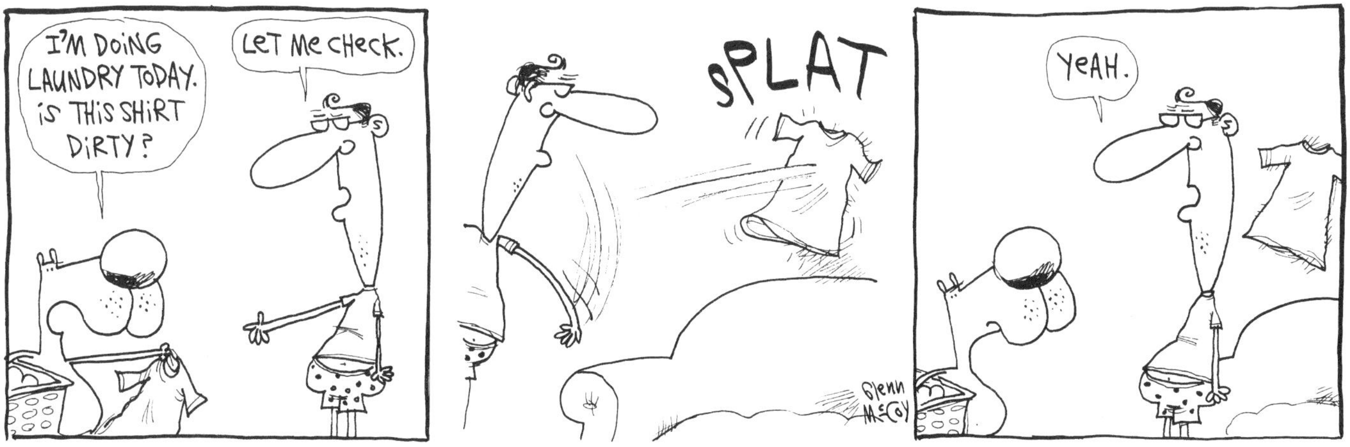
I'M DOING LAUNDRY TODAY. IS THIS SHIRT DIRTY?
LET ME CHECK.
SPLAT
YEAH.
GLENN MCCOY

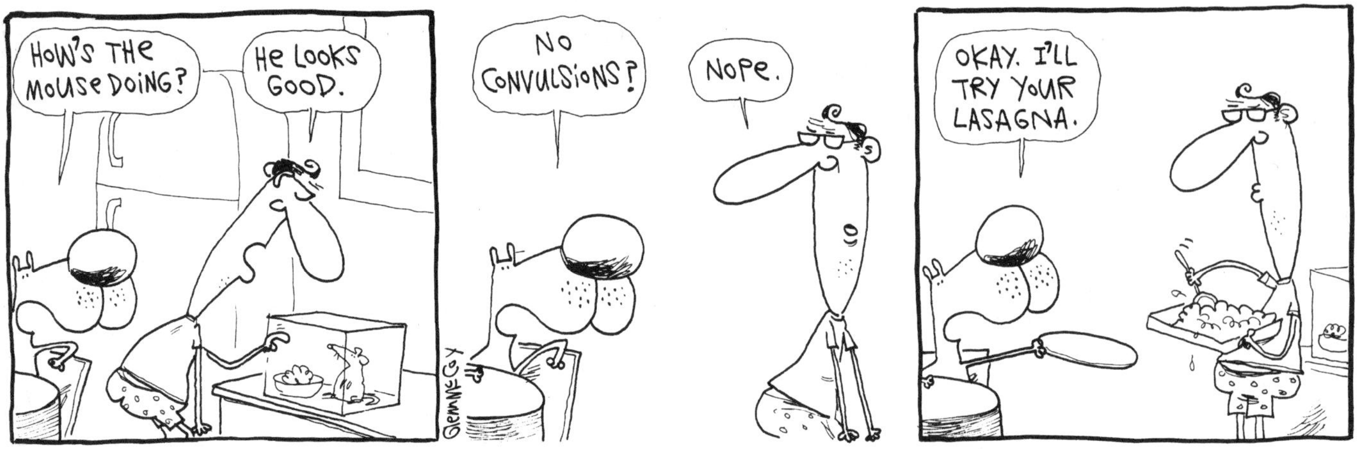
HOW'S THE MOUSE DOING?
He LOOKS GOOD.
Glenn McCoy
NO CONVULSIONS?
NOPE.
OKAY. I'LL TRY YOUR LASAGNA.

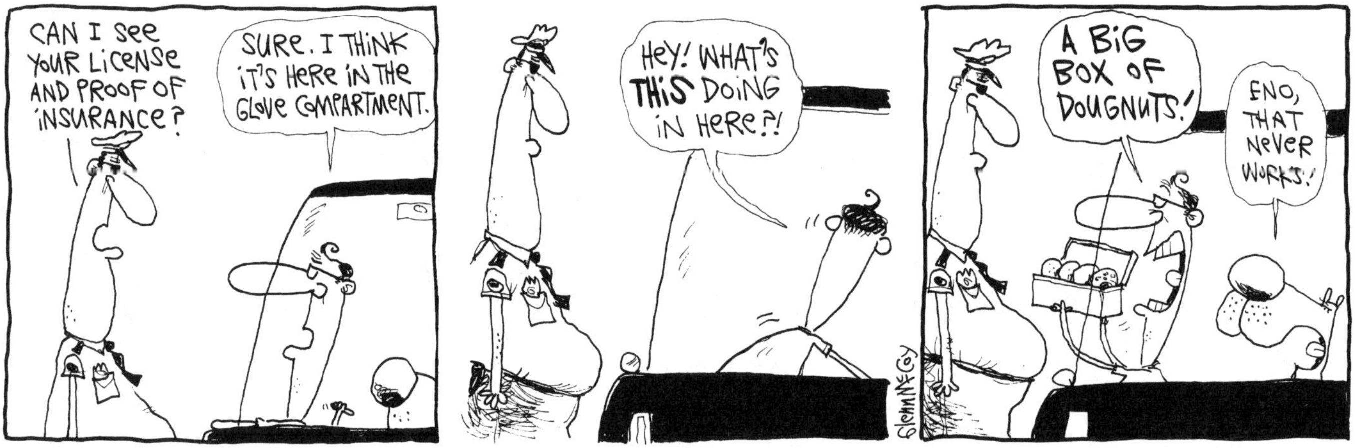
CAN I SEE YOUR LICENSE AND PROOF OF INSURANCE?
SURE. I THINK IT'S HERE IN THE GLOVE COMPARTMENT.
HEY! WHAT'S THIS DOING IN HERE?!
Glenn McCoy
A BIG BOX OF DOUGNUTS!
ENO, THAT NEVER WORKS!

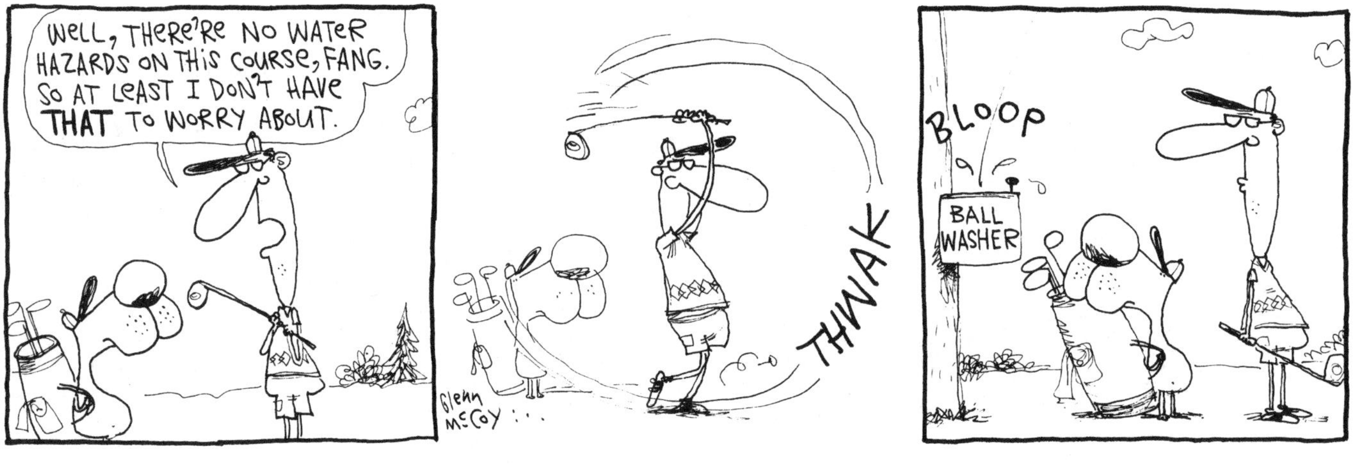
WELL, THERE'RE NO WATER HAZARDS ON THIS COURSE, FANG. SO AT LEAST I DON'T HAVE THAT TO WORRY ABOUT.
THWAK
Glenn McCoy
BLOOP
BALL WASHER

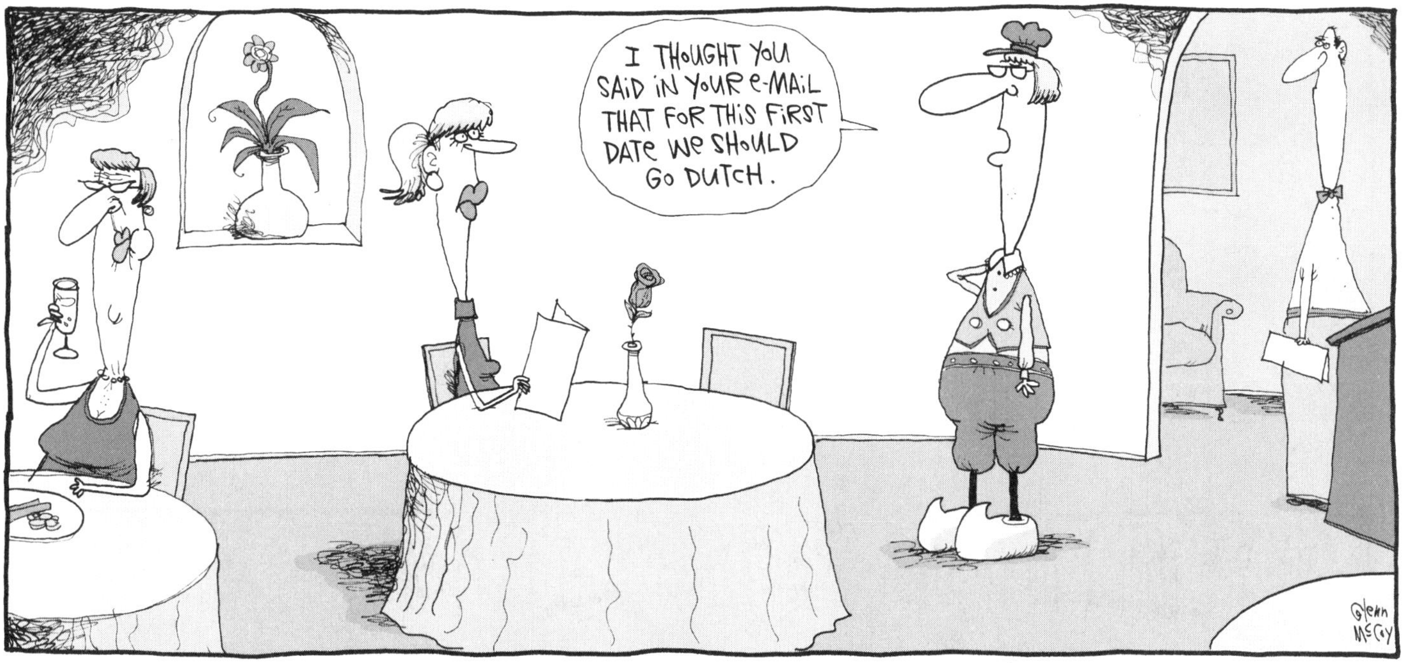
I THOUGHT YOU SAID IN YOUR E-MAIL THAT FOR THIS FIRST DATE WE SHOULD GO DUTCH.
Glenn McCoy

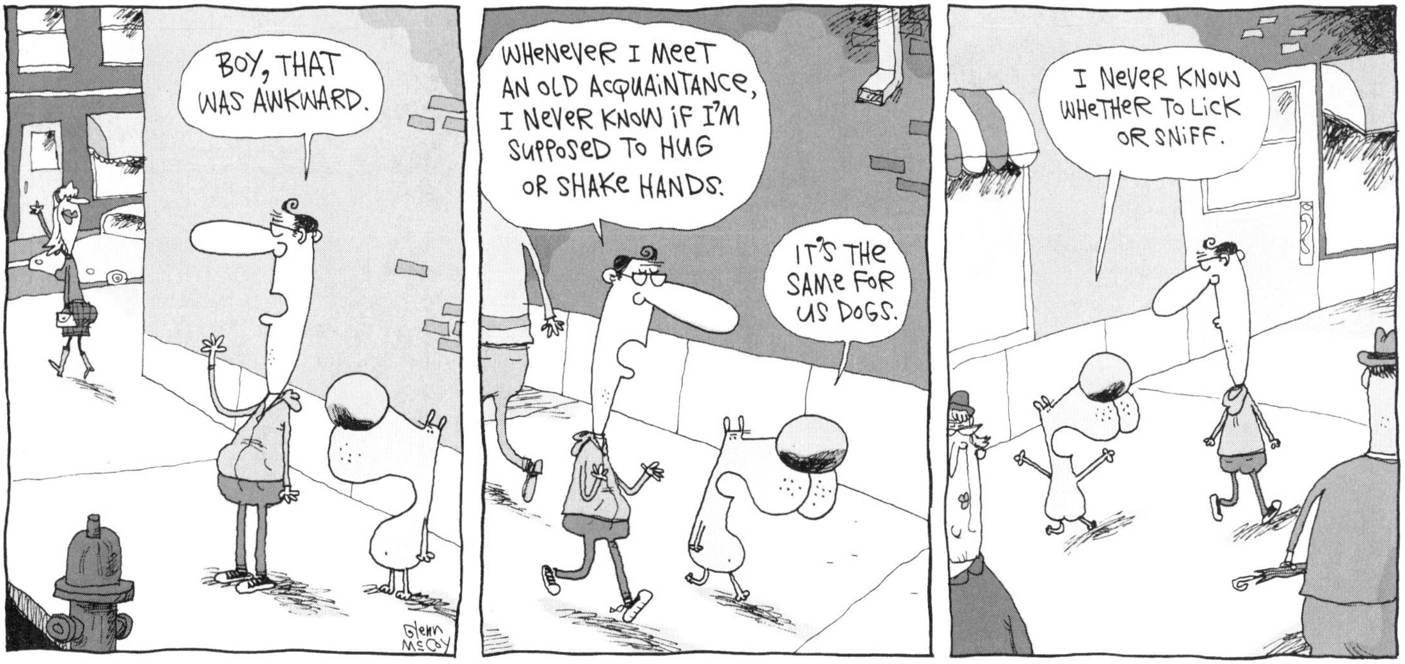
BOY, THAT WAS AWKWARD.
Glenn McCoy
WHENEVER I MEET AN OLD ACQUAINTANCE, I NEVER KNOW IF I'M SUPPOSED TO HUG OR SHAKE HANDS.
IT'S THE SAME FOR US DOGS.
I NEVER KNOW WHETHER TO LICK OR SNIFF.

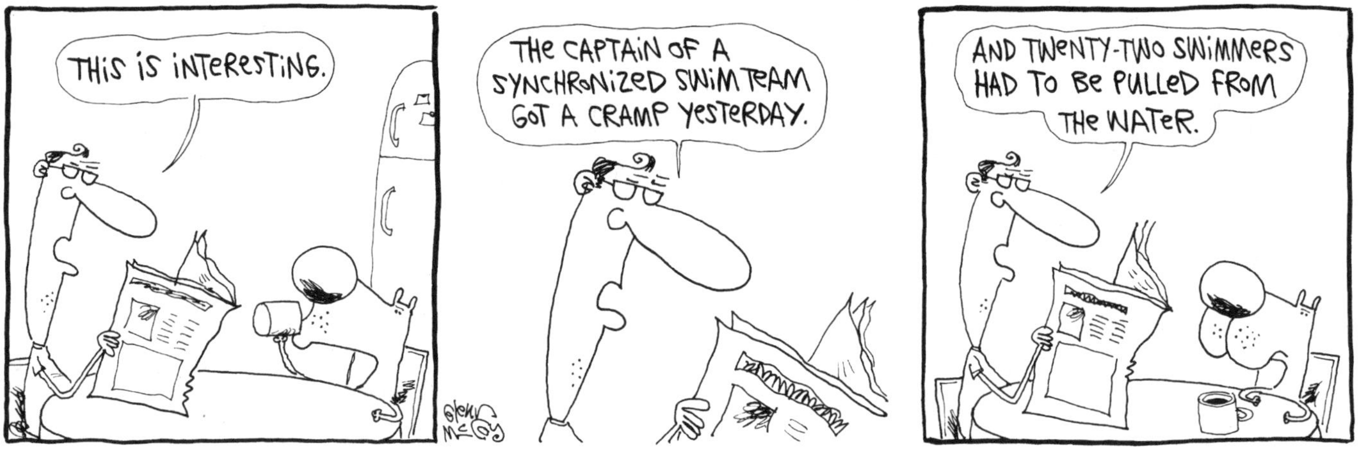
THIS IS INTERESTING.
THE CAPTAIN OF A SYNCHRONIZED SWIM TEAM GOT A CRAMP YESTERDAY.
AND TWENTY-TWO SWIMMERS HAD TO BE PULLED FROM THE WATER.
Glenn McCoy

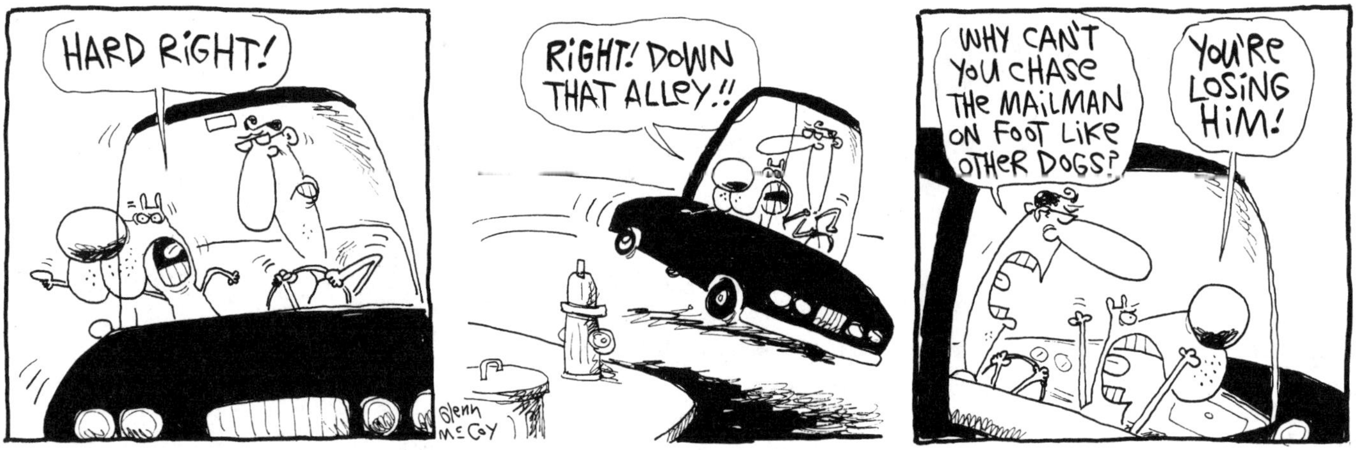
HARD RIGHT!
RIGHT! DOWN THAT ALLEY!!
WHY CAN'T YOU CHASE THE MAILMAN ON FOOT LIKE OTHER DOGS?
YOU'RE LOSING HIM!
Glenn McCoy

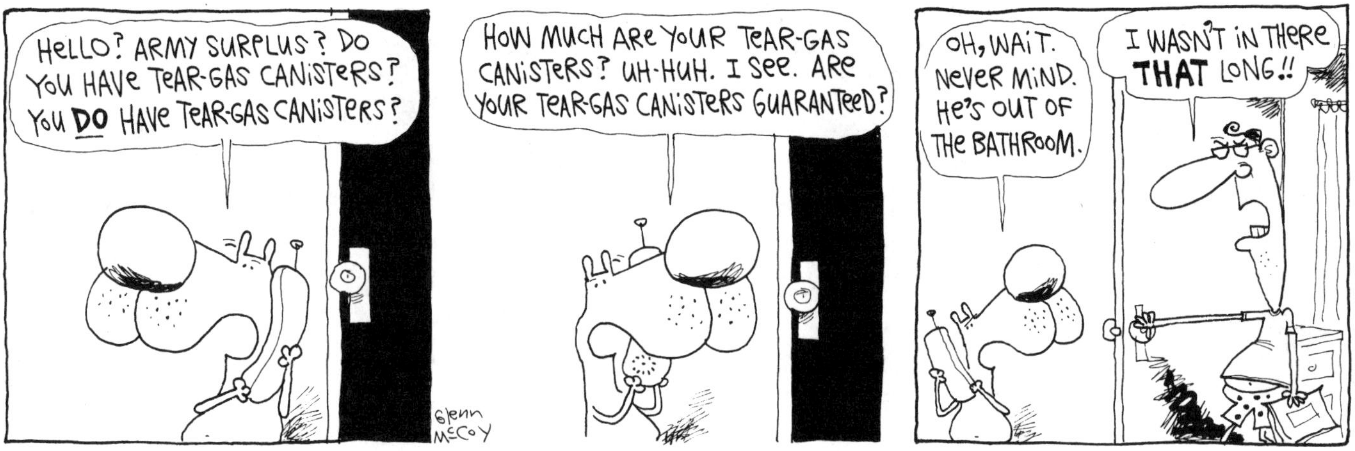
HELLO? ARMY SURPLUS? DO YOU HAVE TEAR-GAS CANISTERS? YOU DO HAVE TEAR-GAS CANISTERS?
HOW MUCH ARE YOUR TEAR-GAS CANISTERS? UH-HUH. I SEE. ARE YOUR TEAR-GAS CANISTERS GUARANTEED?
OH, WAIT. NEVER MIND. HE'S OUT OF THE BATHROOM.
I WASN'T IN THERE THAT LONG!!
Glenn McCoy

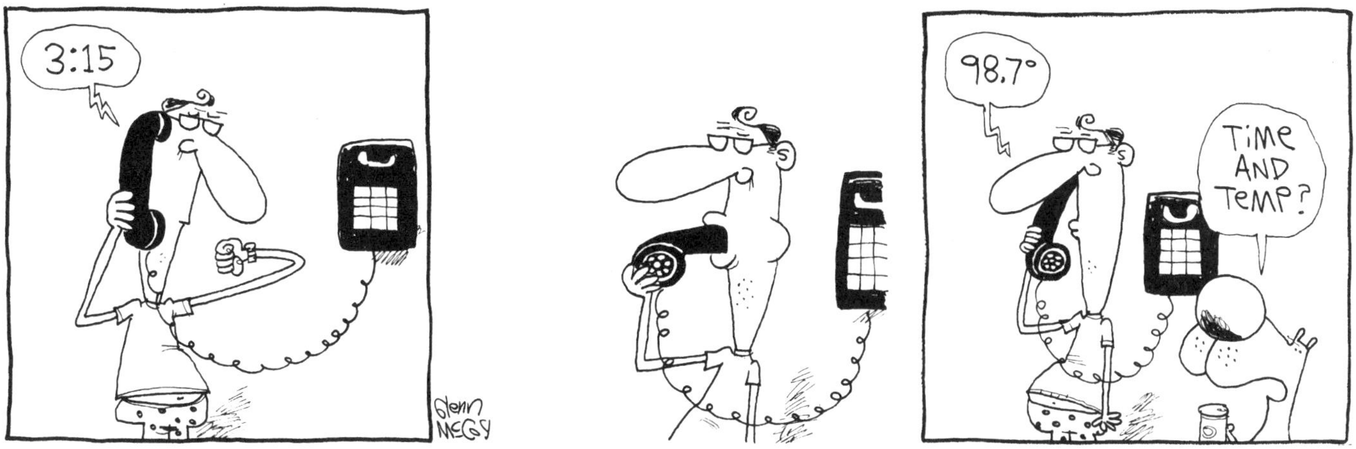
3:15
98.7°
TIME AND TEMP?
Glenn McCoy

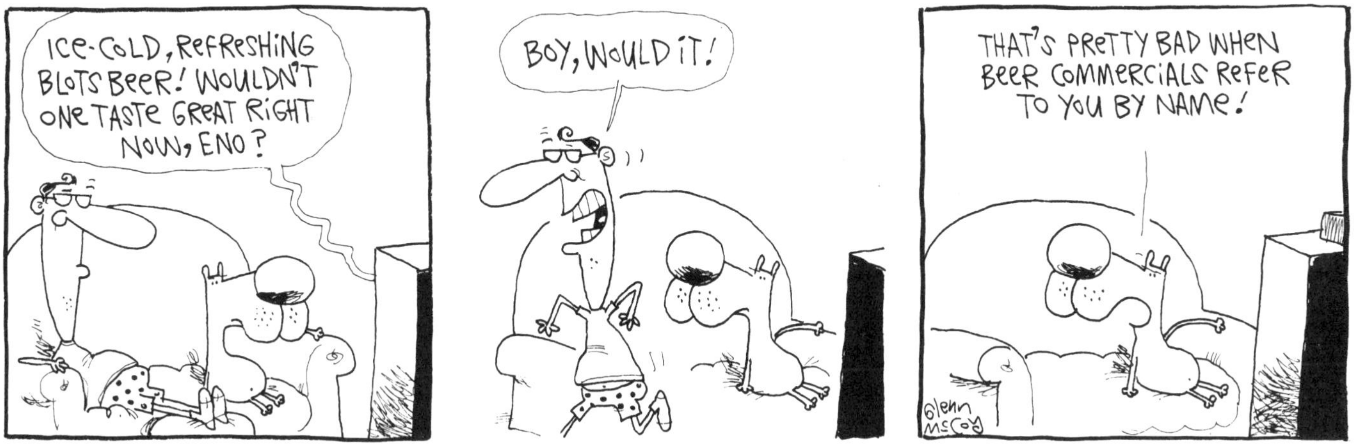
ICE-COLD, REFRESHING BLOTS BEER! WOULDN'T ONE TASTE GREAT RIGHT NOW, ENO?
BOY, WOULD IT!
THAT'S PRETTY BAD WHEN BEER COMMERCIALS REFER TO YOU BY NAME!
Glenn McCoy

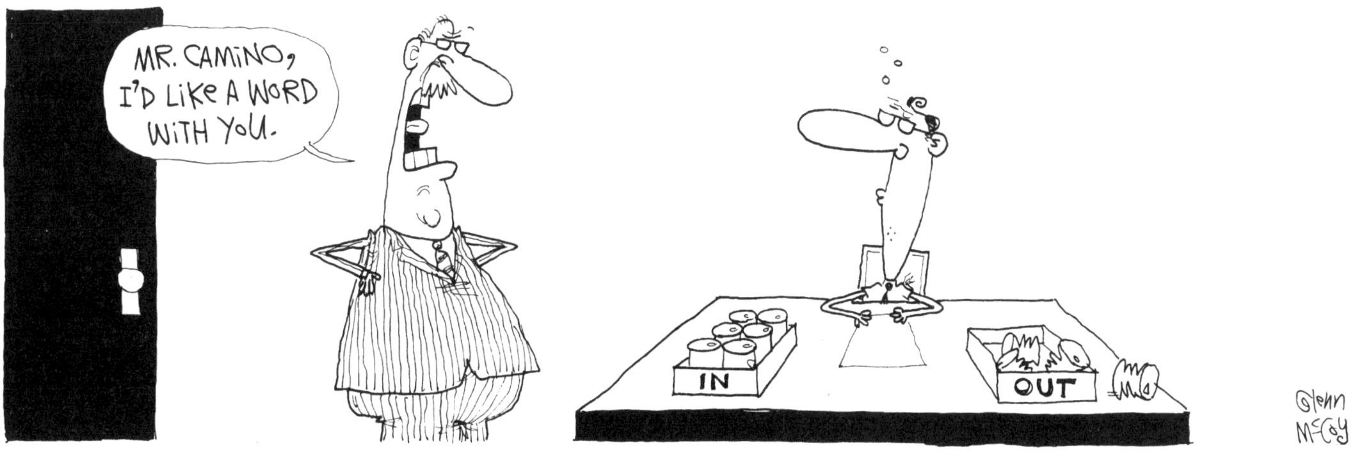
MR. CAMINO, I'D LIKE A WORD WITH YOU.
IN
OUT
Glenn McCoy

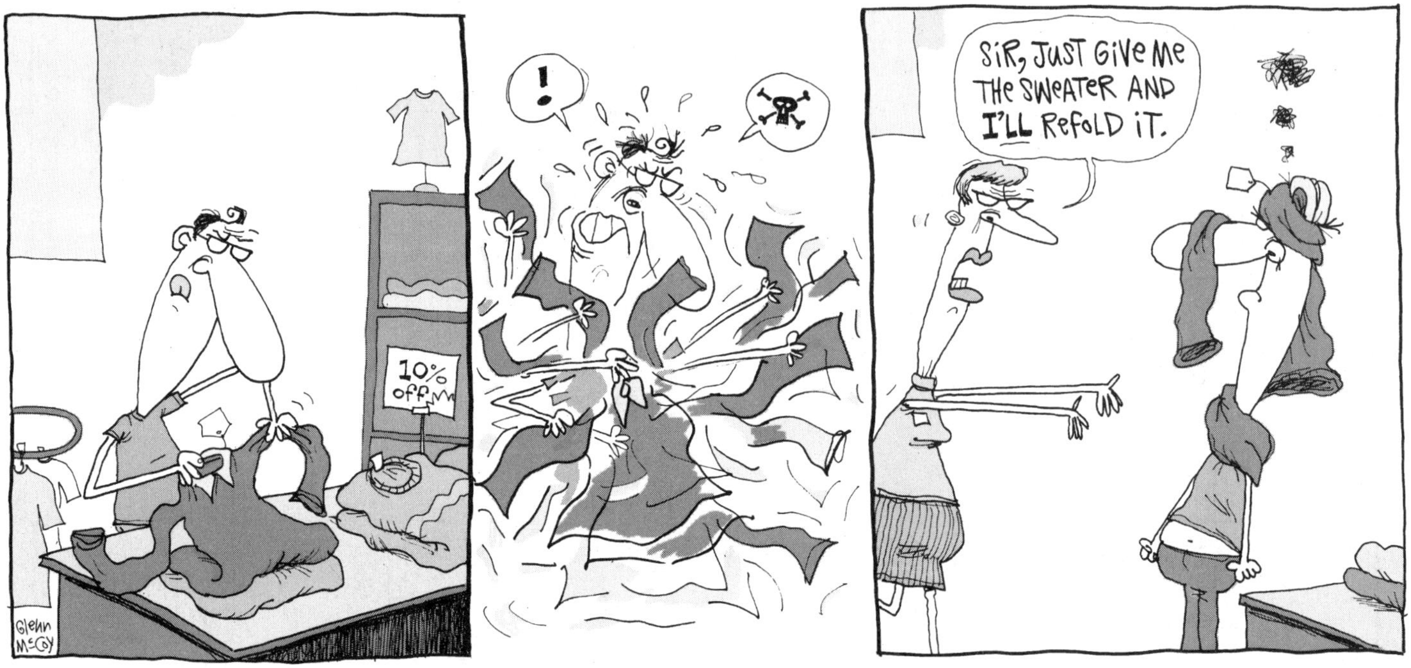
Glenn McCoy
10% off
!
SIR, JUST GIVE ME THE SWEATER AND I'LL REFOLD IT.

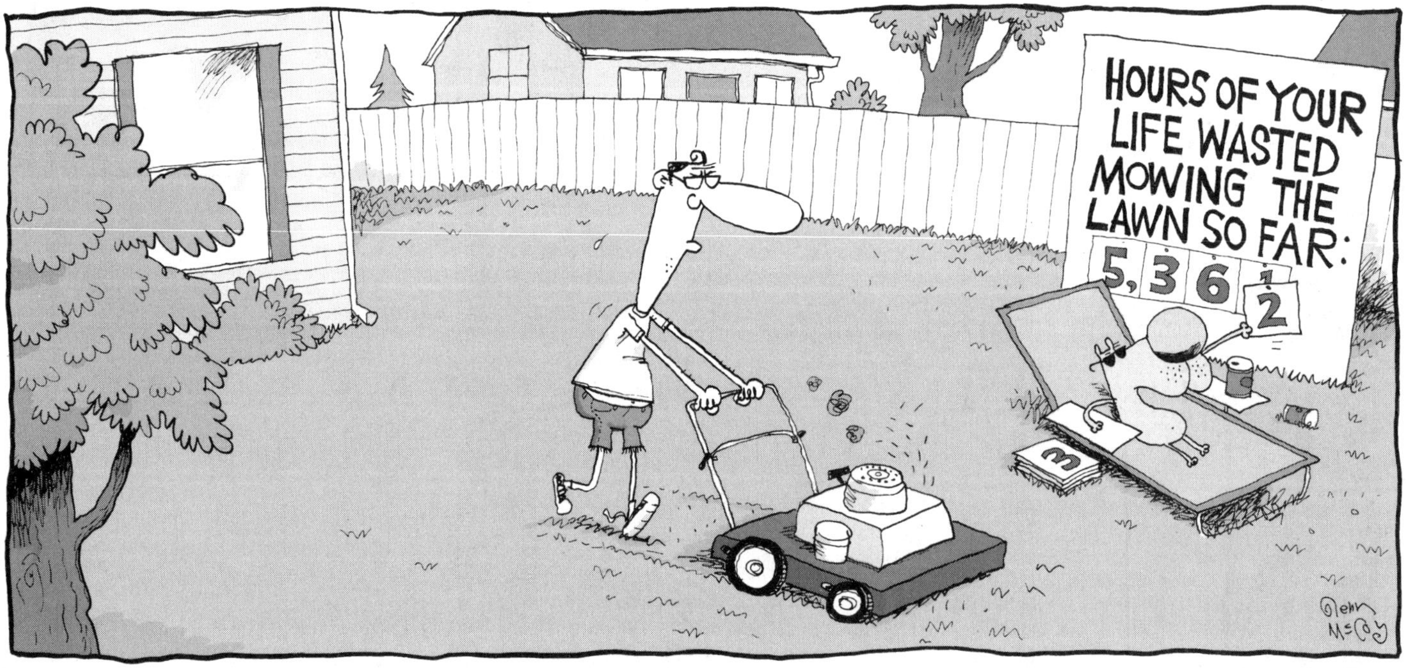
HOURS OF YOUR LIFE WASTED MOWING THE LAWN SO FAR:
5,36 1
2
3
Glenn McCoy

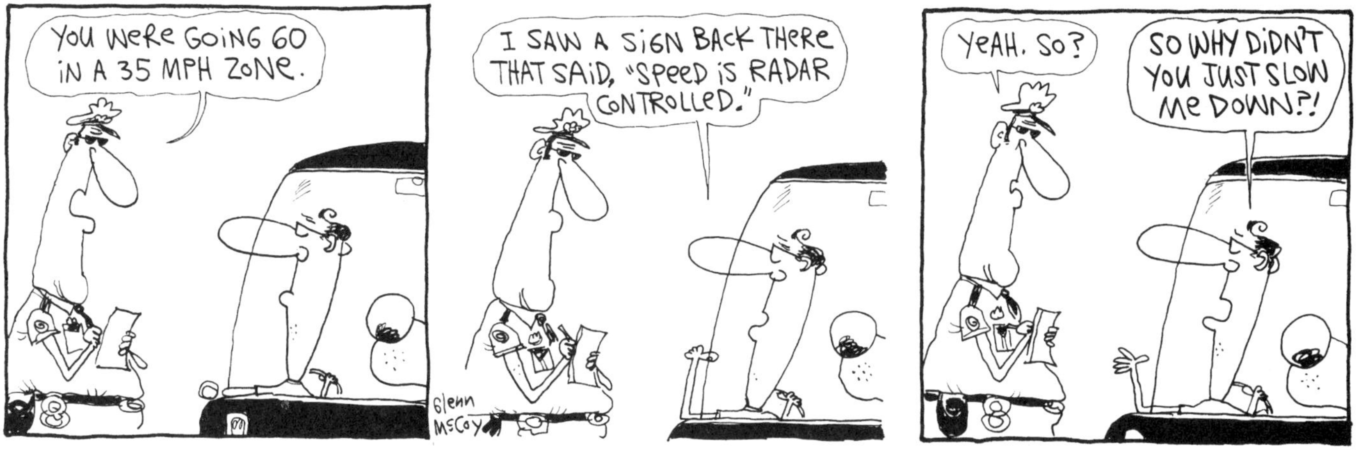
YOU WERE GOING 60 IN A 35 MPH ZONE.
I SAW A SIGN BACK THERE THAT SAID, "SPEED IS RADAR CONTROLLED."
Glenn McCoy
YEAH. SO?
SO WHY DIDN'T YOU JUST SLOW ME DOWN?!

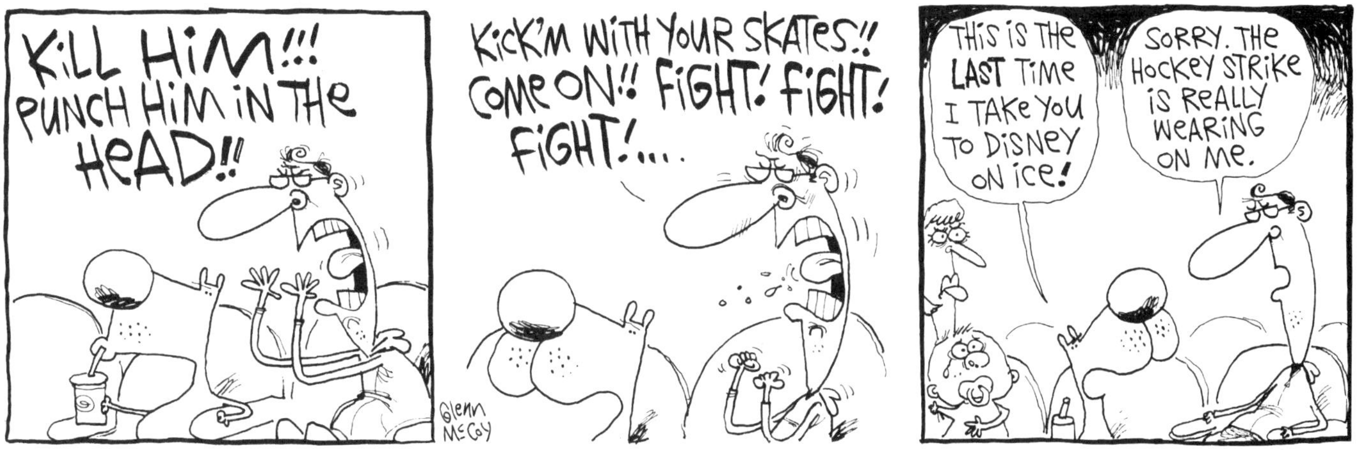
KILL HIM!!! PUNCH HIM IN THE HEAD!!
Glenn McCoy
KICK'M WITH YOUR SKATES!! COME ON!! FIGHT! FIGHT! FIGHT!....
THIS IS THE LAST TIME I TAKE YOU TO DISNEY ON ICE!
SORRY. THE HOCKEY STRIKE IS REALLY WEARING ON ME.

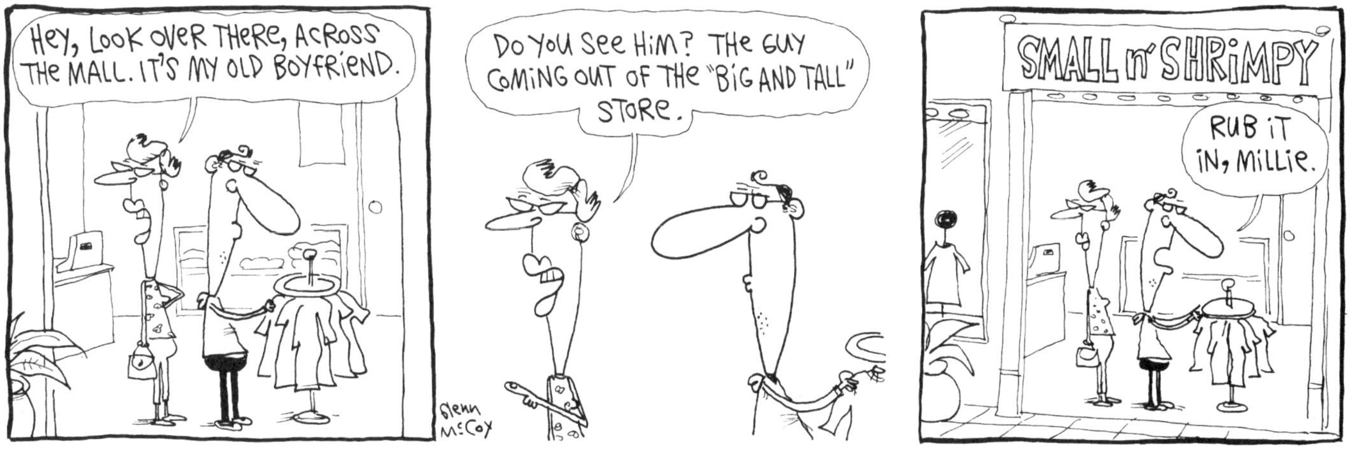
HEY, LOOK OVER THERE, ACROSS THE MALL. IT'S MY OLD BOYFRIEND.
Glenn McCoy
DO YOU SEE HIM? THE GUY COMING OUT OF THE "BIG AND TALL" STORE.
SMALL n' SHRIMPY
RUB IT IN, MILLIE.

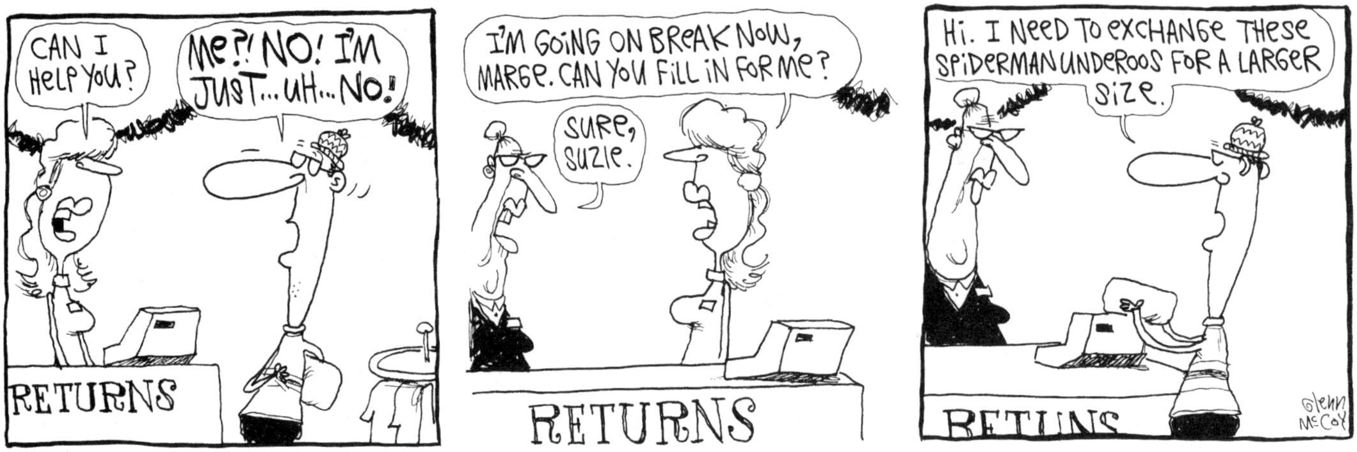
CAN I HELP YOU?
ME?! NO! I'M JUST...UH...NO!
RETURNS
I'M GOING ON BREAK NOW, MARGE. CAN YOU FILL IN FOR ME?
SURE, SUZIE.
RETURNS
HI. I NEED TO EXCHANGE THESE SPIDERMAN UNDEROOS FOR A LARGER SIZE.
Glenn McCoy

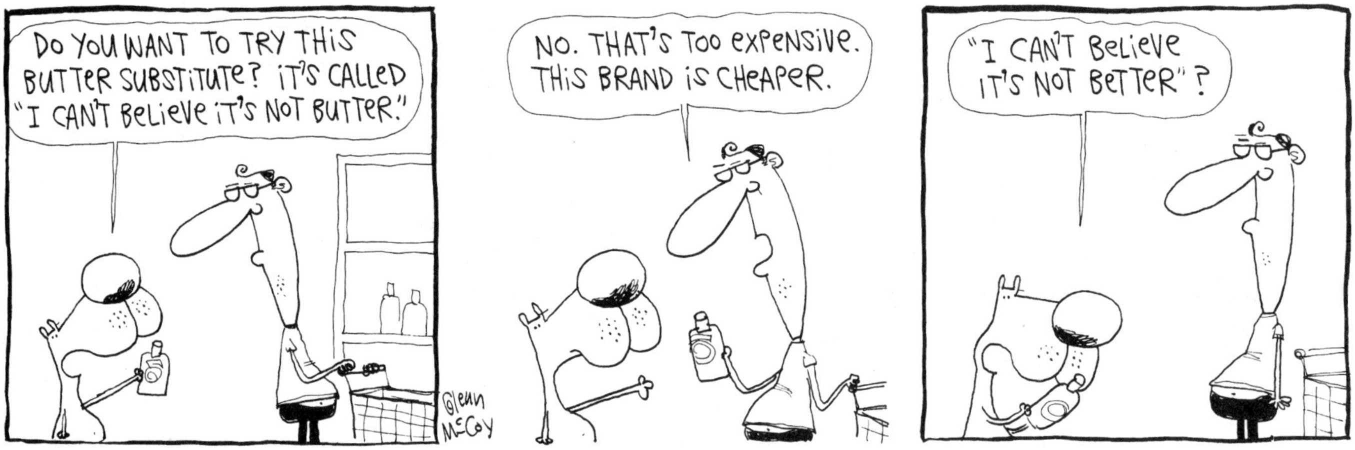
DO YOU WANT TO TRY THIS BUTTER SUBSTITUTE? IT'S CALLED "I CAN'T BELIEVE IT'S NOT BUTTER."
Glenn McCoy
NO. THAT'S TOO EXPENSIVE. THIS BRAND IS CHEAPER.
"I CAN'T BELIEVE IT'S NOT BETTER"?

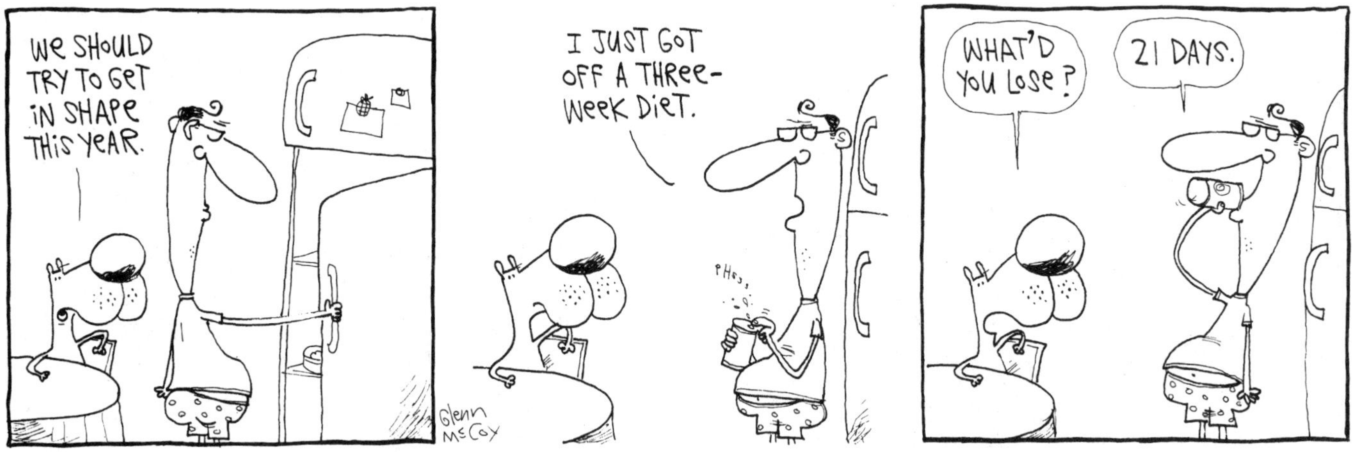
WE SHOULD TRY TO GET IN SHAPE THIS YEAR.
Glenn McCoy
I JUST GOT OFF A THREE-WEEK DIET.
PHSS
WHAT'D YOU LOSE?
21 DAYS.

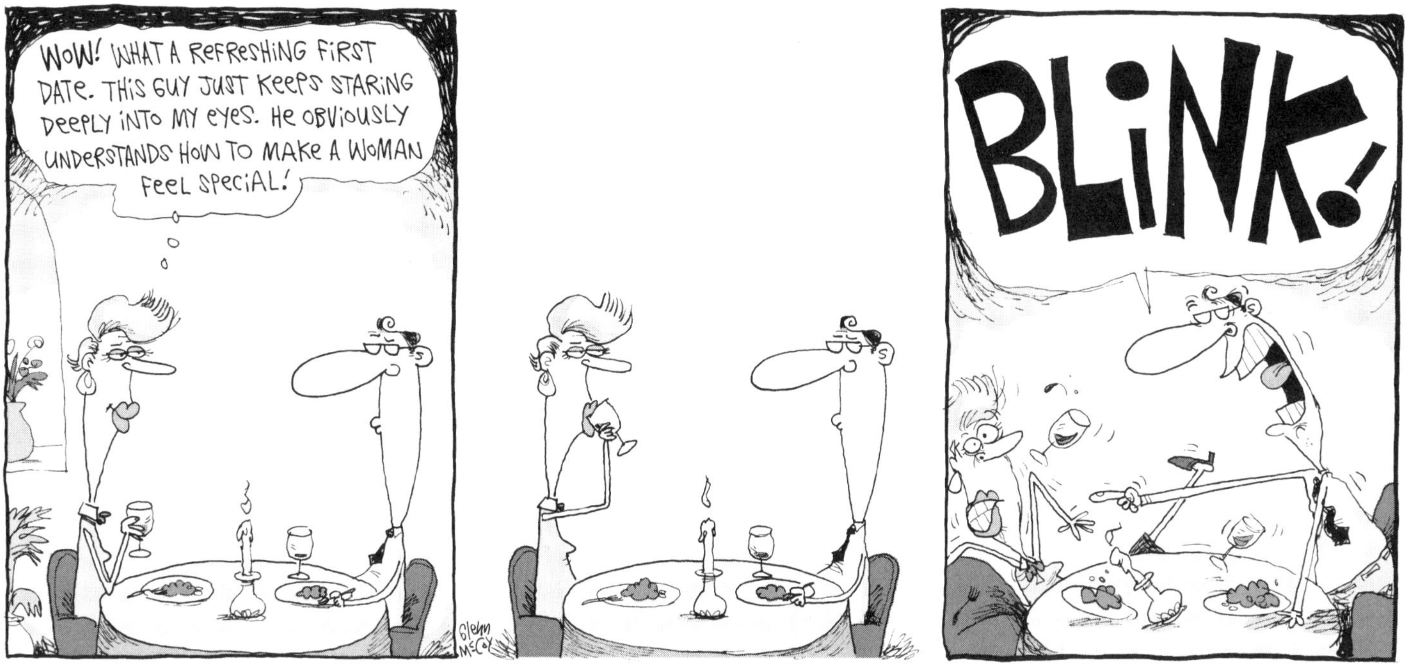
WOW! WHAT A REFRESHING FIRST DATE. THIS GUY JUST KEEPS STARING DEEPLY INTO MY EYES. HE OBVIOUSLY UNDERSTANDS HOW TO MAKE A WOMAN FEEL SPECIAL!
BLINK!

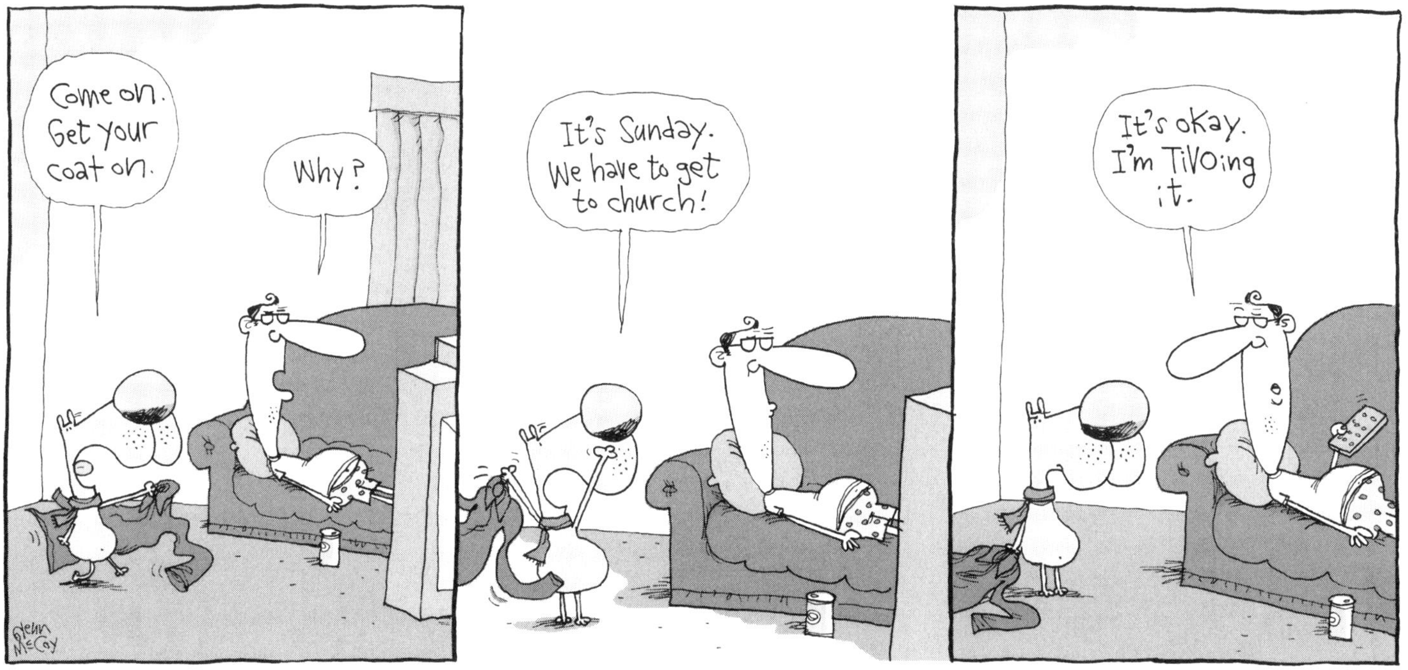
Come on. Get your coat on.
Why?
It's Sunday. We have to get to church!
It's okay. I'm TiVOing it.

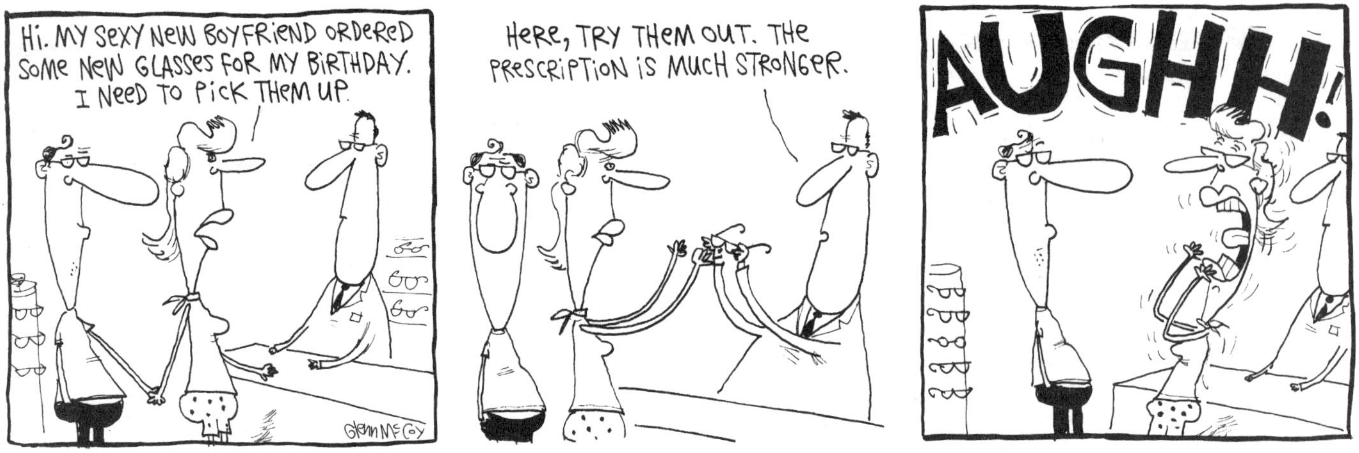
HI. MY SEXY NEW BOYFRIEND ORDERED SOME NEW GLASSES FOR MY BIRTHDAY. I NEED TO PICK THEM UP.
HERE, TRY THEM OUT. THE PRESCRIPTION IS MUCH STRONGER.
AUGHH!
GLENN McCOY

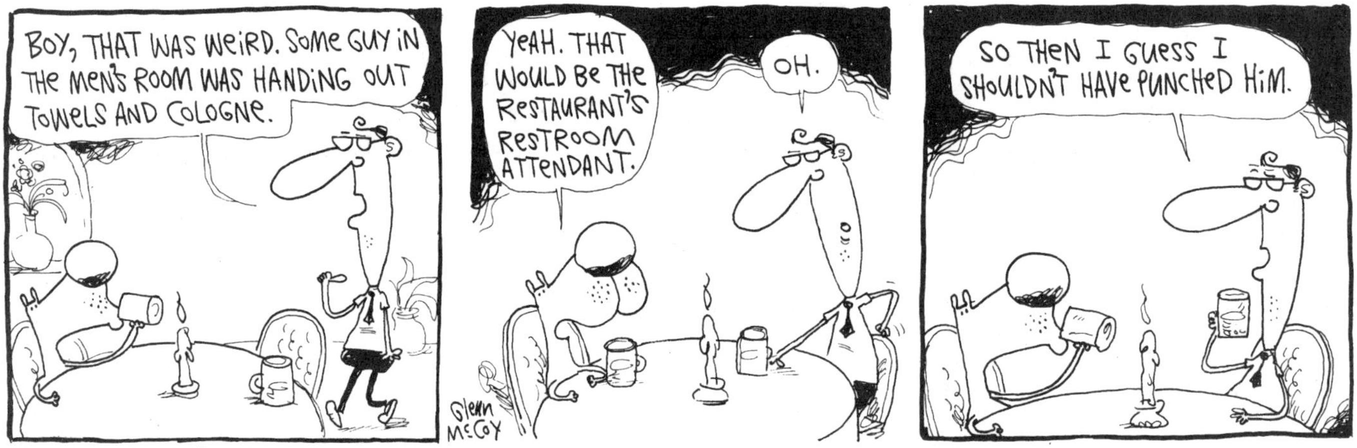
BOY, THAT WAS WEIRD. SOME GUY IN THE MEN'S ROOM WAS HANDING OUT TOWELS AND COLOGNE.
YEAH. THAT WOULD BE THE RESTAURANT'S RESTROOM ATTENDANT.
OH.
SO THEN I GUESS I SHOULDN'T HAVE PUNCHED HIM.
GLENN McCOY

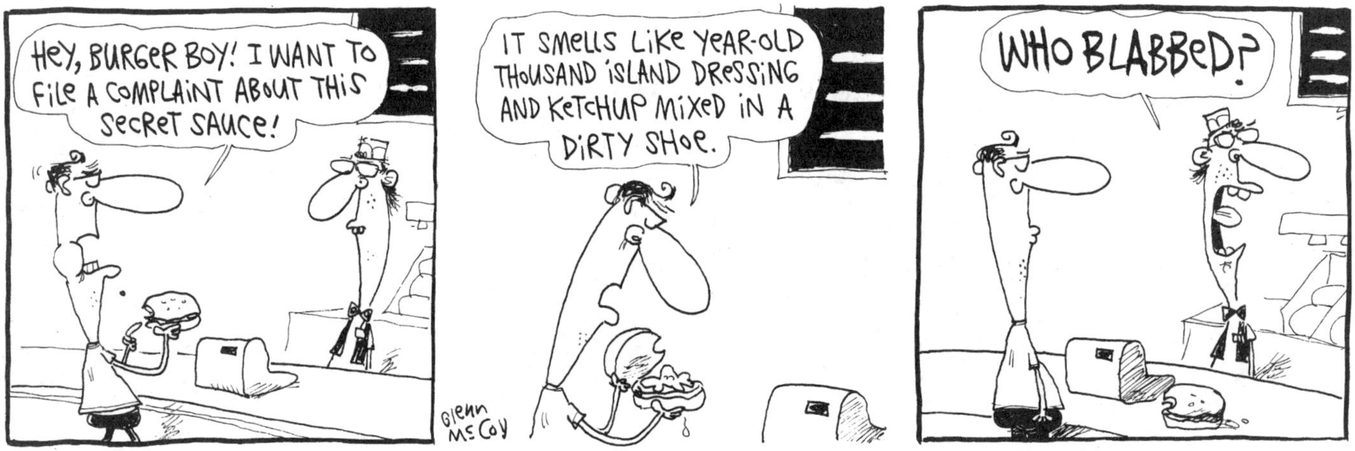
HEY, BURGER BOY! I WANT TO FILE A COMPLAINT ABOUT THIS SECRET SAUCE!
IT SMELLS LIKE YEAR-OLD THOUSAND ISLAND DRESSING AND KETCHUP MIXED IN A DIRTY SHOE.
WHO BLABBED?
GLENN McCOY

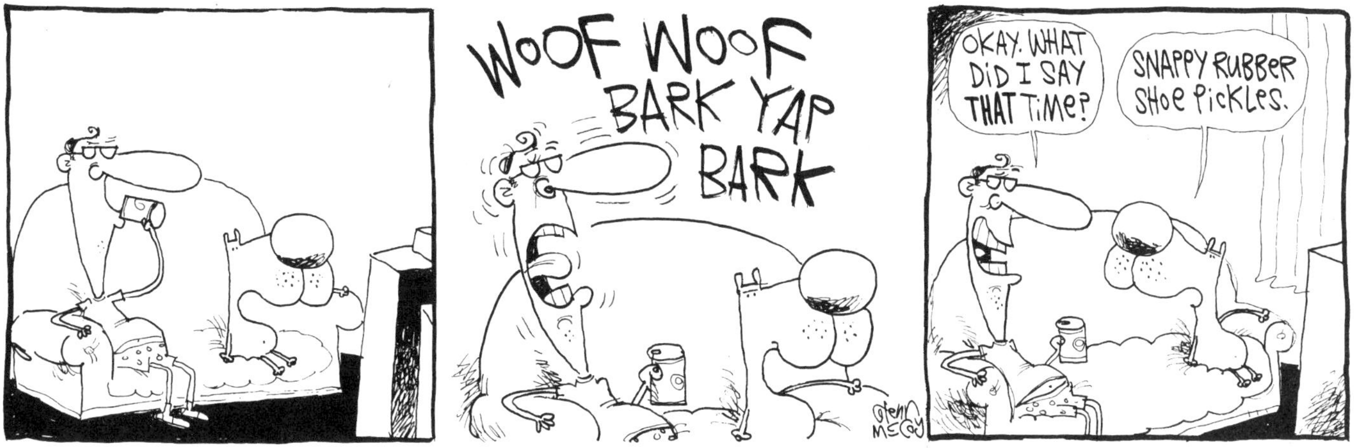
WOOF WOOF BARK YAP BARK
Glenn McCoy
OKAY. WHAT DID I SAY THAT TIME?
SNAPPY RUBBER SHOE PICKLES.

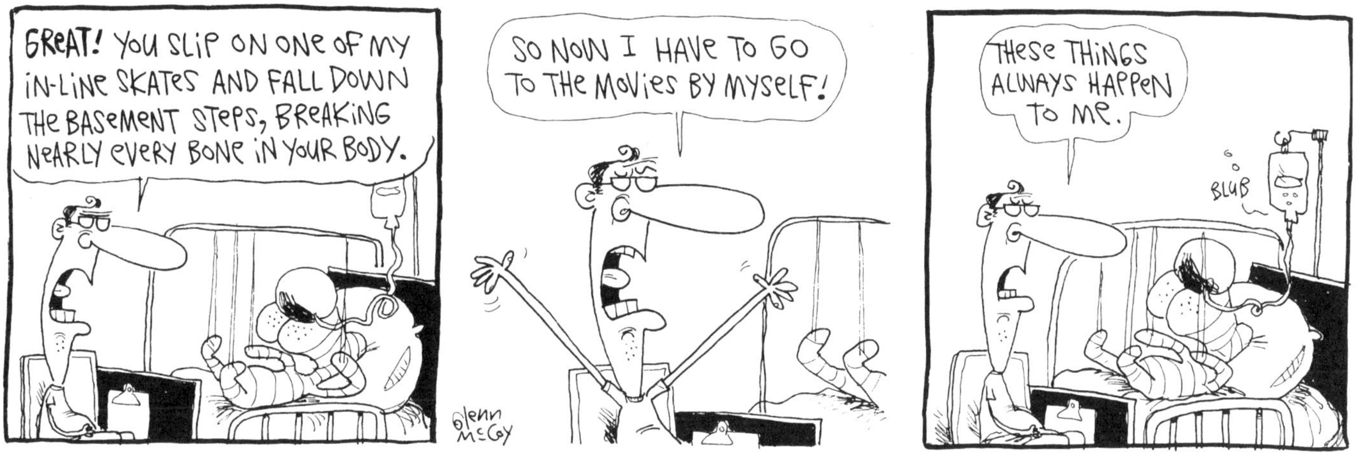
GREAT! YOU SLIP ON ONE OF MY IN-LINE SKATES AND FALL DOWN THE BASEMENT STEPS, BREAKING NEARLY EVERY BONE IN YOUR BODY.
Glenn McCoy
SO NOW I HAVE TO GO TO THE MOVIES BY MYSELF!
THESE THINGS ALWAYS HAPPEN TO ME.
BLUB

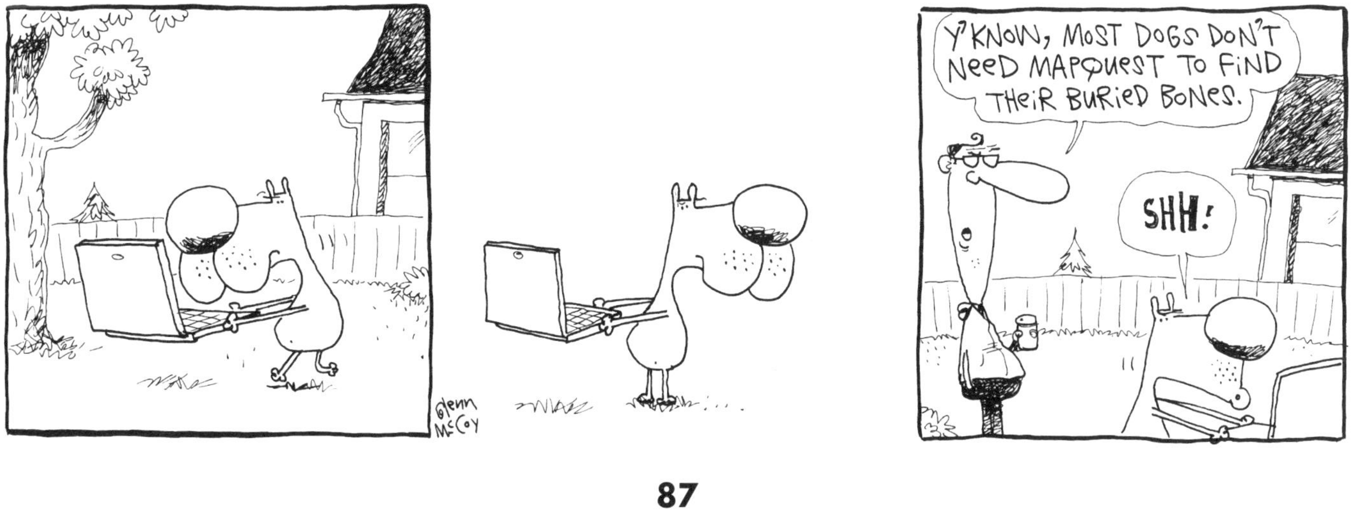
Glenn McCoy
Y'KNOW, MOST DOGS DON'T NEED MAPQUEST TO FIND THEIR BURIED BONES.
SHH!

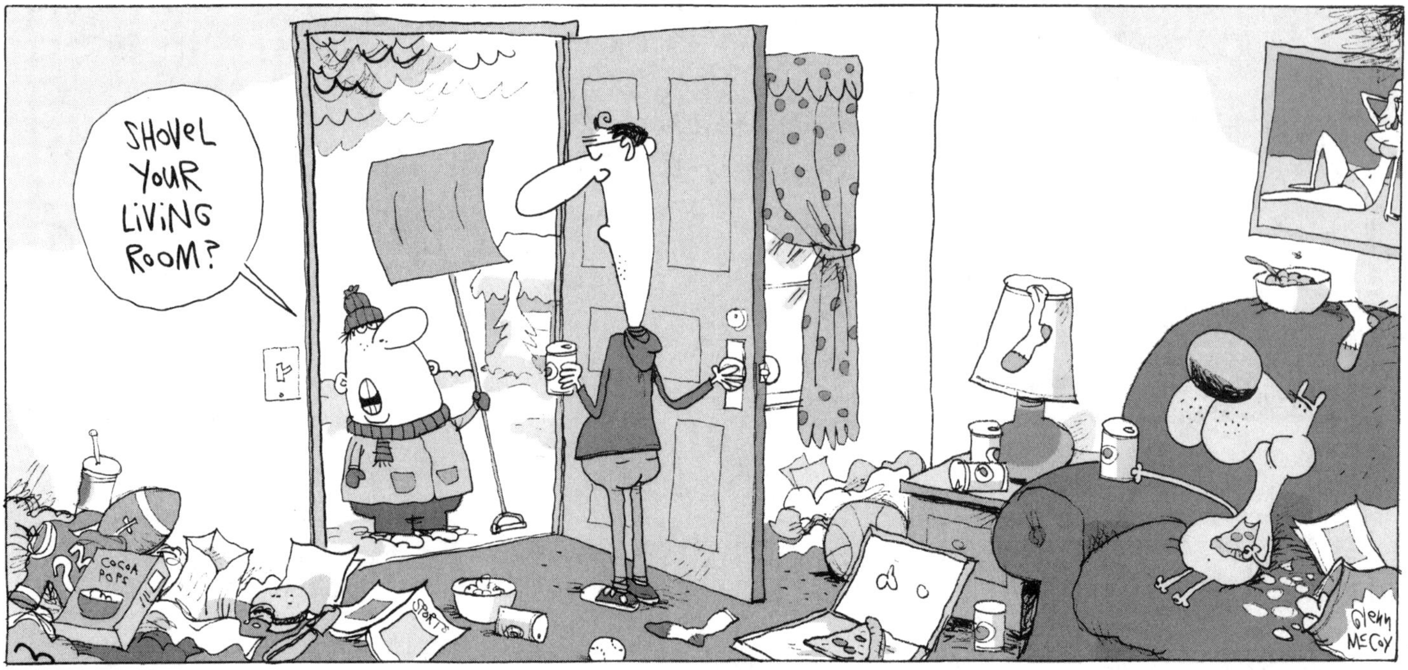
SHOVEL YOUR LIVING ROOM?
GLENN McCOY

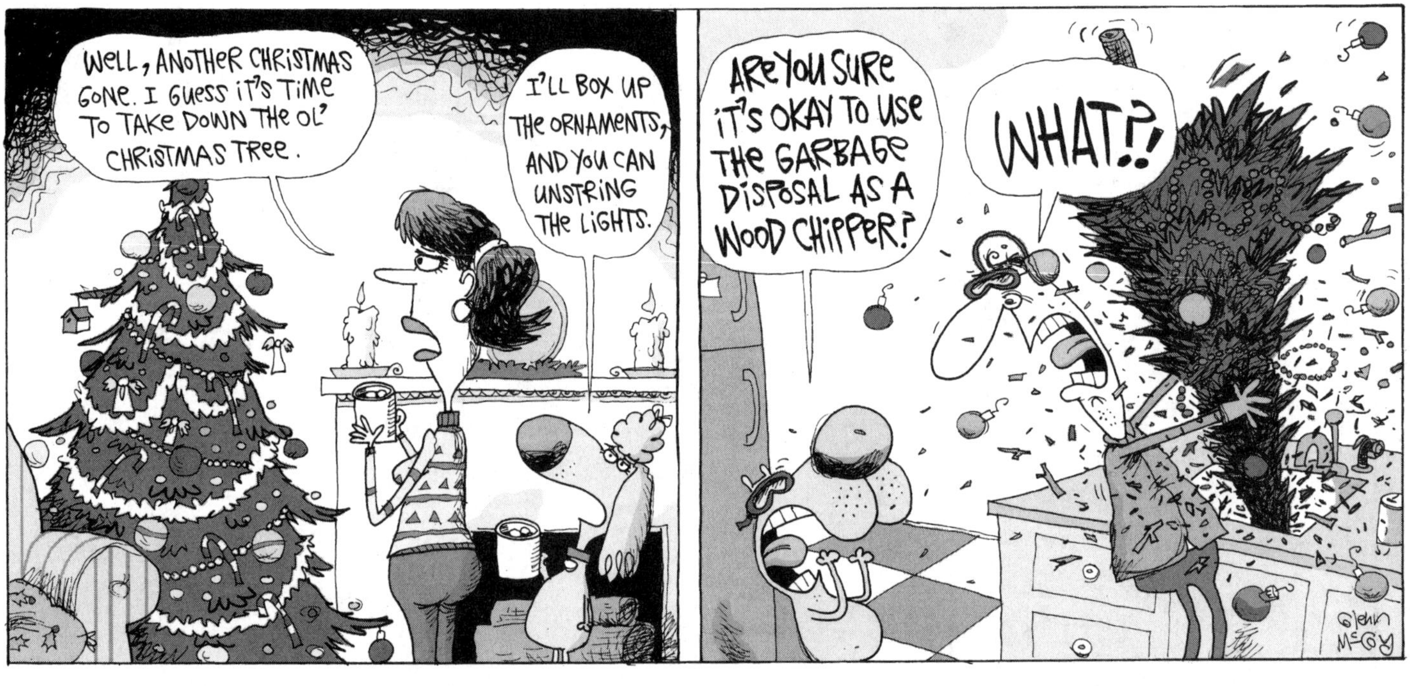
WELL, ANOTHER CHRISTMAS GONE. I GUESS IT'S TIME TO TAKE DOWN THE OL' CHRISTMAS TREE.
I'LL BOX UP THE ORNAMENTS, AND YOU CAN UNSTRING THE LIGHTS.
ARE YOU SURE IT'S OKAY TO USE THE GARBAGE DISPOSAL AS A WOOD CHIPPER?
WHAT!?!
GLENN McCOY

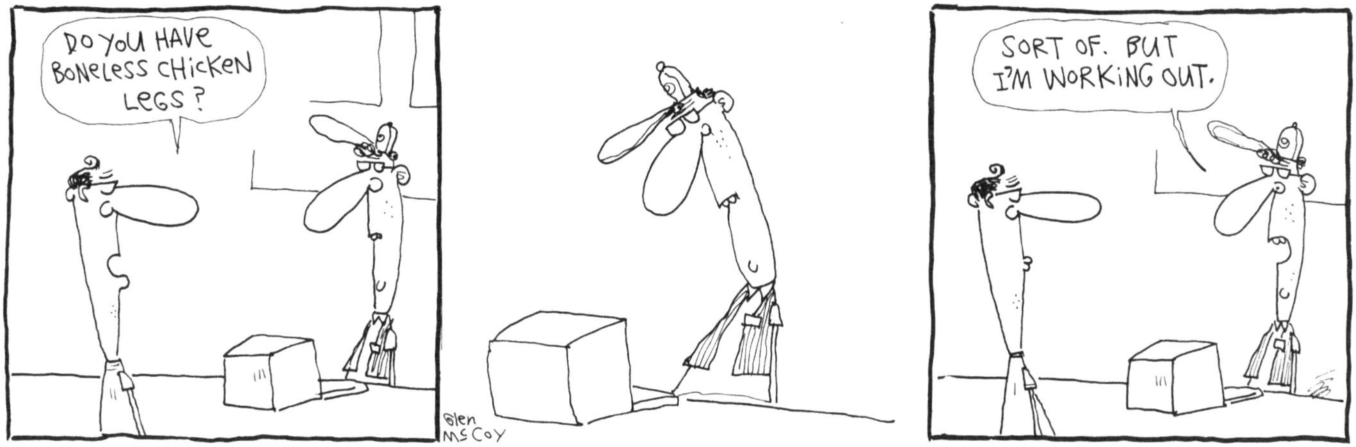
DO YOU HAVE BONELESS CHICKEN LEGS?
SORT OF. BUT I'M WORKING OUT.

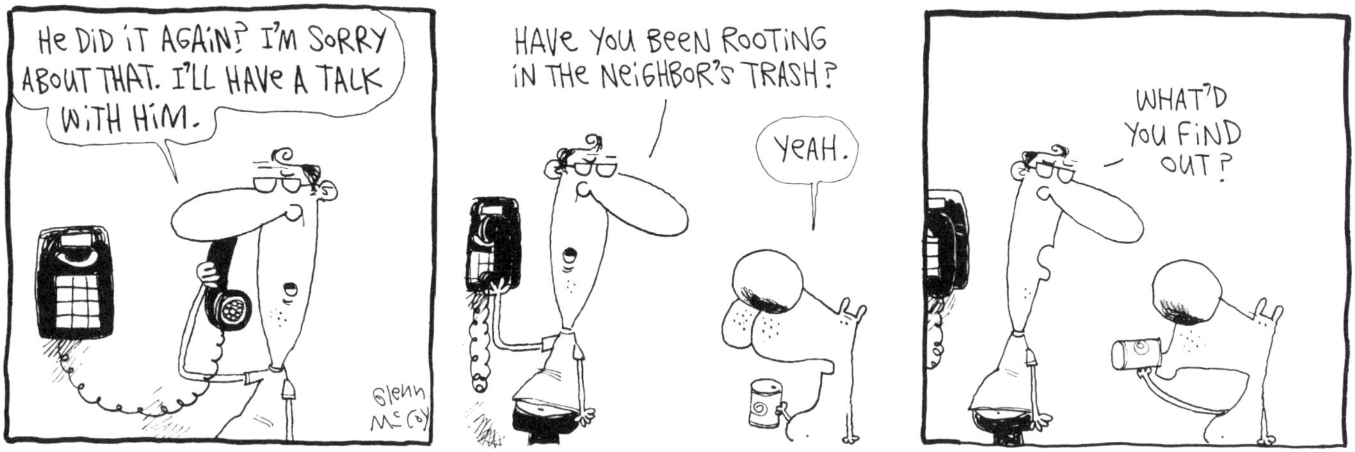
HE DID IT AGAIN? I'M SORRY ABOUT THAT. I'LL HAVE A TALK WITH HIM.
HAVE YOU BEEN ROOTING IN THE NEIGHBOR'S TRASH?
YEAH.
WHAT'D YOU FIND OUT?

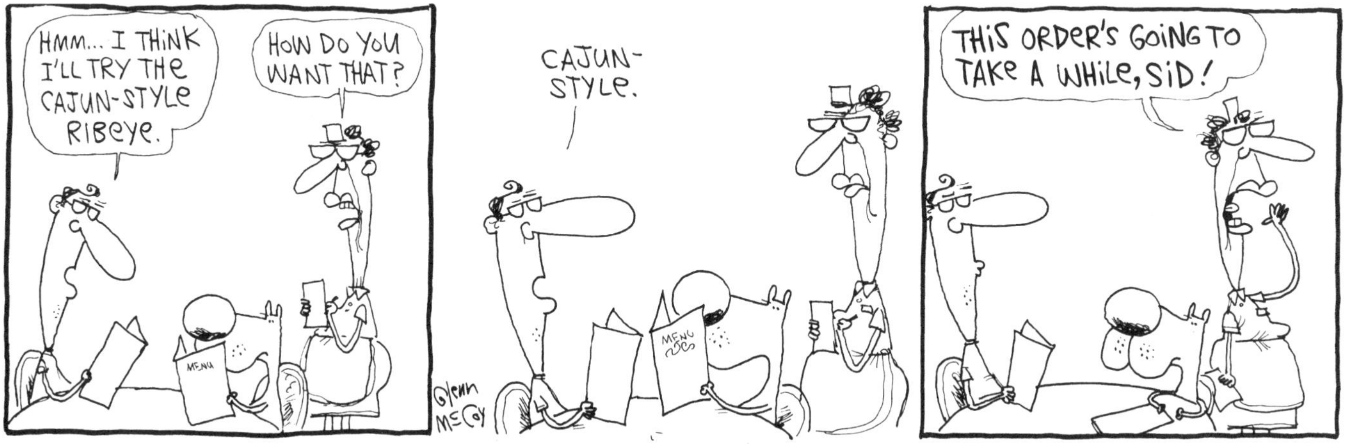
HMM... I THINK I'LL TRY THE CAJUN-STYLE RIBEYE.
HOW DO YOU WANT THAT?
CAJUN-STYLE.
THIS ORDER'S GOING TO TAKE A WHILE, SID!

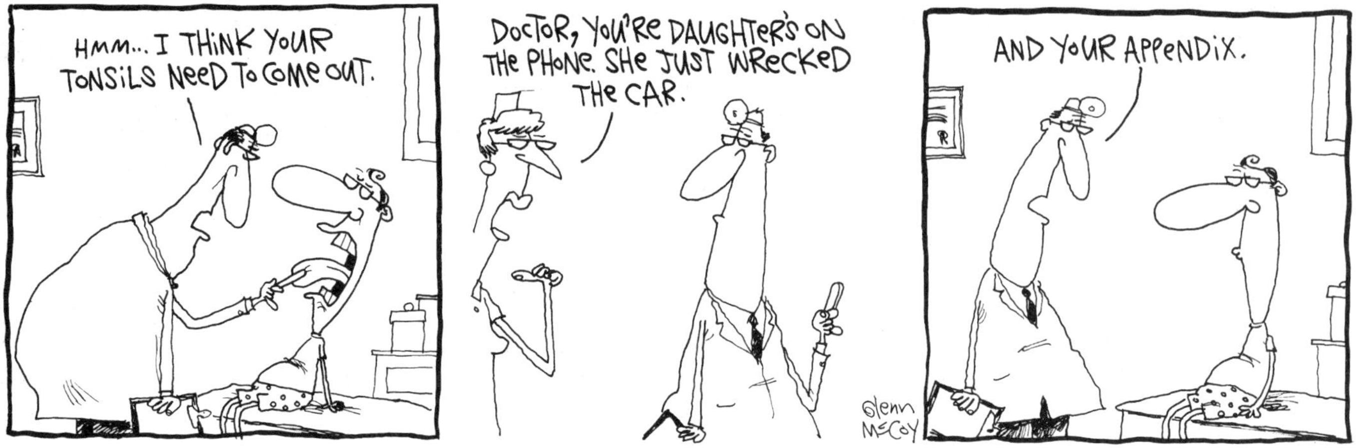
HMM... I THINK YOUR TONSILS NEED TO COME OUT.
DOCTOR, YOU'RE DAUGHTER'S ON THE PHONE. SHE JUST WRECKED THE CAR.
AND YOUR APPENDIX.
Glenn McCoy

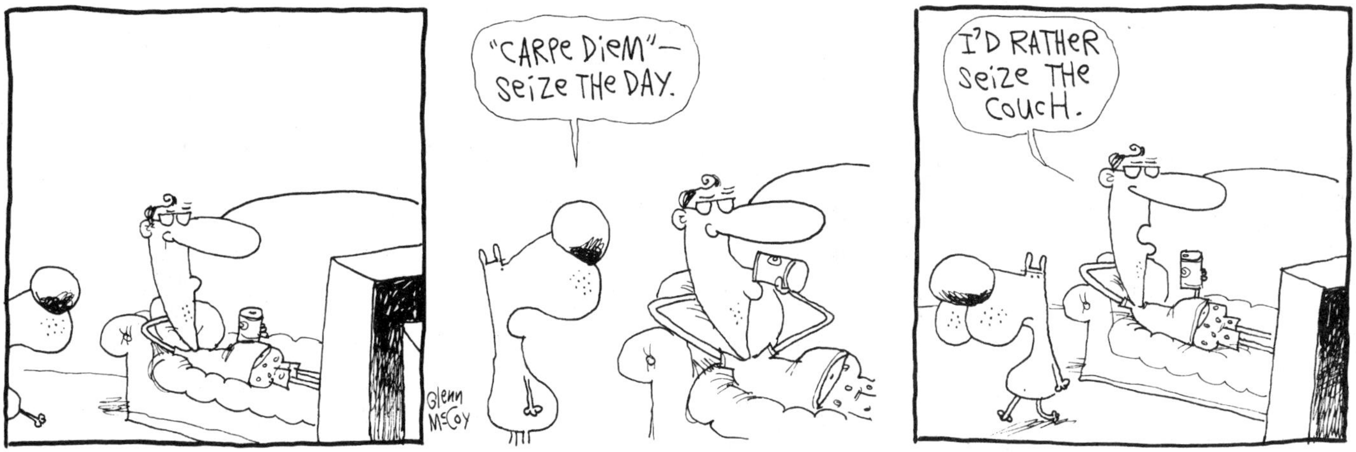
Glenn McCoy
"CARPE DIEM"— SEIZE THE DAY.
I'D RATHER SEIZE THE COUCH.

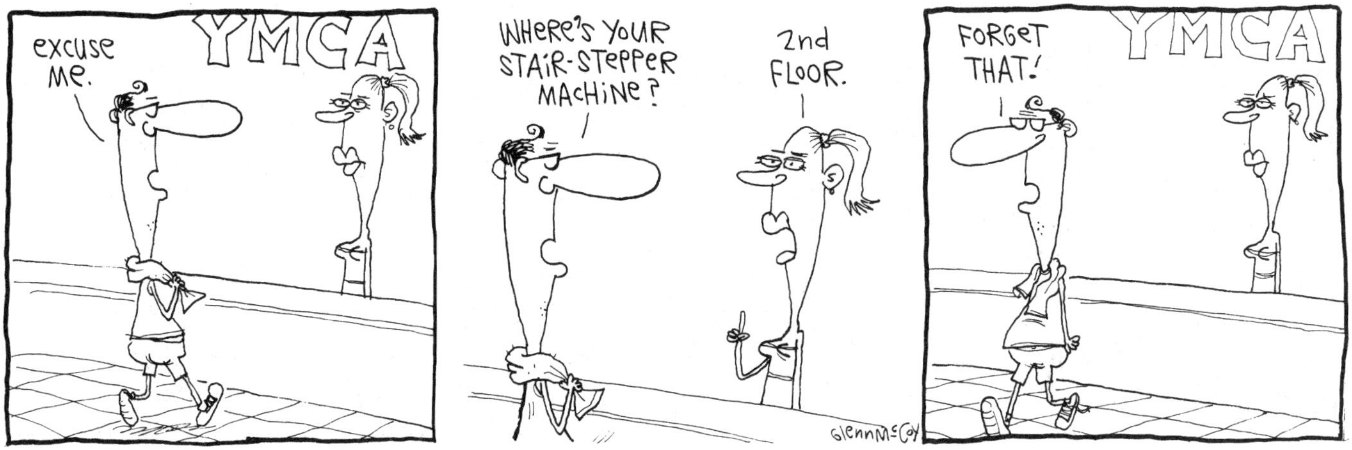
YMCA
EXCUSE ME.
WHERE'S YOUR STAIR-STEPPER MACHINE?
2nd FLOOR.
GlennMcCoy
FORGET THAT!
YMCA

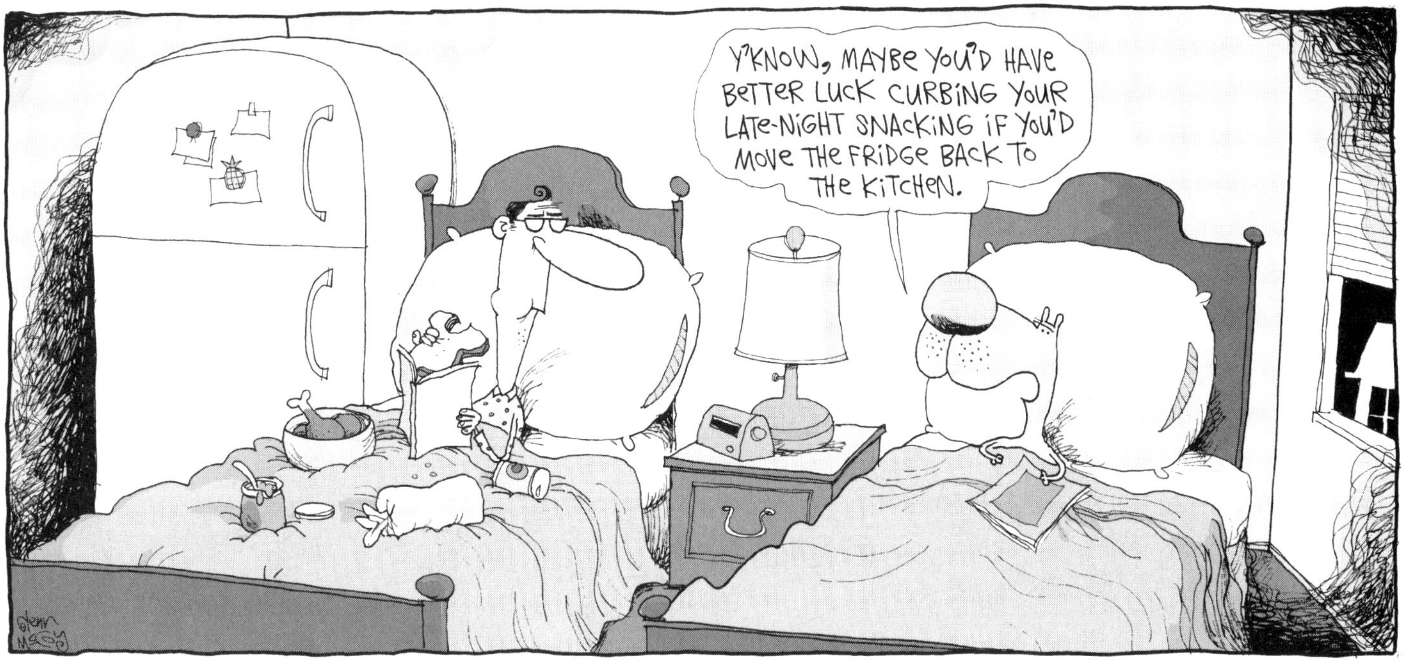
Y'KNOW, MAYBE YOU'D HAVE BETTER LUCK CURBING YOUR LATE-NIGHT SNACKING IF YOU'D MOVE THE FRIDGE BACK TO THE KITCHEN.

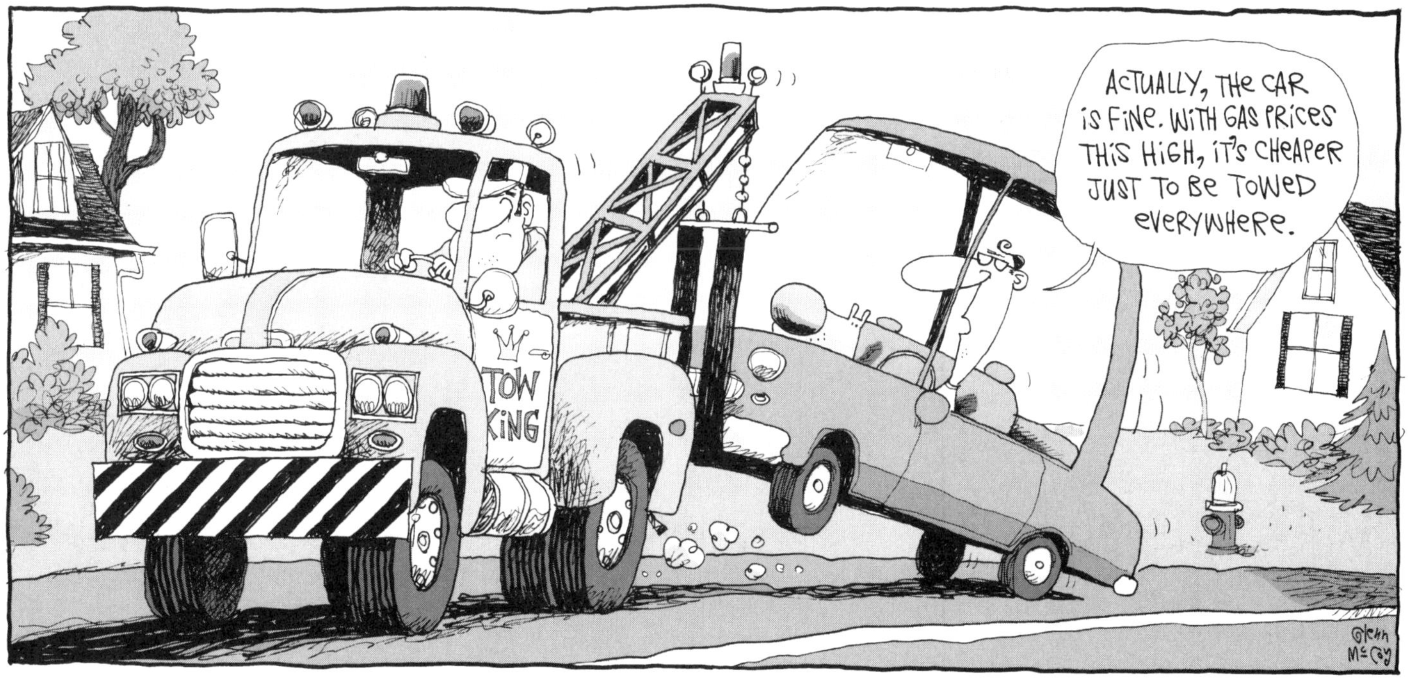
TOW KING
ACTUALLY, THE CAR IS FINE. WITH GAS PRICES THIS HIGH, IT'S CHEAPER JUST TO BE TOWED EVERYWHERE.

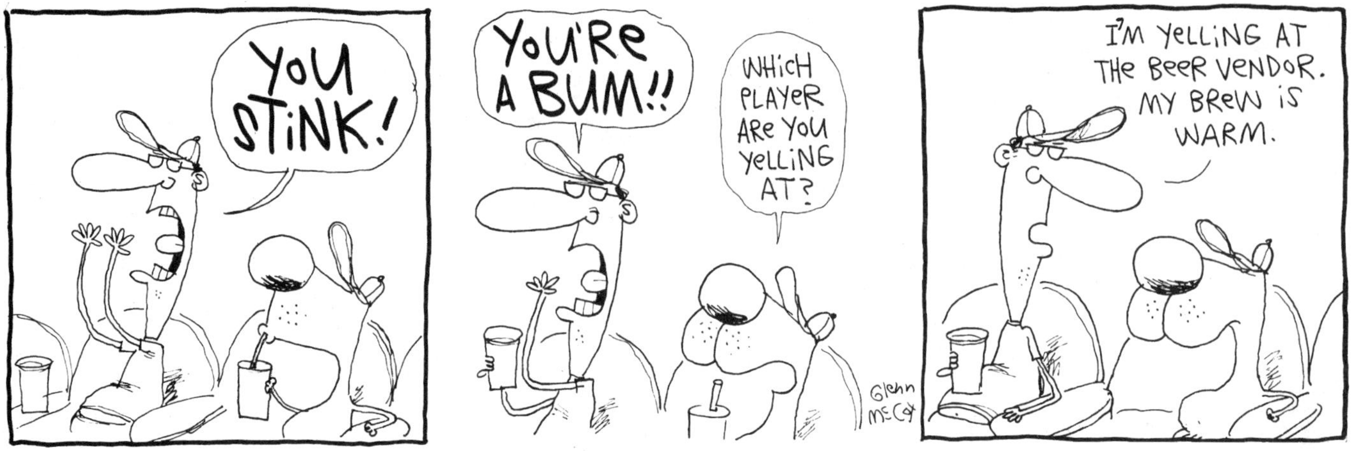
YOU STINK!
YOU'RE A BUM!!
WHICH PLAYER ARE YOU YELLING AT?
Glenn McCoy
I'M YELLING AT THE BEER VENDOR. MY BREW IS WARM.

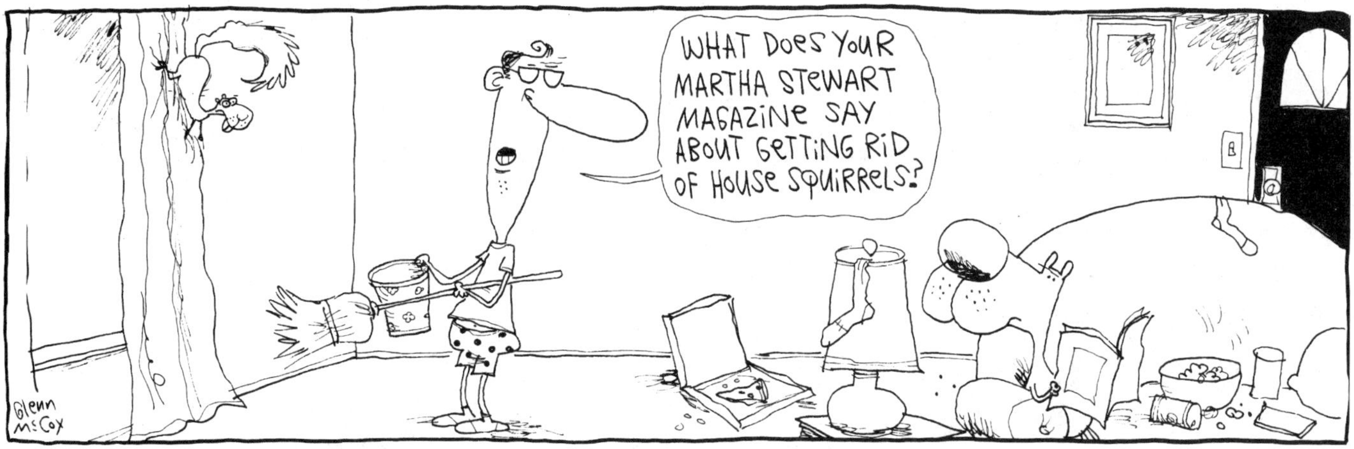
WHAT DOES YOUR MARTHA STEWART MAGAZINE SAY ABOUT GETTING RID OF HOUSE SQUIRRELS?
Glenn McCoy

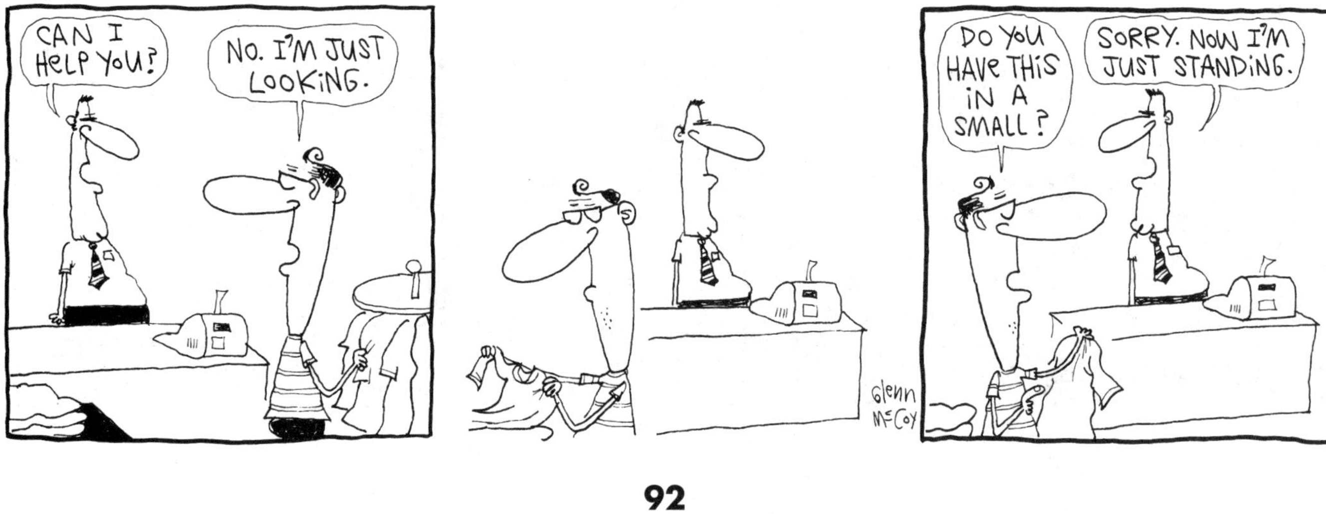
CAN I HELP YOU?
NO. I'M JUST LOOKING.
Glenn McCoy
DO YOU HAVE THIS IN A SMALL?
SORRY. NOW I'M JUST STANDING.

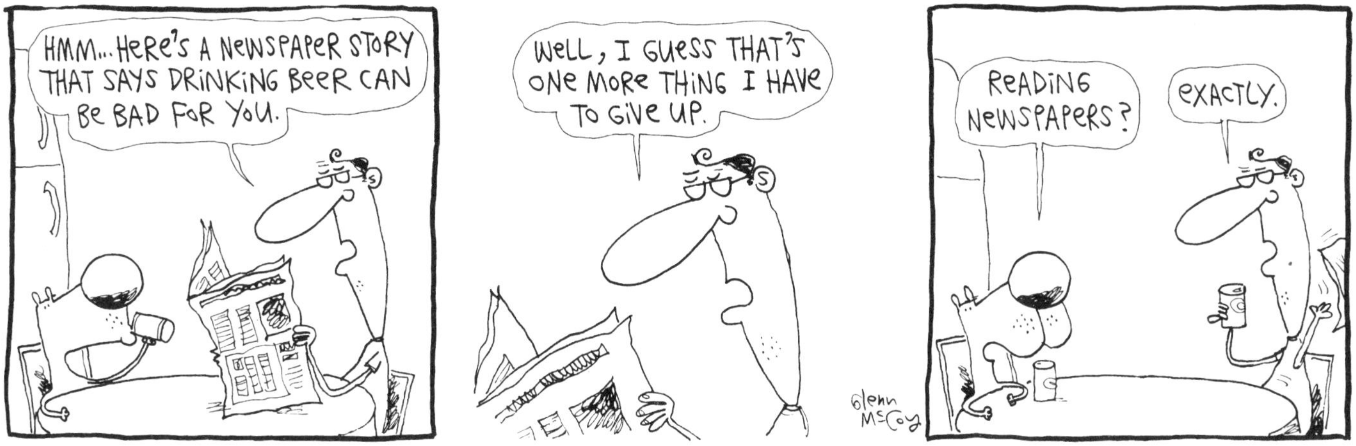
HMM... HERE'S A NEWSPAPER STORY THAT SAYS DRINKING BEER CAN BE BAD FOR YOU.
WELL, I GUESS THAT'S ONE MORE THING I HAVE TO GIVE UP.
READING NEWSPAPERS?
EXACTLY.
Glenn McCoy

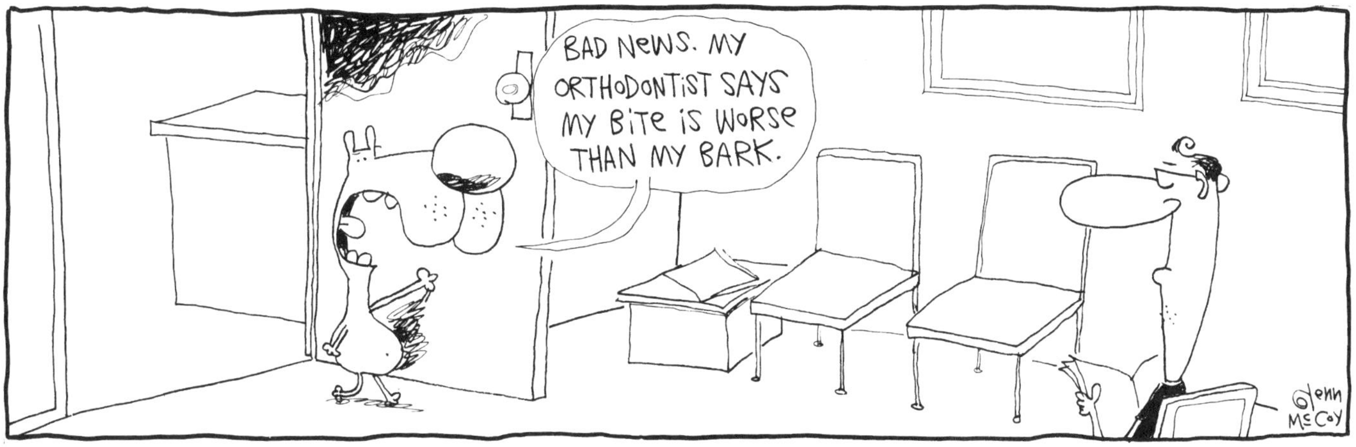
BAD NEWS. MY ORTHODONTIST SAYS MY BITE IS WORSE THAN MY BARK.
Glenn McCoy

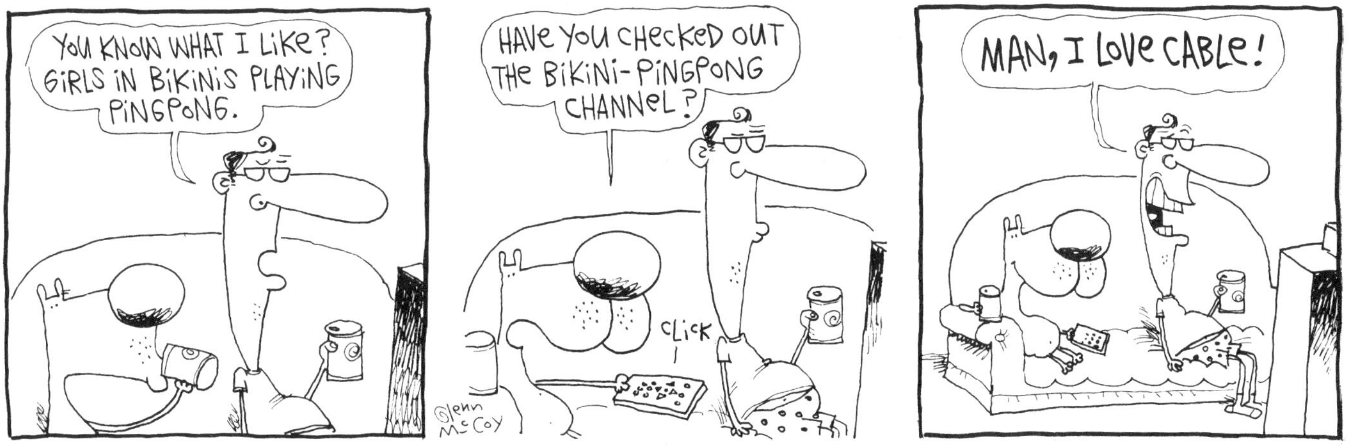
YOU KNOW WHAT I LIKE? GIRLS IN BIKINIS PLAYING PINGPONG.
HAVE YOU CHECKED OUT THE BIKINI-PINGPONG CHANNEL?
CLICK
Glenn McCoy
MAN, I LOVE CABLE!

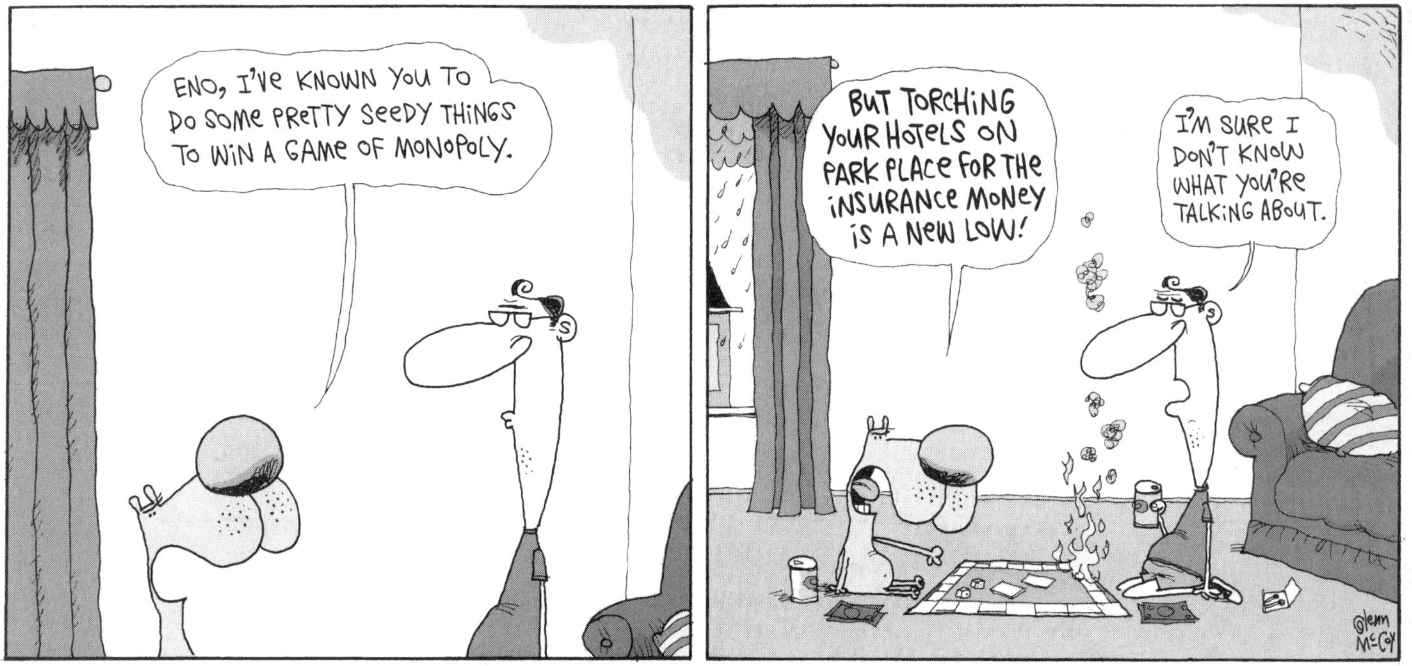
ENO, I'VE KNOWN YOU TO DO SOME PRETTY SEEDY THINGS TO WIN A GAME OF MONOPOLY.
BUT TORCHING YOUR HOTELS ON PARK PLACE FOR THE INSURANCE MONEY IS A NEW LOW!
I'M SURE I DON'T KNOW WHAT YOU'RE TALKING ABOUT.
Glenn McCoy

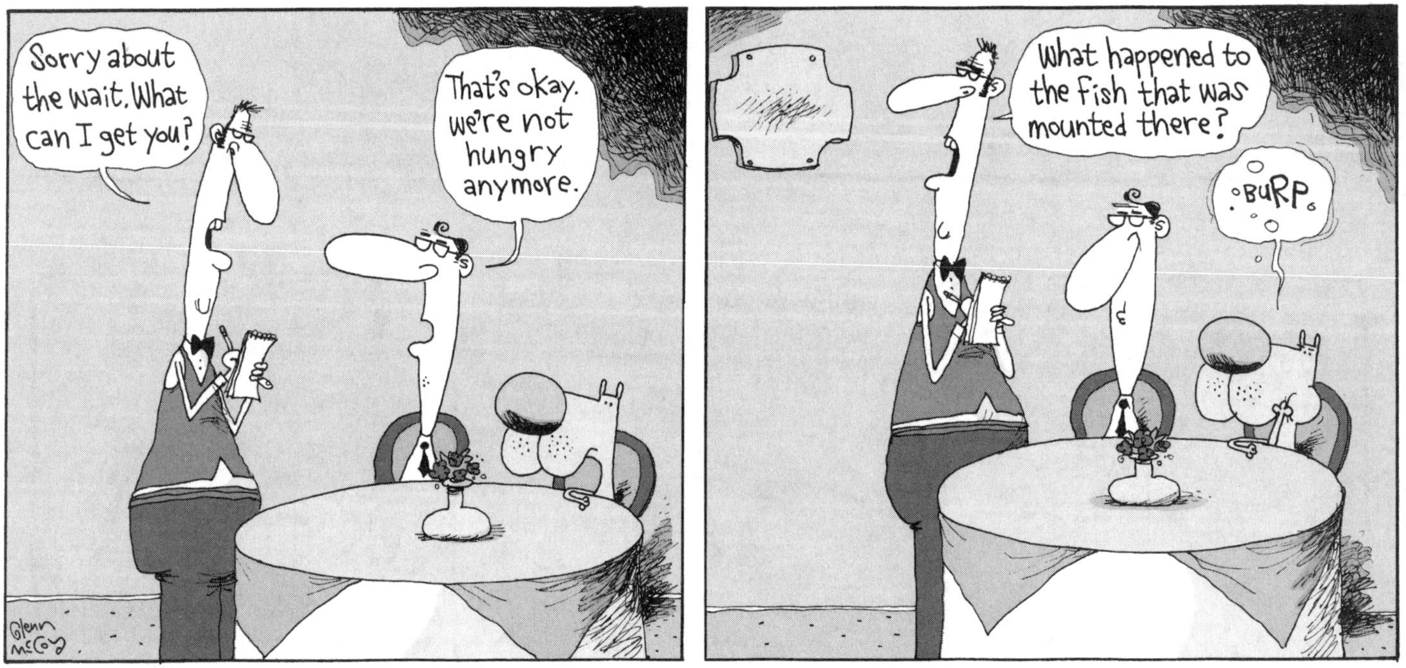
Sorry about the wait. What can I get you?
That's okay. We're not hungry anymore.
Glenn McCoy
What happened to the fish that was mounted there?
BURP

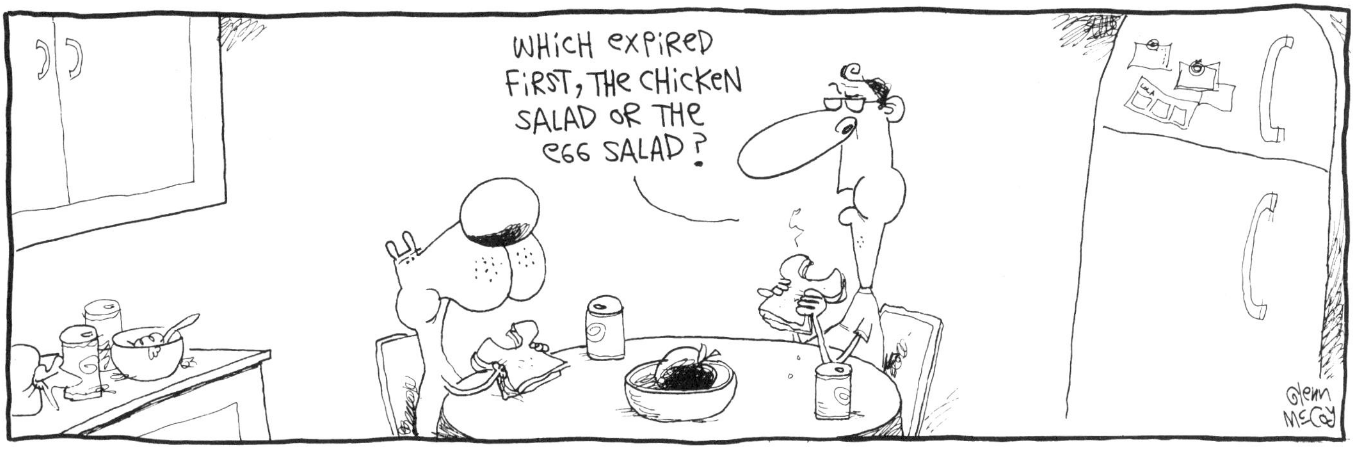
WHICH EXPIRED FIRST, THE CHICKEN SALAD OR THE EGG SALAD?
Glenn McCoy

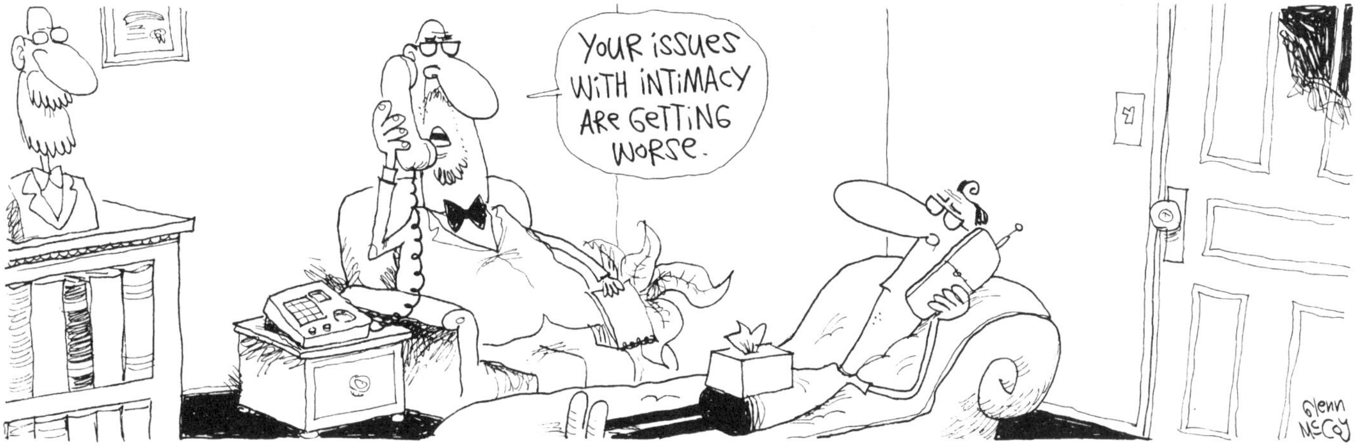
YOUR ISSUES WITH INTIMACY ARE GETTING WORSE.
Glenn McCoy

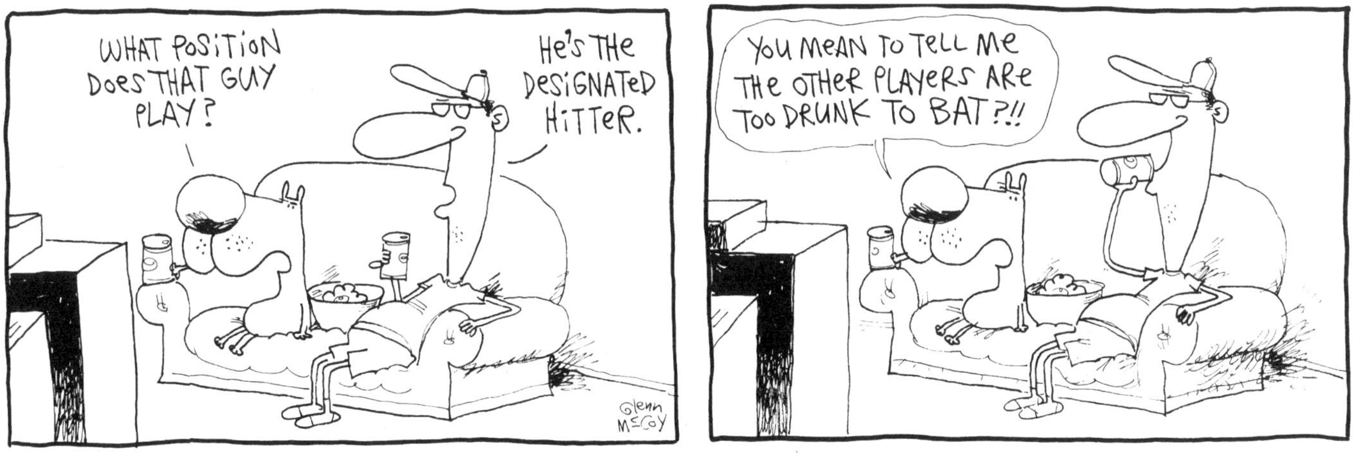
WHAT POSITION DOES THAT GUY PLAY?
HE'S THE DESIGNATED HITTER.
Glenn McCoy
YOU MEAN TO TELL ME THE OTHER PLAYERS ARE TOO DRUNK TO BAT?!!

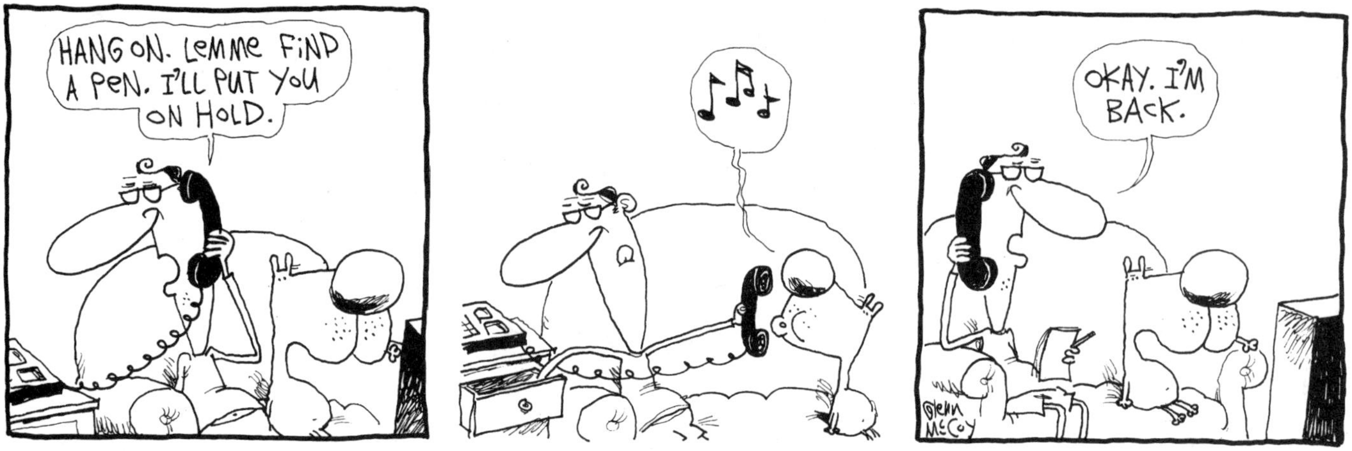
HANG ON. LEMME FIND A PEN. I'LL PUT YOU ON HOLD.
OKAY. I'M BACK.
Glenn McCoy

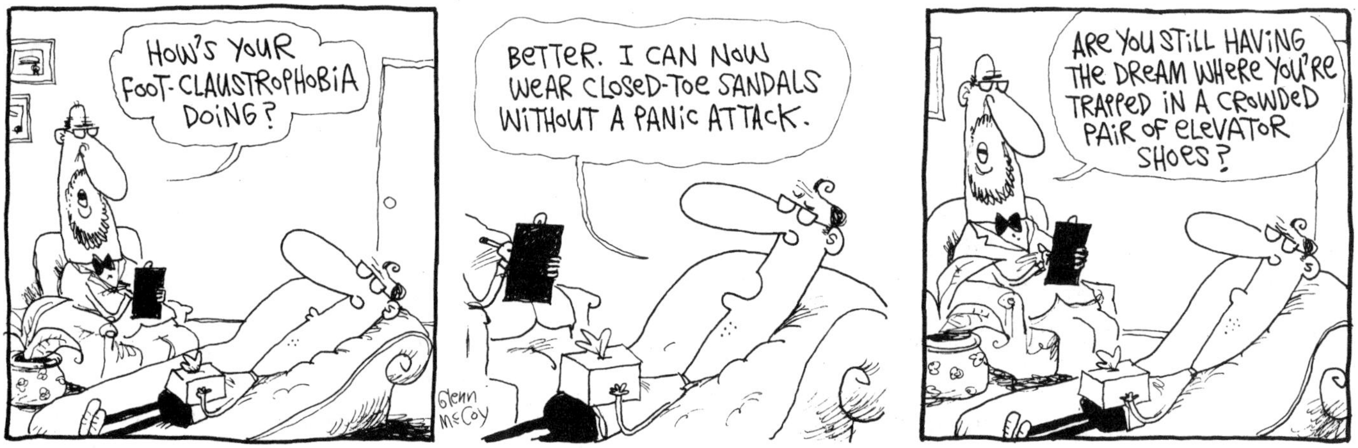
HOW'S YOUR FOOT-CLAUSTROPHOBIA DOING?
BETTER. I CAN NOW WEAR CLOSED-TOE SANDALS WITHOUT A PANIC ATTACK.
ARE YOU STILL HAVING THE DREAM WHERE YOU'RE TRAPPED IN A CROWDED PAIR OF ELEVATOR SHOES?
Glenn McCoy

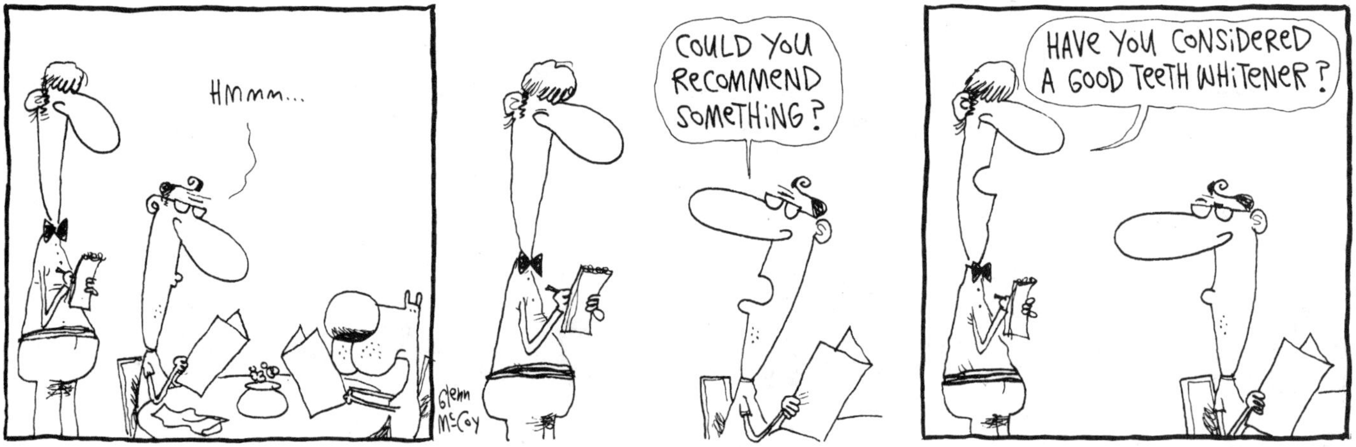
HMMM...
COULD YOU RECOMMEND SOMETHING?
HAVE YOU CONSIDERED A GOOD TEETH WHITENER?
Glenn McCoy

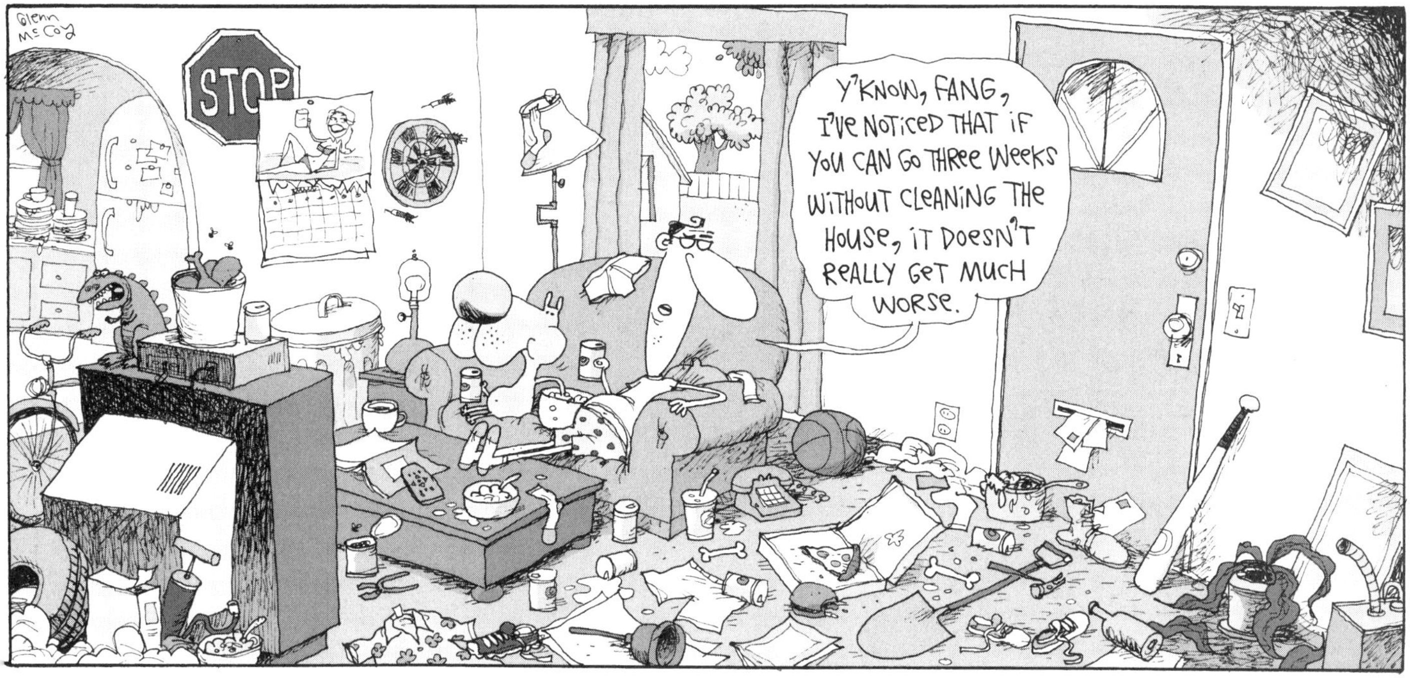
STOP
Y'KNOW, FANG, I'VE NOTICED THAT IF YOU CAN GO THREE WEEKS WITHOUT CLEANING THE HOUSE, IT DOESN'T REALLY GET MUCH WORSE.

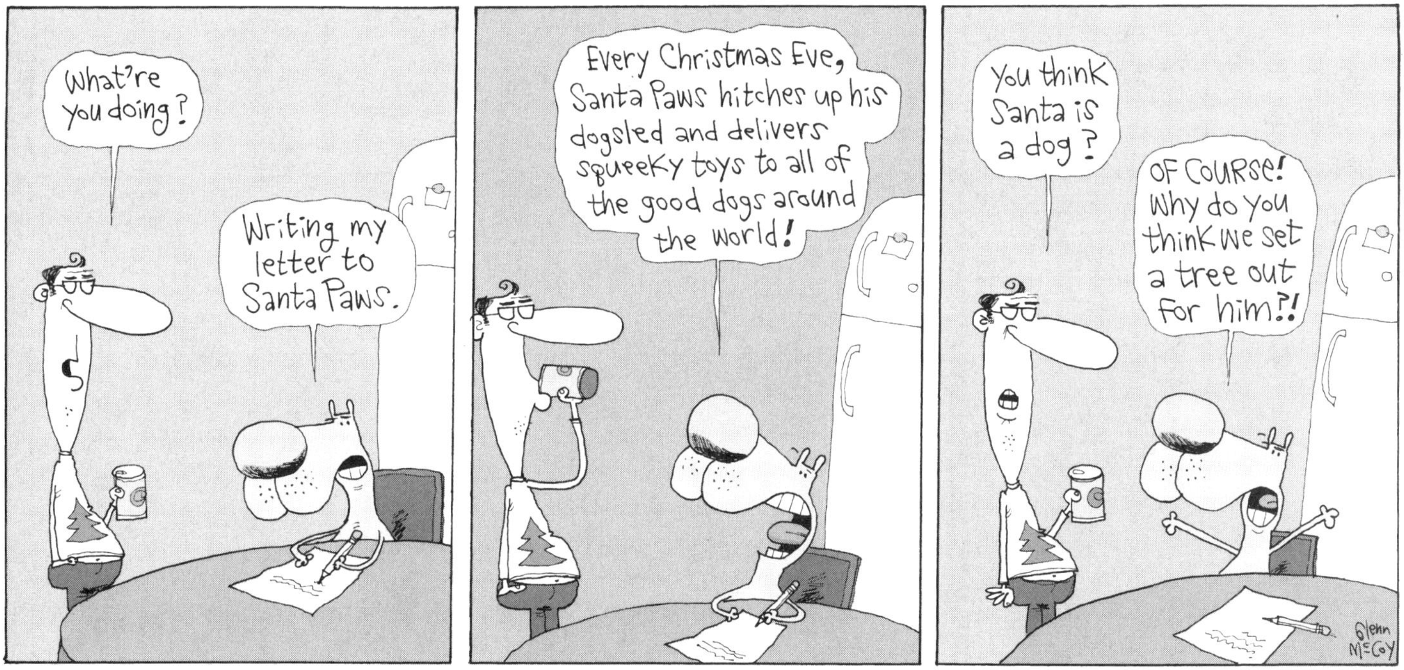
What're you doing?
Writing my letter to Santa Paws.
Every Christmas Eve, Santa Paws hitches up his dogsled and delivers squeeky toys to all of the good dogs around the world!
You think Santa is a dog?
OF COURSE! Why do you think we set a tree out for him?!

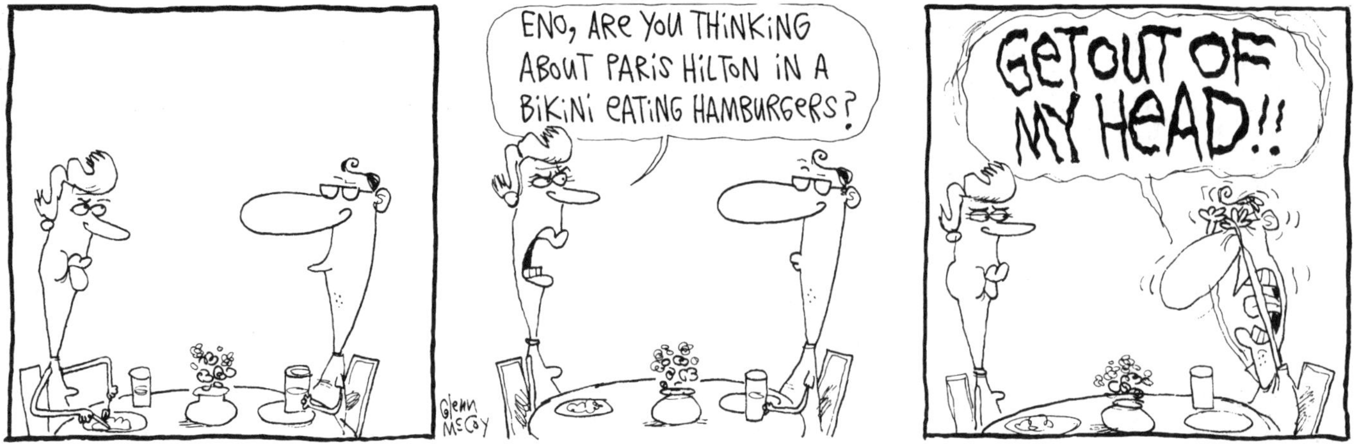
ENO, ARE YOU THINKING ABOUT PARIS HILTON IN A BIKINI EATING HAMBURGERS?
GET OUT OF MY HEAD!!
Glenn McCoy

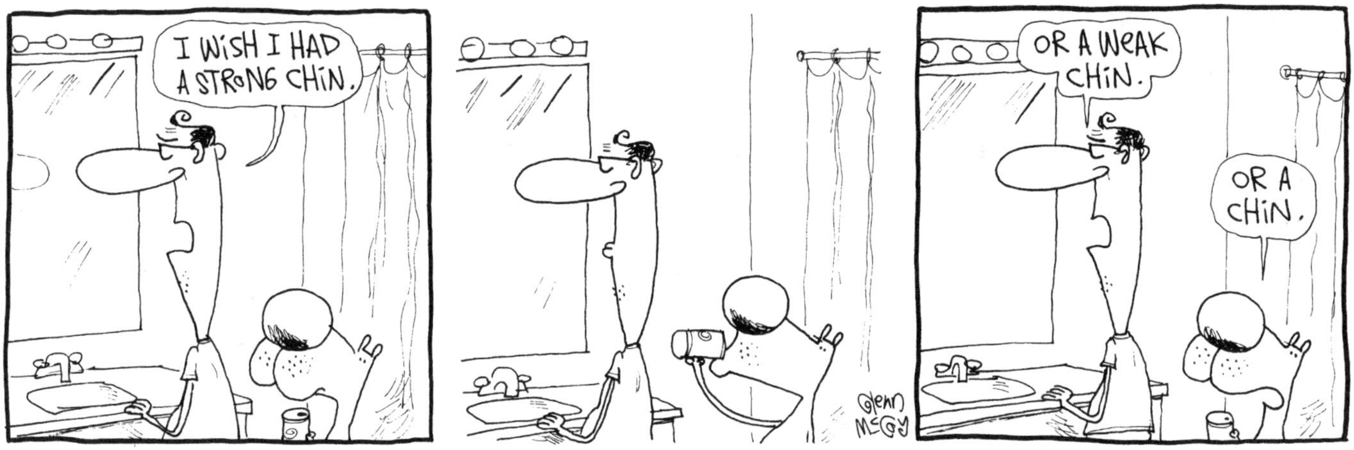
I WISH I HAD A STRONG CHIN.
OR A WEAK CHIN.
OR A CHIN.
Glenn McCoy

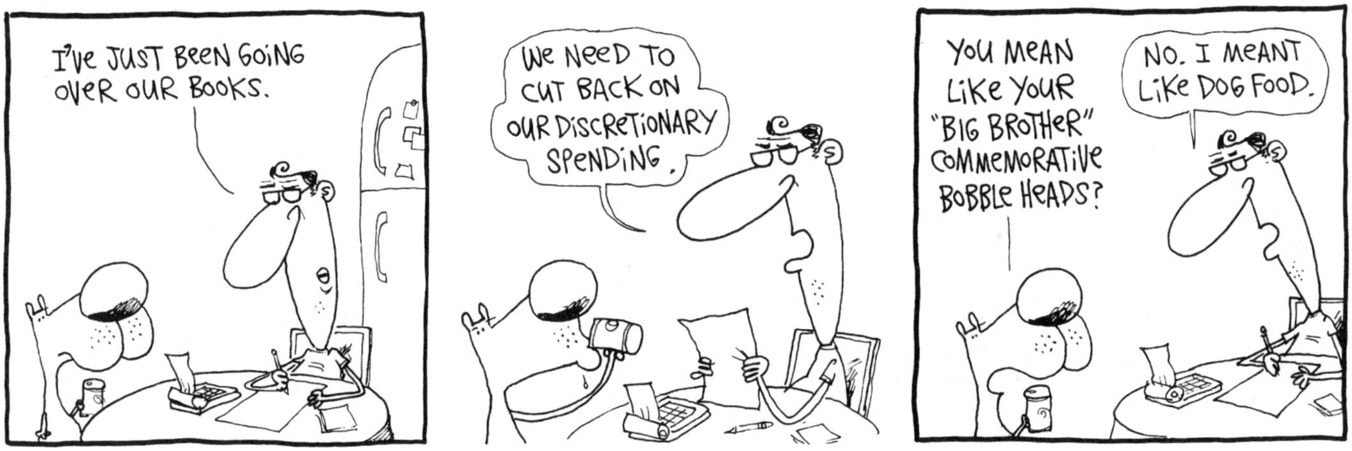
I'VE JUST BEEN GOING OVER OUR BOOKS.
WE NEED TO CUT BACK ON OUR DISCRETIONARY SPENDING.
YOU MEAN LIKE YOUR "BIG BROTHER" COMMEMORATIVE BOBBLE HEADS?
NO. I MEANT LIKE DOG FOOD.

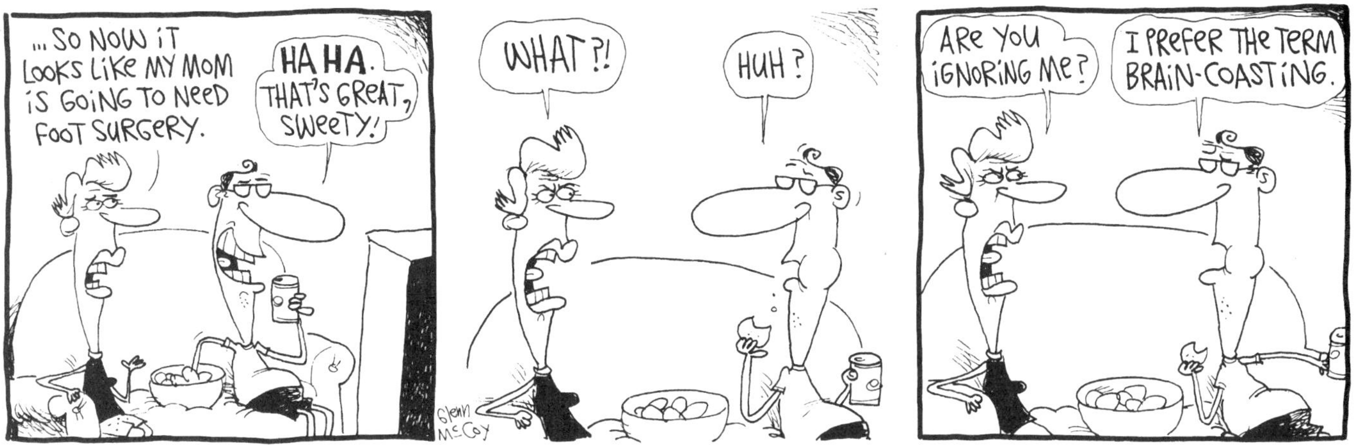
...SO NOW IT LOOKS LIKE MY MOM IS GOING TO NEED FOOT SURGERY.
HA HA. THAT'S GREAT, SWEETY!
WHAT?!
HUH?
ARE YOU IGNORING ME?
I PREFER THE TERM BRAIN-COASTING.

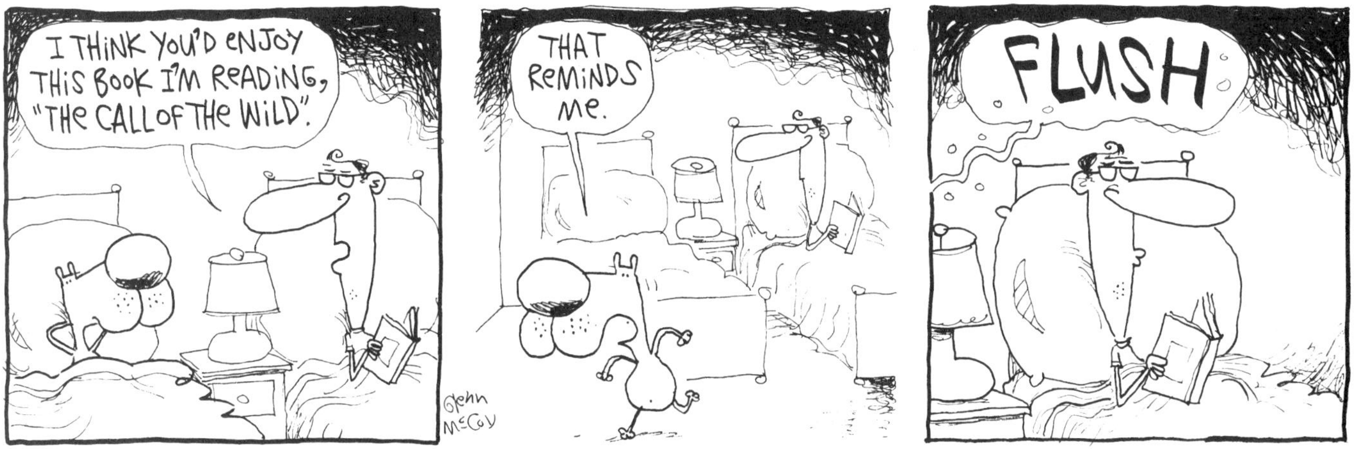
I THINK YOU'D ENJOY THIS BOOK I'M READING, "THE CALL OF THE WILD".
THAT REMINDS ME.
FLUSH

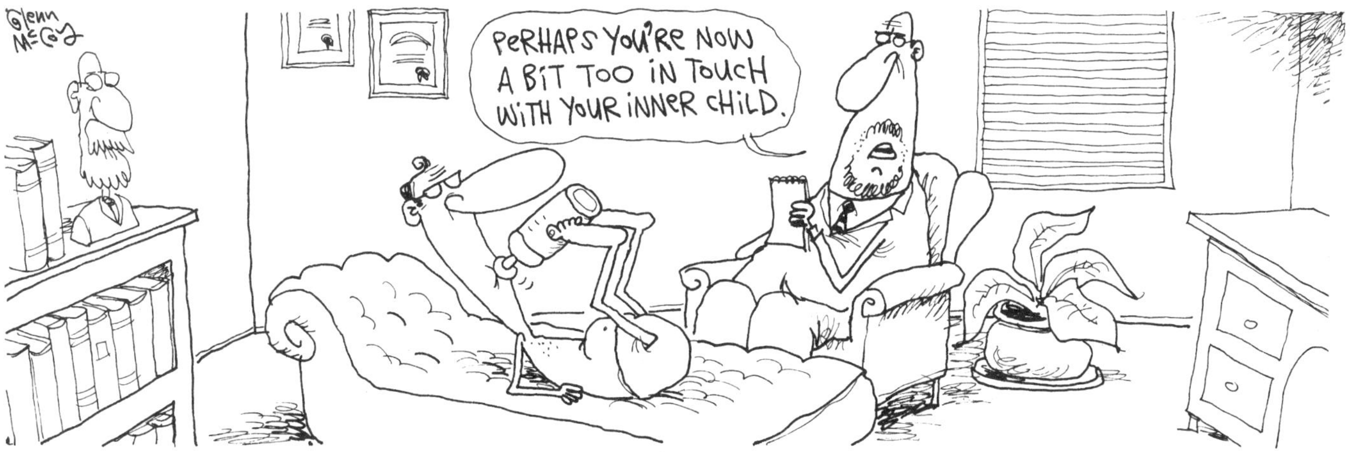
PERHAPS YOU'RE NOW A BIT TOO IN TOUCH WITH YOUR INNER CHILD.

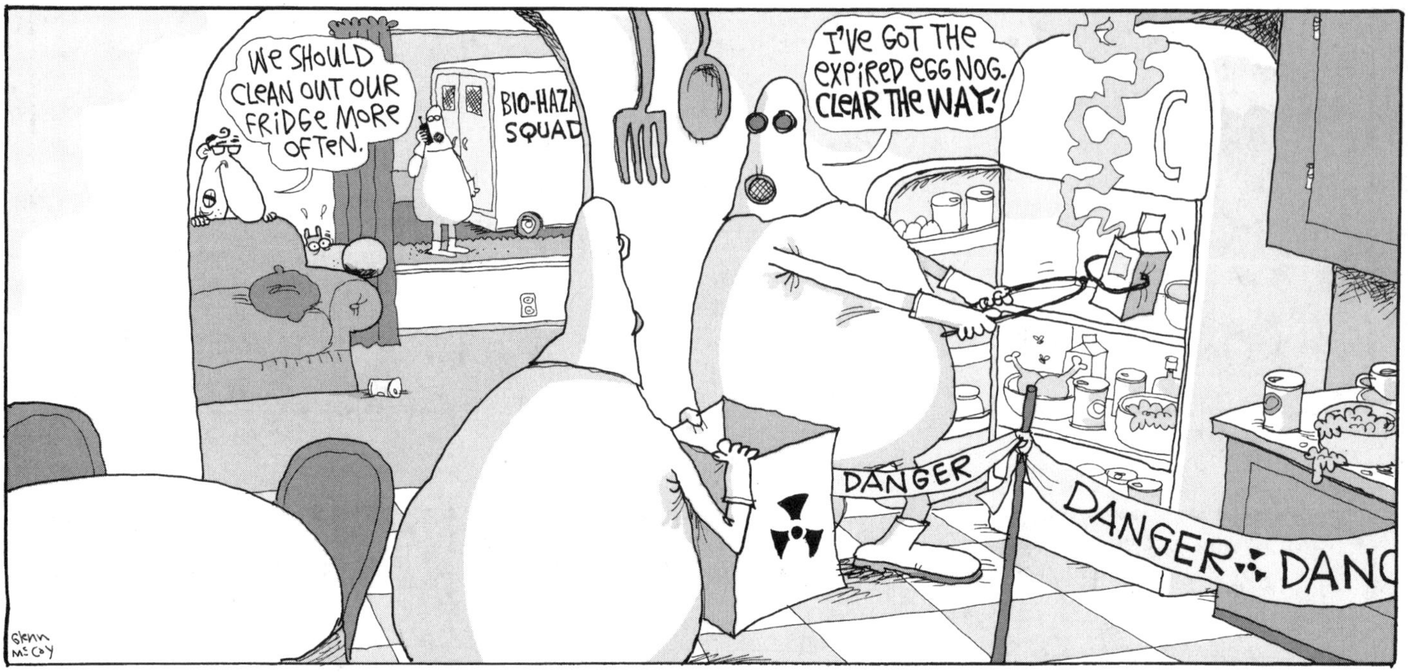
WE SHOULD CLEAN OUT OUR FRIDGE MORE OFTEN.
BIO-HAZA
SQUAD
I'VE GOT THE EXPIRED EGG NOG. CLEAR THE WAY!
DANGER
DANGER
DANC
Glenn McCoy

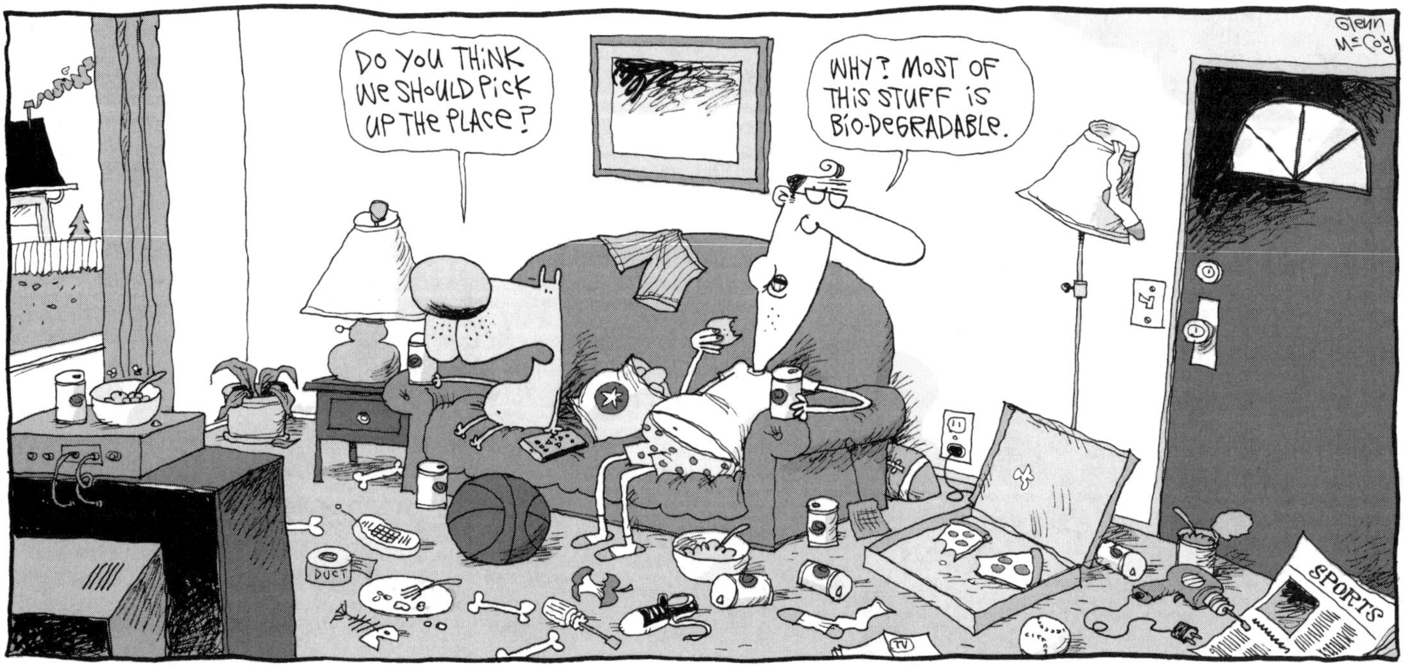
DO YOU THINK WE SHOULD PICK UP THE PLACE?
WHY? MOST OF THIS STUFF IS BIO-DEGRADABLE.
Glenn McCoy
DUCT
TV
SPORTS

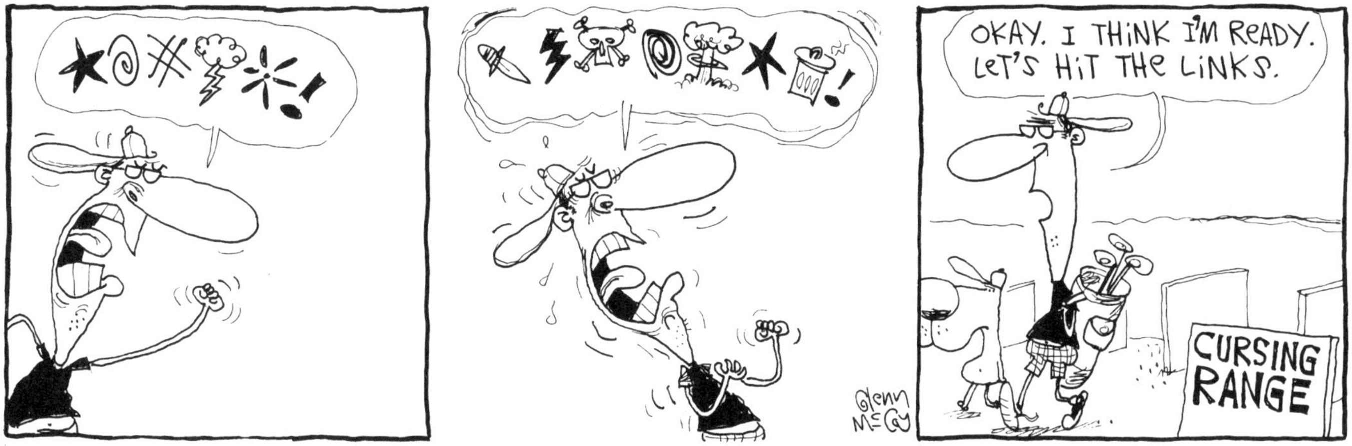
OKAY. I THINK I'M READY. LET'S HIT THE LINKS.
CURSING RANGE

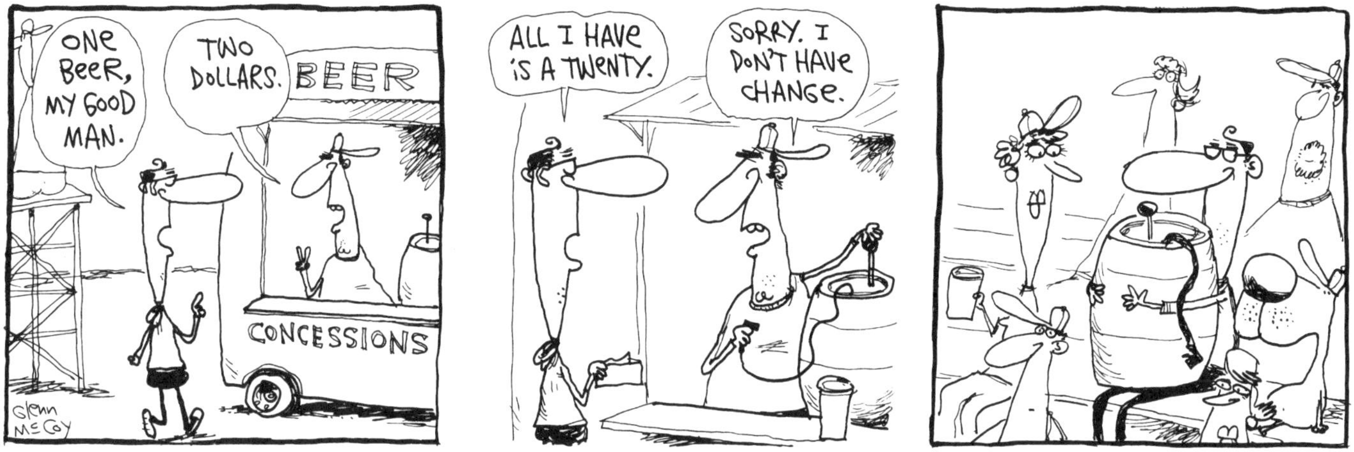
ONE BEER, MY GOOD MAN.
TWO DOLLARS.
BEER
CONCESSIONS
ALL I HAVE IS A TWENTY.
SORRY. I DON'T HAVE CHANGE.

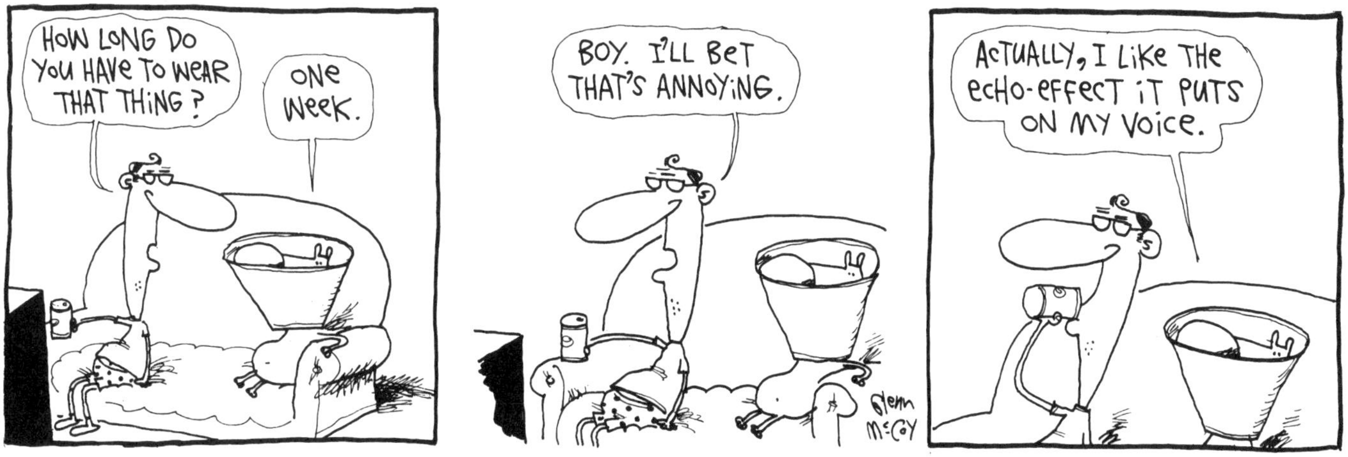
HOW LONG DO YOU HAVE TO WEAR THAT THING?
ONE WEEK.
BOY. I'LL BET THAT'S ANNOYING.
ACTUALLY, I LIKE THE ECHO-EFFECT IT PUTS ON MY VOICE.

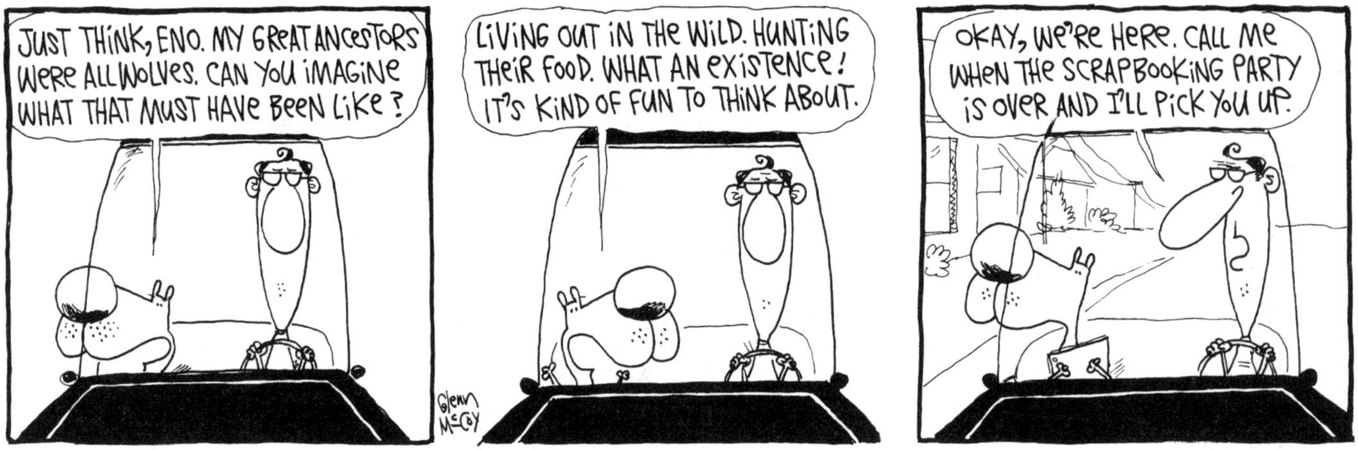
JUST THINK, ENO. MY GREAT ANCESTORS WERE ALL WOLVES. CAN YOU IMAGINE WHAT THAT MUST HAVE BEEN LIKE?
LIVING OUT IN THE WILD. HUNTING THEIR FOOD. WHAT AN EXISTENCE! IT'S KIND OF FUN TO THINK ABOUT.
OKAY, WE'RE HERE. CALL ME WHEN THE SCRAPBOOKING PARTY IS OVER AND I'LL PICK YOU UP.
Glenn McCoy

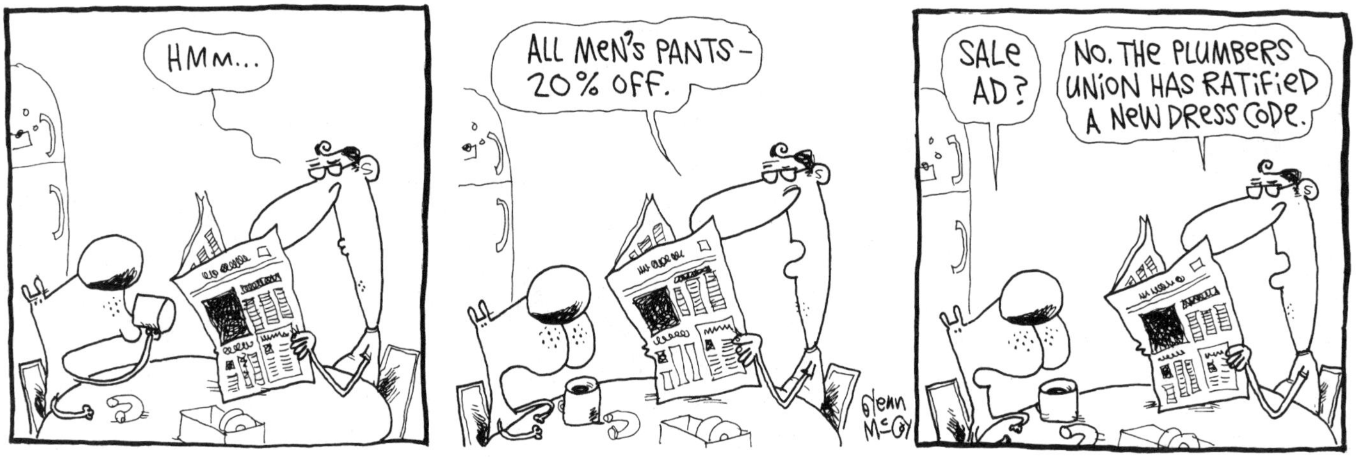
HMM...
ALL MEN'S PANTS— 20% OFF.
SALE AD?
NO. THE PLUMBERS UNION HAS RATIFIED A NEW DRESS CODE.
Glenn McCoy

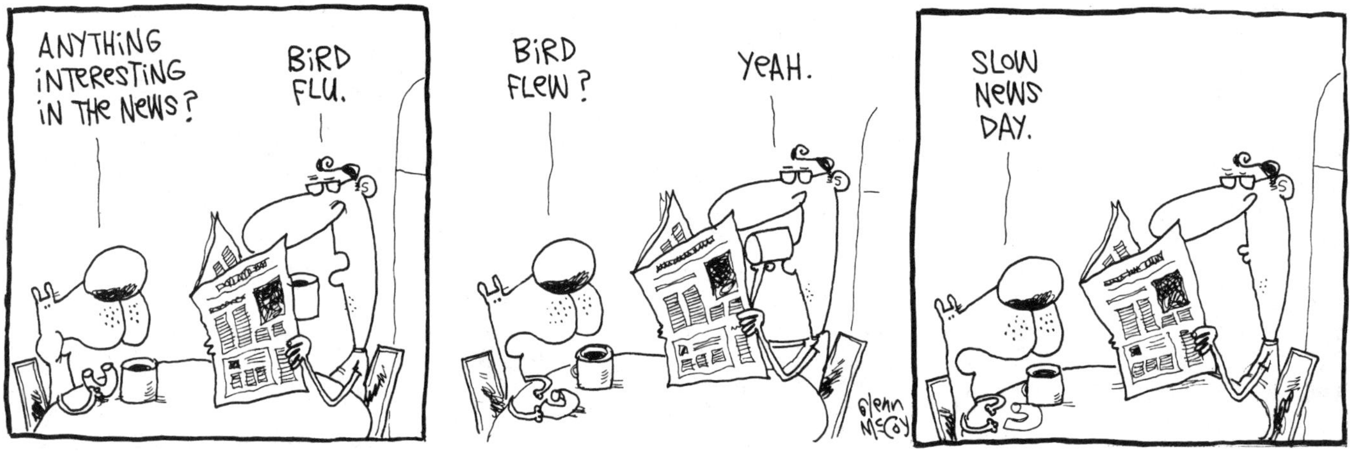
ANYTHING INTERESTING IN THE NEWS?
BIRD FLU.
BIRD FLEW?
YEAH.
SLOW NEWS DAY.
Glenn McCoy

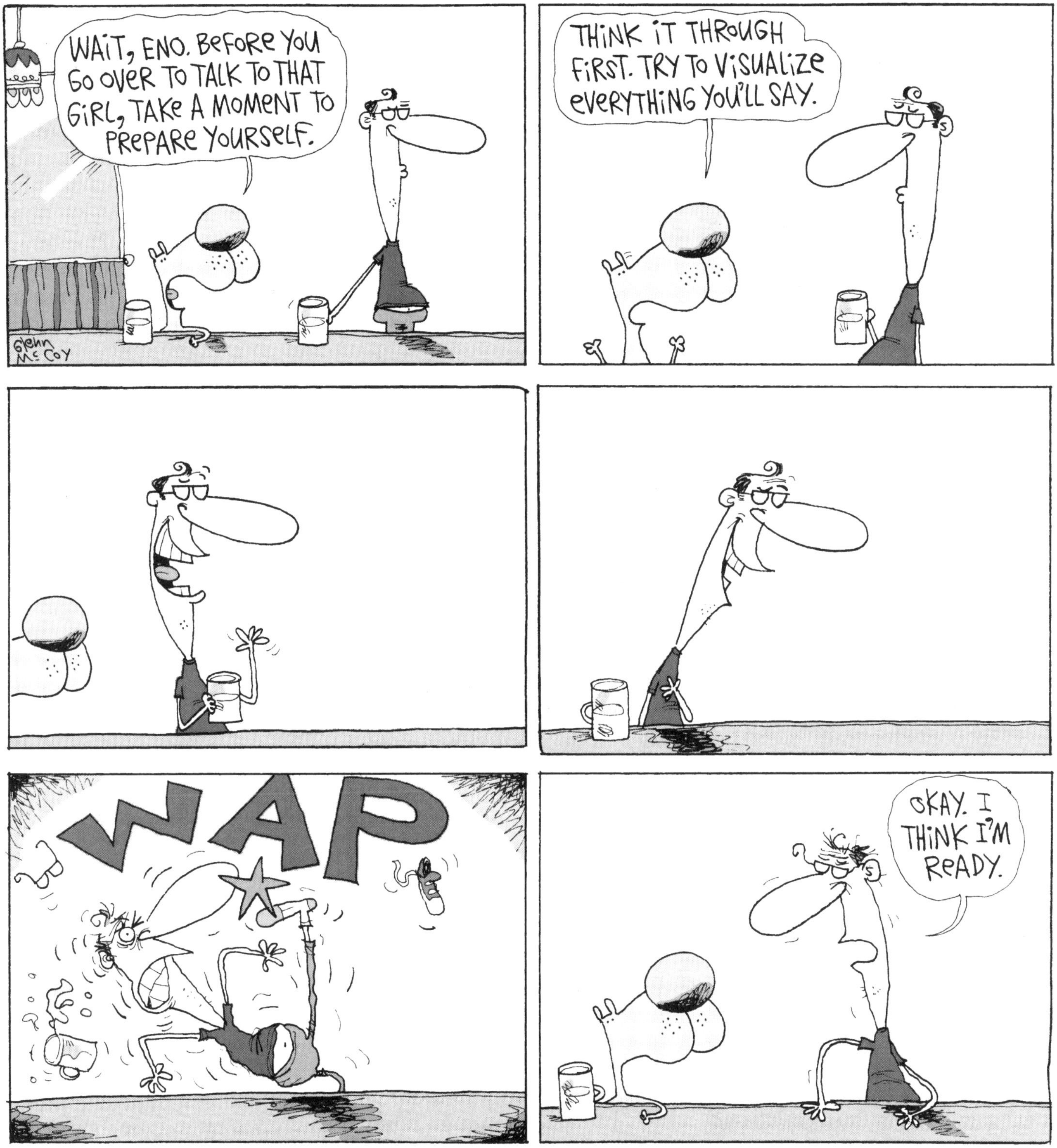
WAIT, ENO. BEFORE YOU GO OVER TO TALK TO THAT GIRL, TAKE A MOMENT TO PREPARE YOURSELF.
Glenn McCoy
THINK IT THROUGH FIRST. TRY TO VISUALIZE EVERYTHING YOU'LL SAY.
WAP
OKAY. I THINK I'M READY.

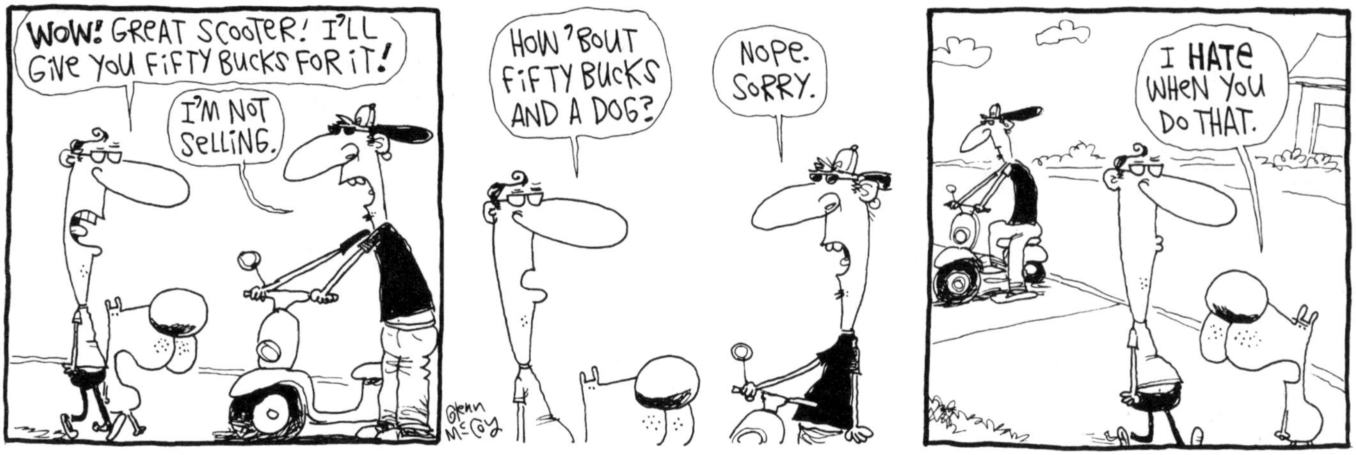
WOW! GREAT SCOOTER! I'LL GIVE YOU FIFTY BUCKS FOR IT!
I'M NOT SELLING.
HOW 'BOUT FIFTY BUCKS AND A DOG?
NOPE. SORRY.
I HATE WHEN YOU DO THAT.
Glenn McCoy

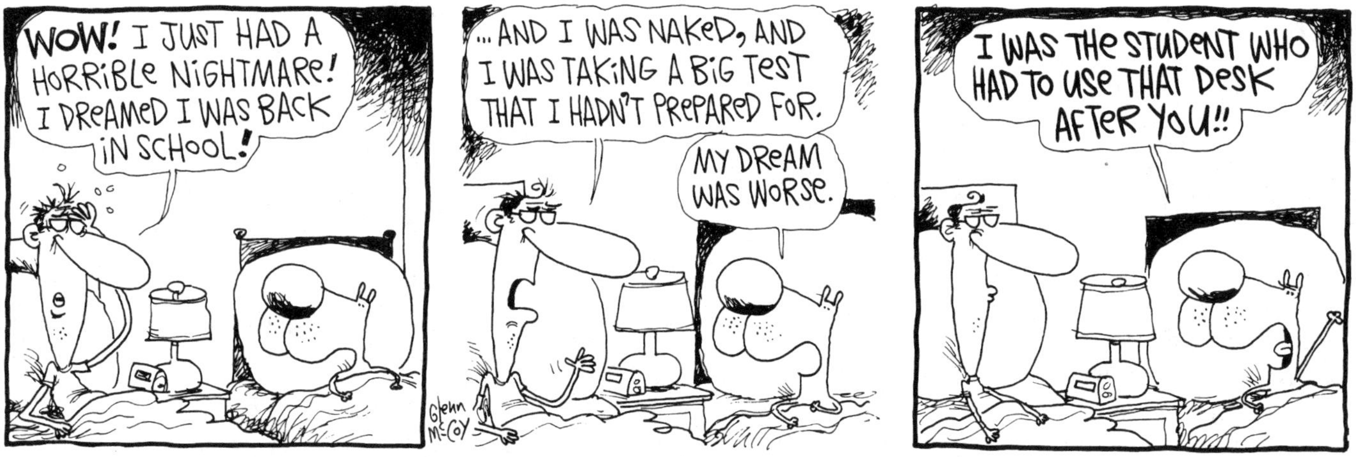
WOW! I JUST HAD A HORRIBLE NIGHTMARE! I DREAMED I WAS BACK IN SCHOOL!
...AND I WAS NAKED, AND I WAS TAKING A BIG TEST THAT I HADN'T PREPARED FOR.
MY DREAM WAS WORSE.
I WAS THE STUDENT WHO HAD TO USE THAT DESK AFTER YOU!!
Glenn McCoy

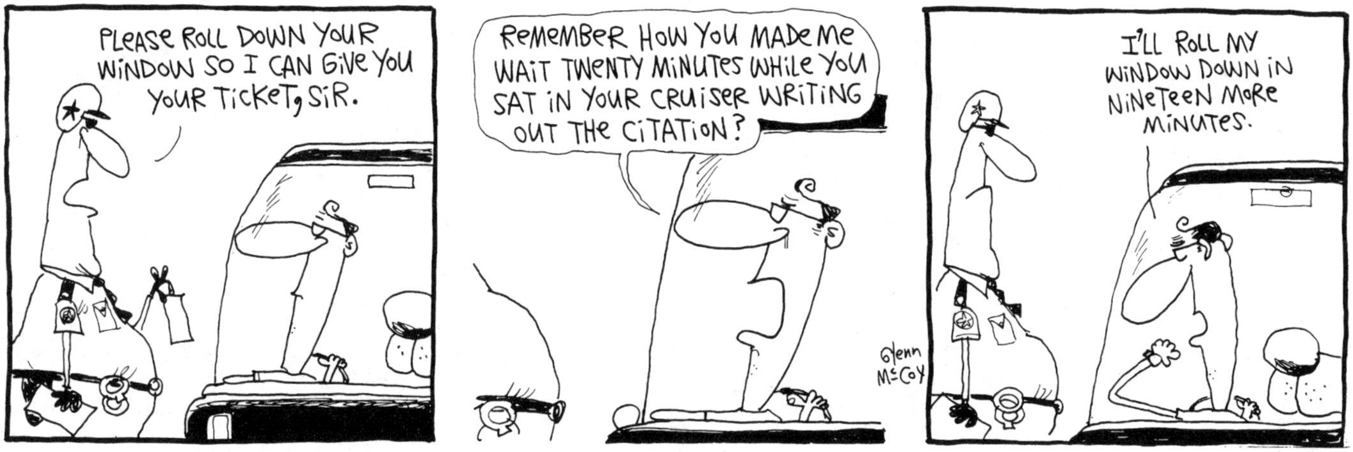
PLEASE ROLL DOWN YOUR WINDOW SO I CAN GIVE YOU YOUR TICKET, SIR.
REMEMBER HOW YOU MADE ME WAIT TWENTY MINUTES WHILE YOU SAT IN YOUR CRUISER WRITING OUT THE CITATION?
I'LL ROLL MY WINDOW DOWN IN NINETEEN MORE MINUTES.
Glenn McCoy

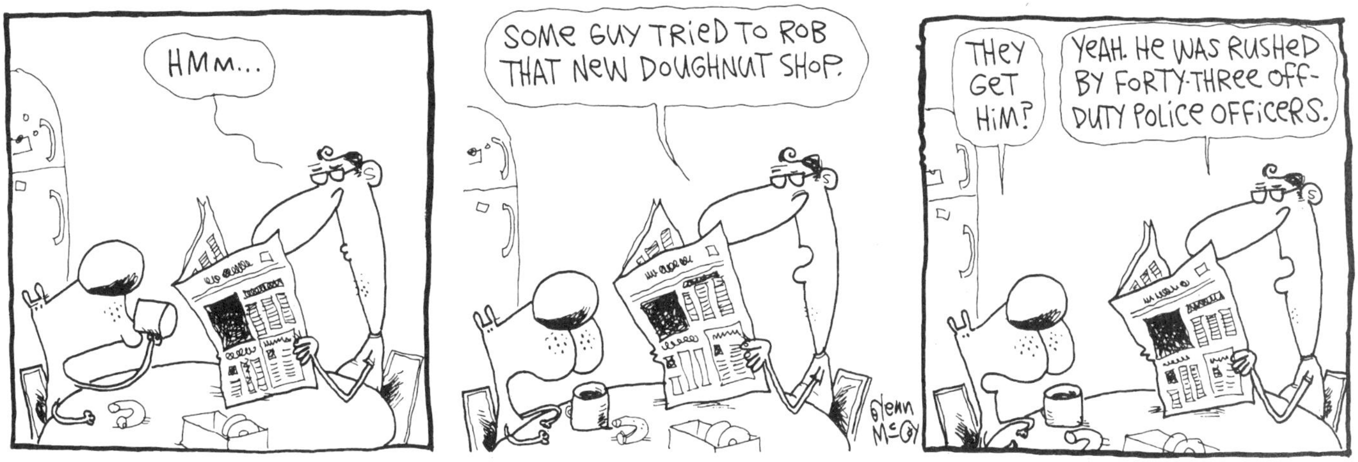
HMM...
SOME GUY TRIED TO ROB THAT NEW DOUGHNUT SHOP.
THEY GET HIM?
YEAH. HE WAS RUSHED BY FORTY-THREE OFF-DUTY POLICE OFFICERS.
Glenn McCoy

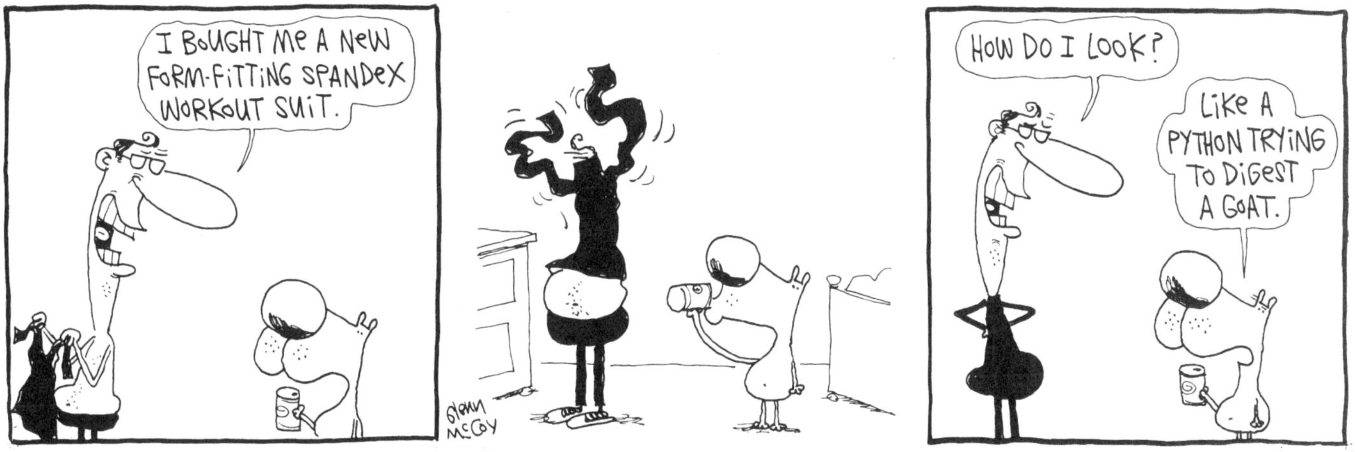
I BOUGHT ME A NEW FORM-FITTING SPANDEX WORKOUT SUIT.
Glenn McCoy
HOW DO I LOOK?
LIKE A PYTHON TRYING TO DIGEST A GOAT.

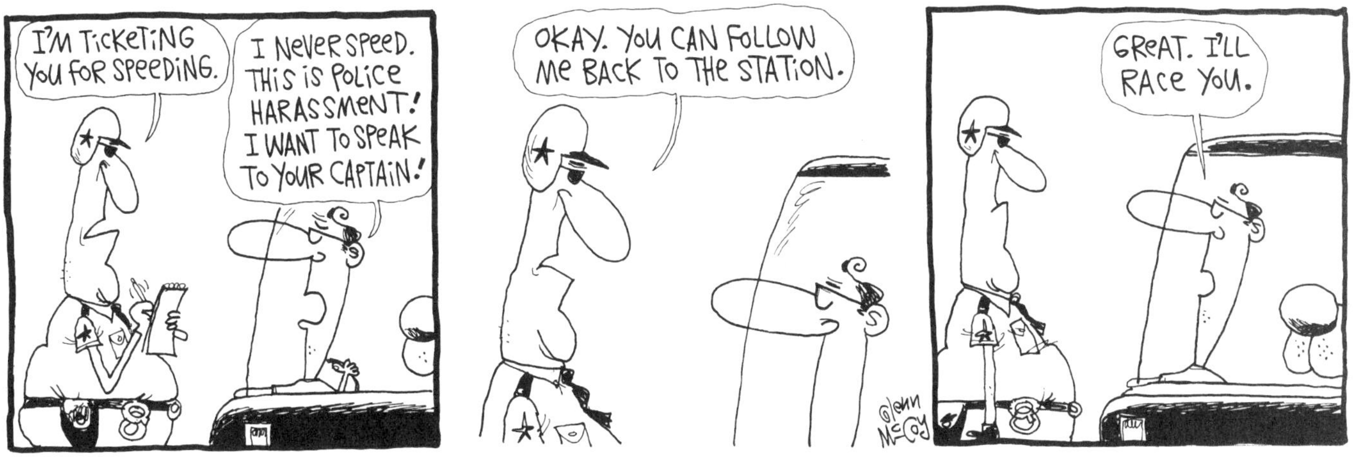
I'M TICKETING YOU FOR SPEEDING.
I NEVER SPEED. THIS IS POLICE HARASSMENT! I WANT TO SPEAK TO YOUR CAPTAIN!
OKAY. YOU CAN FOLLOW ME BACK TO THE STATION.
Glenn McCoy
GREAT. I'LL RACE YOU.

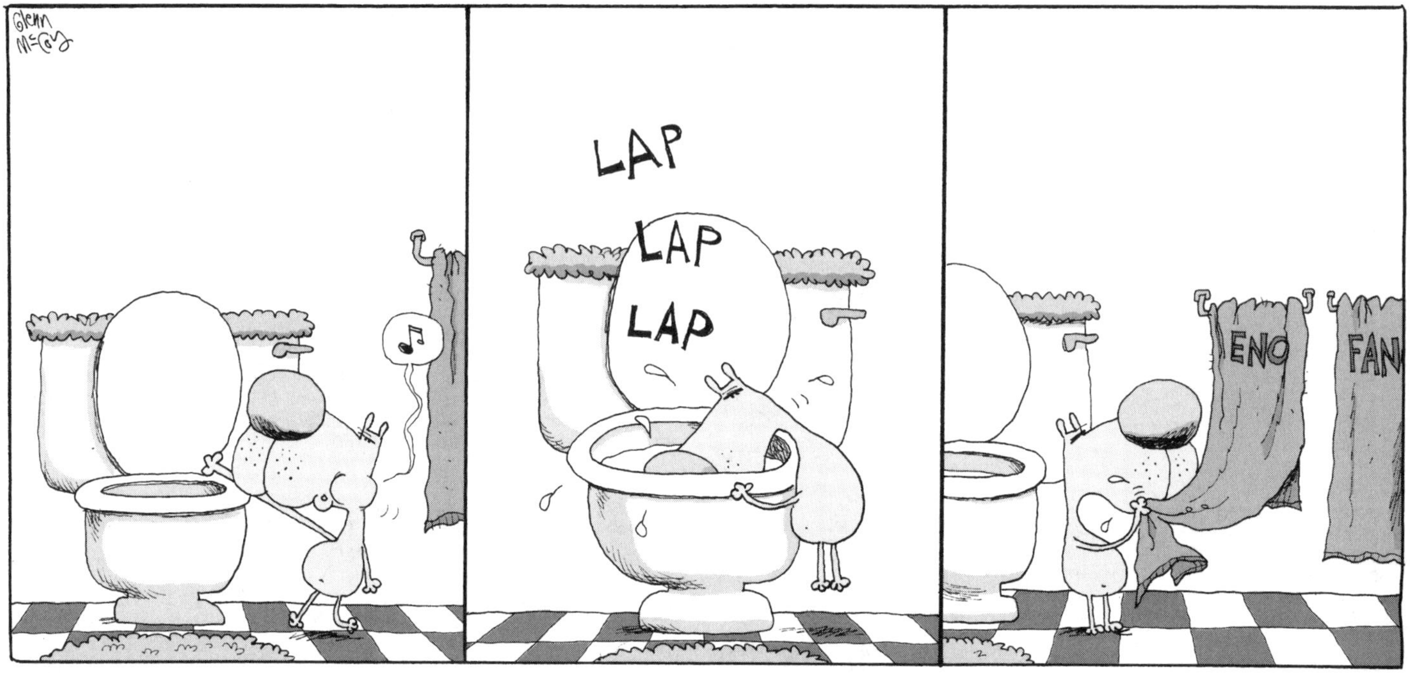
Glenn McCoy
LAP
LAP
LAP
ENO
FAN

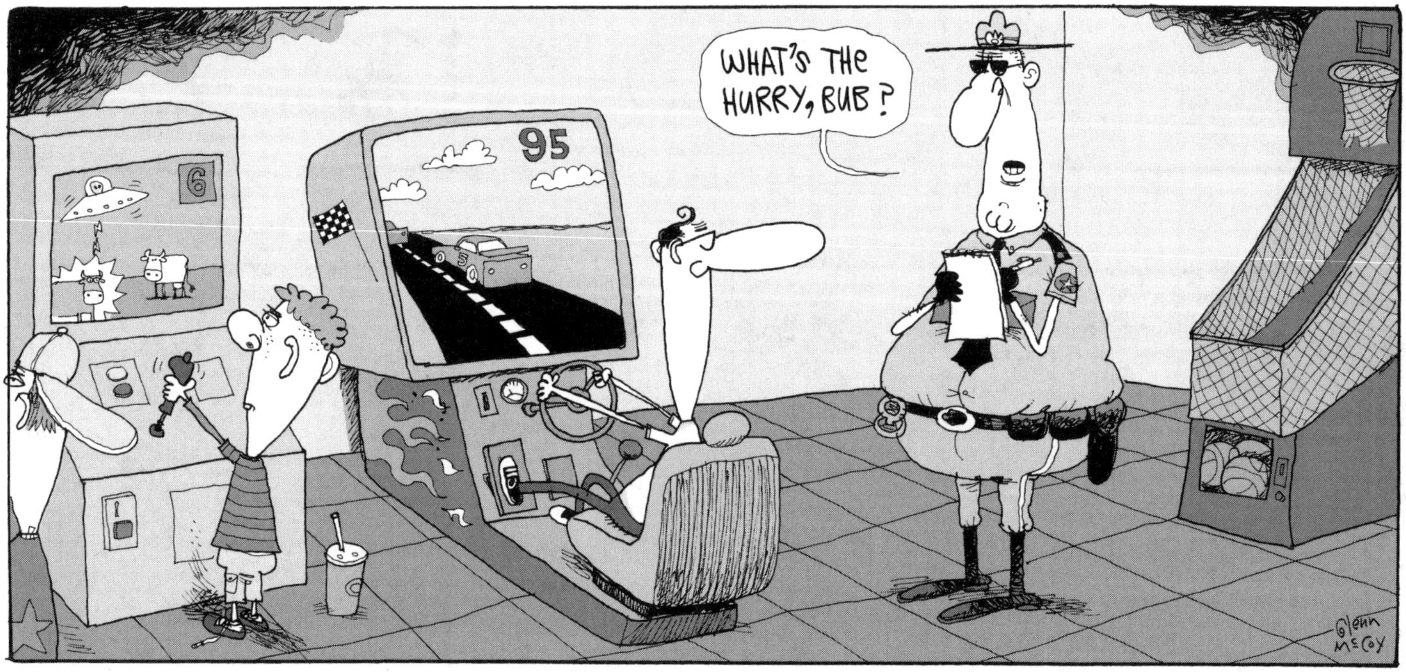
WHAT'S THE HURRY, BUB?
95
6
Glenn McCoy

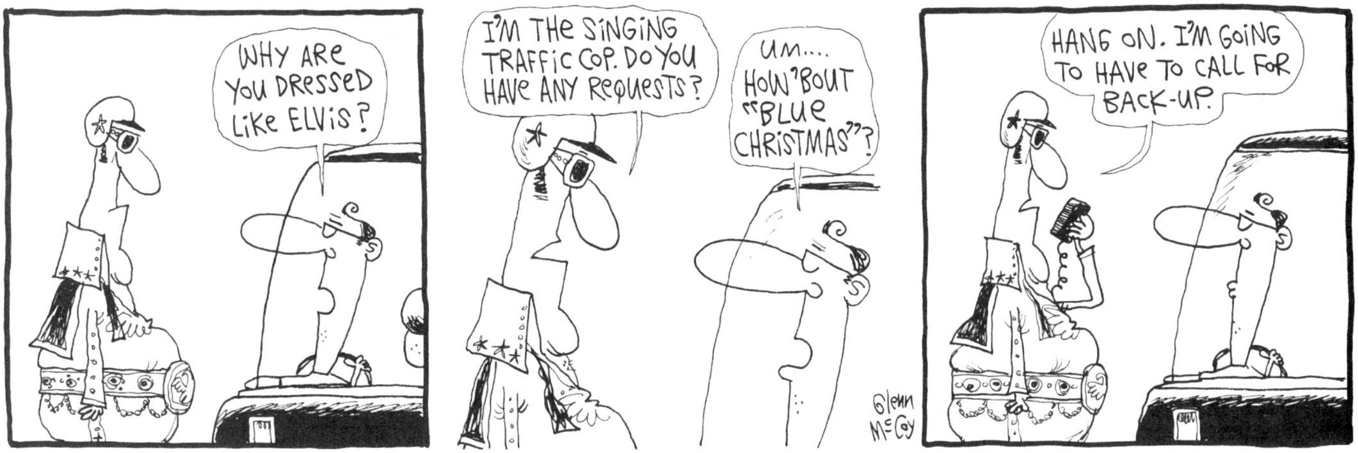
WHY ARE YOU DRESSED LIKE ELVIS?
I'M THE SINGING TRAFFIC COP. DO YOU HAVE ANY REQUESTS?
UM.... HOW'BOUT "BLUE CHRISTMAS"?
HANG ON. I'M GOING TO HAVE TO CALL FOR BACK-UP.
Glenn McCoy

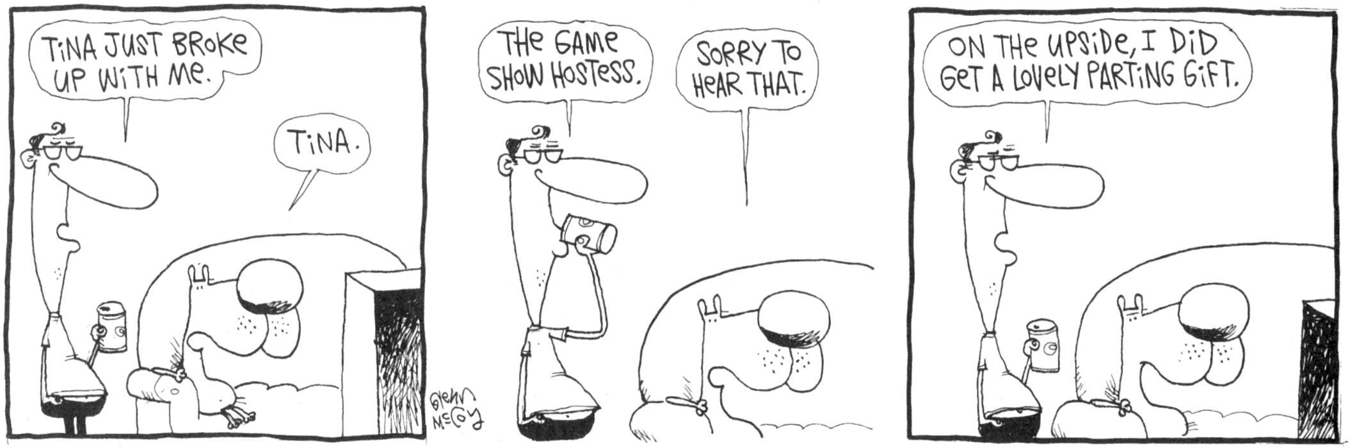
TINA JUST BROKE UP WITH ME.
TINA.
THE GAME SHOW HOSTESS.
SORRY TO HEAR THAT.
ON THE UPSIDE, I DID GET A LOVELY PARTING GIFT.
Glenn McCoy

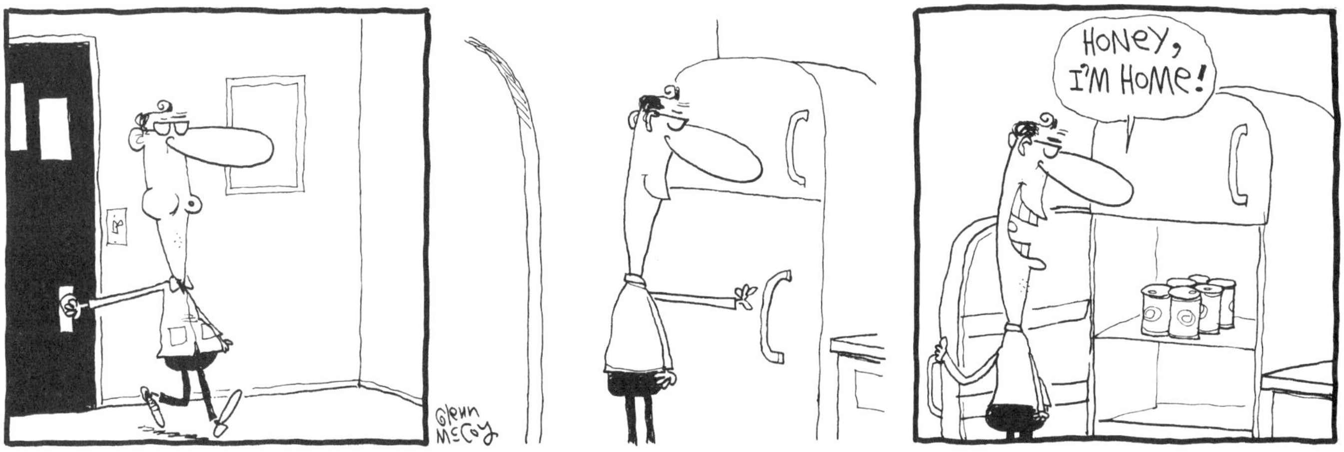
Glenn McCoy
HONEY, I'M HOME!

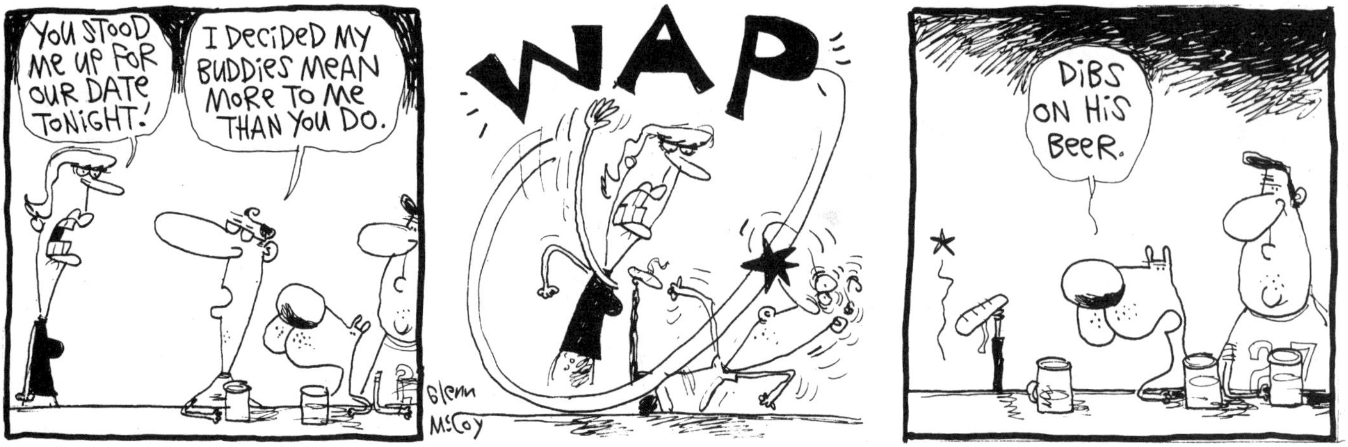
YOU STOOD ME UP FOR OUR DATE TONIGHT!
I DECIDED MY BUDDIES MEAN MORE TO ME THAN YOU DO.
WAP
DIBS ON HIS BEER.
Glenn McCoy

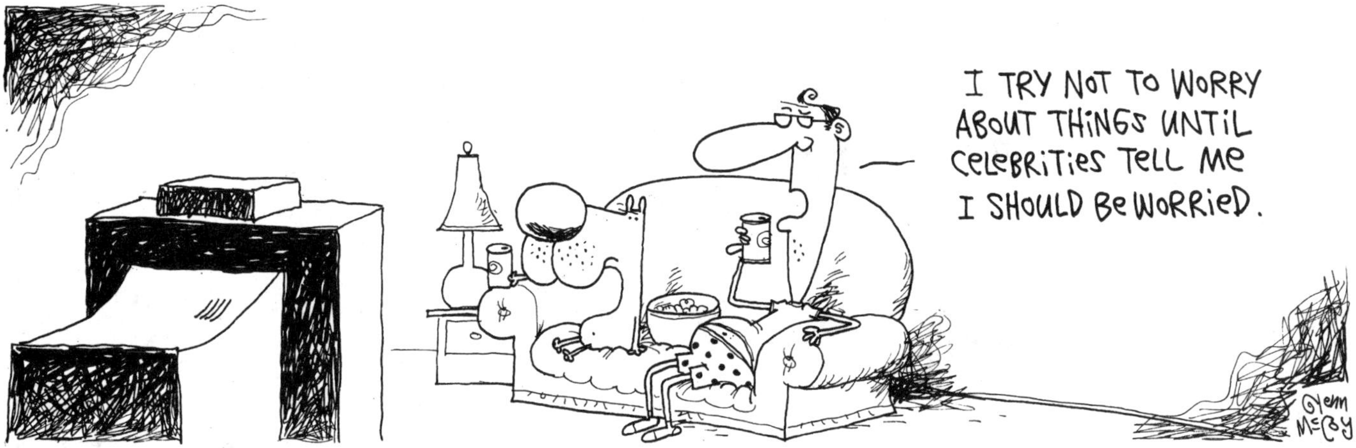
I TRY NOT TO WORRY ABOUT THINGS UNTIL CELEBRITIES TELL ME I SHOULD BE WORRIED.
Glenn McCoy

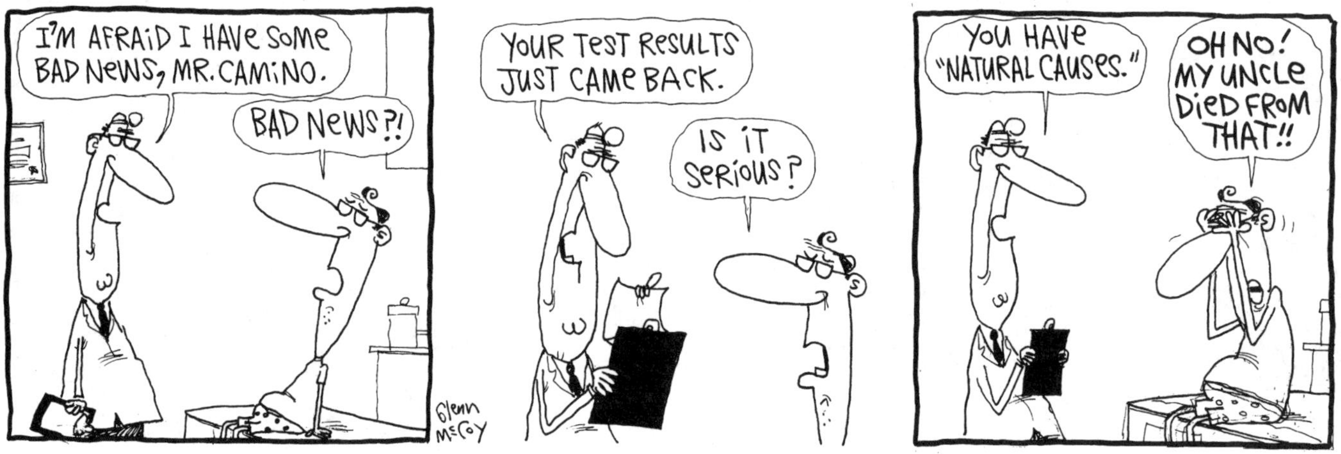
I'M AFRAID I HAVE SOME BAD NEWS, MR. CAMINO.
BAD NEWS?!
YOUR TEST RESULTS JUST CAME BACK.
IS IT SERIOUS?
YOU HAVE "NATURAL CAUSES."
OH NO! MY UNCLE DIED FROM THAT!!
Glenn McCoy

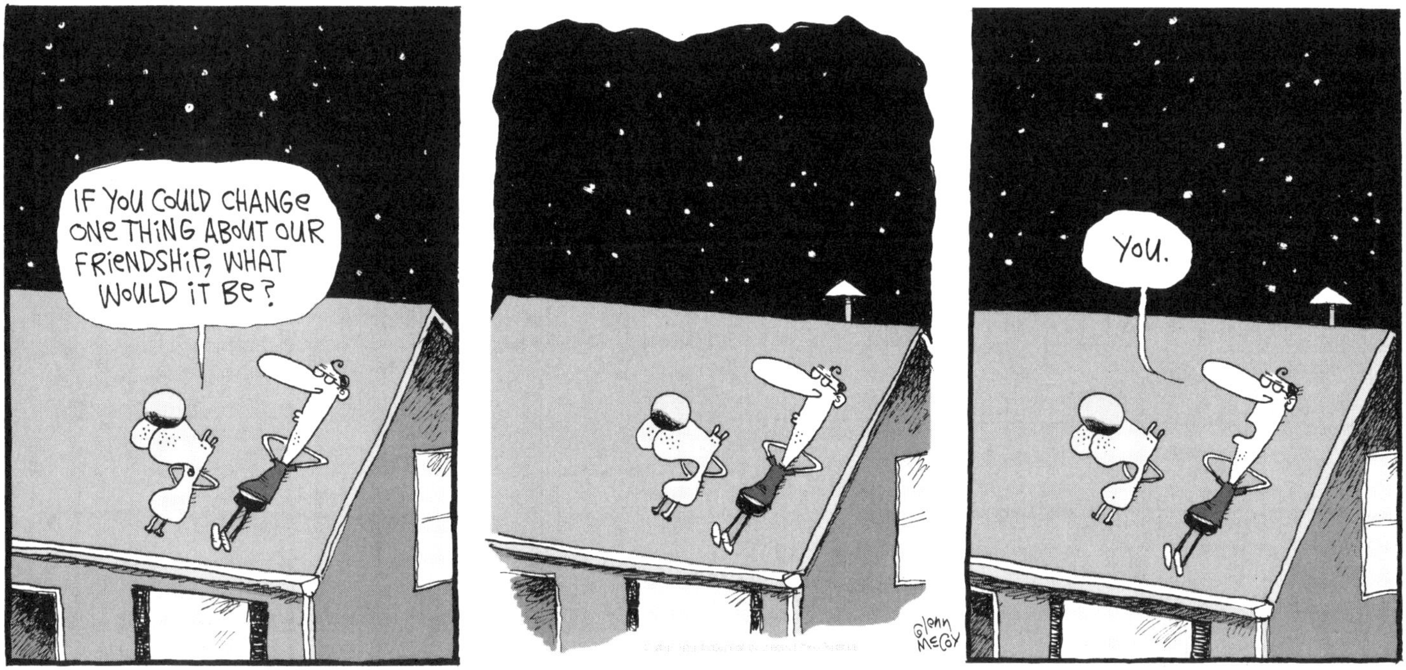
IF YOU COULD CHANGE ONE THING ABOUT OUR FRIENDSHIP, WHAT WOULD IT BE?
YOU.

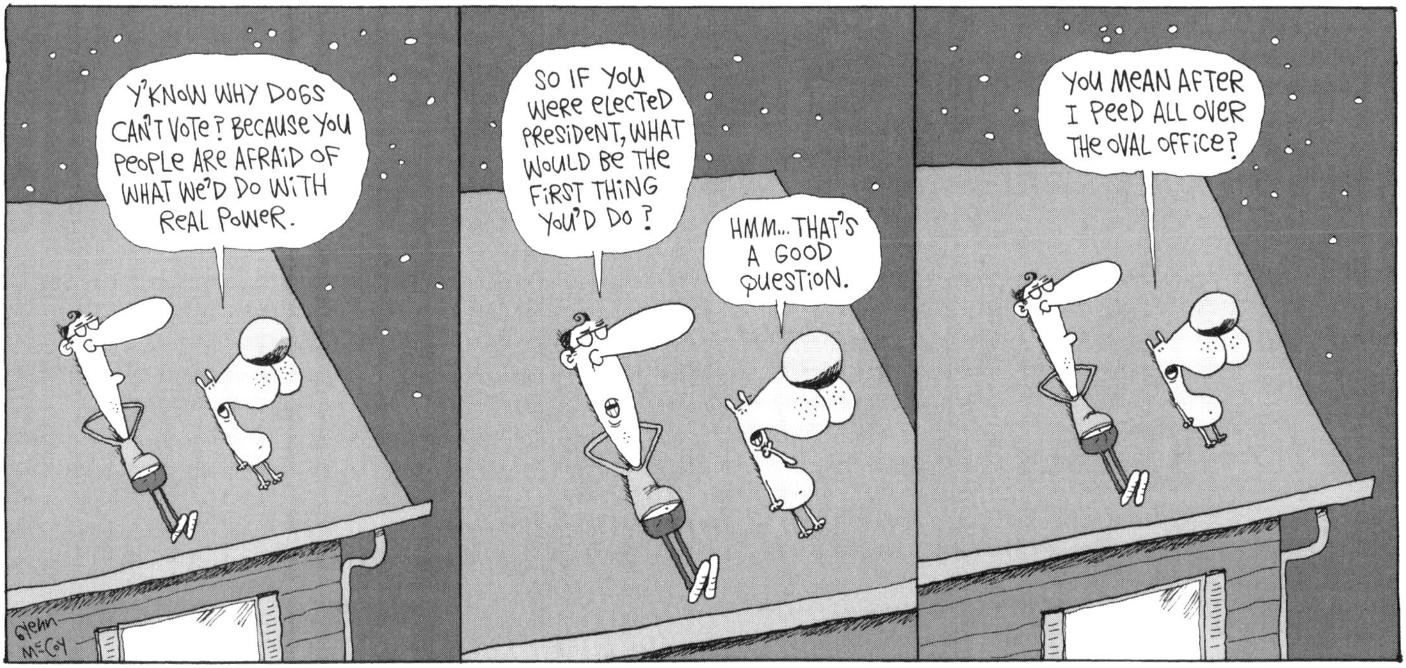
Y'KNOW WHY DOGS CAN'T VOTE? BECAUSE YOU PEOPLE ARE AFRAID OF WHAT WE'D DO WITH REAL POWER.
SO IF YOU WERE ELECTED PRESIDENT, WHAT WOULD BE THE FIRST THING YOU'D DO?
HMM... THAT'S A GOOD QUESTION.
YOU MEAN AFTER I PEED ALL OVER THE OVAL OFFICE?

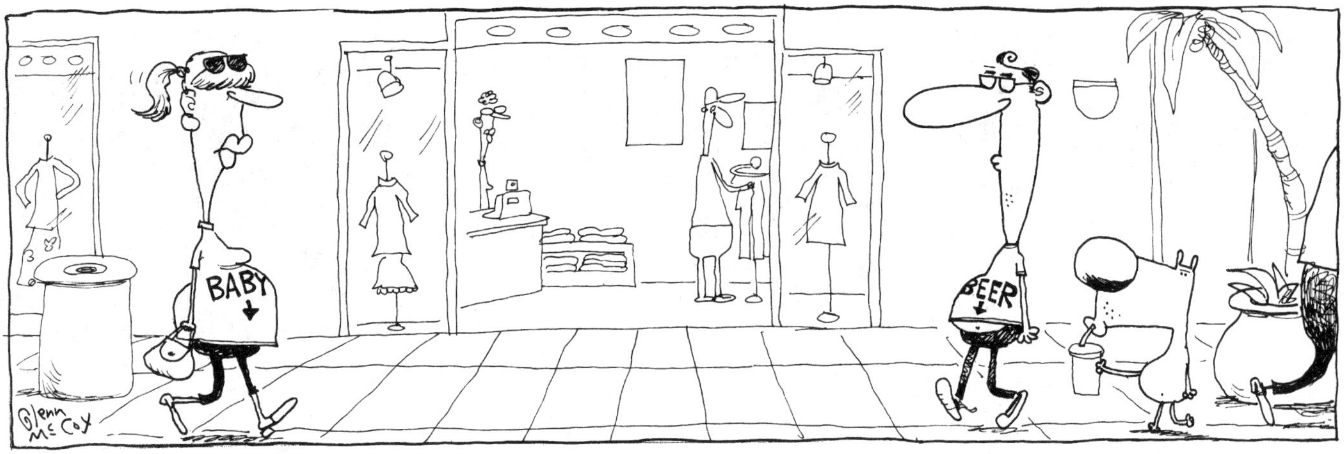
BABY
BEER

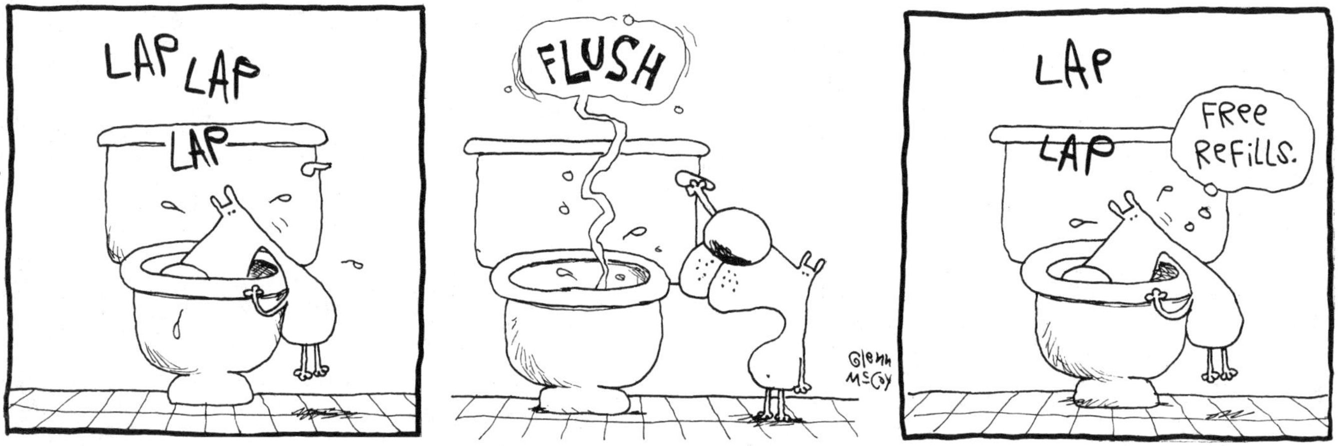
LAP LAP
LAP
FLUSH
LAP
LAP
Free Refills.

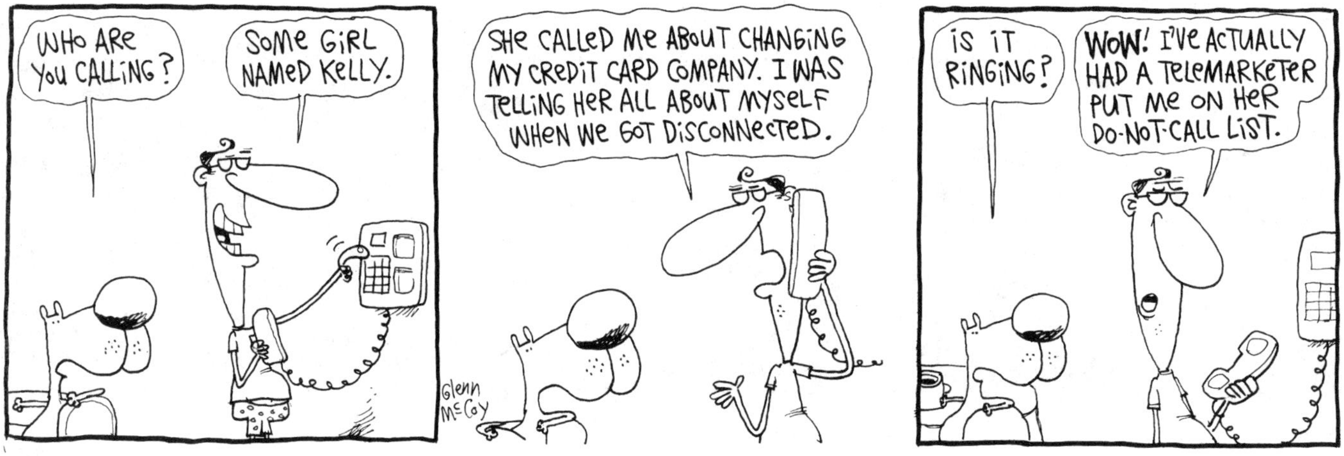
WHO ARE YOU CALLING?
SOME GIRL NAMED KELLY.
SHE CALLED ME ABOUT CHANGING MY CREDIT CARD COMPANY. I WAS TELLING HER ALL ABOUT MYSELF WHEN WE GOT DISCONNECTED.
IS IT RINGING?
WOW! I'VE ACTUALLY HAD A TELEMARKETER PUT ME ON HER DO-NOT-CALL LIST.

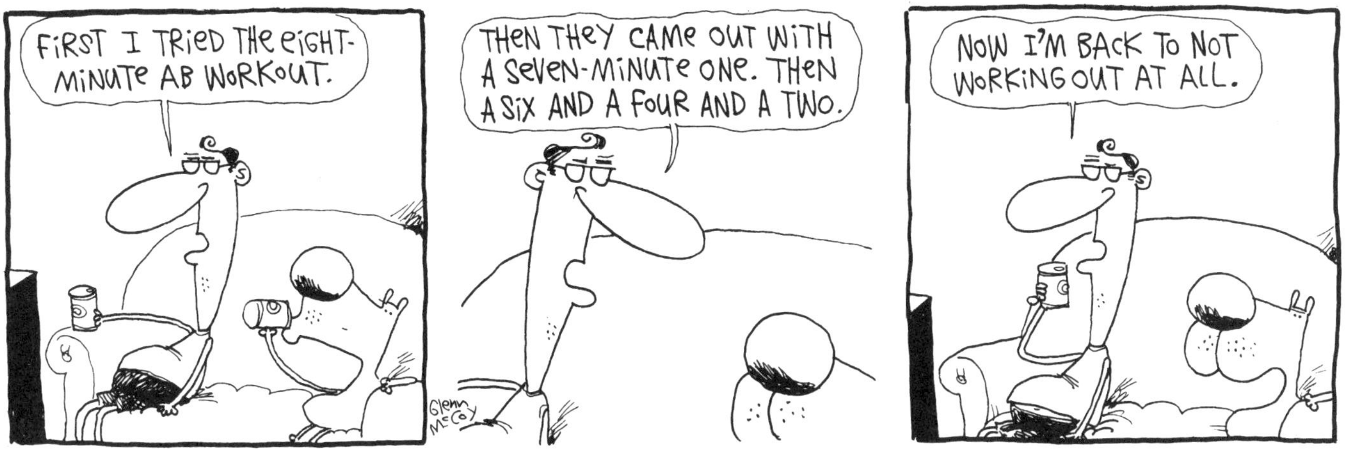
FIRST I TRIED THE EIGHT-MINUTE AB WORKOUT.
THEN THEY CAME OUT WITH A SEVEN-MINUTE ONE. THEN A SIX AND A FOUR AND A TWO.
NOW I'M BACK TO NOT WORKING OUT AT ALL.
Glenn McCoy

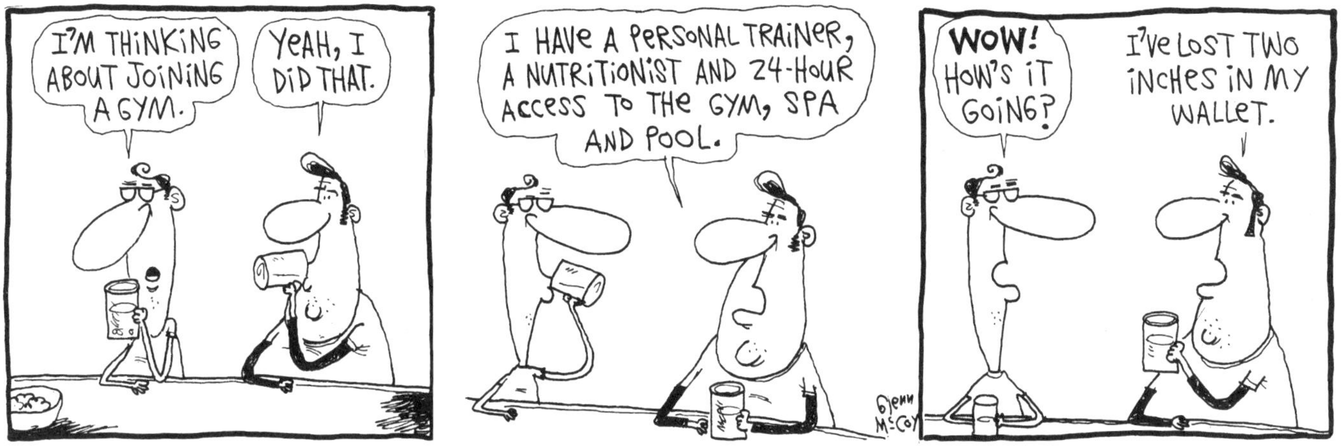
I'M THINKING ABOUT JOINING A GYM.
YEAH, I DID THAT.
I HAVE A PERSONAL TRAINER, A NUTRITIONIST AND 24-HOUR ACCESS TO THE GYM, SPA AND POOL.
WOW! HOW'S IT GOING?
I'VE LOST TWO INCHES IN MY WALLET.
Glenn McCoy

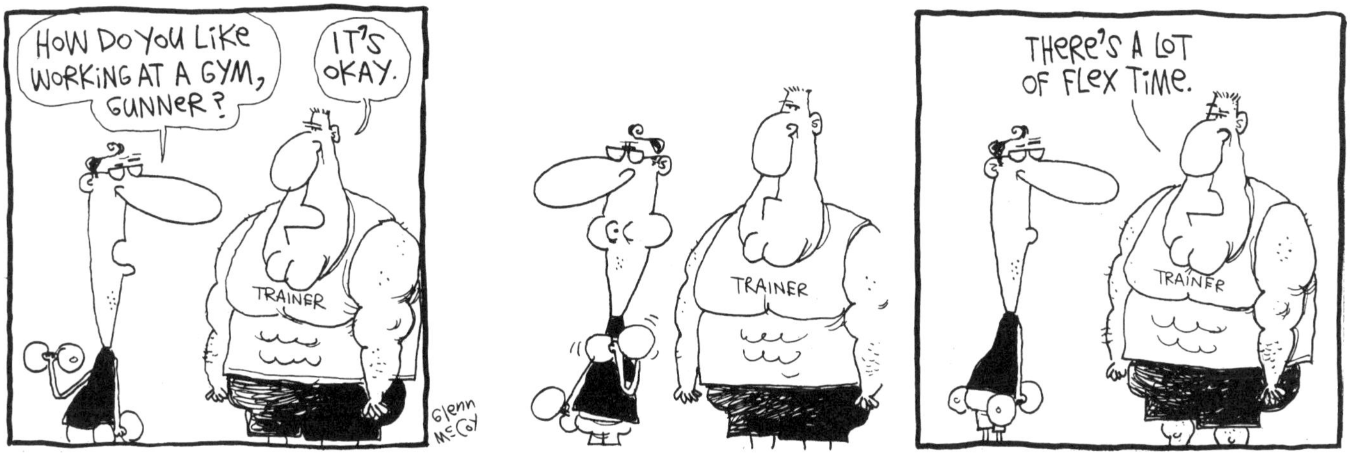
HOW DO YOU LIKE WORKING AT A GYM, GUNNER?
IT'S OKAY.
TRAINER
Glenn McCoy
TRAINER
THERE'S A LOT OF FLEX TIME.
TRAINER

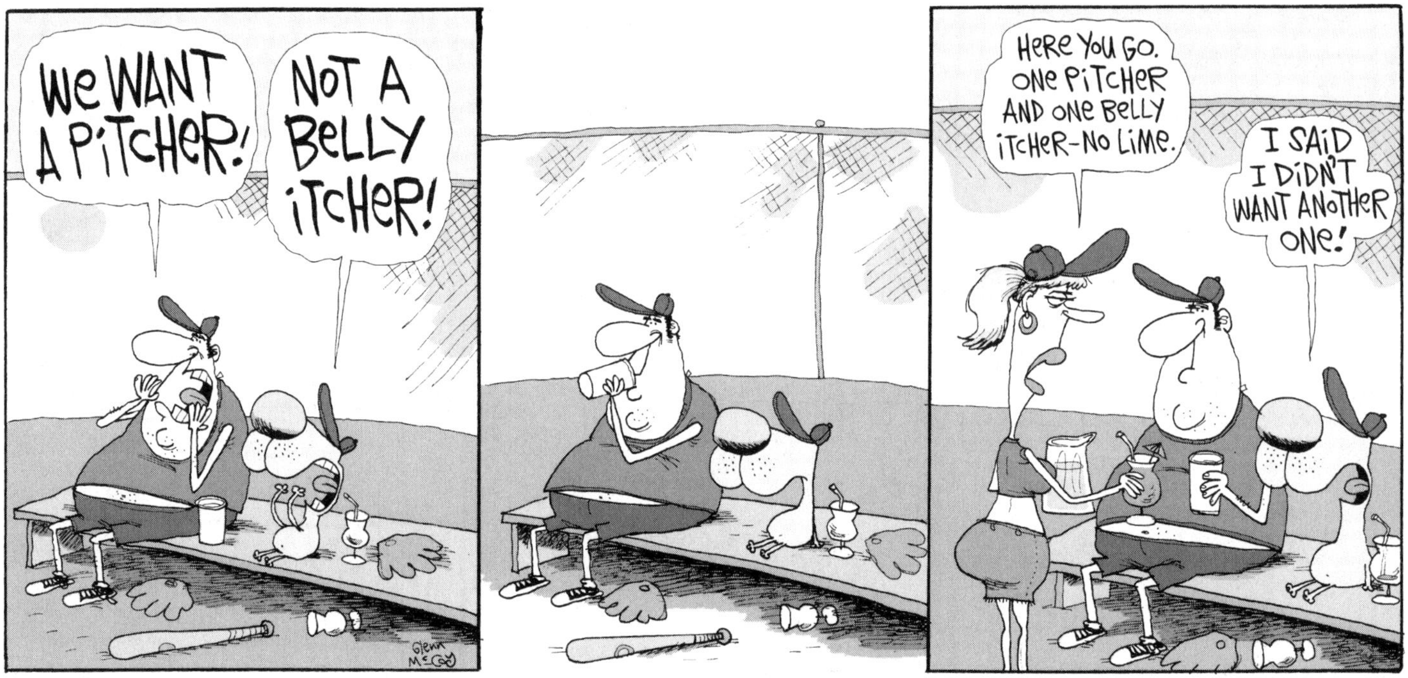
WE WANT A PITCHER!
NOT A BELLY ITCHER!
HERE YOU GO. ONE PITCHER AND ONE BELLY ITCHER–NO LIME.
I SAID I DIDN'T WANT ANOTHER ONE!
Glenn McCoy

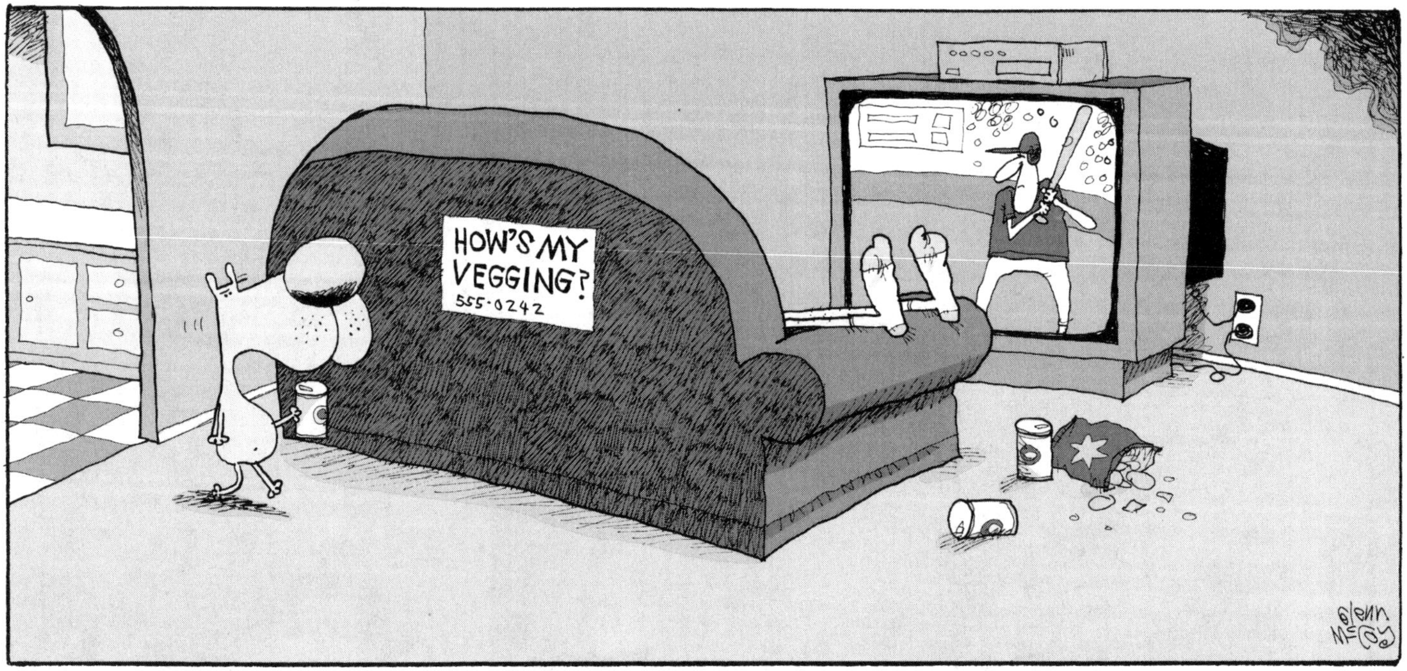
HOW'S MY VEGGING?
555-0242
Glenn McCoy

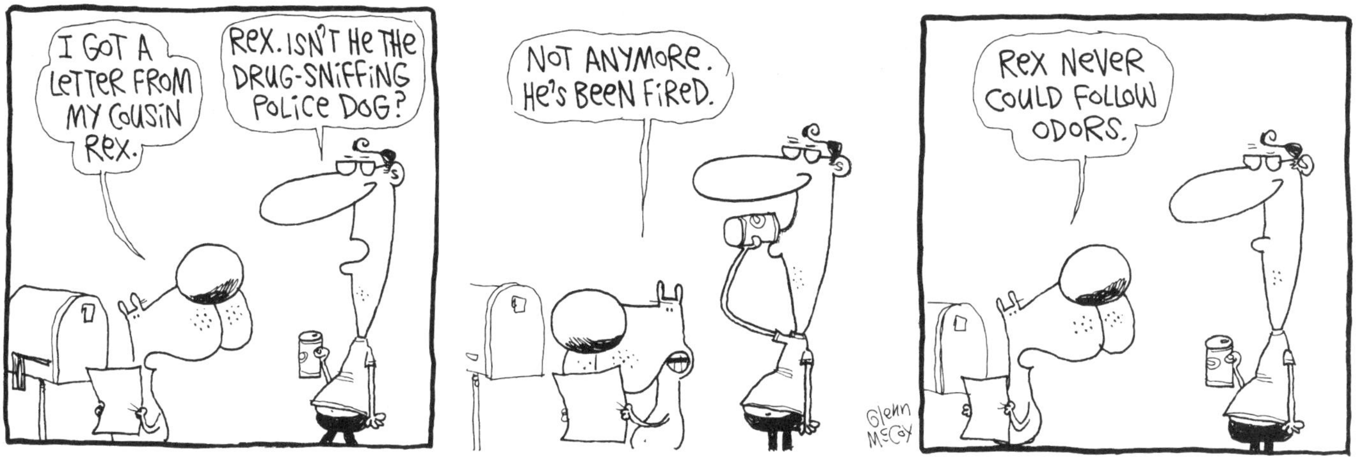
I GOT A LETTER FROM MY COUSIN REX.
REX. ISN'T HE THE DRUG-SNIFFING POLICE DOG?
NOT ANYMORE. HE'S BEEN FIRED.
REX NEVER COULD FOLLOW ODORS.
GLENN McCOY

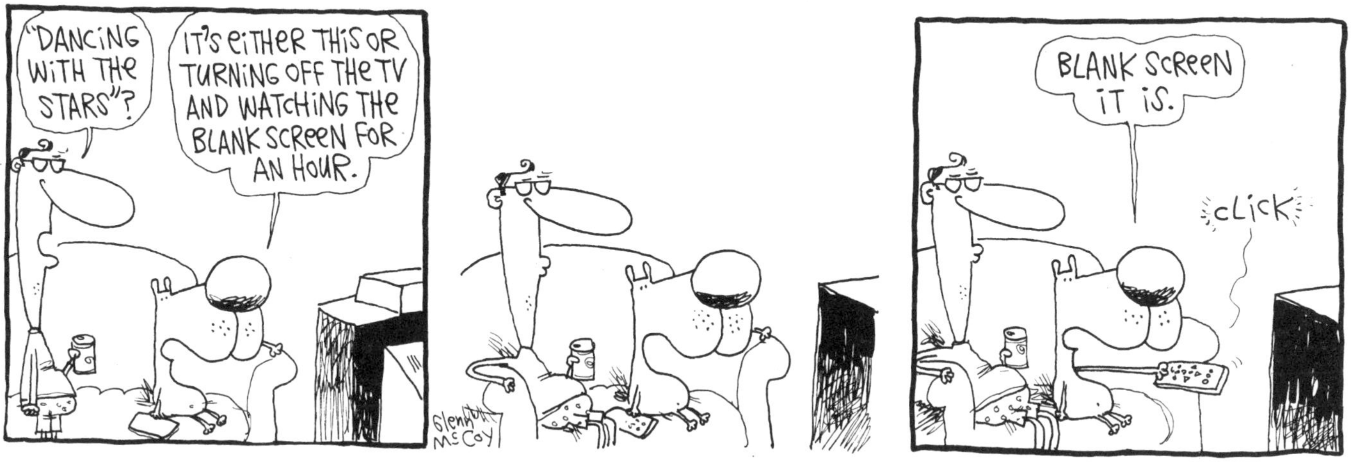
"DANCING WITH THE STARS"?
IT'S EITHER THIS OR TURNING OFF THE TV AND WATCHING THE BLANK SCREEN FOR AN HOUR.
GLENN McCOY
BLANK SCREEN IT IS.
CLICK

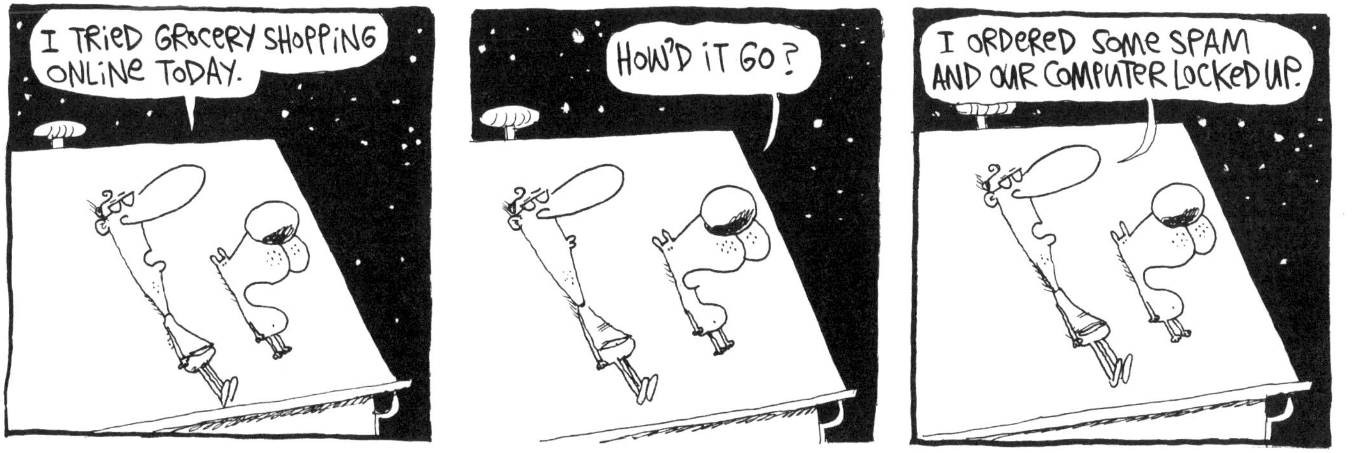
I TRIED GROCERY SHOPPING ONLINE TODAY.
HOW'D IT GO?
I ORDERED SOME SPAM AND OUR COMPUTER LOCKED UP.

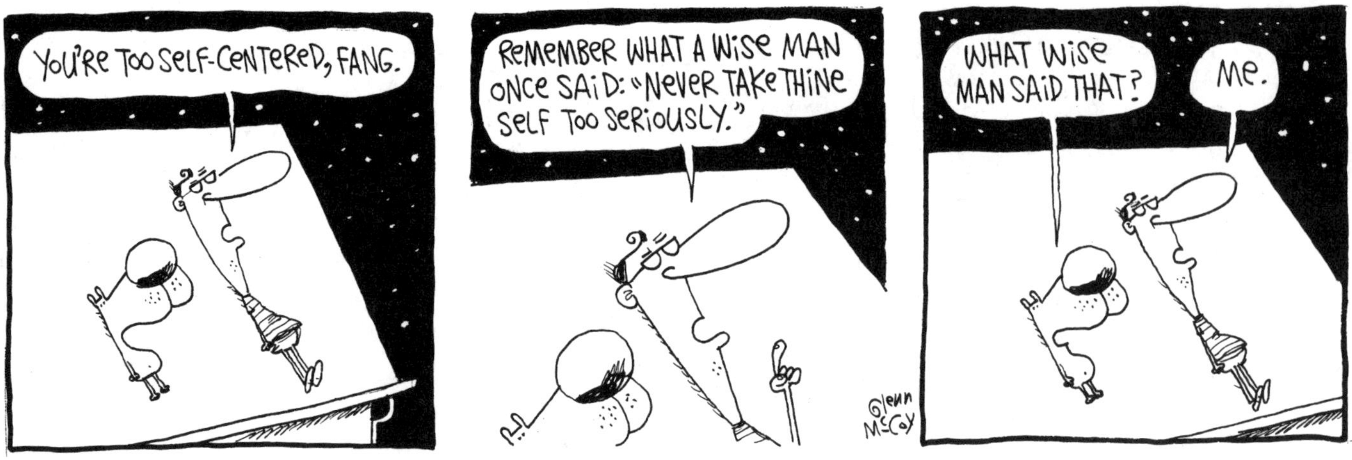
YOU'RE TOO SELF-CENTERED, FANG.
REMEMBER WHAT A WISE MAN ONCE SAID: "NEVER TAKE THINE SELF TOO SERIOUSLY."
WHAT WISE MAN SAID THAT?
ME.
GLENN McCOY

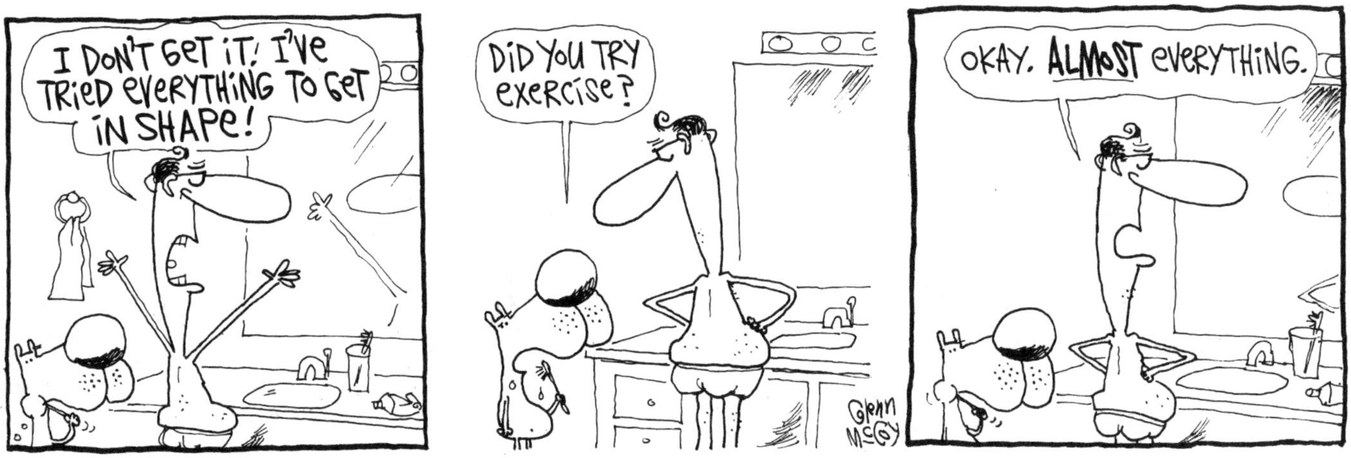
I DON'T GET IT! I'VE TRIED EVERYTHING TO GET IN SHAPE!
DID YOU TRY EXERCISE?
OKAY. ALMOST EVERYTHING.
GLENN McCOY

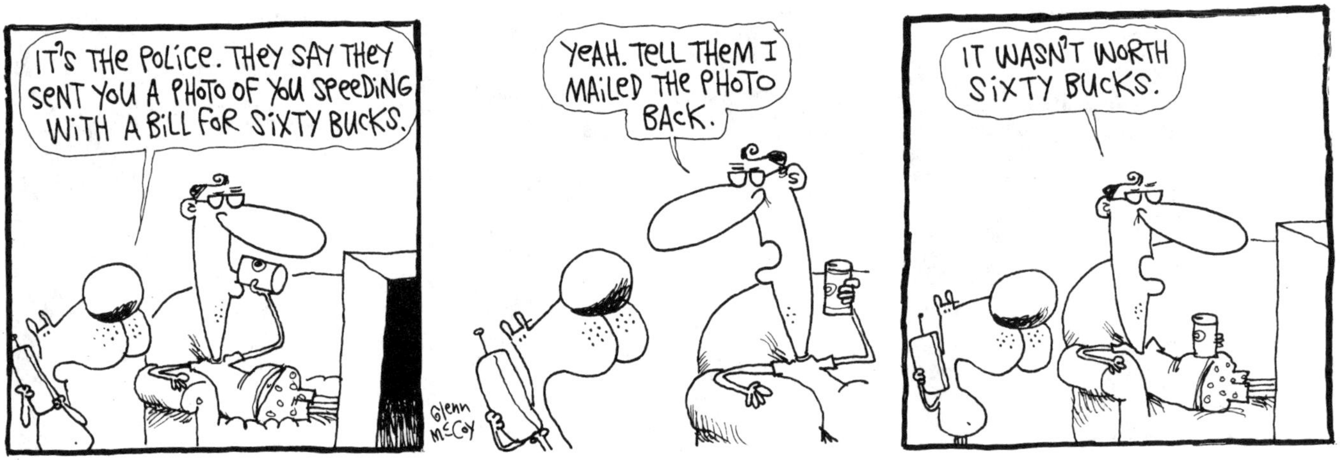
IT'S THE POLICE. THEY SAY THEY SENT YOU A PHOTO OF YOU SPEEDING WITH A BILL FOR SIXTY BUCKS.
YEAH. TELL THEM I MAILED THE PHOTO BACK.
IT WASN'T WORTH SIXTY BUCKS.
GLENN McCOY

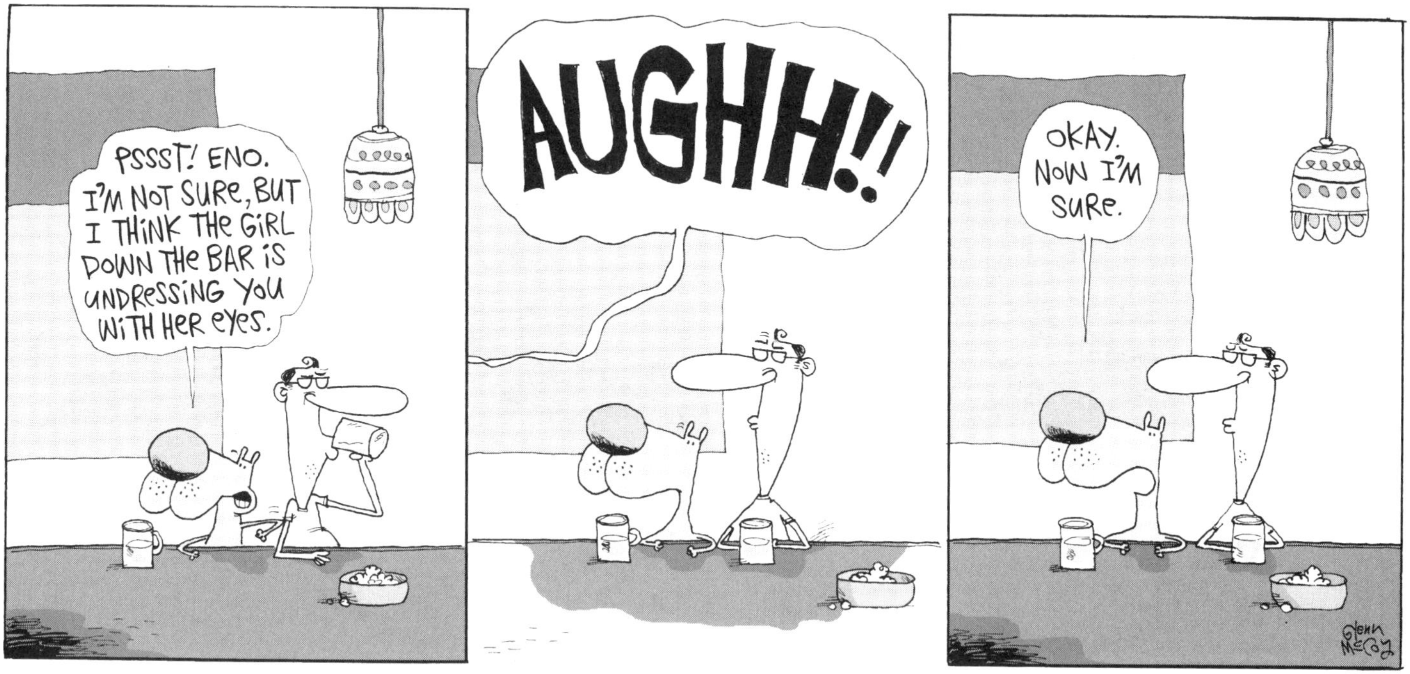
PSSST! ENO. I'M NOT SURE, BUT I THINK THE GIRL DOWN THE BAR IS UNDRESSING YOU WITH HER EYES.
AUGHH!!
OKAY. NOW I'M SURE.

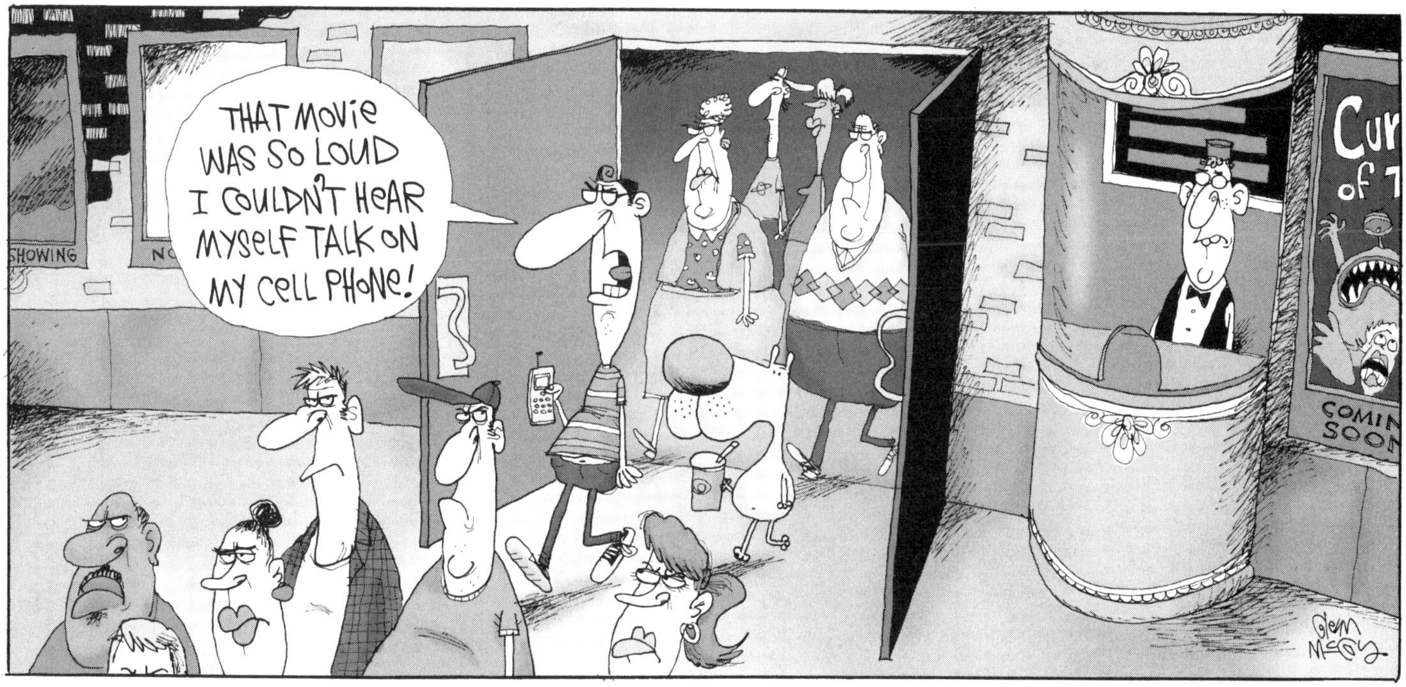
SHOWING
THAT MOVIE WAS SO LOUD I COULDN'T HEAR MYSELF TALK ON MY CELL PHONE!

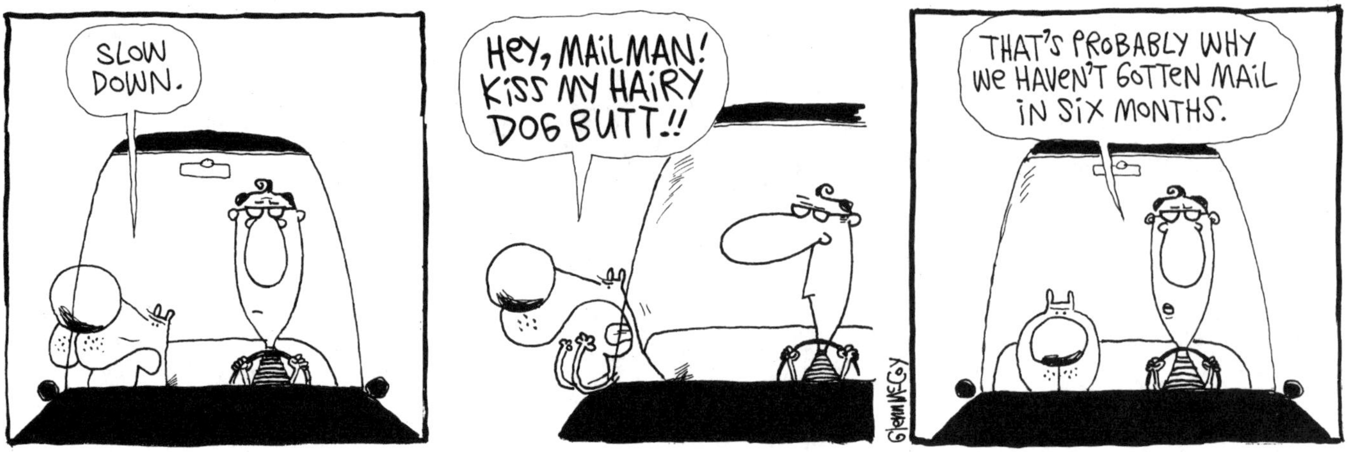
SLOW DOWN.
HEY, MAILMAN! KISS MY HAIRY DOG BUTT!!
THAT'S PROBABLY WHY WE HAVEN'T GOTTEN MAIL IN SIX MONTHS.

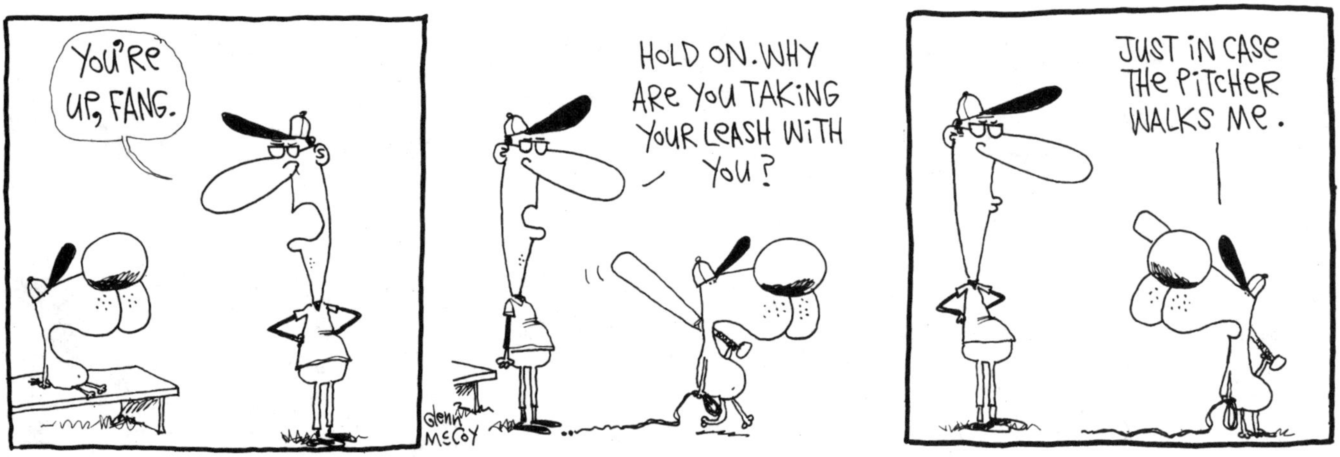
YOU'RE UP, FANG.
HOLD ON. WHY ARE YOU TAKING YOUR LEASH WITH YOU?
JUST IN CASE THE PITCHER WALKS ME.

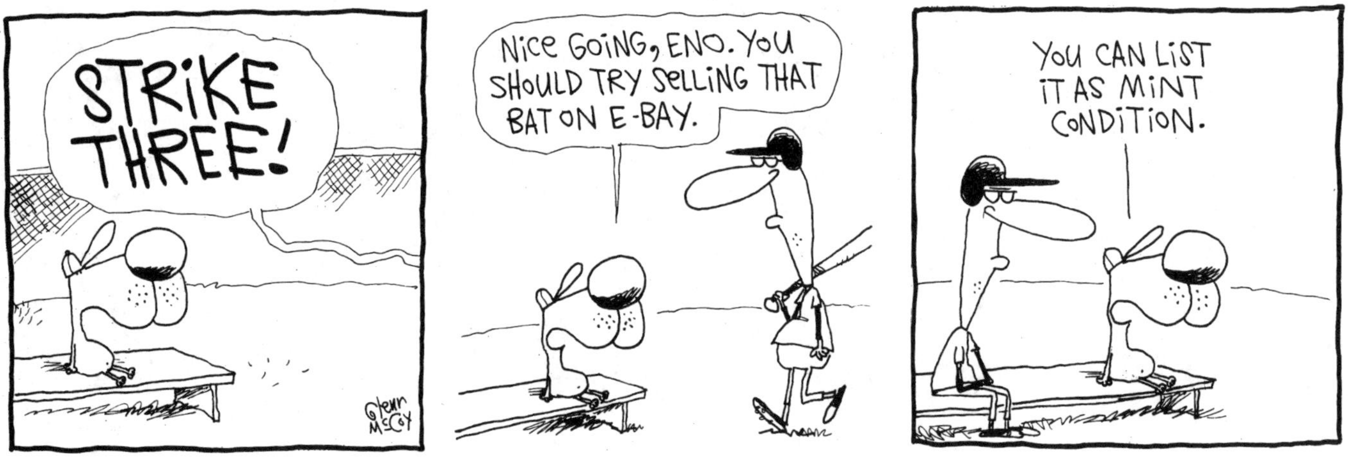
STRIKE THREE!
NICE GOING, ENO. YOU SHOULD TRY SELLING THAT BAT ON E-BAY.
YOU CAN LIST IT AS MINT CONDITION.

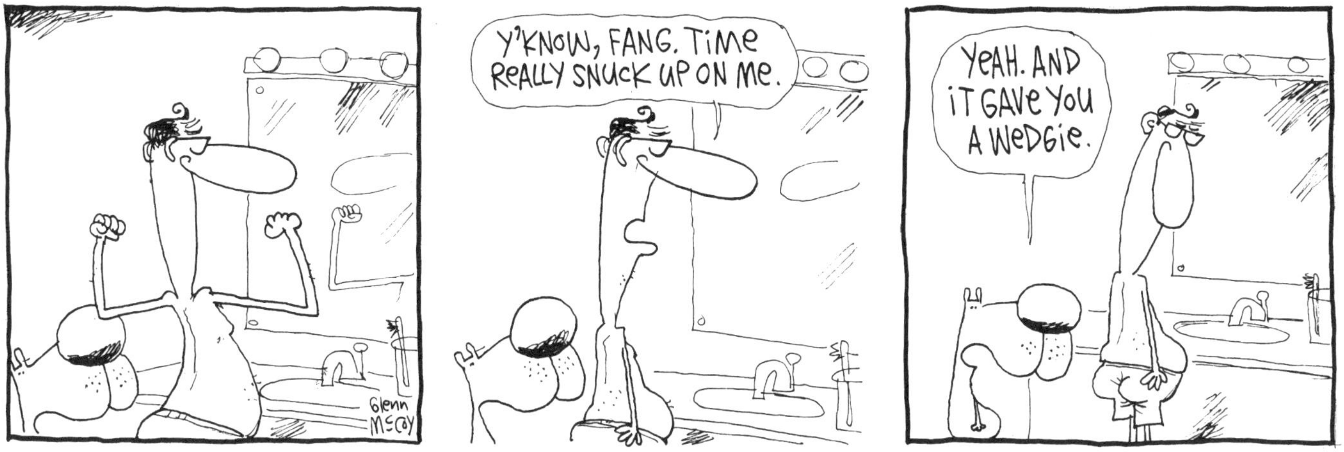
Glenn McCoy
Y'KNOW, FANG. TIME REALLY SNUCK UP ON ME.
YEAH. AND IT GAVE YOU A WEDGIE.

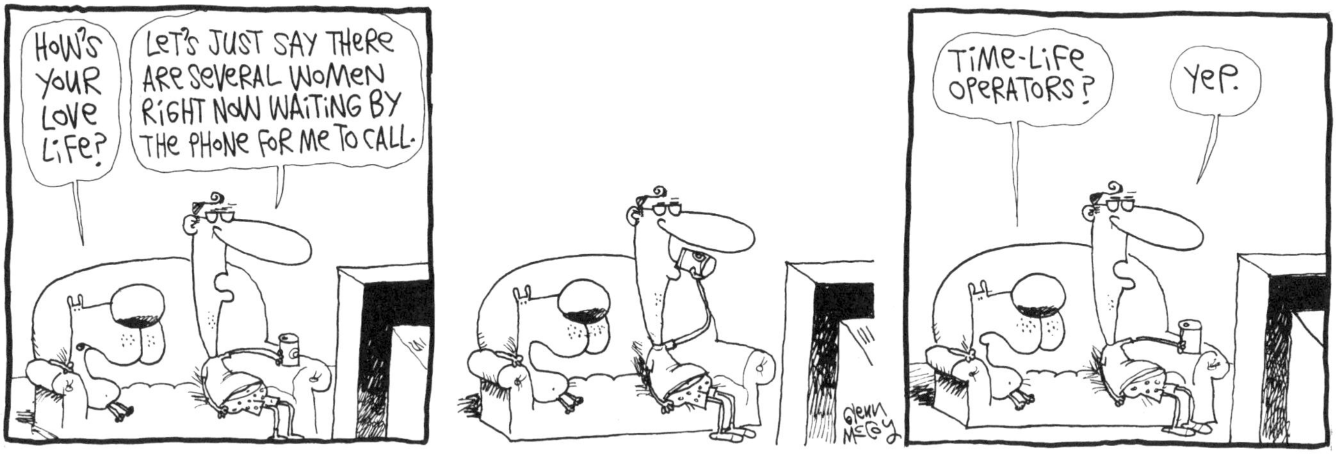
HOW'S YOUR LOVE LIFE?
LET'S JUST SAY THERE ARE SEVERAL WOMEN RIGHT NOW WAITING BY THE PHONE FOR ME TO CALL.
Glenn McCoy
TIME-LIFE OPERATORS?
YEP.

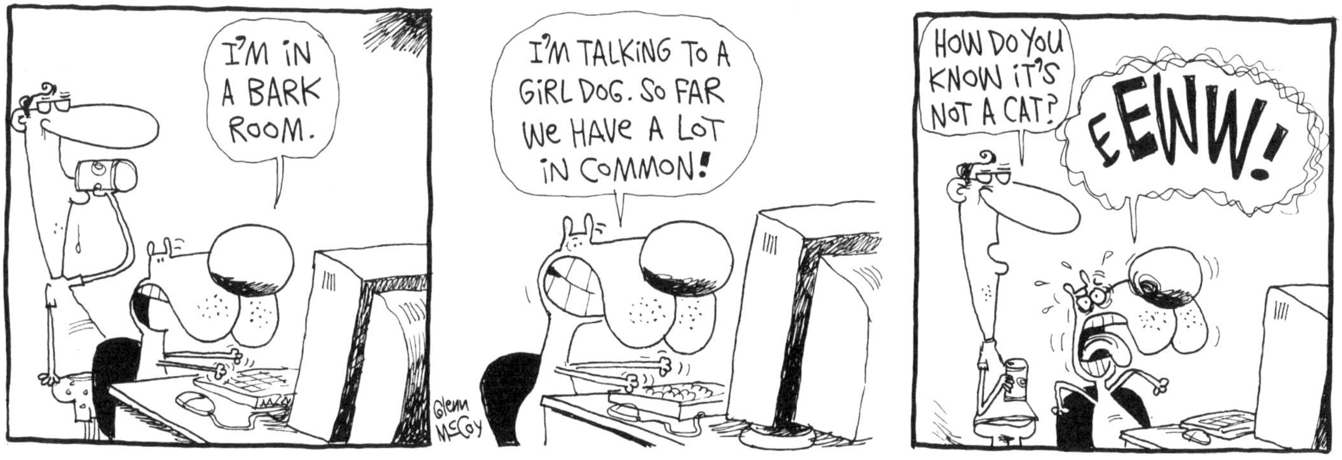
I'M IN A BARK ROOM.
Glenn McCoy
I'M TALKING TO A GIRL DOG. SO FAR WE HAVE A LOT IN COMMON!
HOW DO YOU KNOW IT'S NOT A CAT?
EEWW!

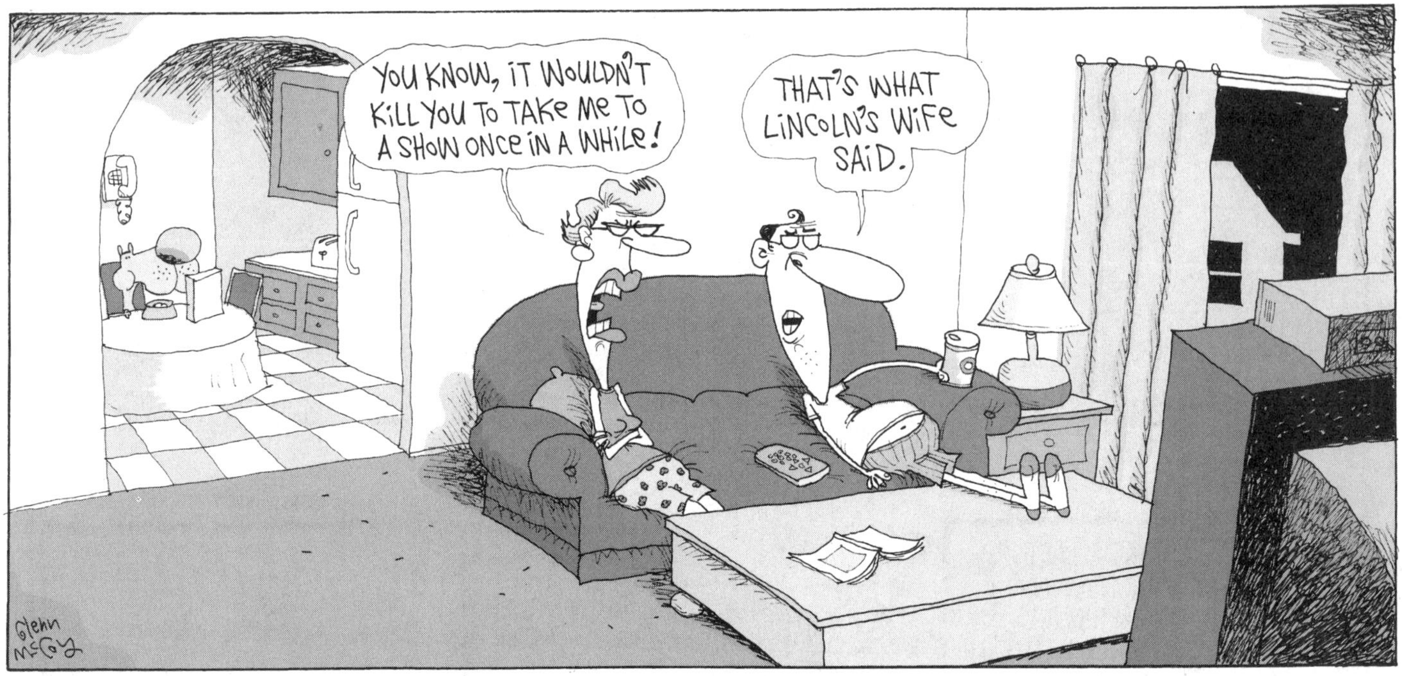
YOU KNOW, IT WOULDN'T KILL YOU TO TAKE ME TO A SHOW ONCE IN A WHILE!
THAT'S WHAT LINCOLN'S WIFE SAID.
Glenn McCoy

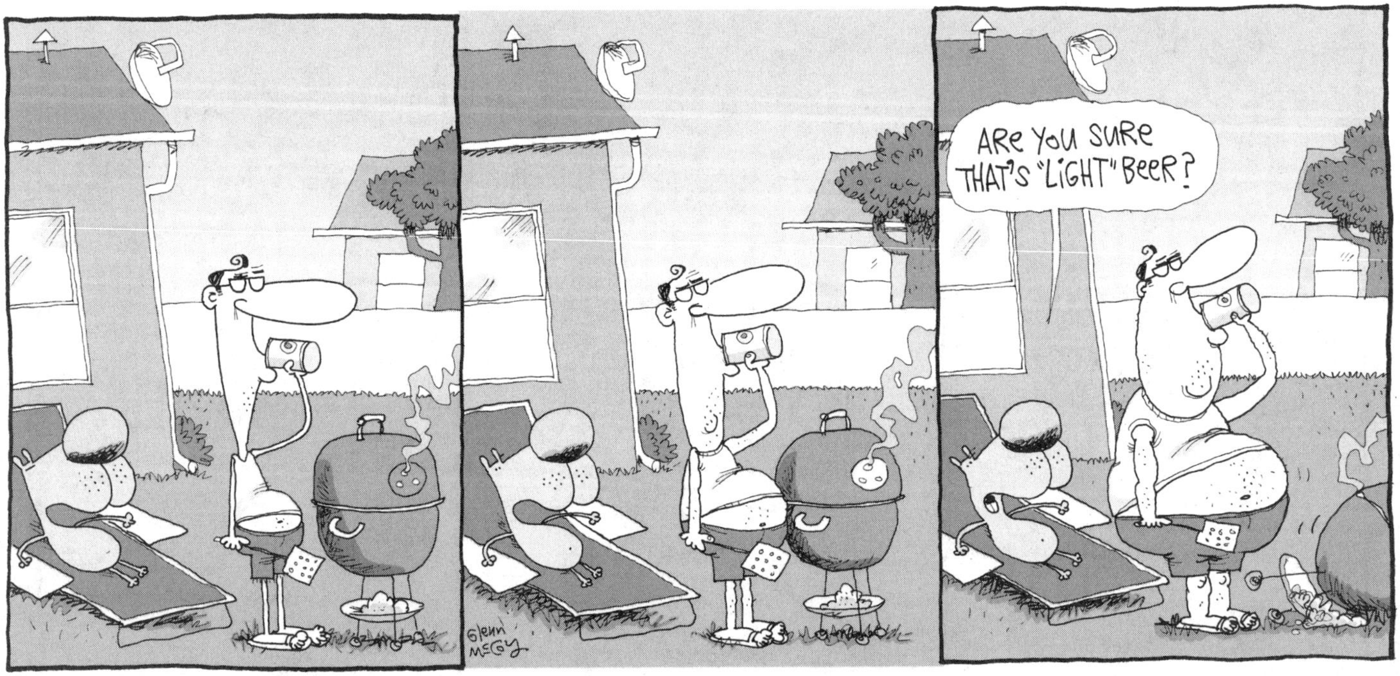
Glenn McCoy
ARE YOU SURE THAT'S "LIGHT" BEER?

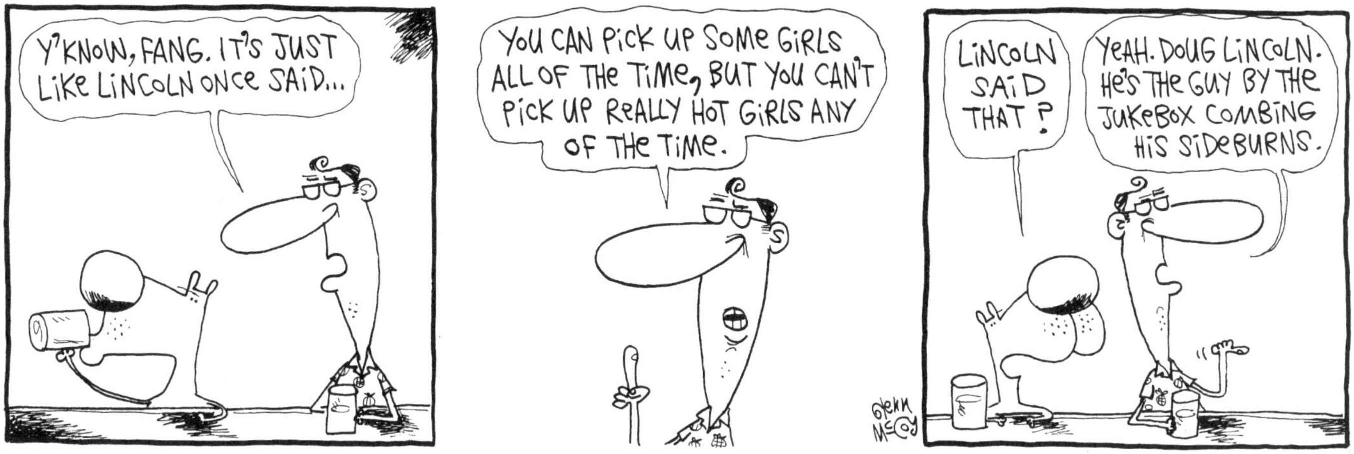
Y'KNOW, FANG. IT'S JUST LIKE LINCOLN ONCE SAID...
YOU CAN PICK UP SOME GIRLS ALL OF THE TIME, BUT YOU CAN'T PICK UP REALLY HOT GIRLS ANY OF THE TIME.
LINCOLN SAID THAT?
YEAH. DOUG LINCOLN. HE'S THE GUY BY THE JUKEBOX COMBING HIS SIDEBURNS.
GLENN McCOY

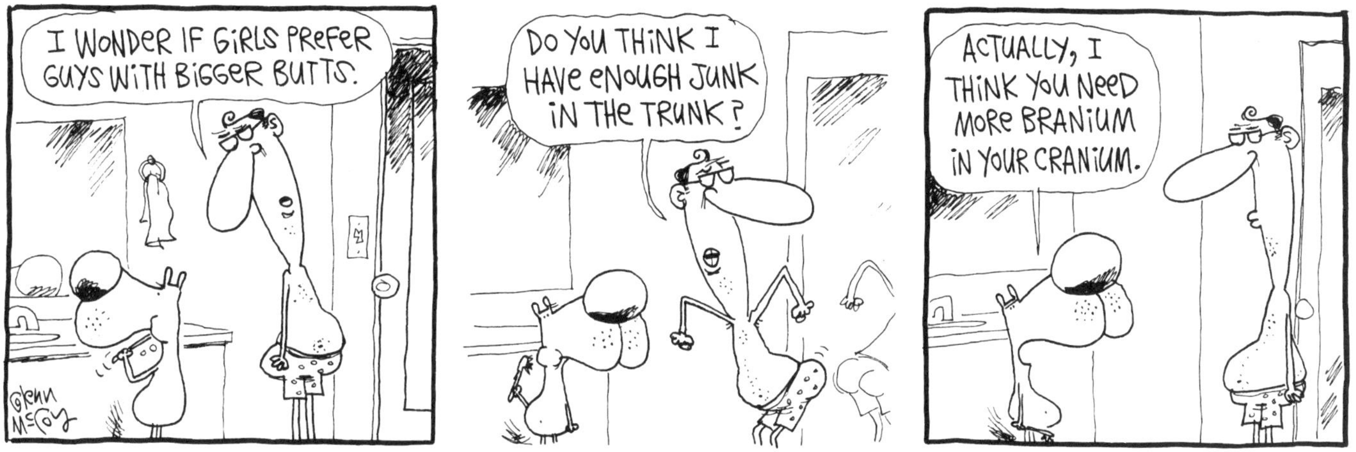
I WONDER IF GIRLS PREFER GUYS WITH BIGGER BUTTS.
GLENN McCOY
DO YOU THINK I HAVE ENOUGH JUNK IN THE TRUNK?
ACTUALLY, I THINK YOU NEED MORE BRANIUM IN YOUR CRANIUM.

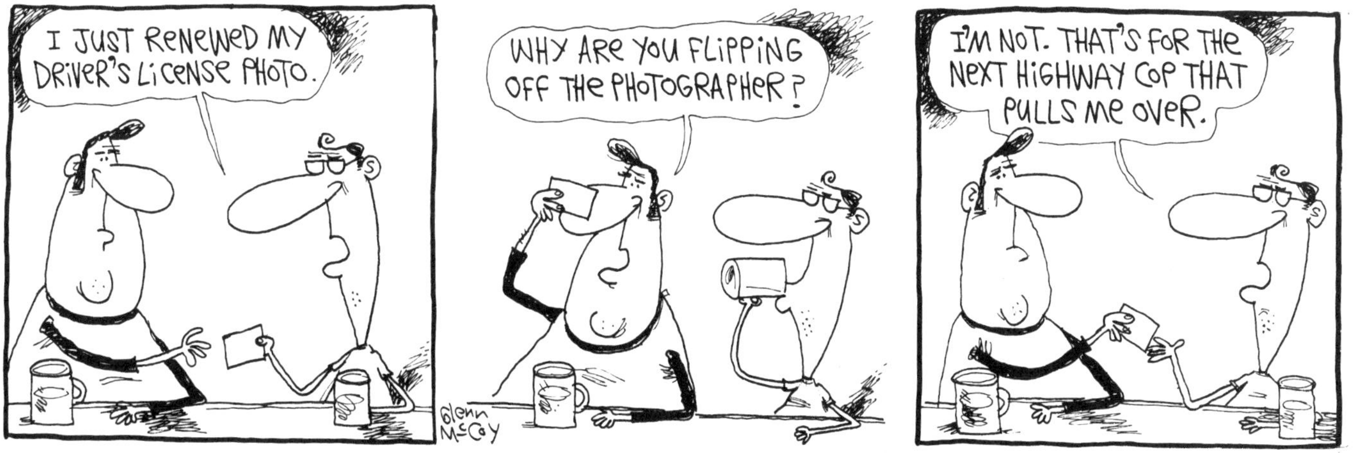
I JUST RENEWED MY DRIVER'S LICENSE PHOTO.
WHY ARE YOU FLIPPING OFF THE PHOTOGRAPHER?
GLENN McCOY
I'M NOT. THAT'S FOR THE NEXT HIGHWAY COP THAT PULLS ME OVER.

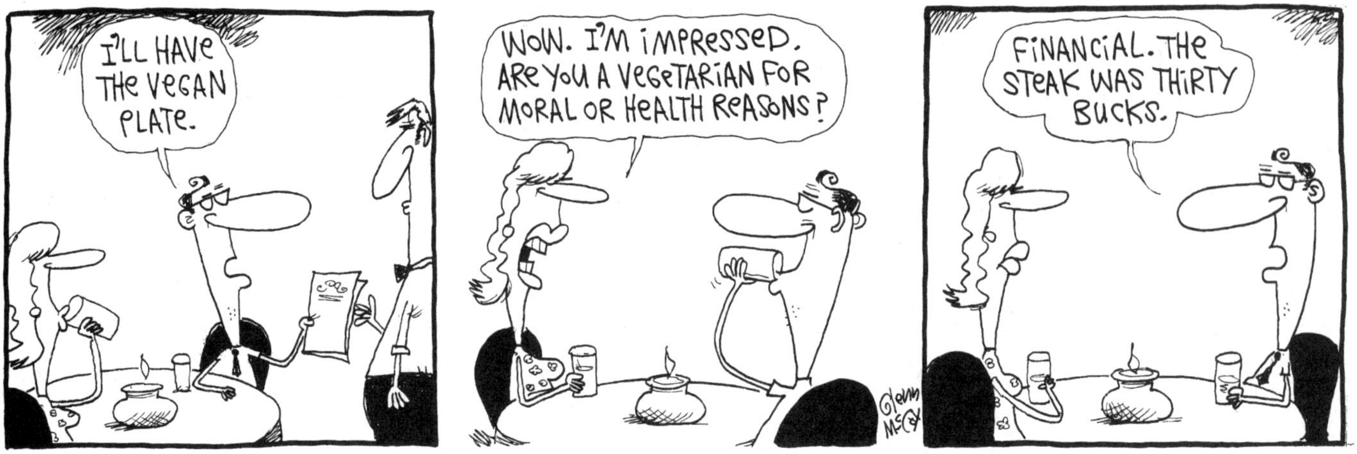
I'LL HAVE THE VEGAN PLATE.
WOW. I'M IMPRESSED. ARE YOU A VEGETARIAN FOR MORAL OR HEALTH REASONS?
FINANCIAL. THE STEAK WAS THIRTY BUCKS.
Glenn McCoy

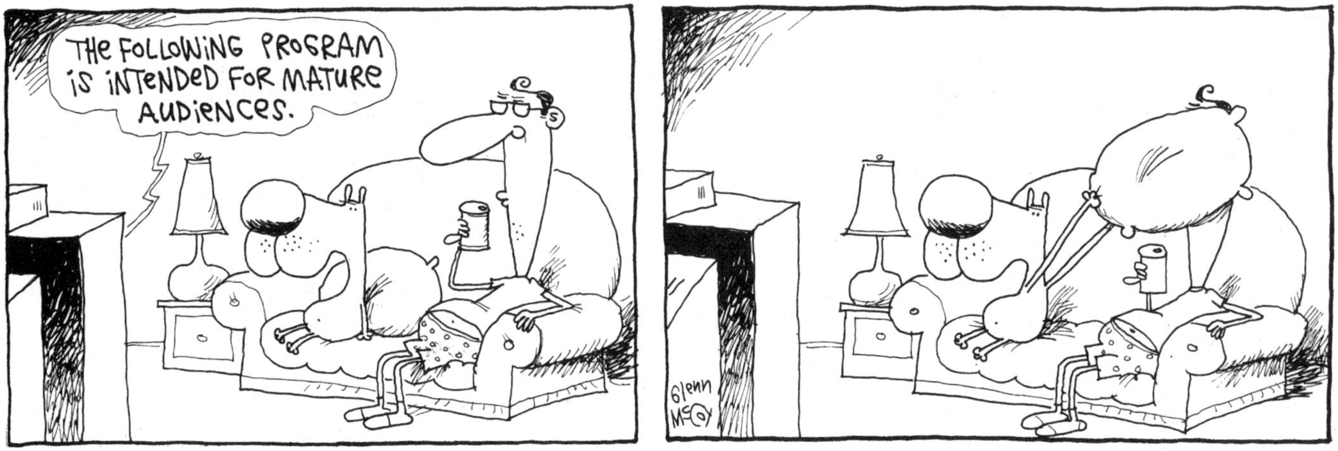
THE FOLLOWING PROGRAM IS INTENDED FOR MATURE AUDIENCES.
Glenn McCoy

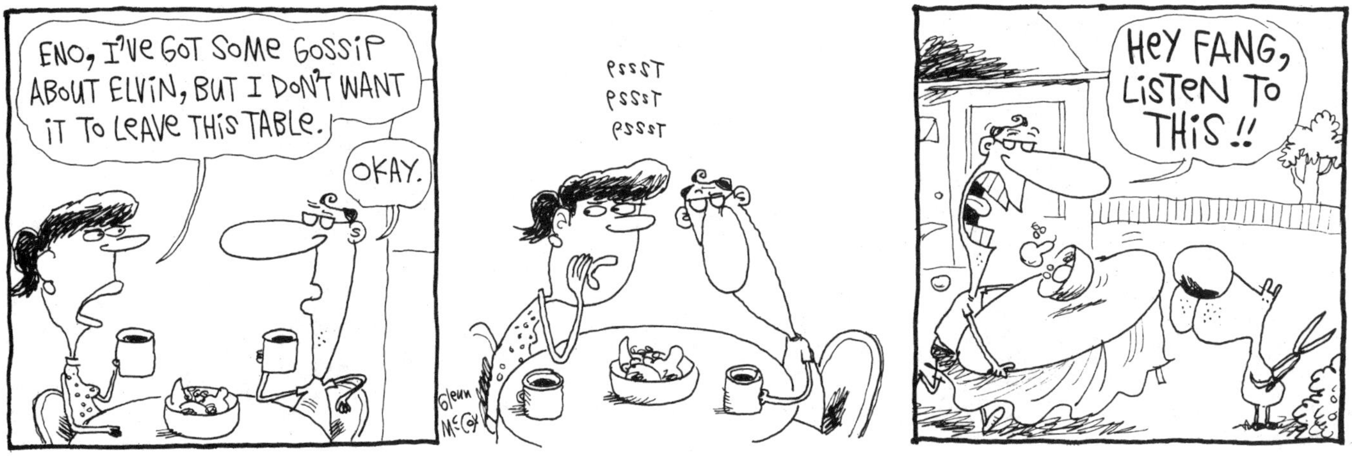
ENO, I'VE GOT SOME GOSSIP ABOUT ELVIN, BUT I DON'T WANT IT TO LEAVE THIS TABLE.
OKAY.
PSSST PSSST PSSST
HEY FANG, LISTEN TO THIS!!
Glenn McCoy

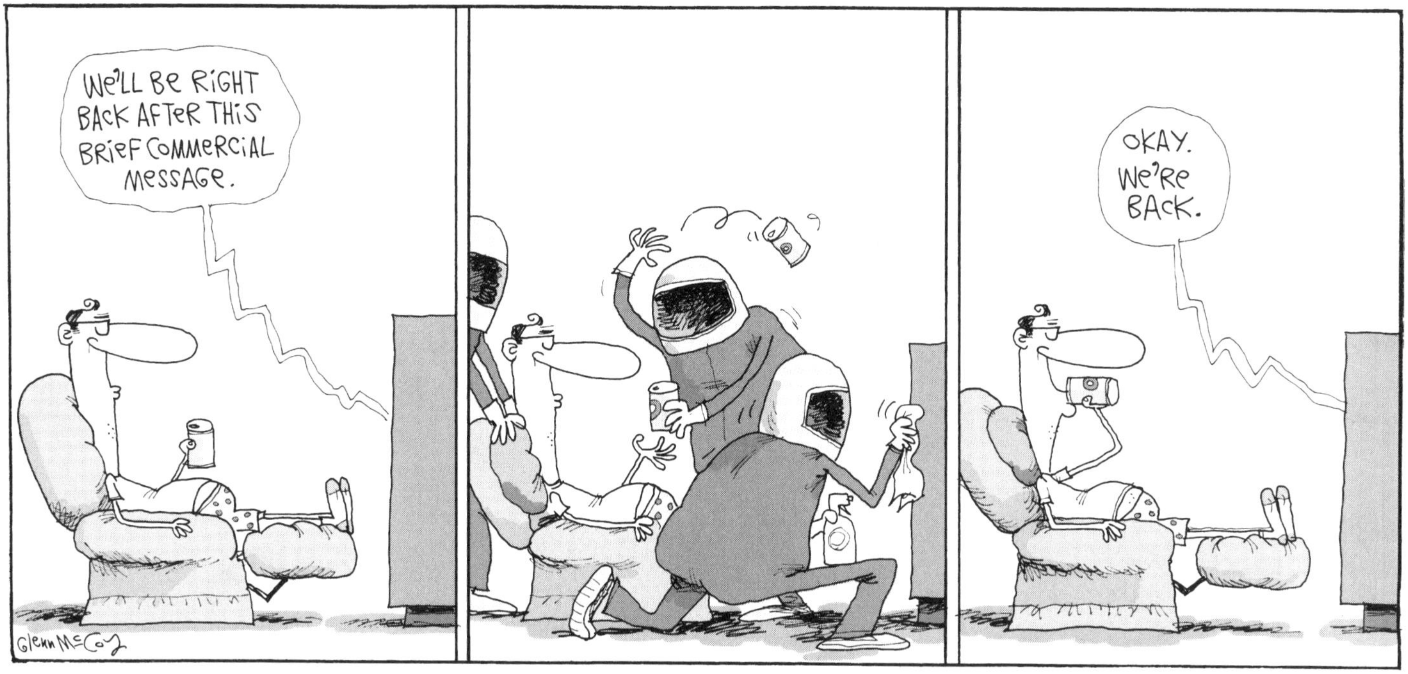
WE'LL BE RIGHT BACK AFTER THIS BRIEF COMMERCIAL MESSAGE.
OKAY. WE'RE BACK.
Glenn McCoy

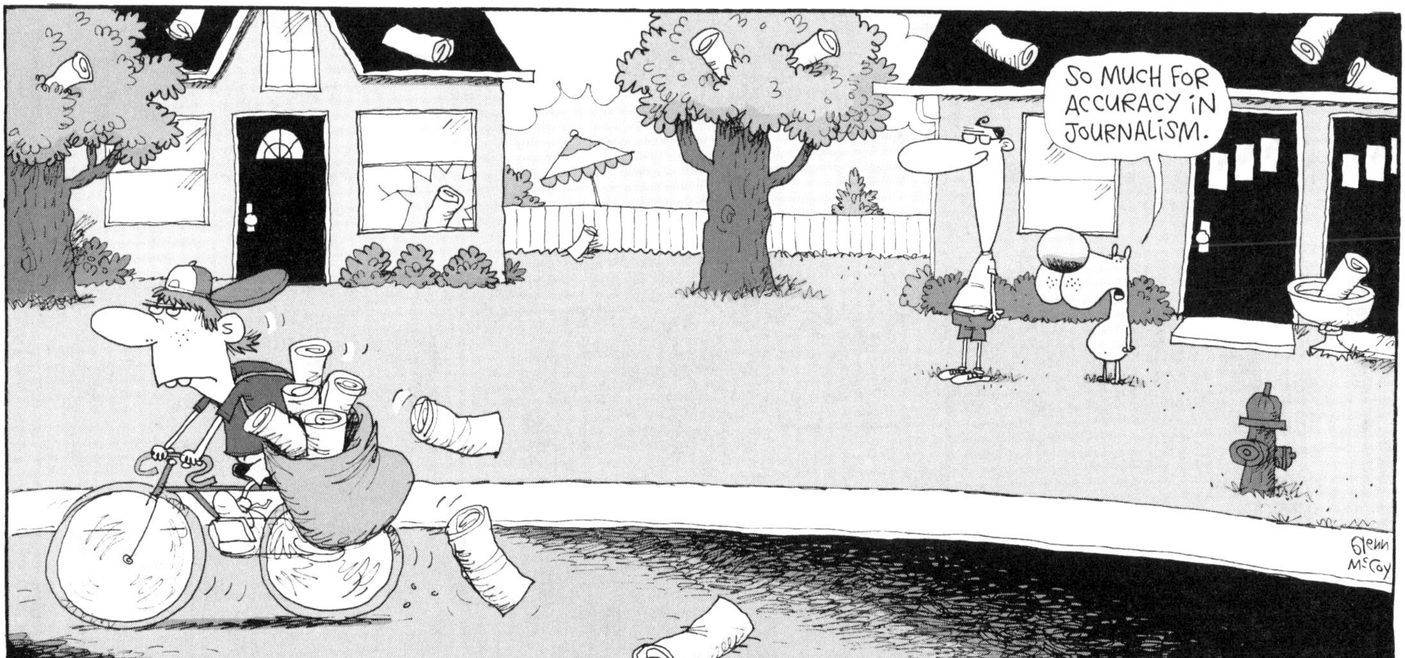
SO MUCH FOR ACCURACY IN JOURNALISM.
Glenn McCoy

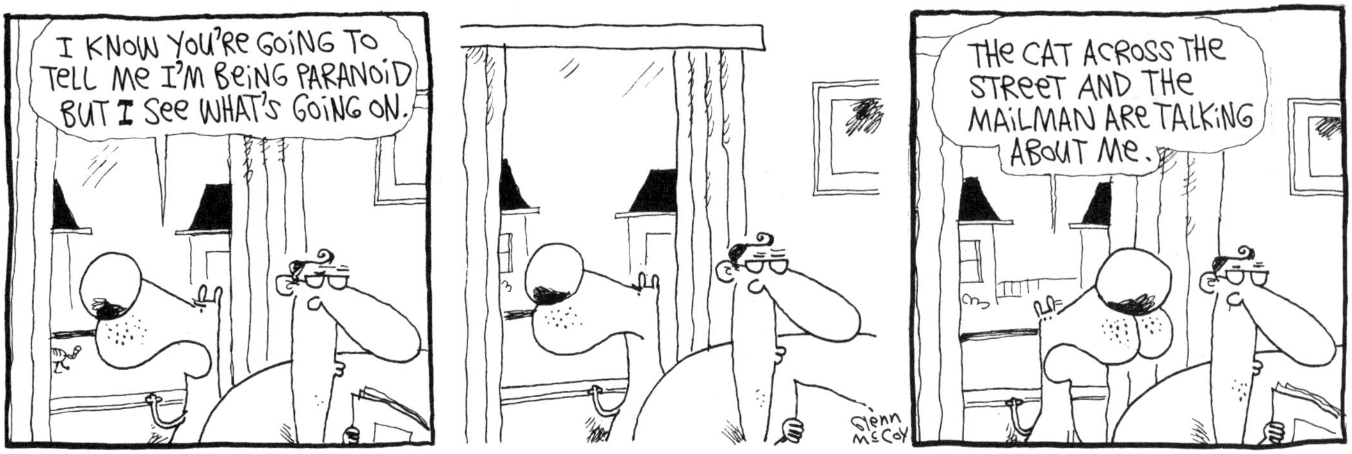
I KNOW YOU'RE GOING TO TELL ME I'M BEING PARANOID BUT I SEE WHAT'S GOING ON.
THE CAT ACROSS THE STREET AND THE MAILMAN ARE TALKING ABOUT ME.

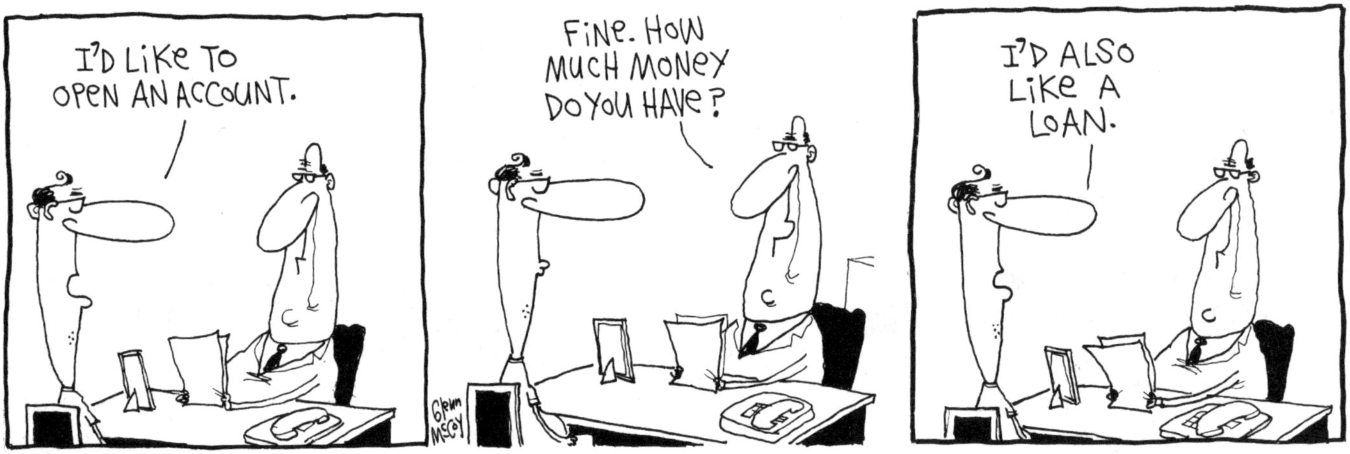
I'D LIKE TO OPEN AN ACCOUNT.
FINE. HOW MUCH MONEY DO YOU HAVE?
I'D ALSO LIKE A LOAN.

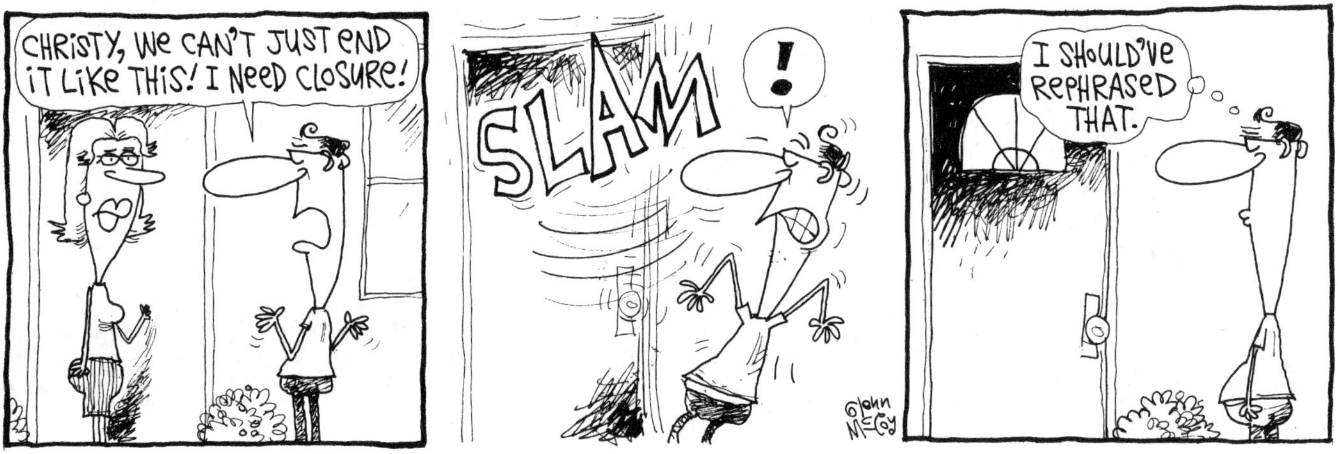
CHRISTY, WE CAN'T JUST END IT LIKE THIS! I NEED CLOSURE!
SLAM
!
I SHOULD'VE REPHRASED THAT.

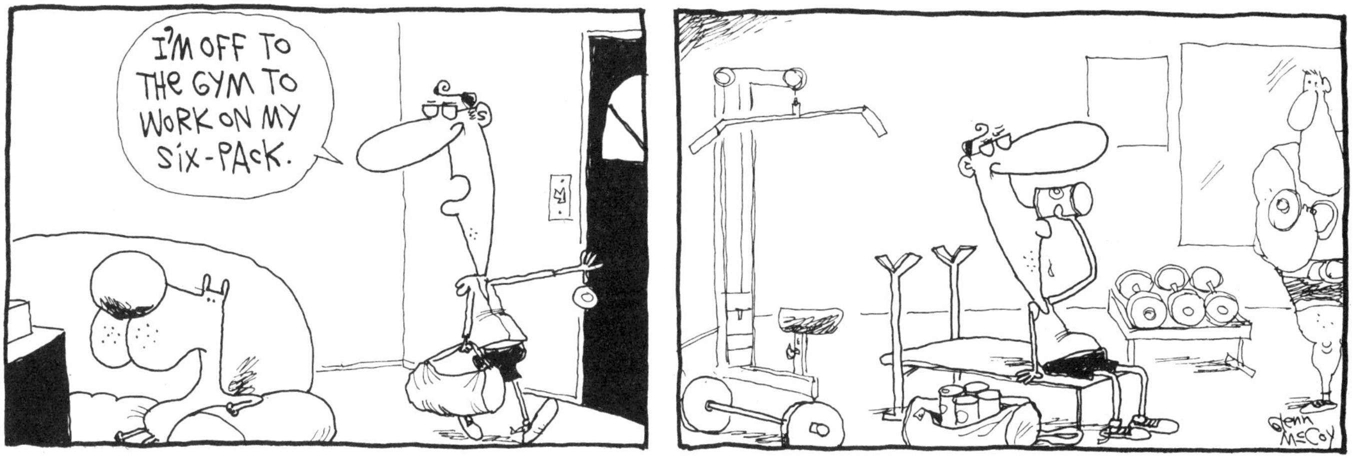
I'M OFF TO THE GYM TO WORK ON MY SIX-PACK.
Glenn McCoy

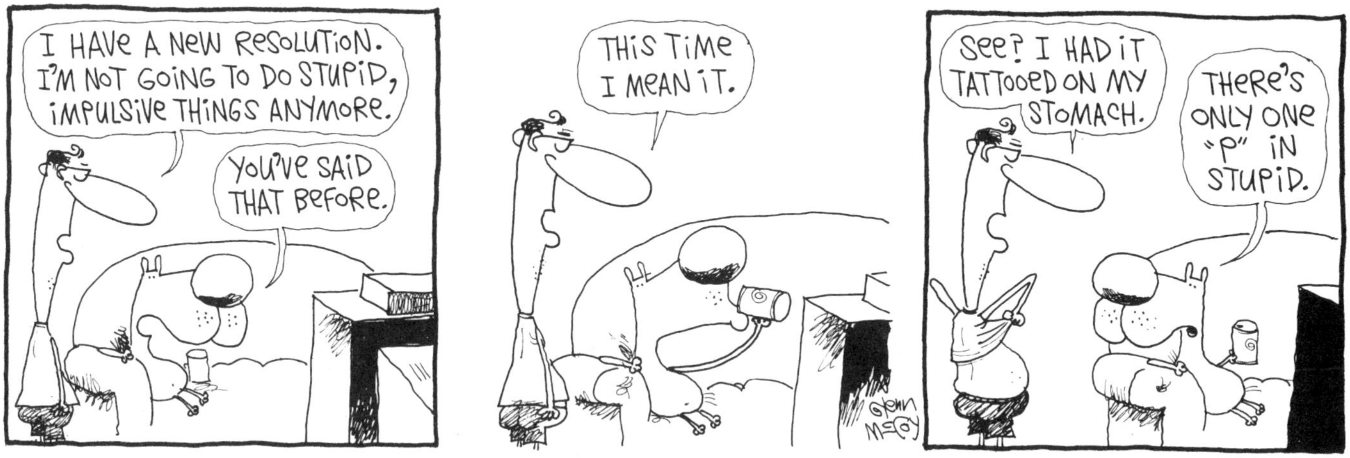
I HAVE A NEW RESOLUTION. I'M NOT GOING TO DO STUPID, IMPULSIVE THINGS ANYMORE.
YOU'VE SAID THAT BEFORE.
THIS TIME I MEAN IT.
Glenn McCoy
SEE? I HAD IT TATTOOED ON MY STOMACH.
THERE'S ONLY ONE "P" IN STUPID.

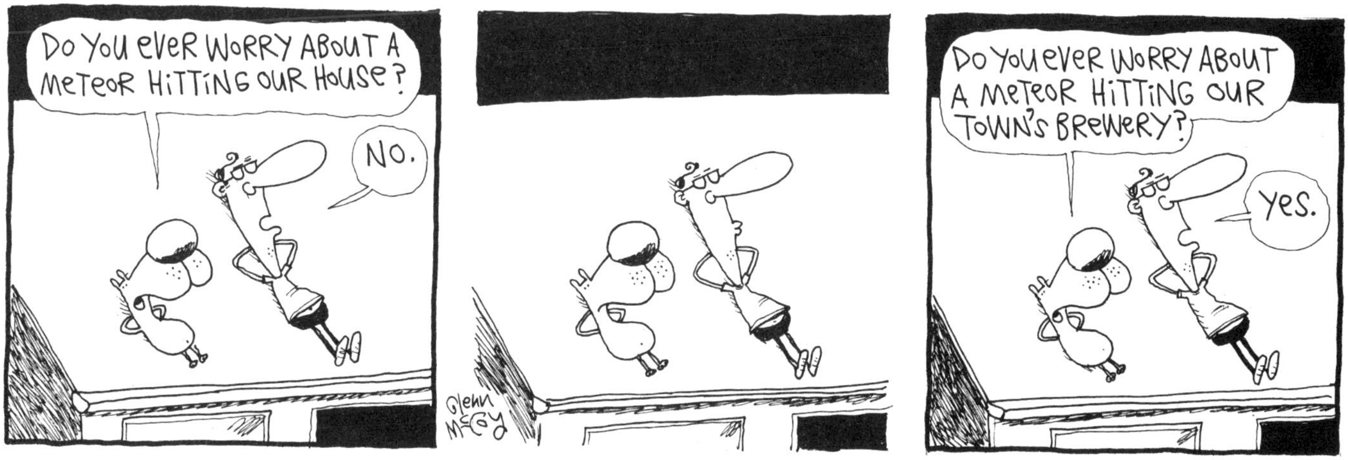
DO YOU EVER WORRY ABOUT A METEOR HITTING OUR HOUSE?
NO.
Glenn McCoy
DO YOU EVER WORRY ABOUT A METEOR HITTING OUR TOWN'S BREWERY?
YES.

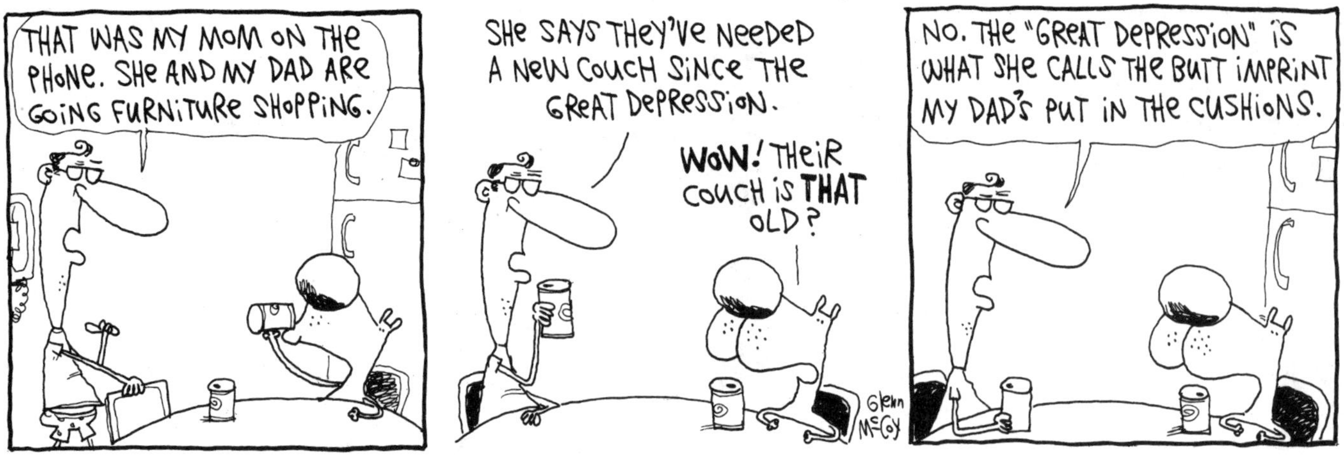
THAT WAS MY MOM ON THE PHONE. SHE AND MY DAD ARE GOING FURNITURE SHOPPING.
SHE SAYS THEY'VE NEEDED A NEW COUCH SINCE THE GREAT DEPRESSION.
WOW! THEIR COUCH IS THAT OLD?
NO. THE "GREAT DEPRESSION" IS WHAT SHE CALLS THE BUTT IMPRINT MY DAD'S PUT IN THE CUSHIONS.
Glenn McCoy

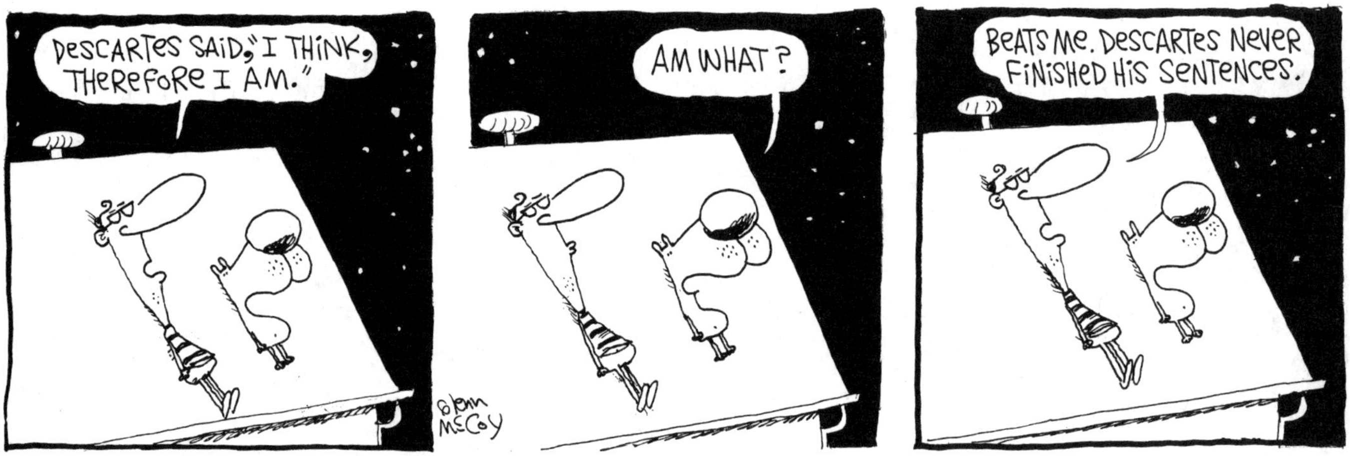
DESCARTES SAID, "I THINK, THEREFORE I AM."
AM WHAT?
BEATS ME. DESCARTES NEVER FINISHED HIS SENTENCES.
Glenn McCoy

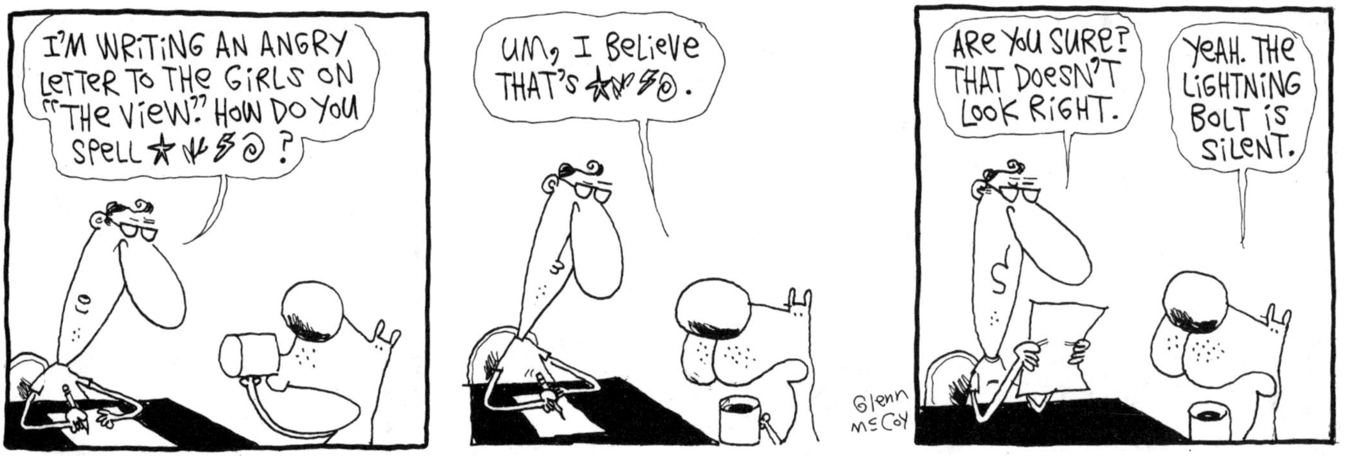
I'M WRITING AN ANGRY LETTER TO THE GIRLS ON "THE VIEW." HOW DO YOU SPELL ?
UM, I BELIEVE THAT'S .
ARE YOU SURE? THAT DOESN'T LOOK RIGHT.
YEAH. THE LIGHTNING BOLT IS SILENT.
Glenn McCoy

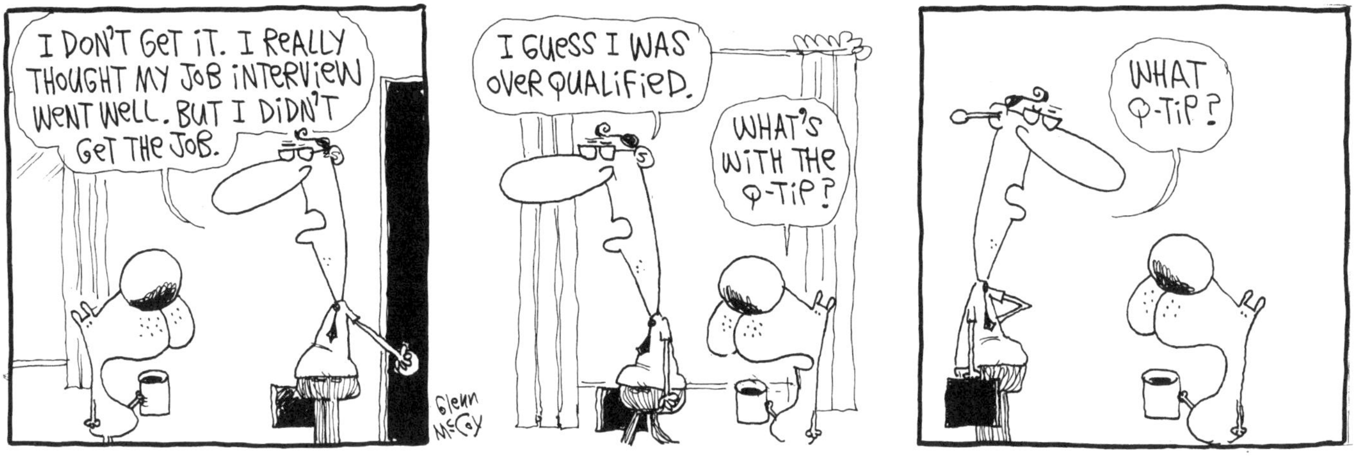
I DON'T GET IT. I REALLY THOUGHT MY JOB INTERVIEW WENT WELL. BUT I DIDN'T GET THE JOB.
Glenn McCoy
I GUESS I WAS OVERQUALIFIED.
WHAT'S WITH THE Q-TIP?
WHAT Q-TIP?

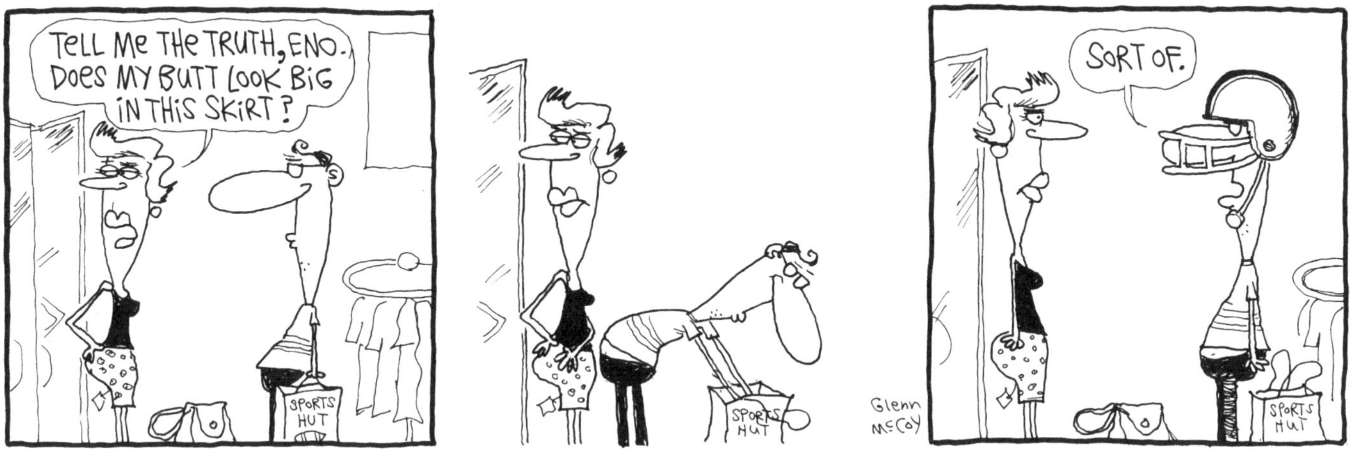
TELL ME THE TRUTH, ENO. DOES MY BUTT LOOK BIG IN THIS SKIRT?
SPORTS HUT
SPORTS HUT
Glenn McCoy
SORT OF.
SPORTS HUT

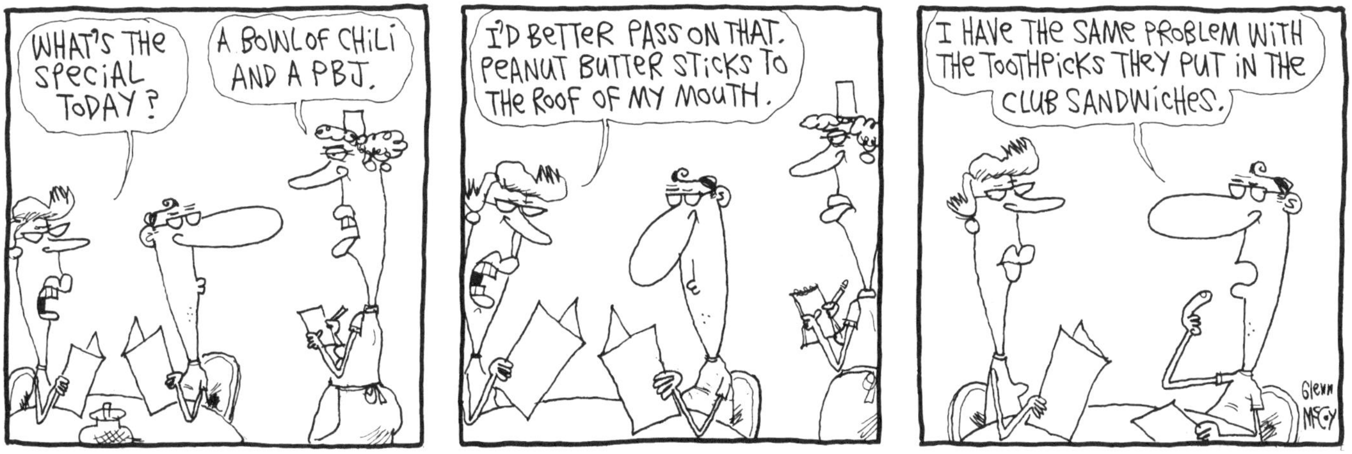
WHAT'S THE SPECIAL TODAY?
A BOWL OF CHILI AND A PBJ.
I'D BETTER PASS ON THAT. PEANUT BUTTER STICKS TO THE ROOF OF MY MOUTH.
I HAVE THE SAME PROBLEM WITH THE TOOTHPICKS THEY PUT IN THE CLUB SANDWICHES.
Glenn McCoy

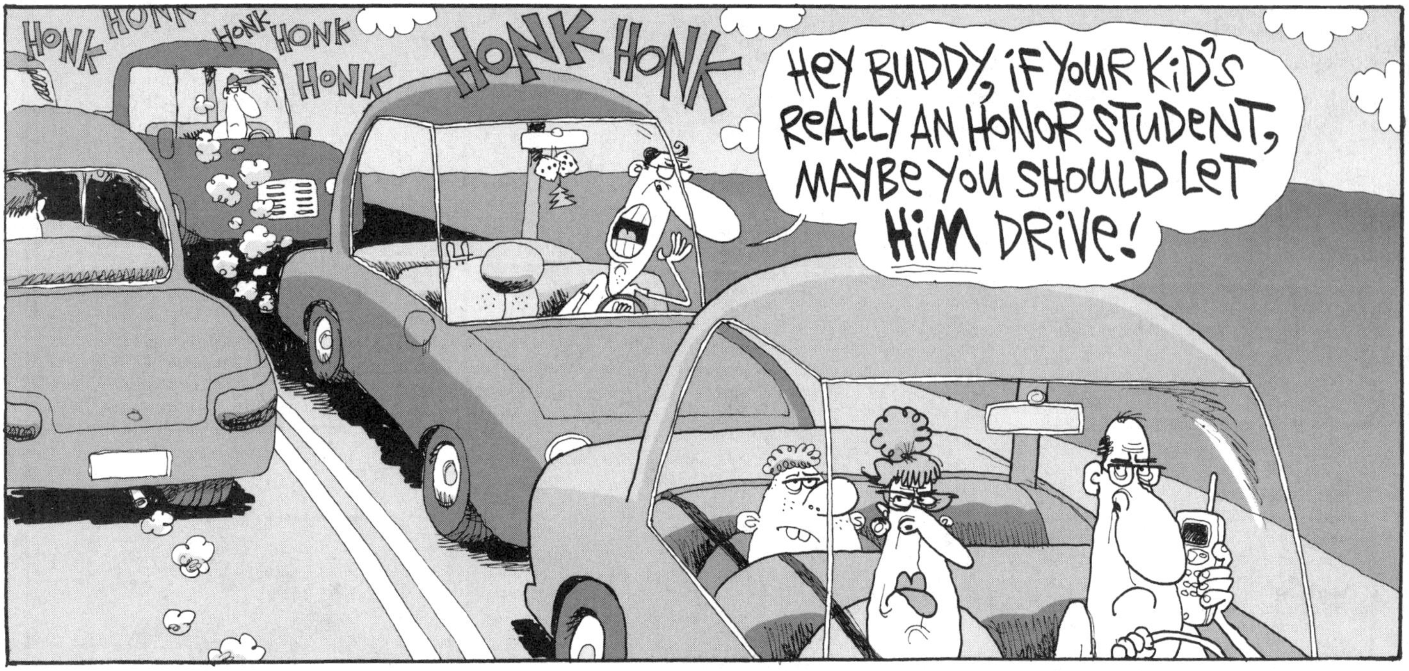
HONK HONK
HONK HONK
HONK
HONK HONK
HEY BUDDY, IF YOUR KID'S REALLY AN HONOR STUDENT, MAYBE YOU SHOULD LET HIM DRIVE!

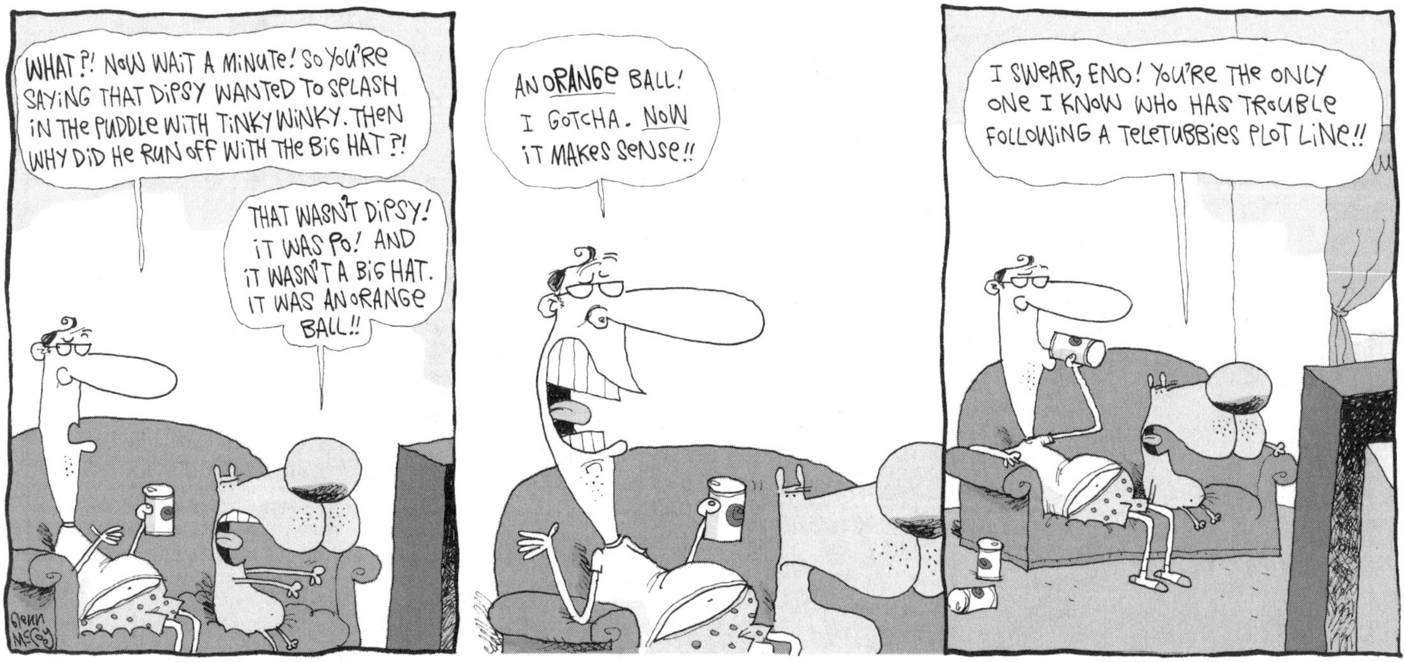
WHAT?! NOW WAIT A MINUTE! SO YOU'RE SAYING THAT DIPSY WANTED TO SPLASH IN THE PUDDLE WITH TINKY WINKY. THEN WHY DID HE RUN OFF WITH THE BIG HAT?!
THAT WASN'T DIPSY! IT WAS PO! AND IT WASN'T A BIG HAT. IT WAS AN ORANGE BALL!!
AN ORANGE BALL! I GOTCHA. NOW IT MAKES SENSE!!
I SWEAR, ENO! YOU'RE THE ONLY ONE I KNOW WHO HAS TROUBLE FOLLOWING A TELETUBBIES PLOT LINE!!
Glenn McCoy

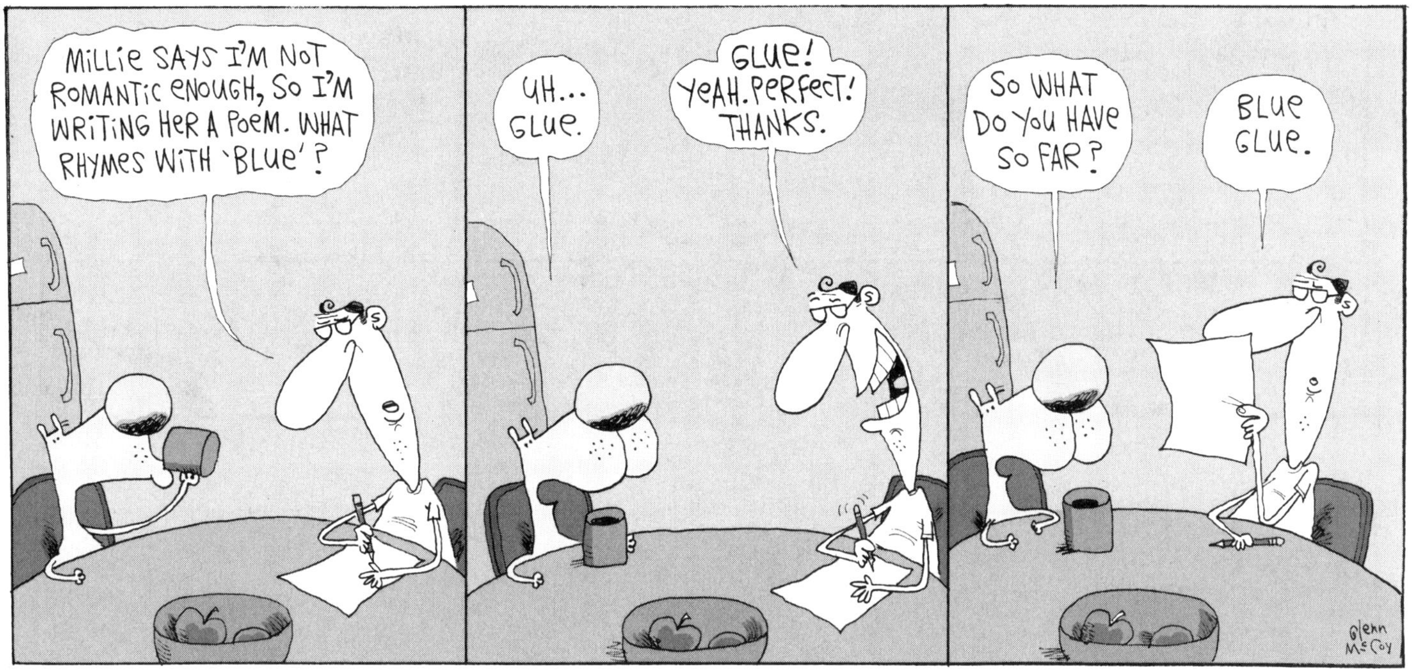
MILLIE SAYS I'M NOT ROMANTIC ENOUGH, SO I'M WRITING HER A POEM. WHAT RHYMES WITH 'BLUE'?
UH... GLUE.
GLUE! YEAH. PERFECT! THANKS.
SO WHAT DO YOU HAVE SO FAR?
BLUE GLUE.
Glenn McCoy

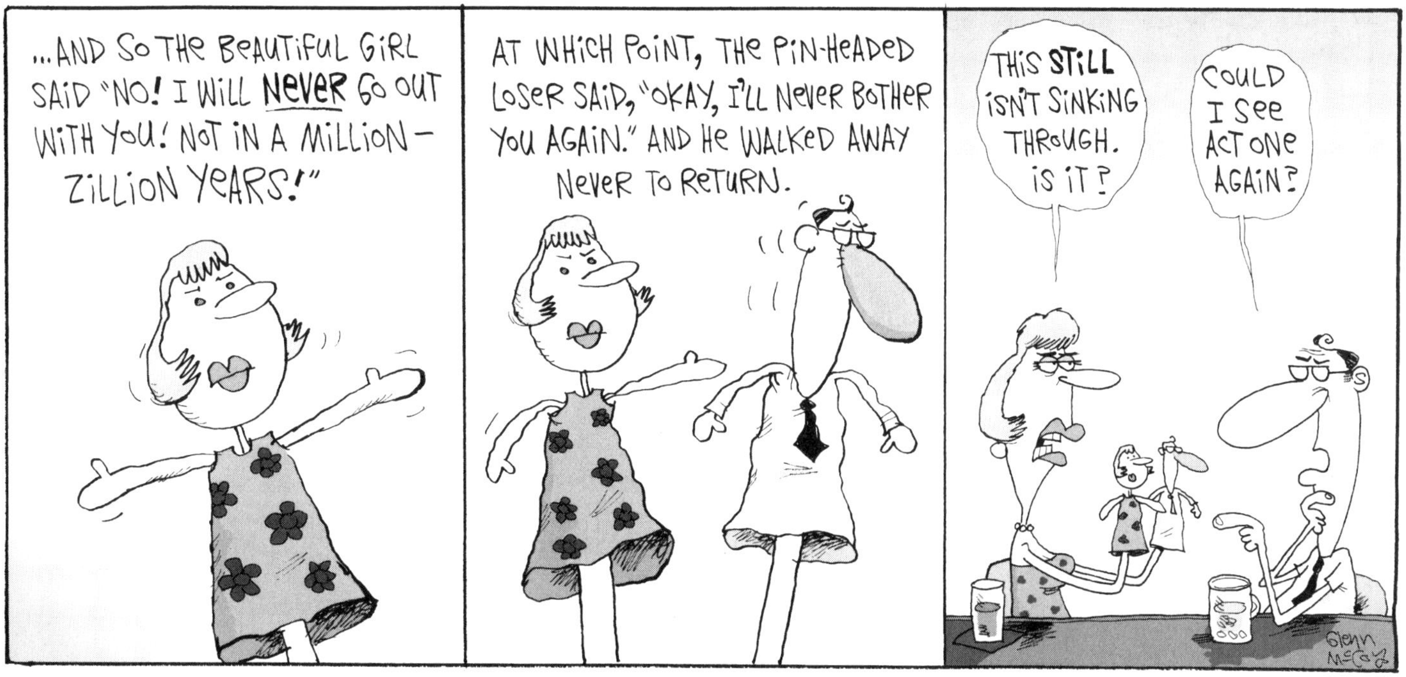
...AND SO THE BEAUTIFUL GIRL SAID "NO! I WILL NEVER GO OUT WITH YOU! NOT IN A MILLION-ZILLION YEARS!"
AT WHICH POINT, THE PIN-HEADED LOSER SAID, "OKAY, I'LL NEVER BOTHER YOU AGAIN." AND HE WALKED AWAY NEVER TO RETURN.
THIS STILL ISN'T SINKING THROUGH. IS IT?
COULD I SEE ACT ONE AGAIN?
Glenn McCoy

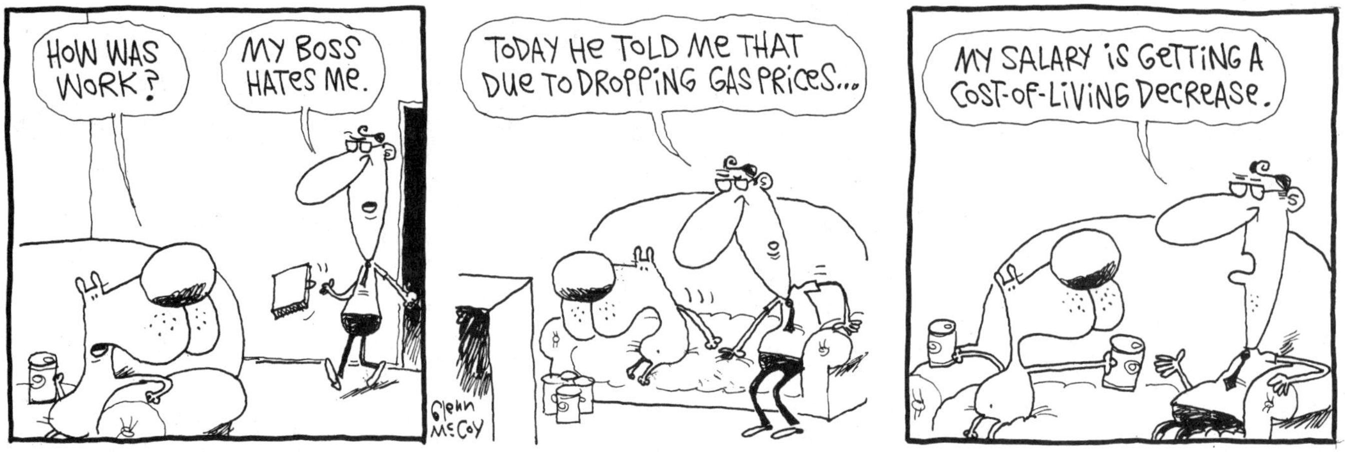
HOW WAS WORK?
MY BOSS HATES ME.
TODAY HE TOLD ME THAT DUE TO DROPPING GAS PRICES...
MY SALARY IS GETTING A COST-OF-LIVING DECREASE.
Glenn McCoy

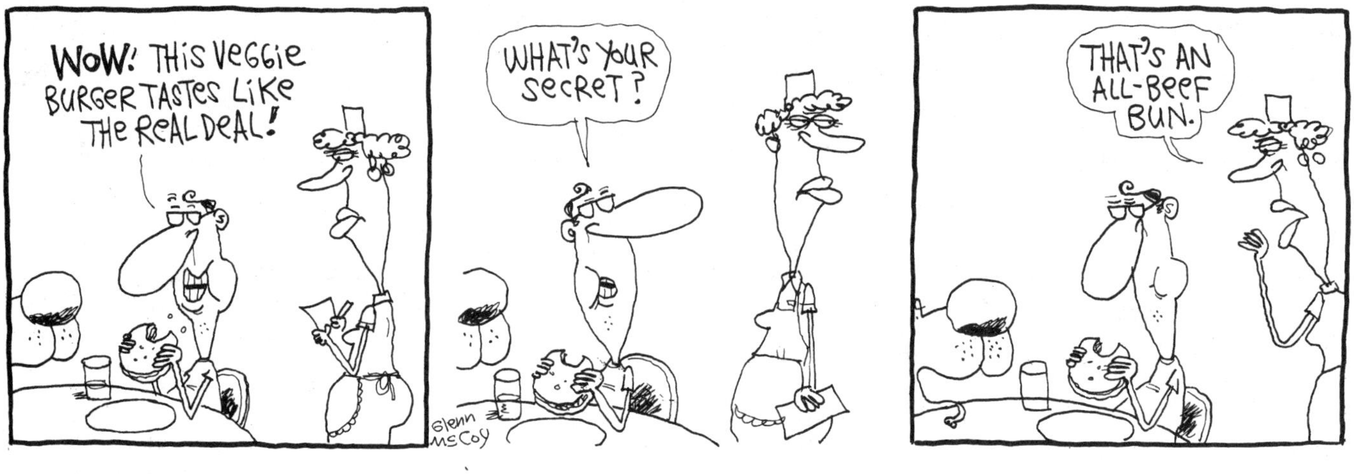
WOW! THIS VEGGIE BURGER TASTES LIKE THE REAL DEAL!
WHAT'S YOUR SECRET?
THAT'S AN ALL-BEEF BUN.
Glenn McCoy

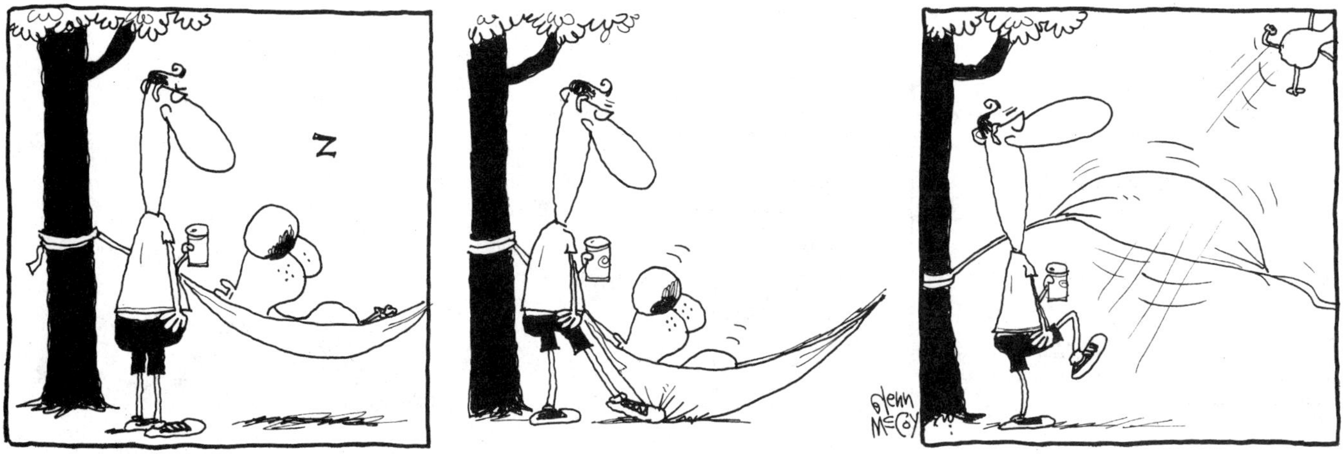
Z
Glenn McCoy